C. J. Ehrehart
June 1852

A COMMENTARY ON THE BOOK OF PROVERBS.

BY

MOSES STUART,

LATELY PROFESSOR OF SACRED LITERATURE IN THE THEOLOGICAL SEMINARY AT ANDOVER, MASS.

NEW YORK:

M. W. DODD, BRICK CHURCH CHAPEL.

1852.

ANDOVER: JOHN D. FLAGG,
STEREOTYPER AND PRINTER.

PREFACE.

THE history of the present undertaking is brief and simple. After completing my Commentary on Ecclesiastes, I felt specially attracted toward another book, (that of the Proverbs), by reason of its close affinity with Ecclesiastes, in a variety of respects. The *gnomic* form of much that is in the latter book, naturally produced in my mind, after having spent so much time upon it, an interest in respect to the other book, which is filled with gnomes. A large circle of clerical friends, (many of whom had once been my pupils), who are now moving in extensive spheres of usefulness, and enjoying the approbation of highly respected churches, gave me, early in the summer of the present year, cheering and animating encouragement to proceed in the writing of a Commentary on the Proverbs. My own inclination and choice had already, in a measure, anticipated their friendly request; for when that reached me, I had gone on more than half-way through the book, in the writing of the Commentary. Other friends and brethren, also, have since approved and encouraged the undertaking. A kind Providence has spared my life, when I had little reason to expect its continuance: and from time to time, after repeated partial interruptions of my labors, (during some of which I was led seriously to doubt whether I should ever be able to renew them), I have been enabled to complete what I had begun, if not according to my wishes, yet according to my best ability.

In the composition of the work which follows, I have felt even a deeper interest than I had anticipated. As to the *Hebrew* in which it is written, it bears the unmistakable stamp of *antiquity*. Nothing can be more diverse in this respect than the Proverbs and the Preacher. A true lover of the old Hebrew must needs enjoy the reading of the Proverbs. Then, in the next place, such a book as this, which records so many hundreds of short, pointed, pithy sayings, or maxims, must exhibit much of the common conversational idiom of the Hebrews. Moreover, many of the nicer and more difficult points, in respect to Hebrew Grammar, are here developed, as we should naturally conclude they would be; for proverbial sayings generally take large liberties as to the forms, idioms, and syntax of any language. The student, who is desirous of mastering such difficulties, will acquire much useful training in the accurate investigation of the idioms in the book before us. Nowhere, in the Hebrew Scriptures, is knowledge of this kind more often required than here. And it is in the study of this book, that the masterly Syntax of Ewald, in regard to the most obscure and difficult points of the Hebrew language, affords peculiar, and in general, adequate aid, — aid which can scarcely be found to such an extent in any other work of this nature. I acknowledge myself indebted to him, for illustrations of some points elsewhere either overlooked or imperfectly exhibited. There is scarcely any anomaly in the Hebrew Scriptures, on which he has not touched; and not only so, but adduced illustration and confirmation of his method of solving it.

Ernesti, almost a century ago, said that *no interpretation, which is at variance with the laws of grammar and of idiom, can be the true one*. The reason is obvious. To be at all understood, the sacred writers must of course conform to the *usus loquendi* of their times. The laws of grammar, so called, do nothing more than exhibit *facts* respecting the *usus loquendi* of any language. They are not laws which grammar makes, but laws which it discovers and exhibits. If, then, we do not attain to a right understanding of these laws, we of course must, to a certain extent, be ignorant of the *usus* in question; and when we are thus ignorant, how can we interpret with any good measure of assurance, that we are in the right? We may give credit to the learning and judgment of others, but we cannot trust our own.

On such a ground of exegesis as that mentioned above, I have aimed that the following work should have its basis. There has never been, consciously on my part, any endeavor to dictate what the sacred writer *ought to say*, but merely to find out *what he has said*. And to do this, all guessing, conjecture, or imagination must be dismissed, and must stand aside. My reverence for God's Word is such, that when I find out what his servants have said and sanctioned, I regard it as of more value than all which any uninspired interpreter can say. Hence my partiality for a simple *commentary of explanation*, at least for the use of all preachers of the gospel. A commentary merely hortatory and practical, they should themselves be able to make. They ought not to depend on others, in this case. But to find the real nucleus, out of which this practical commentary is to be developed, one must of necessity betake himself to the aid of grammatico-historical exegesis. The present work is designed to aid such an undertaking, to facilitate the labor of the student, and to spare him as much of time in regard to the investigation of materials, as is practicable, when this is to be carried through by his own efforts.

I believe I may venture to assert that there is no real difficulty as to form, idiom, or syntax, in the book of Proverbs, on which I have not touched, and which I have not endeavored to explain. Hence the saving of time, as I would hope, to the reader. The *materials* are gathered for him; they are fitted for *structure*; and he has only to apply his own efforts, in order to erect and complete the structure designed. It has been my intention always to conduct him so as that he may see with his own eyes, if he will use them; and, moreover, see as clearly as if he had expended his time in collecting for himself the materials now made ready to his hand. *Ex cathedra dicere* is not designedly the order of the day, in the following work. Nothing is intended to be established by mere assertion or assumption, but every opinion given is designed to be defended by facts and reasons. Of these, the reader has as good a right to judge as the writer.

Brief I have aimed to be. I have been so, specially in the Commentary. I have not labored to explain what can be made no plainer than it already is. Smaller difficulties are briefly and summarily discussed. In a few cases only, has a kind of exegetical dissertation been deemed necessary ; and these are treated with all needful and becoming amplitude.

In a large number of cases, where the language is figurative, or peculiarly compressed, or elliptic, or hyperbolic in the mode of expression, I have subjoined to each verse a summary of what I deemed to be the real sentiment designed to be expressed, in plain and simple English idiom. The *expert* in commentary will not be displeased with this; the *tyro* will, as I would hope, gratefully accept of such aid, and avail himself of it.

I have become more and more attached to a close translation of the original, as a most important aid in the study of a Hebrew book. Our idiom better expresses the Hebrew, than any other modern European language, or than the older Latin or Greek. De Wette has made a noble translation of the Scriptures into the German ; and this language stands next to our own, in exhibiting the power of the Hebrew idiom. But I have forborne habitually to consult his version of the book in question, because I wished to give my own impressions of the meaning of the Hebrew, without any embarrassment. De Wette, however, may well be consulted by the student; but now and then I have found in him evidence that he had not always mastered some of the peculiar idioms of the book, nor always investigated specialities of syntax in it. I have, therefore, forborne to consult him, with less reluctance than I should have felt, without having come to the knowledge of these facts. I hardly need to say that my aim has been to keep close to the original, and to employ pure and simple *English* words in my version. The latter will speak for itself. I have more often hesitated in order to find a Saxon word which is not vulgar, instead of a word derived from the Latin or Greek, than from almost any other cause. After all, I have been forced, at times, upon the latter class of words, either to avoid vulgarism, or to give the nicer shade of meaning demanded by the Hebrew. E. g. the meaning of שָׂבַע is *to satisfy*, and also *to satiate*. In cases where the latter meaning is plain, our version has given *filled*, or *satisfied*, neither of which convey the Hebrew shade of meaning. I have been obliged, therefore, to use *satiate;* for I could not say *stuffed*, *crammed*, or the like. But then, this is no more a *Latinism* than *satisfy;* and it may be employed with equal propriety. In all cases where a real equivalent Saxon word presented itself — a word in good repute — I have preferred it. It is such a usage of our English translators, which has made our common version an immortal monument of the noble Anglo-Saxon.

A good and faithful *translation* is of itself, for the most part, an adequate interpretation. Hence its importance. That in such a book as that of Proverbs, our English translators should have sometimes erred, being furnished with no other knowledge than what the lexicons and grammars afforded them two centuries ago, is much less a matter of wonder, than that they should so generally have been in the right. No apology however is needed, as I trust, at the present time, for differing from them in a few cases, where new light has been poured upon grammar, idiom, or the general subject of Hebrew antiquities.

Thus much for the *history* and *manner* of my present work. A word as to the book itself, which is the subject of commentary, and I have done.

The book of Proverbs, I venture to assert, has a deep *historical* interest, as well as a moral, social, industrial, and pious one. Solomon doubtless did not *make* or *compose* all the proverbs contained in it. Many of them he selected, digested, and arranged. But the mass of the book passed through his hands, or at least through his mind; and therefore it has his sanction. But there can be little doubt, that by far the greater part of the book originated among the Hebrew people as such. Most of the maxims are plainly the offspring of sound common sense, of much experience, and of acute discrimination. They bear the evident stamp of serious, thinking, and devout minds. I have spoken of them as a *selection.* There is good reason for thus speaking; inasmuch as in 1 Kings 4 : 32, we are told that Solomon " spake three thousand proverbs." If now he drew from these, in order to compose one book of Proverbs, he must have *selected;* for the present book contains less than one thousand. The internal testimony of the book discloses the certainty, that the proverbs of other wise men besides Solomon are contained in it. The store, then, of Hebrew proverbs must have been very great, in the time of Solomon.

Let this however be as it may, there can be no doubt that this book had great currency among the Hebrews. It fell in, therefore, with the feelings and views of that people. It is here, then, that we come to see the *historical* element of the book. It is a picture — a vivid picture — of *the internal Hebrew man;* of his genius, feelings, practical reasonings, morals, industry, social condition, internal relations, comity, and, in a word, of the whole state of the Hebrews, and their rank among the society of nations. What is generally popular and approved among the masses of any people, must be that which is congruous with their civil, social, and moral condition. What they thought, and felt, and said, on all the great problems relating to a social state and the respective rights of men, in regard to their mutual relations and dependencies, or in respect to their moral and religious views and feelings, — all this is completely before us, in the picture drawn in the book of Proverbs. Not that there were no dissenters from many of its maxims; for there were doubtless bad men among them, at that time; and the like have been found in every age and among every nation. But the mass of the people must have been of a different character; for how else could they relish and heartily approve of such a manual of ethics, of sobriety, chastity, industry, and economy, as the book before us contains? In this book, then, is virtually contained the history of their mental and moral state and progress, — a history more minute, more graphic, more extensive, and, I may add, more interesting, than all the *external* histories of the nation taken together.

And what story does this tell of the Hebrew people, in the days of Solomon? One, I venture to say, that the proverbs of no nation destitute of the Bible ever did or can tell. I have pursued this course of thought to some length in my Introduction to the book; and I have also compared a considerable mass of the Arabic and Greek proverbs with those in the book before us. The reader may now judge in some measure for himself, whether foreign nations had any good reason to despise the Hebrews. All the heathen moralists and proverbialists joined together cannot furnish us with one such book, as that of the Proverbs in the sacred Scriptures.

The subject is one of deep interest, to all who wish to acquire an intimate knowledge of the mental and moral state of the Hebrews in ancient times. If the preceding remarks are all well grounded, then is it plain, that this book gives a better insight into their manners and morals, than all their histories, not even excepting the sacred ones. If the student will carefully peruse the book with this view of the matter before him, he will find himself richly repaid in the end, by coming at most interesting developments of the Hebrew national character.

The book in its *present* form, was a thing of gradual accomplishment. "The words of the wise," in 22 : 17, seq.; the additions made by "the men of Hezekiah," 25 : 1, seq.; and the compositions of Agur and Lemuel, 30 : 1, seq., 31: 1, seq.; are all witnesses to the correctness of this statement. But all these topics are amply discussed in the Introduction.

I have only to add, that I have purposely adapted my work to *beginners in Hebrew study*. Hence the minute and careful solution of all which is *abnormal*, either in form, idiom, or syntax. It is of little or no use to pursue the study of the original Scriptures, without aiming at minute philological accuracy. Half-way between this and a mere popular preaching commentary, is the least satisfactory way of all. It is too high for the common reader, and too low for the accurate inquirer. It therefore satisfies neither.

Should a kind Providence still preserve me in life, with the power of action, I think seriously of endeavoring, at some future period, to *write a commentary on this book, altogether adapted to common readers*, that is, to the great mass of our population. There is no book on earth of deeper interest, in a social, moral, industrial, and economical point of view, than the book of Proverbs. May and should it not have a wider diffusion, and be more read and studied, and better understood ? I believe it may, if it shall be duly provided with popular and appropriate illustrations. I hesitate, indeed, as to my own competency duly to perform this task ; but I cannot hesitate as to cherishing an ardent desire that it should be speedily and well performed.

MOSES STUART.

Andover, 1852.

INTRODUCTION.

---

§ 1. *Name of the Book.*

THE full name of the book is מִשְׁלֵי שְׁלֹמֹה, *Proverbs of Solomon,* which constitute the first two words that present themselves in the text to the reader. More commonly, only the first of these words is employed to designate the book; and accordingly, מִשְׁלֵי is the running title in our Hebrew Bibles; and in our English ones, the common appellation given to it is PROVERBS. The Talmud, and all the later Jews, exhibit the like usage. In Baba Bathra however (fol. 14. 6), the name סֵפֶר חָכְמָה, i. e. *Book of Wisdom,* is given both to this book and to that of Coheleth or Ecclesiastes.

In the Greek Christian fathers, we find not only *παροιμίαι Σαλομῶντος*, (a literal translation of the first compound Hebrew name), but very frequently meet with *σοφία*, as a title for the book; or, as Gregory Nazianz. has it (Orat. xi.), we also meet with *ἡ πανάρετος σοφία*. This last designation is also given by Clement of Rome (i. 57); and Eusebius (Hist. Ecc. iv. 22) speaks of Hegesippus, Irenaeus, and others, as giving to Proverbs the same title. Semler thinks this to be the title of an apocryphal book of Proverbs, (Pref. to Vogel's edit. of Schultens on the Prov.); but without any valid reason. Thus much however is true, viz., that the Christian fathers apply *πανάρετος σοφία* also to the book of

Sirach and the Wisdom of Solomon; see Cotelerius in Epist. Clem. i. 57. It seems probable, that the Jews, before the writing of the Talmud, were accustomed, in common parlance at least, to call the book חָכְמָה; probably because of the peculiar *wisdom* of Solomon, its main author, or because Wisdom makes so conspicuous a figure in it, and is often introduced as a personage speaking. It was natural, therefore, to name her words *σοφία*. And so, in imitation of this title of the book, we have a late apocryphal one which is entitled *σοφία Σολομῶντος*. In this way we may see a sufficient reason, why (in Baba Bathra as quoted above) the name *Book of Wisdom* was employed.

Our English word *Proverbs*, however, or the German *Sprüche*, does not accurately express מִשְׁלֵי. A *proverb* usually means a short and pithy saying which is often employed, and commonly with point and special significancy. But this proverb may be either *prose* or *poetry;* and more usually with us, it is the former. Not so as to מִשְׁלֵי. The word מָשָׁל means *comparison*, *resemblance*, *similitude*. But, as applied to the book of Proverbs, it should not be taken as meaning, that this composition in a peculiar manner abounds in the use of figurative or tropical language or similitudes. In fact, Proverbs is quite distinguished from the Psalms and Prophets, by the comparative infrequency of such language. The *comparison* or *similitude*, in the present case, belongs not so much to the kind of diction, as to the *poetic parallelisms* everywhere employed. Scarcely a single proverb is completed in one clause, or short sentence. Nearly every verse is *bimembral;* a few only are trimembral; and still fewer have four or more clauses. But whether there are two, or three, or more clauses, they are always adjusted to each other by the like measure or metre. Being placed side by side, being of the like length, and usually standing in the closest connection, they form a *basis of similitude*, even in their external form. Their internal structure helps to confirm this idea. The parallelisms are either *synonymous*, or *antithetic*, or *synthetic*. The first repeat, in the second clause, the same or the like sentiment which is developed in the first clause; the second place the two clauses in *contrast*, or *antithesis*; and the third *continue* the sentiment begun in the first clause, by adding something in the second, either confirmatory or explanatory, or else something which advances the movement of thought. In this case, the parallelism is one of *measure*, or *metre*, rather than one of meaning. Hence the position side by side, (in the last case as well as in the others), the like length of the clauses, and at least the general correspondence of meaning, all naturally lead to and suggest the name מְשָׁלִים. This name, moreover, is appropriately given to a book which consists wholly of language so adjusted and measured, that all parts suggest the idea either of *comparison* or of *similarity*.

It is easy now, in this light, to see the special significancy of the *Hebrew* name; while our English one does not serve at all to characterize the *manner* of the book, (as the Hebrew designation does), but merely its *matter*. Most of the latter (but not all) is, indeed, of a proverbial and gnomic cast; but the Hebrew name shows that this matter has put on a special and *poetic* costume, in respect to measure and arrangement. But we have no English word which will exactly correspond with the Hebrew. We may as well abide, therefore, by the common usage, and name the book, as is wont, the PROVERBS.

§ 2. *Leading Divisions of the Book.*

Independently of striking differences in the style and mode of composition, in various portions of the book, there are some palpable boundaries, which are evidently designed to separate one part from another. For example, there are at least *six different titles*, which serve to show where a new, separate, and different composition begins, if they do not indicate a new and different writer.

Prefixed to the book stands a *general title*, introductory to the whole, and comprehensive of the whole. This is in chap. 1: 1—7. First, we have the name, *Proverbs of Solomon*, which in this case is *generic*. Then follows a designation of the general design and object of the book, which comprehends all parts of it. The book not only teaches how to acquire wisdom and instruction, to know justice and judgment, but also "to understand *the words of the wise, and their dark sayings*," v. 6. Accordingly, where the special *proverbs of Solomon* (included in 10 : 1—22 : 16) break off, *the words of the wise* constitutes a new title, 22 : 17. *Dark sayings*, or *enigmas*, is also specially significant, and has reference, in all probability, to the closing part of the book, where are many of this character. But of this, more in the sequel.

Of the general title, then, in 1: 1—7, we are now prepared to make some estimate. It is plain, that it stands at the head of a collection, which embraces some things not written by Solomon, but by other wise men. That this general title was affixed by a later compiler, will also appear more plainly in the sequel; for this general title evidently alludes to *all* the various contents of the book. At the same time, it may, and perhaps does, serve to introduce the first part of the work, which comprises 1: 8—9 : 18, for two titles might be deemed superfluous. This first division is separated from all the rest of the book, by both manner and matter. In what particular way these serve as a line of distinction or separation, must be a subsequent question; for at present we are concerned only with the *titular* signs of distinction.

The second portion of the book, chap. 10: 1—22: 16, commences with a new and simple title, viz., *The Proverbs of Solomon*. In style and character these are, as we shall hereafter see, very discrepant from the first nine chapters. The subordinate and internal divisions of this second part, it concerns us not at present to notice.

The third division begins with 22: 17, where the pupil is admonished to hear THE WORDS OF THE WISE. These too are peculiar in their manner, and somewhat in their matter, and they extend from 22: 17 to the end of chap. 24. We shall hereafter see, that they exhibit plain marks of an authorship different from that of Solomon. They may have passed under his revision; but they differ much from his proverbial style. There too, as before, is a subordinate division, commencing with 24: 23, and ending with the same chapter.

The fourth division is made by the title in 25: 1, "*These are the Proverbs of Solomon, which the men of Hezekiah king of Judah copied out.*" These have, as we might expect, many traits in common with the second or *Solomonic* division, in 10: 1—22: 16. They exhibit, also, various discrepancies of manner, which show that the plan of collecting and arranging here, was different from that which predominates through the whole of the second division. There are some evident tokens that this fourth division was copied out, by the sacred scribes of Hezekiah, from different collections or volumes of Proverbs, current at that period. What belonged to Solomon, in those collections, seems to have been selected by the scribes from among other proverbs, and then brought together by them into one little volume. The evidence here becomes quite clear, that our present book of Proverbs was not completed, in respect to the final and entire compilation, until nearly three centuries after Solomon; (Solomon † 975; Hezekiah † 698). Before the labor of selecting and copying out, performed by the pious king's scribes, the contents of Prov. 25: 1—29: 27, would seem to have been circulated in connection with books of proverbs, different from the second division of the compound book now before us, viz. 10: 1—22: 16. A title, which gives us a history like that here given, is rarely, if at all, found anywhere else in the Scriptures.

The fifth division consists of chap. 30; which, as its title indicates, appears to be the work of Agur, a son of the queen of Massa. But if no special title had designated this chapter as coming from a hand different from that of Solomon, yet the contents themselves would offer satisfactory proof of this. The style and manner are altogether different from anything else in the book of Proverbs, or in the Old Testament.

The sixth division consists properly of the words of Lemuel, in chap. 31: 1—9; but if we make the division more general, it embraces the whole of the last chapter. Yet a subdivision, in this case, seems necessary, since the eulogy of the virtuous woman, in 31: 10—31, is entirely different from anything else in the whole book. The song is *alphabetical*, i. e. each successive clause begins with each successive letter in the alphabet. This is artistic beyond any other example in the book; but still the piece is one of the most simple and beautiful specimens of lyric eulogy that can be found in the Hebrew writings. *Who wrote it?* is a question for discussion in the sequel. It would seem probable (see Comm. on 30: 1), that Agur and Lemuel were *brothers*, and sons of the same queen of Massa; and not improbably, moreover, the beautiful picture of the "virtuous woman" was drawn by the hand of that fortunate and excellent mother. What Lemuel writes, is in fact and confessedly only a repetition of the excellent advice which his mother gave him; and she, who could give such advice, might also draw the picture in question.

The reader must not be startled with the apprehension, that we are about to bring in *foreigners* and unknown persons, as writers of a part of the Hebrew Scriptures. If he will turn to the Comm. on 30: 1, he may find reason to believe, that *Massa* was held and inhabited by *the sons of Simeon*, i. e. by Hebrews, during the reign of Hezekiah, and probably for some time afterwards; see 1 Chron. 4: 41—43. Inasmuch as chaps. xxx. xxxi. stand last in the book, and after the portion copied out by the men of Hezekiah king of Judah, it is probable that they were obtained last of all, by the final compiler of the book. I speak of *compiler*, because the inscription in 25: 1, shows beyond all doubt, that the collection of the whole, and the uniting of them in one compact body, was a work performed at least about three centuries later than the time of Solomon.

§ 3. *Why is one common name given to the whole?*

Certainly not, as we have seen, because that Solomon wrote the whole; for the testimony of the book itself decides against this, beyond any appeal. And if it did not, the contents of the book would speak against universal sameness of authorship. Still, Solomon appears to have been the principal author. Chap. 10: 1—22: 16 are plainly his; and so 25: 1—29: 27. These constitute a very large portion of the book. From chap. x. to the end of the work, we have only four and a half chapters which appear to have come from other hands. More difficult is it to decide respecting the first division, viz., 1: 8—9: 18. The general title (1: 1—7), as we have seen above, refers to other words than those of Solomon, viz., *the words of the wise*, comp. 22: 17—24: 34; and under these we may also arrange chaps. xxx. xxxi., for Agur, Lemuel, and the queen-mother, were doubtless among the *wise*. But whether the general title to the whole compilation, (inasmuch as it refers to the different parts of the whole), specifically designates also the first nine chapters, is a question about which one may be at a loss. If the title should be interpreted, as designating what follows immediately as belonging to Solomon alone, then it would seem very strange, that this title should be formally repeated again, in 10: 1. What need of this, in case there was no distinction between what precedes, and what follows, as to authorship? Nay, the very fact that such a title stands in 10: 1, creates, as it has been alleged, a doubt of course, whether what precedes belongs to Solomon. The natural implication, it is said, would seem to be, that what had preceded did not belong to him. And if to this we add the circumstance, that 1: 1—7 is, to all appearance, merely a *generic* title of the whole book, then, it is further said, we seem to have no evidence before us, as to the authorship of 1: 8—9: 18. Yet this is not quite so conclusive, as it seems at first view to be. The plain truth is, that 10: 1, seq. is so wholly different in its tone and texture from what precedes, that it doubtless belonged originally to a little book by itself, which had the title that now stands connected with it. Solomon may then have written some, or (so far as this matter is concerned) even all, of what precedes, since no adequate evidence against this can be made out from the title in 10: 1. But it seems equally probable, (as we shall see by and by), that there may be works of more than one author in Part I. Still, the name of Solomon may be given to the whole book, for a reason like to that which makes the book of Psalms to be styled *David* in the New Testament, and also leads us to speak every day of *David's Psalms*, meaning thereby the whole book of Psalms, although David did not write much more than half of the book. The *Proverbs of Solomon* is a short, a good, and an easy name for the whole,—a name which rests on the ground of the old maxim: *A potiori nomen fit.* Solomon wrote most of the book. Solomon was the author of at least three thousand proverbs, 1 Kings 4: 32; he was therefore a great master of gnomic lore; he was wise above all other men, and the book of Proverbs extols wisdom more than any other book; and finally, he was the great exemplar or pattern in the art (if I may so speak) of gnomic writing; and so the book may well be named as it now is. If it is not all Solomon's, it is nearly all after the general manner of Solomon; and from him, as the highest master of gnomic composition, it may appropriately receive its name.

§ 4. *Arrangement and Characteristics of Part* I., *including* 1: 8—9: 18.

(1) As arranged in the Hebrew, this part consists of two hundred and forty-seven verses. Nearly all of these are *simple parallelisms*, i. e. they consist of two members or clauses in each verse. Only eleven *triplets* are found, in the whole.[1] The distribution of the parallelisms, as to the different species of them, is very unequal. If I have reckoned rightly, there are two hundred and nine *synonymous* parallelisms; thirty-six *synthetic;* and only four *antithetic*, which last are all in one group, viz.: 3: 32—35. In the whole two hundred and forty-seven verses, we have only eleven exceptions to *bimembral* parallelism; and these contain each three clauses.

(2) From this survey of the kinds of parallelism, it is evident that Part I. differs widely from the style and manner of Part II. Here, c. 10—15 exhibit one hundred and eighty-six *antithetic* verses, and only twenty-three *synthetic ;* while c. 16—22: 16 reverse this order, and exhibit twenty-four *antithetic*, and one hundred and fifty-nine *synthetic*. But in neither of these two divisions of Part II. do we find the *synonymous* parallelism at all; while in Part I. there are two hundred and nine to thirty-six synthetic and four antithetic. These parallelistic distinctions, therefore, between the two divisions, are of a most palpable and striking

[1] These are in 1: 22, 23, 27. 3: 3. 4: 4. 5: 19. 6: 3, 13. 7: 23. 8: 13. 9: 2.

nature. Specially is this the case with c. 10—15, where the *antithetic* equals one hundred and eighty-six, the *synthetic* are only twenty-three, and *there are no synonymous parallelisms.* Yet this last species makes up almost the entirety of Part I. What bearing this may have on the *sameness* of authorship in both cases, will come in due time to be discussed.

(3) Part II., i. e. 10: 1—22: 16, contains only three verses, (19: 7, 23. 21: 20), where the *triplet* is employed; and even in these, there is synthetic parallelism. In this division, moreover, *no subject is continued so as to comprise more than one verse or sentence.* This last circumstance is very striking, when contrasted with Part I. Here the same subject is continued, in 2, 3, 4, 5, 10, 15, and even up to 25 verses; and this occurs so constantly, that *connected and in some degree prolonged discourse* is, we may well say, altogether the usual order of the day.[1] I find only four cases out of the whole in which a subject is completed by one verse, viz. 3: 30, 33—35. This certainly is very remarkable, and has nothing like to it in *extent*, in any other portions of the book of Proverbs, and very little which is like to it even in *kind.* Only 23: 29—35. 24: 30—34. 27: 23—27. 31: 3—7, 10—31, afford specimens (all excepting one are brief) of the like nature, throughout all the rest of the book. Most distinctly marked, then, is Part I., as to treating subjects *continuously*, and constituting a kind of short discourse, rather than a gnome; for this is the character and tenor of the composition in this Part. All these things seem to plead strongly for different authors; but the

[1] E. g. (1) 8 and 9, 10—19, 20—33. (2) 1—9, 10—15, 16—19, 20—23. (3) 1 and 2, 3 and 4, 5 and 6, 7 and 8, 9 and 10, 11 and 12, 13—18, 19 and 20, 21—24, 25 and 26, 27—29, 31 and 32. (4) 1 and 2, 3—6, 7—9, 10—13, 14—19, 20—22, 23—27. (5) 1 and 2, 3—14, 15—21, 22 and 23. (6) 1—5, 6—11, 12—15, 16—19, 20—23, 24—35. (7) 1—5, 6—27. (8) 1—11, 12—36. (9) 1—6, 7—9, 10—12, 13—18.

discussion of this question must be deferred, for a little time.

(4) A subordinate and artistic classification appears, here and there, in groups of *tens*. So 1: 10—19. 3: 1—10, 11—20. 4: 10—19. 8: 12—21, 22—31. The like of this we meet with nowhere else, in this book. I call it *artistic*, because, somewhat like that of the *alphabetical* Psalms, such an arrangement appears to be purposely made, for the sake of aiding the memory.

(5) Many paragraphs in Part I. are headed with the address: *My son.*[1] *This appears nowhere in Part* II., and but very rarely in the latter part of the book. But this address does not stand at the head of every new and distinct paragraph, although it serves to distinguish paragraphs so far as it goes. It is easy, however, to distinguish them by the subject-matter of their contents, without the aid of such an address. This is another striking point of difference between Parts I. and II., on which we must touch again hereafter.

(6) Some of the most extended sentences in all the Bible, are found in Part I. For example, the whole of chap. ii. (twenty-two verses) is in reality but one sentence. Then again, examine 1: 29—33, which is virtually of the same description; and so 6: 20—26. 7: 6—20. 8: 22—31. 9: 13—18, with many others of less extent indeed, but still longer than is elsewhere common in the book of Proverbs. This is, at least, a circumstance that must be brought into the account, when we come to inquire about *authorship*.

(7) The name of אֱלֹהִים occurs nowhere in Proverbs, except in 2: 5, 17, and in the little work of Agur, 30: 5, 9. Everywhere else יְהוָה is employed, to designate the *Godhead*. To speak in the language of some recent critics, the authors were *Jehovists*, and not *Elohists*. And such being the case,

---

[1] E. g. 1: 8, 10. 2: 1. 3: 1, 11. 4: 10, 20. 5: 1. 6: 1, 20. 7: 1.

would it not seem probable, that this second chapter came from the hand of a person, who was different from the other writers? We must weigh this in the sequel.

(8) The poetic character of some portions of Part I., is greatly elevated above the rest of the book, with the exception, perhaps, of 31: 10—31, which contains the exquisite eulogy of a virtuous woman. In solemn and awful grandeur, 1: 20—33 is hardly surpassed by any monitory passage of the sublime Isaiah. Indeed, it reminds one of many passages of a like nature in this prophet. There we have that lofty and glowing description of Wisdom, in 8: 12—36, hardly surpassed by any scriptural writer. Such is the all-pervading spirit of the poet which breathes through it, that on an aesthetical ground it can well claim a high preëminence. Then, in 7: 6—27, is a picture of the "strange woman," which for vivacity, simplicity, and graphic power, has seldom been exceeded. Nothing can be more discrepant than these pieces are, from the poetry which pervades not only Part II., but the whole book, with some two or three exceptions of a very limited extent. The cause of this difference in style is not merely the different subject-matter of Part I. and that of the rest of the book; for there is plainly another and *different spirit* in the lofty aspirations of the first portion of the book from that of the rest. One is constrained to feel that he is in different company, when he reads Part I., and then the rest of the Proverbs. Still, as there is almost always some room for debate, where *taste* merely is concerned, we must not place so much reliance on this aesthetical judgment, as on plain and simple matters of fact.

(9) In case the compositions of different authors are comprised in Part I., there is still a pervading unity of design in the whole. The principal design of all is, to lead the young in the way of happiness and peace; to warn them against the dangers and attractive temptations which often assail them; and to show them that they will be safe only

by acquiring that heavenly wisdom, which will guide them in attaining to the highest good. There are indeed, here and there, a few brief passages which are apparently isolated; e. g. 3: 30—35. But almost throughout the whole, the main objects which have been stated are in view.

We have now before us the design and the individual characteristics of Part I. We seem, then, in some good measure, to have prepared the way for the discussion of the questions which yet remain.

§ 5. *Where and by whom was Part* I. *composed?*

We put first the question: Is it the work of *one* writer, or of *several?*

Some facts in respect to Part I. seem to have an important bearing on this question. It is a fact, that the same subject, specially in regard to two prominent topics, is very often *repeated;* and this not merely by slight allusions and recognitions *en passant*, but by formal and protracted discussions or representations. For example: The "strange woman" is not only described, with warnings and admonitions subjoined in 2: 16—19, but in the fifth chapter the subject is resumed, and carried on through the whole of it. In 6: 20—35, it appears again with very considerable detail. But even this does not suffice. Chap. 7: 1—27, resumes the subject, and carries it on through all the minutiae of temptations. But while one is by this time ready to think, that nothing more can be said in regard to the *strange woman*, she makes her appearance once more, in 9: 13—18. It is indeed true, that all these descriptions vary from each other, in many respects. The *costume* is not at all the same throughout. But the *person* is the same in all.

What are we now to say, in view of this? Is there any tolerable probability, that the same writer, within so short a compass, repeated his subject at length *five* different times?

Certainly this is not the usual method of writing, among intelligent men; and surely not in a continuous composition. In a large volume, repetitions may occur through forgetfulness, and the writer may be pardonable for them. But that such oblivion could come over a writer, in a composition so brief as that of Part I., is hardly to be credited. Why did he not say all that he had to say on this subject, in *one continuous* composition? There seems to be no assignable good reason for so often quitting and resuming the same subject. Certainly, it makes rather strongly against the *unity* of authorship, when we find these repetitions so frequently made. It is a much more probable solution of the difficulty, to suppose that the compositions of different writers on the same subject, are brought together here by a compiler, and united in one piece. It was a subject in the time of Solomon, which must have assumed a grave and threatening aspect. The golden age of that king, was one in which wealth and splendor, and luxury, and consequently sensuality, very much abounded. At least, if we are to judge of it by Solomon's own example, we must surely come to such a conclusion. This state of things seems to have roused up holy seers and men of God. In different ways they attacked a prevailing vice; and the compiler of the book of Proverbs, or perhaps Solomon himself, seems to have selected the most urgent and persuasive appeals of these men, and, for the sake of impression, combined them all in one book. Hence the repetitions; and these are indeed so frequent, that we can scarcely deem it probable that they were made by one and the same writer.

But the example of repetitions on the subject of incontinence, does not stand alone. There is another, which at least is equally conspicuous. I refer to that of *Wisdom*. In 1 : 20—33, her awful warnings are uttered. In chap. ii., she is found again giving her instructions. In 3 : 13—20, is a most attractive and beautiful picture of her. In chap. iv.

she again appears as an instructor. In v. and vi. she warns against various vices, specially against sloth and incontinence. In chap. vii. she again admonishes and advises in respect to the latter vice. In chap. viii. she is *personified,* and a most magnificent description of her is given. In ix. she reappears once more, and employs all her powers of persuasion to attract learners, and make them docile. The repetition here is on the whole even more frequent than in the former case, although the descriptions, in this case, excepting in chap. viii., are not so protracted as in the first case. Still, it is hardly supposable, that one and the same writer would have repeated the same subject so often, within so limited a piece of composition. It is, at least, easier to account for such repetition, on the ground that *several* writings are here combined, than on the ground that here is *only one* and the same writer.

More especially must we feel constrained to adopt such a solution here, because the discrepancy of style is so great between different portions of Part I. Read, for example, 1 : 20—33, and then compare this with any other piece in this first part. That in chap. viii. may equal or surpass it as to the sublime of poetry, but hardly in the powerful impression which it makes. But that the two pieces are wide asunder in *manner,* is evident at first sight, and particularly to any one familiar with the original Hebrew.

Admitting, then, what we seem to be constrained to admit, viz. that there are several authors concerned with Part I.; who were they? And was Solomon one of them?

On the first question we have no more to say, than that they are not specifically disclosed in chaps. i—ix. Nor has any history known to us given an account of them. We judge, then, only as led by the force of *internal evidence,* arising from the many repetitions of the same subject, and the difference among them in point of style. I say *style,* and not *diction* merely, because the diction itself, although slightly varied, has no such diversity as to afford any good basis for sound critical reasoning against sameness of authorship. One thing may be said in passing, in respect to diction, viz. that the whole book most clearly belongs not to the very late Hebrew. It is quite a different book from Coheleth. Chaldaisms and Syriasms may indeed, in a few cases, be found in it, but not more than in any piece of Old Testament poetry which is of equal length. It seems quite clear from the general tenor of the diction throughout the book, that it must have been written in the middle age of the Hebrew, i. e. between the time of Solomon and that of Josiah. There is a strong probability that most of it was in writing long before the time of Hezekiah; for his sacred scribes added no new compositions of their own, but merely copied out some of Solomon's works, which already existed in other and previous volumes. That there was still remaining very much which they did not copy, is clear from the fact, that Solomon wrote three thousand proverbs (1 K. 4: 32); while, in the whole book of Proverbs now before us, there are only nine hundred and seventeen verses, and of course considerably fewer proverbs, since many of them consist of two or more verses each.

Writers contemporary with Solomon would be likely of course to employ a *diction* similar to his; but the style of each individual would be different from that of the others; and such a difference as it is natural to suppose, we may easily find in Part I. I concede it to be possible, that the same individual might, at different times, have composed the various pieces in Part. I.; because the discrepance between the parts is not sufficient of itself to settle the question decisively about sameness or severalty of authorship. But other reasons combine with this, to make probable a *diversity* of authorship.

I must request the reader, in view of this, to cast his eye again on Nos. 1 and 2 above; where he will see, that nearly the whole of Part I. is made up of *synonymous* parallelisms, while in Part II., (the expressly acknowledged genuine work of Solomon), there is none at all of this kind of writing. It is possible, that a writer, in consequence of a special and designed plan, might purposely adopt these different modes of writing. But plans of so artificial a nature are not common in ancient writings, and specially in the biblical ones. The discrepance is so great in this case, that some design of this kind in the writer must be made probable, or else we must attribute that discrepance to difference of authorship. Then again, it is a fact (see No. 3), that all of Part II. exhibits *the completion of a subject within the compass of one and the same verse;* while in Part I. there are only four verses which resemble Part II. in this respect. It may have been through design, for this plainly is possible; but, on the other hand, everything wears the appearance of being written without any particular plan of this kind; and if so, it is natural to suppose a *diversity* of authorship.

The groups of *tens* in Part I. (No. 4), and the frequent addresses, *My son*, (No. 5), which are nowhere found in Part II., serve to widen the discrepancy of manner between the two writings. The extended and very long sentences in Part I. (No. 6), to which there is no resemblance in Part II.; and also the use of *Elohim* in Part I., and there only as it respects the mass of the composition (No. 7); help to widen the same breach. And, as we have just seen above (No. 9), the poetic spirit and range in Part I. is widely different from that in Part II. As I have already said, it is *possible* that the same man, through special design, might write in this varied manner; but is this a *probable* thing? It seems to me that it is not. I see no difficulty in ascribing to the prophets and holy men of Solomon's time, the composition of some parts of i—ix.; for then they stand on the same ground as to *authority* with that of Solomon's writings; and the supposition of diverse authors removes most or all of the difficulties which have been brought to view. Why then may we not admit it?

But supposing we do admit it; is Solomon, who unquestionably wrote Part II., to come in for a share in Part I.? Are not the discrepancies of style and mode of arrangement so great between the two, as to preclude the idea of Solomon's authorship as to any portion of Part I.?

We must call to mind here, that Solomon was an extensive and very prolific writer. He not only composed three thousand proverbs, but wrote one thousand and five songs, besides his treatises (we know not how many) on botany and zoology. "Would they had all been spared to us!" we are prone to say. Then we might peruse, to their full extent, the writings of the wisest man in ancient times. But a holy Providence knows what is best; and it is quite probable, that we now have the most select and profitable part of the wise king's writings. But to return; a man who wrote so much, and on such a variety of things, must have possessed an uncommon power of composing, and this power was exercised in a variety of ways. This being admitted, we might say, perhaps, that the last portion of Part I., viz. chaps. 6:20—9:18, (which seems to be but one extended discourse), may have come from the hand of Solomon. It is, at all events, well worthy of him. Chaps. vii. viii. and a part of ix., are in a style of finish, beauty, and magnificence, which well becomes the celebrated and learned king. This differs, I readily concede, quite widely from Part II.; but we must call to mind, that the *kind* of writing is entirely different. The proper *gnomic* does not at all belong to Part I.; while all of Part II. is gnomic. The vivid picture in chap. vii., and the lofty strains of chap. viii., well become what we may suppose to have been the genius and mental power of such a king.

But why not extend the like reasoning to the whole of Part I.? Because this would present the inexplicable difficulties already adverted to and described above, viz. those which would attach to a repetition of the same subject so often, and in such a narrow space, by the same individual writer. We have acknowledged the *possibility* of one and the same authorship throughout; but the *probability* against it is too strong to be overcome by anything short of some positive evidence; and this we have not.

But what of the *inscription* or *introduction*, 1: 1—7? Does not this attribute the *whole* to Solomon? This subject has been already discussed (§ 2. § 3.); and we have seen that this introduction has reference to the *whole book*, some parts of which, (e. g. 22 : 17—24 : 34 and xxx. xxxi.), are surely not from Solomon's pen. We have seen, then, that the inscription is *generic*, and not specific; and that the book is *Solomon's* in a like (or even in a stronger) sense than the book of Psalms is *David's*. It does not follow, therefore, from this inscription, that we are obliged by it to ascribe all, or even any, of Part I. to Solomon. But inasmuch as other authors are not here expressly intimated, we may well suppose that Solomon himself brought Part I. into its present form, by selecting from other prophets or holy men of God, what would well accord with his great design, viz. to recommend wisdom, and to show its high importance. Hence the repetitions; hence the discrepancies of style. And if he not only wrote 6 : 20—9 : 18, but compiled the rest, well might the work be attributed to Solomon. There is nothing in the language or manner of Part I., or in any portion thereof, which gives us any hint that a part of the composition is later than the time of Solomon. There is not one word in it, for example, of warning against *idolatry*, the crying sin of all times after that of Solomon. How could this have been omitted, when other sins are here censured in language of the gravest rebuke? Everything in this part of the book looks like belonging to the age of Solomon, and nothing is against this view of the matter. And surely it will be admitted that Solomon performed a very appropriate work, when he compiled Part I. as an introduction to his own in Part II.

I cannot prove that my supposition is true by any direct testimony; neither can any one prove that it is not true. But in the absence of specific history, or testimony, it seems to me that a very probable case has been fairly made out; and at all events one which relieves us from most of our critical difficulties.

As to the other question proposed at the beginning of this section, viz. *when* was Part I. composed? it is of course answered by the preceding remarks on the authorship, in case they are well grounded. The *time* was the age of Solomon.

§ 6. *Characteristics of Part* II., 10 : 1—22 : 16.

The great question of authorship is here decisively answered, by the inscription to the piece as it stands in 10 : 1. There is no critical ground for suspecting that this inscription is incorrect. The *time* when it was written, is of course also settled. What remains is, to exhibit the distinctive characteristics of the writing now before us.

(1) The piece itself seems to be divided, or distinguished as to its method, into two leading portions, viz. x—xv. (which I shall name A.), and xvi—xxii. 16, (named B.). I refer to the *kinds of parallelism* respectively employed in each part, A. and B. The part A. has one hundred and eighty-six *antithetic* parallelisms, and twenty-three *synthetic*; while, on the other hand, the part B. has twenty-four only of the first kind, and one hundred and fifty-nine of the latter, (see § 4. 2). In the first, the *antithetic* is altogether predominant; in the second, the *synthetic*. What led to such an evident diversity of manner in the two parts, we are unable to say. It seems probable, however, that, at first, the two compositions were *separate*, and were composed at different times, although

by the same writer. *Diversity* may have been an object designed to be accomplished by the change of parallelisms. In other respects than that of the different kinds of parallelism, there is very little, in regard to any discrepancy, that deserves particular notice. We shall soon see that the same general characteristics belong, for the most part, to both divisions.

(2) All throughout the piece is of one tenor, as to *the completion of sentences by a single verse;* for every verse forms an independent and complete sentence. Rarely is there ever a similarity of subject in two or more continuous verses, so as to connect them even in a loose way. And so palpable is this trait, that the *order* of the verses might be almost indefinitely changed, without any serious injury to any part of the piece. Even the two parts of the same verse very rarely run into each other, so as to form one composite sentence. The exceptions to this are nearly all in one single chapter, viz. in 20: 10, 11, 12, 14, 19, 21, 30. Such a rigid method, from beginning to end, both in A. and B., shows that the writer had a special design in view, viz. to insert only such proverbs as were complete in one verse, whatever the kind of parallelism might be. This method, although of frequent occurrence in the sequel of the book, is nowhere else so rigidly observed as here.

In A., as we have seen, almost the whole of the verses are of the *antithetic* order; and in B., of the *synthetic*. The general rule as to completing the sense, is common to both parts; and so is it also in regard to the respective length of the parallelisms; but in B., there are very few examples of the *antithetic* kind. In 21. 15, 20, 26, 28, 29, 31. 22: 3, are included nearly, if not quite, all the cases of this nature. This does not indeed show a difference of authorship, but merely a different design in the writer as to method, in A. and B. It looks very much as if originally there were two *libelli*, the one for *antithetics*, and the other for *synthetics*. It is impossible to examine the whole matter minutely and critically, without coming to the conclusion, that such an arrangement is *designed*, and not accidental. But one author, however, is admissible in the present case, because the general principle of systematic arrangement, in other respects, is so uniform throughout, and so entirely consistent, as to imply that the whole plan proceeded from one and the same mind.

(3) There is another characteristic exhibited in some passages of Part II., which shows a peculiar *artistic* (if I may so call it) construction. This is, that the same word or words, or one or more words of the like import, which are leading and important words, are arranged consecutively in two or more verses, and repeated in each, although the general tenor of meaning in the verses themselves is different. For example: In 10: 6, 7, we find צַדִּיק and רְשָׁעִים in both verses. So in 10 : 14, 15, מְחִתָּה, stands in both ; so 10 : 16, 17, לְחַיִּים; 10: 18, 19, שִׂפְתֵי and שְׂפָתָיו; 10 : 20, 21, both צַדִּיק and לֵב; 10: 28, 29, רְשָׁעִים; 10: 31, 32, תַּהְפֻּכוֹת. All these (in one chapter) look like *designed* arrangement. So also 11: 8, 9, נֶחֱלָץ and יֵחָלֵצוּ; 11: 10, 11, קִרְיָה and קֶרֶת; 11: 25, 26, בְּרָכָה; 11: 30, 31, צַדִּיק. Again, in 12 : 5, 6, 7, רְשָׁעִים; 12: 15, 16, אֱוִיל. In 14: 12, 13, אַחֲרִיתָהּ; 14: 17, 18, אִוֶּלֶת; 14: 26, 27, יִרְאַת יְהוָֹה. In 15: 31, 32, תּוֹכַחַת. In 16 : 27, 28, 29, אִישׁ. In 18: 6, 7, כְּסִיל; 18 : 10, 11, עֹז and עֻזּוֹ; 18 : 18, 19, מִדְיָנִים. — These are specimens. More might be added; but these will suffice. Such a thing is evidently the result of *designed* grouping; and probably it was done in order to aid the memory of the pupil.

The like to this, and for a like purpose, may be seen in 15: 33 and 16: 1—7, 9, 11, where the word יְהוָֹה occurs ten times in succession. So in 16 : 10, 12, 13, 14, 15, מֶלֶךְ occurs (partly in the plural) five times. And the like to all this is sometimes found in the Psalms, probably thus composed for the sake of easy remembrance.

A few (very few) cases occur, of like matter in two continuous verses ; even then each may be taken separately, and be disconnected without injuring either verse. But there is no general plan in such an arrangement ; and each verse, although similar, is in fact independent of the other.

There is, moreover, throughout Part II., a general correspondence in the measure or length of the clauses, or verses. Generally, the first clause has four words, and the second three ; but sometimes they stand four and four, and five and three ; and in a few cases, three and three. In a few cases, also, where small words are attached to larger ones by a Maqqeph, there are nine, and even ten and eleven words ; see 17: 2, 8. 19 : 18. 21: 1.

In some cases, (but few), there is, in the second clause, a virtual repetition of the sentiment of the first ; e. g. in 11: 7. 14 : 19, 26. 16 : 16. 17 : 6. 18 : 3. Sometimes (very rarely) the second clause is exegetical of the first ; as in 15 : 3. In a few cases, the second clause gives the reason or ground of the first ; e. g. 16 : 26. 21: 7. Comparatives by *as* sometimes appear ; as in 10 : 26. 11 : 32 (כְּ being implied). The comparative degree by מִן is not unfrequent ; as in 15 : 16, 17. 16 : 8, 19. 17 : 10. 21 : 19.

We must not omit to mention, that there is a considerable number of cases, in which there is a *repetition* of a preceding proverb, in a different place. Thus 14: 12, and 16 : 25, (comp. 21: 2). 21: 9 and 19 ; and so a repetition of *one clause* of a verse ; e. g. 10 : 1 and 15 : 20 ; 10 : 2 and 11: 4 ; 10 : 15 and 18 : 11 ; 15 : 33 and 18 : 12 ; and specially is this identical as to one clause, in 11: 21 and 16 : 5 ; 14 : 31 and 17 : 5 ; 19 : 12 and 20 . 2.

This last circumstance suggests to our consideration, that there were various sources from which Part II. must probably have been derived. We cannot well suppose that Solomon sat down to the composition of Part II. as he would in order to write chap. viii., i. e. his eulogy on Wisdom. In the last case, he probably drew directly from his own conceptions, without reliance on any other writing. But in the case of mere gnomes or popular proverbs, he was in quite a different position. Many, perhaps most, of these proverbs were such as common sense and long experience had for substance already suggested to the minds of intelligent men. They were floating among the common people, and subjected thereby to more or less disfigurement or change. Solomon's mind, under divine influence, could easily recognize such of these proverbs as were true and useful; and, acknowledging them to be so, he transferred them into *written* language, so that they might be rendered permanent in their true and proper sense, and be thus guarded against alterations. These common maxims of life, thus sanctioned by him when in such a state, became *authoritative* and general truths. Of course, we may properly assign the *authorship* of them to him; for he selected them, adopted them, and published them as consonant with his own views. They were only of *traditional* currency before this; but now they became a part of Scripture, under the sanction of Solomon.

We are obliged, as it seems to me, to account in this way for the many *repetitions*, in Part II., of the same things. One sole concipient writing, purely from his own mind, in a composition like this, would never have repeated the same things so often, and within so limited a space. His memory could scarcely be so treacherous, as to forget what he had just said. The only probable way, then, in which these repetitions came to be introduced, was through the medium already described. If Solomon wrote three thousand proverbs, he must have been a great lover of *gnomic* lore, and probably must have read everything of that nature which was then in circulation. Doubtless, at times, he selected whole paragraphs from other collections, and, transferring them to his own, just as they were, and because he assented to the truth of them, he transcribed them in the state in which they stood in other Mss. In this way, we may suppose many of the maxims in

Part II. to have been transferred from other collections of gnomes, and when the transfer was made, it was (as usual in ancient times) made without curtailing or expunging. Hence came about the repetitions in question, because they were connected with other matter which was not repetitious. We may suppose, that most well-read persons of that day would recognize at once what was new, and what had been transferred. We cannot now do what they could then do; but we can easily see how the whole matter of repetition might take place; and that without supposing the wise king to have forgotten himself, or rather, to have forgotten what he had just written. The proverbs transferred from common life into Part II., are now of course just as valid, by the sanction of Solomon, as they would have been, had he composed them all *de novo.*

I see no other probable way of accounting for the phenomenon in question. It seems hardly feasible to make out the probability of a *de novo* composition; and specially at the expense of taxing the writer's memory with failure, and denying him a consciousness of what he had just written. But as the matter has now been represented, we find no serious difficulties attendant upon the repetition of the same gnome. It does seem probable, at least, that some such cause occasioned the repetition now in question; for the only motive of *repetition,* independent of this consideration, must have been the special importance of the matter repeated. But investigation will show, that in the present instance it could not have sprung from this source, because the things repeated, to say the least, are not more important than many other things not repeated.

We must call to mind here, that Solomon wrote or composed some three thousand proverbs; while in the book before us, less than one third part of these are contained. He might then, in compiling Part II., have selected much from his own previous *libelli.* Who can show even a probability that he did not? Still, one would naturally suppose that, in selecting and transferring his own compositions, he would take more liberty of omitting what was repetitious, than he would when extracting from others. Most probably, then, the *repetitions* occur in cases of extracting from others, while we may still believe that Solomon selected much from his own previous writings, which was adapted to his design in the writing of Part II.

(4) Ewald (as usual) finds a *ὕστερον πρότερον* in the order of Parts I—IV. He arranges them thus. (1) Part II. (2) Part IV. (3) Part I. (4) Part III. Hitzig cleaves to the present order of parts, in our Hebrew Scriptures. Such being the case, we may well believe, since the difference between them is so great, that the reasons of Ewald for his arrangement are not of a very cogent nature; more specially so, since Bertheau has shown (Einl. § 3), that there are no valid arguments for such an arrangement. Part II., which Ewald ranks as the oldest, he attributes to a period of two hundred years after the death of Solomon. Part IV., which he ranks next, was composed, as the inscription shows, in the time of Hezekiah, i. e. about three hundred years after Solomon. Still later, as he avers, came Part I., which he ranks as the *third* in order; and last of all, Part III., that is, 22: 17—24: 34.

I shall but briefly discuss this matter, inasmuch as the whole thing seems to me quite arbitrary. Ewald alleges, (1) That there is a great diversity between Parts I. and II., as to their form or manner. — This, we have not only acknowledged, but also have shown at length above. But this proves nothing as to the *time* of composition. Contemporary writings may be, and often are, exceedingly diverse. He says that Part II. has the air of *antiquity*, i. e. it is characterized by even measure, sentences complete in one verse, and strongly marked parallelisms. But conceding this, (which indeed is true), on the ground which we occupy it does not touch the case. Solomon, as we have seen, probably selected proverbs from those in common use, and reduced them to writing. The older they were, the better; for in this case the currency of them would meet with no objection. All nations, in their more uncultivated state, are attached to gnomic sayings, and abound in them. Cultivated nations more seldom form new proverbs. Before books are written, *gnomes* are the *books* of the multitude. The intelligence of keen observers strikes out many a true and happy thought, which is the result of oft-repeated experience. So with the Hebrews at all events, who were surely a talented nation. A large portion of Part II. may have been traditionally current, before Solomon's day; and well may his book, containing more or less of selections from proverbs long current, wear to us the air of great antiquity. But this is nothing to the purpose of showing, that Part II. was *written* long before the other Parts. The truth is, that the difference in manner between Parts I. and II., is apparently a matter of design. In other words, the writer or writers of Part I. intended to write *continued* and *connected* discourses; while the compiler of Part II. intended just the contrary. But this is a matter which has nothing to do with the *time* when these Parts were respectively written.

(2) Ewald objects to the first two Parts being *coetaneous*, that *the difference in language* between them is very great.

But even if we allow this, it cannot prove anything of consequence. If much of Part II. consists of proverbs long in use, it of course exhibits more or less of the older language. Besides this, the fact that the gnomes in Part II. are all made up of one sentence each, and that they are brief, pointed, compressed, popular maxims, is enough to account for variation, in some measure, from the diction of the continuous and connected discourses in Part I. To establish his point, Ewald produces some four or five words and phrases in Part II., which are not found in Part I. But this proves nothing; for different compositions and different subjects of course demand different language. On the other hand, there are many leading and characteristic expressions and words, which are common to Parts I. and II. For example: מַרְפֵּא, יָפִיחַ, פֶּרַע, לֹא יִנָּקֶה, עֵץ חַיִּים, חָכְמוֹת (plur.) זָרָה *adulteress*, תַּהְפֻּכוֹת, שִׁלַּח מָדוֹן, חָרַשׁ רַע, עָרַב and תָּקַע put together, נָלוֹז, אַחֲרִית, אִישׁוֹן and many others. If any one will take his Hebrew Concordance, and trace these words in it, he will see that they belong in common to Parts I. and II. This is enough to overwhelm all the cases produced by Ewald, of peculiar usage in Part II.; even if they were in point as far as they go. Every one who reads and compares, will see that there are very many expressions which are alike in both Parts. The compositions, as we have seen, are in all probability not all from the same hand; but that they are *contemporaneous*, or nearly so, seems to be impressed on the diction and on the thoughts everywhere to be met with.

(3) Ewald asserts, that the external relations apparent in Parts I. and II., are diverse and unlike.

In proof of this, he appeals to the case of lawless marauders wandering through the country, as brought to view in 1: 11—19. 2: 12—15. 4: 14—17. It is true, however, that the very nature of the composition in Part II., (all of it introducing and concluding a subject in each verse), renders such a prolonged description as we find in Part I. impossible. But 12: 6 compared with 1: 11, will show that both Parts recognize one and the same thing as to predatory excursions. The passage in 3: 31, which cautions against envying those who *oppress*, Ewald thinks peculiar to Part I. But the numerous passages in Part II., which threaten the rapid loss of unjust gain, and the speedy perishing of the wicked who are rich, surely correspond to and expand the idea in 3: 31.

These, then, are all the reasons which Ewald finds, to disprove *contemporaneousness*. Yet these are surely but a broken reed to lean upon. On the other hand; what will he say to the *thoughtless suretyship* which is described and censured, in 6 : 1—4, and also in like way, in 11: 15. 17: 18. 20 : 16 ? All this seems to indicate a sameness of period for both compositions.

The result, then, seems plainly to be this, viz., that Parts I. and II. were written at or near the same period ; that in all probability they passed through the hands of Solomon, as both compiler and original author ; and as we have direct testimony to his authorship in respect to Part II., in the sense above explained, so we have probable evidence from the position and nature of Part I., and its adaptedness as an introduction to the book, that it was put in its present place by the wise king, and of course sanctioned by his authority, even if it were not compiled in part by him. If the last three chapters of Part I. are his composition, (and this they would seem to be), then is it altogether probable that he *compiled* the rest. The general introduction in 1: 1—7, seems to come from the hand of the *latest* compiler of the book, as it relates, in part, to portions of the work written some three hundred years after the time of Solomon.

In this general conclusion, as to the contemporaneous rise of Parts I. and II., Bertheau seems fully to agree. At least he deems Ewald's arguments as making nothing against this. Hitzig adopts the present order of the Parts as the true one; and he observes, in confirmation of this, that the five books of the Psalms were originally collected and arranged as they now stand.

§ 7. *Characteristics of Part* III., 22: 17—24: 34.

The general inscription in 1: 1—7, refers to THE WORDS OF THE WISE, as one thing which the book is designed to teach, v. 6. Here now, in 22 : 17, we find that *same title*, in an exhortation to give a hearing ear to such words: "Hear *the words of the wise.*" Again, in 24: 23, some additions to *the words of the wise* are said to be made; and these are contained in 24: 23—34. Here, then, we have at least two collections of those *words of the wise.* In the first, the compellation, *My son,* is several times repeated; but in the second part it does not at all appear.— Our next question is: How is Part III. characterized?

(1) In Part III., the construction of the verse or metre is nothing like so regular as in Part II. We have indeed here (as there) verses of eight, seven, and six words; but they stand mingled with others of eleven words, (22: 29. 23: 31, 35); of fourteen words, (23: 29); and even of eighteen words, (24: 12). In some of these instances, distinct traces of proper parallelism can hardly be discovered. They are a kind of measured prose.

Here, moreover, the parallelisms are all *synthetic,* excepting only 24: 16, which is *antithetic.* Here also sentences completed in one verse are the *exception,* (and a small one); those in two or more, are the *rule.* Very often, three verses are combined in a sentence, e. g. 23: 1—3, 6—8, 19—21. In one case, 24: 30—34, we have five verses; and in 23: 29—35 (virtually one compound sentence) we have even seven verses. All this makes a great variety and a miscellaneousness in the composition. In general, Part III. is strikingly different from anything which precedes it.

(2) Here, as in Part I., we have the address: *My son.* And where this is not prefixed to a paragraph, an address is often made to the second person singular, *thou.*

(3) As to the *arrangement* of the proverbs here, sometimes those similar in their tenor are brought together; e. g. 23: 15, seq. But in general, no pains appears to have been taken to make out arrangements regularly consecutive. Neither the compiler, nor the original concipients, seem to have felt the necessity of subjecting themselves to the ordi-

nary gnomic rules; for in some places we have, as it were, short parables; e. g. 23: 29—35. 24: 30—34.

On the whole, then, the discrepancy between Part III. and the preceding Parts, is striking, and would of itself raise doubts in the mind of the reader, as to identity of authorship in each of the Parts. But when to all this is superadded the distinctive titles in 22: 17, and 24: 23, it would seem that there is little room for critical doubt, that the authors of Part III. are different from that or those of the preceding Parts. But,

(4) *When was Part* III. *first written?* Ewald places it as contemporaneous with Part I., i. e. according to him, about one hundred years later than Part II. We have seen that he gives no satisfactory reasons for assigning an earlier period to Part II., and a later one to Part I. So far as language or phraseology is concerned, there is much reason to believe that all three Parts are nearly of the same age. E. g. תָּקַע and עָרַב are joined here, as in Parts I. II.; 22: 26 and 6: 1. 17: 18. So Parts II. III. have many expressions in common; e. g. שִׁלְּחִים, 22: 21 and 10: 26; שׁוּחָה עֲמוּקָה, (an adulteress), 22: 14 and 23: 27; תַּחְבֻּלוֹת, 24: 6 and 11: 14. 20: 18; יִקְּבוּהוּ עַמִּים, 24: 24 and 11: 26, (the latter having לְאוֹם); רַע עַיִן in 23: 6, and טוֹב עַיִן in 22: 9. Ewald says, that the warning against sedition, 24: 21, is peculiar to Part III.; but 17: 11 and 16: 14 show that this subject is fully recognized in Part II. Thoughtless and hasty suretyship is denounced in 22: 27, and in 20: 16 also is the same thing virtually the subject of reprobation. On the score of language, then, no striking differences can be made out, but, as we have seen above, quite the contrary.

(5) *By whom was Part* III. *compiled?* To this question we can give no definite answer, because the title (in 22: 17) does not name any author. Was the compiler, then, probably the same who compiled Parts I. II.? We cannot answer this

question with any pretensions to certainty; but there is a probability still in this case, which appears somewhat strong. The compiler presents *himself* as speaking, only in 22 : 17—21. The rest of the piece contains *the words of the wise.* But the compiler's own words are too few for us to draw any conclusions from them. The address or exhortation in them is of a tenor like to that of the addresses in Part I.; although the *style* of one portion of the address, viz., in 22 : 19—21, is different from that in the addresses of Part I. The discrepancies and the resemblances in general have already been stated. There can be hardly any room to doubt, that *the words of the wise* (22 : 17) forms a new category, standing at the head of something superadded. The only question is — Did Solomon, (in case he compiled Parts I. II., as seems quite probable), also add Part III. to the others which he had compiled? For my own part, I feel quite disposed to answer this question in the affirmative. It need not follow from this, that Solomon himself compiled the different portions of Part III., or even that he wrote the exhortation in 22 : 17—21. He might have lighted on this collection, with its introduction, made by some prophet or man of God in his time, and, approving of it, have appended it to Part II., his principal work. But that Part III. is not his own proper composition, seems to be quite probable from the discrepance of this Part from the others, in respect to metres, length of parallelisms, and other external marks of distinction. Specially is this made probable by the fact, that emphasis is often made in Part III., by the express repetition of the pronoun; e. g. אַף אַתָּה in 22: 19; אַף הִיא, 23 : 14, 15, 19, 20. 24: 6, 27, 32. This usage is very rare elsewhere, in the whole book.

We may easily believe that Solomon, who had such an attachment to gnomic lore, meeting with Part III. in its present form, and so made ready as it were to his hand, selected it to be added to his own little volume. Some of it may even have been taken from other parts of his own works. At all events, however this may be, we cannot well suppose that it was added to Parts I. II. after the time of Hezekiah, when Part IV. was added; see 25 : 1. Had not Part III. already been in existence before this, it would of course have been *put after* what is now Part IV. in the compilation ; for had it been in existence, and not been already united to Parts I. II., then it was almost a matter of course for the men of Hezekiah to have put Solomon's work, now in Part IV., immediately after Part II., so that all the writings of Solomon might be connected together. We can imagine no motive why late compilers should insert Part III. between Part II. and the present Part IV. It would of course have been postponed.

We may then take it as altogether probable, that Parts I—III. were first collected and put together, and were in circulation, and probably had long been so, when the *men of Hezekiah* made an addition, by collecting from various writings of Solomon that stood in other collections, that which now belongs to Part IV., and joining this with the other preceding Parts. We may account for the sameness of one clause in 20 : 18 and 24 : 6, and so of one in 11 : 14 and 24 : 6, by the supposition, that the compiler of Part III. had drawn from sources which contained some things belonging to Solomon. Particularly may this principle be applied to 6 : 10, 11 and 24 : 33, 34. The first was either in some composition adopted by Solomon, and incorporated with Part I., or else came from some of Solomon's *libelli* of proverbs, which do not appear in his works now extant. The compiler of Part III. met with the same *libellus*, and extracted 24 : 33, 34, from it. The same writer, in the same continuous book, would scarcely have made such repetitions. On any other ground than the one now suggested, they can hardly be accounted for.

By whomsoever composed, Part III., although it differs much from the preceding one, cannot well be placed *below* the preceding Part. It is full of life and power, and in point of graphic description, it is not exceeded by anything in the whole book; see, for example, 23 : 29—35. 24 : 30—34.

One word on a subordinate division of Part III., which commences with a new title in 24 : 23, running thus: לַחֲכָמִים גַּם אֵלֶּה, i. e. *these also belong to the wise*, the ל being a ל *auctoris*, as in the Psalms. The גַּם settles the question, that there is a new addition appended here. It compares well with the preceding division, both in spirit and in manner. It was indeed well worthy of reception. The probability of course is, that it was derived from a source different from that of the preceding division. The גַּם shows the design of the compiler, viz. that the two portions of Part III. should be inseparably connected.

§ 8. *Characteristics of Part* IV. *chap.* xxv—xxix.

The *authorship*, and of course the *time* of compilation, is here made certain. This Part contains *the Proverbs of Solomon, which the men of Hezekiah, king of Judah, copied out*, 25 : 1. *The men of Hezekiah* must of course mean, the sacred scribes in the service of the king, or his counsellors. Among these doubtless were many excellent men, who would zealously perform such a labor. The verb הֶעְתִּיקוּ, rendered *copied out*, lit. means, *to transfer from one place to another*. In respect to a *writing*, this must mean, *to transcribe*, or *to copy*. Sept., very happily: *ἐξεγράψαντο*. This shows that other volumes, or portions of volumes, comprising the gnomic compositions of Solomon, were then in circulation, besides what is contained in Parts I. II. above. From them the scribes of the pious king made a selection, and chaps. xxv—xxix. is the fruit of this selection. We must notice the characteristics.

(1) In respect to *parallelisms*, there are ninety-three *synthetic*, and thirty-five *antithetic* ones, but no synonymous members of verses. In respect to the metres, they very

much resemble those in Part II., the verses mostly consisting of eight, seven, and six words. In some cases, two closely connected verses contain of course many more; e. g. 25: 6, 7, comprise twenty words; and 25: 21, 22 amount to eighteen words. The antithetic verses (=35) are strenuously and regularly antithetic. But in chaps. xxv—xxvii., most of the verses are *comparisons*, either in the strict, or in the freer sense. In many, we can hardly make out a parallelism; e. g. 25: 8, 9, 10, 21, 22. 26: 18, 19. 27: 1. 29: 12. Yet there is a *symmetry* even here, in respect to the form of the clauses. We meet here with repeated instances of a proverb extended to several verses; which is altogether different from Part II. There are some passages, e. g. 26: 23, 28, and 27: 23, 27, which have a lofty poetic spirit, quite different from that of common gnomes.

(2) There is a striking resemblance in Part IV. to Part II., in regard to the repetition of the same word or phrase in different verses. E. g. 25: 1 and 2, מְלָכִים; 25: 4 and 5, הָגוֹ; 25: 8, 9, 10, רִיב; 25: 11, 12, זָהָב; 25: 19, יוֹם צָרָה, and 25: 20, יוֹם קָרָה; 26: 3—12, כְּסִיל (sing. or plur.) in each of the ten verses; 26: 13—16, עָצֵל in each verse; 26: 20, 21, עֵצִים; 27: 1, 2, תִּתְהַלֵּל and יְהַלֶּל; 27: 5, 6, אַהֲבָה and אוֹהֵב. So in 27: 7, 9, מָתוֹק and מֶתֶק; 28: 4, 7, 9, תּוֹרָה; 28: 3, 6, רָשׁ; 28: 2, 16, יַאֲרִיךְ; 28: 12, 28, קוּם רְשָׁעִים; 29: 2, 16, בִּרְבוֹת צַדִּיקִים and בִּרְבוֹת רְשָׁעִים; 28: 14 and 29: 1, מַקְשֶׁה; 29: 8, 10, אַנְשֵׁי. All this looks like designed selection and arrangement, in such a way as to attract attention, and to help fix passages in the memory; and this may be called *Solomonic;* for it is very common in Part II.

(3) The point of striking difference between Part II. and IV. is, that in the latter, there are many cases of two or more verses connected in one sentence, which is never the case in Part II.; e. g. 25: 6 and 7, 9 and 10, 21 and 22. 26: 18 and 19. 27: 15 and 16. Moreover, in 26: 23—28, there are six verses united; and in 27: 23—27, there are five.

(4) Part IV. shows that the men who compiled it were different from the compiler of Part II. One and the same compiler or author would never have repeated, in Part IV., so many things which are said in Part II. Compare, for example, the following passages: 25 : 24 with 21 : 9; 26 : 13 with 22 : 13; 26 : 15 with 19 : 24; 26 : 22 with 18 : 8; 27 : 13 with 20 : 16; 27 : 15 with 19 : 13; 27 : 21 with 17 : 3; 28 : 6 with 19 : 1; 28 : 19 with 12 : 11; 29 : 22 with 15 : 18, (and more there are of the same kind which it is needless to cite). No one continuous writer ever would have repeated himself so often. But others, who selected from his works, might easily come to insert such repetitions, because they stood connected with other matter that surrounded them, and which was cited.

Different is the case in regard to repetitions of Part III., viz. *the words of the wise.* We find only one instance of this, viz. 28 : 21 and 24 : 23. In respect to repetitions of itself in Part IV., there is only one example, viz. 26 : 12 and 29 : 20; but even here, there is so much variation of the latter from the former, that a case of repetition can hardly be made out. So in 28 : 12, 28 : 28, and 29 : 2, there is the like general sentiment, but the costume is different.

On the whole it is clear, from the view given above of repetitions in Parts II. and IV., that the compilers of both drew from the same original sources, whether they were the works of Solomon, or of others. And these close resemblances serve to confirm what 25 : 11 asserts, viz. that Part IV. is made up, or compiled, from the works of Solomon.

Ewald says, that the *diction* of Part IV. serves to show that it sprung from *Northern* Palestine. But as he has not given specific examples, nor any reasons for such an opinion; as there is nothing in history respecting Hezekiah, which serves to confirm the notion, that he sent sacred scribes thither in order to collect proverbs; and specially, as we can discover no diagnostics in this case of a provincial dialect;

I do not see any ground for such an assertion. Most of all did Solomon's works circulate at and near Jerusalem; and there, most probably, were found the works from which Part IV. is selected.

Finally, this Part, although *compiled by the men of Hezekiah*, has Solomon for its *real author;* and therefore is of the same authority as the preceding Parts of the book.

§ 9. *Characteristics of Part* V. *chap.* xxx.

In the Commentary on 30 : 1, the title to this Part is fully discussed; and the attempt is made to show, that the most probable meaning of v. 1 is this: "The words of Agur, the son of her who was obeyed in Massa," [i. e. of the queen of Massa]. It is there shown, that Massa was probably a region or city, lying east of the gulf of Akaba, once possessed by the Amalekites, who at last were expelled by *the sons of Simeon*. These last settled down in the room of the expelled, during the time of Hezekiah, whose scribes copied out Part IV. of the book of Proverbs; 1 Chron. 4 : 41—43. It seems natural, then, to suppose that Parts V. and VI. must have been united to the book of Proverbs, after Part IV. had been joined to it; and the arrangement itself speaks for this. Whether the addition was made by the same *men of Hezekiah*, who selected and added Part IV., we have no means of determining with certainty. But in itself it seems quite probable. It is clear, that Agur was a son of the queen of Massa; and, as king Hezekiah reigned some twenty-nine years, and as the Simeonites may have made their conquest of Massa and settled there in the earlier part of his reign, they may, as living in a distant country, have had, and probably they did have, an Emir or prince of their own to rule over them; and this prince may have been the father both of Agur and Lemuel, for they seem to be brothers, and sons of the same mother; see on 30 : 1. The queen in question, may have been such in consequence of the demise of her husband, who gave her his throne; and on this account, as chap. xxx. was written during her reign, Agur is spoken of as being her son. A distinguished woman she must have been, according to 30 : 1, 31 : 1. It is not said of Agur, however, that he was a *king;* yet of *Lemuel* (probably his older brother) this is said, 31 : 1. But as Agur was the son of a queen, he of course was a *prince.*

Chap. xxx., then, came in all probability from the hand of a *Hebrew.* So the language itself of course indicates. There is nothing specially *provincial* in the diction; although the form and manner of the composition is altogether *sui generis.* If the sacred scribes of Hezekiah selected this composition of Agur, and judged it meet to be joined to the rest of the book of Proverbs, we should be satisfied that it properly belongs there.

(1) In regard to the *parallelisms* here, all but three are of the *synthetic* order. Three are partially *antithetic.* In regard to the *quantity* or space assigned to one and the same subject, some are completed in one verse; others in two; more frequently there are three verses, as in 18—20, 21—23; sometimes four, as in 24—28, and once even six, 1—6. The length of the verses here is often widely discrepant from that in Part II.; for here are verses of eleven, twelve, thirteen, and even twenty-four words (v. 4).

Strict correspondence of the parallelisms is not regarded much here. Many of them, likewise, are but little more than measured prose, excepting the poetic spirit which reigns in them. This, and the kind of metre belonging to them, probably contributed to place this composition in a book of poetic proverbs.

There are some things in chap. xxx. which are altogether peculiar. The repeated reckoning there of *two* things (v. 7); of four things in vs. 11—14; then of three increased by a fourth in vs. 15, 18, 21, 29; then of four things in v. 24; is unlike in extent to anything else in the whole Bible, excepting in Amos i. and ii., where we have *three* and then a *fourth* added, eight times in succession. There is, in our text, a kind of play of the fancy upon the numbers; and the gradual increase, first from two to three, then to three with an appendix, and then four, shows a design or plan of arrangement in the writer's mind. It is plain, indeed, that the design of Agur is not to develop merely maxims or rules of conduct. In fact, there is little of precept here, excepting it be obtained in the way of making out deductions from what is said in the representations of things. Some of the matter is very grave, and attains to a high moral sublimity; see vs. 2—6, where the unsearchable nature of God and the excellence of his truth are strikingly developed. Then come some excellent sentiments, in vs. 7—9. Then follow four classes of individuals, who seem to be held up to indignation, vs. 11—14. Next, we have one of the חִידוֹת (enigmas), which seem to be plainly adverted to in the general introduction to the book, 1: 6. It is difficult to make out the moral of vs. 14, 15. The *insatiability* of the things named there belong to mere natural objects, and has no moral character. It is probable, that under these חִידוֹת is couched some moral truth, which is designedly left for the reader to discover if he can. Perhaps the passage relates to avarice; perhaps to sensual appetites which are nourished, and which grow stronger by indulgence. More difficult still would it be, to find out the design of vs. 18, 19, were it not that v. 20 gives us some clue. The amount of what is here said seems to be, that wickedness may sometimes be so concealed, that no traces of it can be discovered by any one, besides those who commit it. The design of vs. 21—23 is like that of vs. 11—14, viz. to hold up to our dislike several *incongruous* things. On the other hand, in vs. 25—28, there are four notable examples of sagacity and active industry and order, which are designed to stimulate us. Last of all, come exemplars of comeliness and strength. Nothing in all these particulars seems to be dependent on the manner of their consecution. They are seized as they occur to the mind, while it is employed in the excogitation of something which is designed to be enigmatical. Consequently, there is no mutual connection between them, and each is independent of the other. And after all that we can do in the way of inquiry, such passages as vs. 15, 16, and also vs. 29—31, remain in a good measure among the real חִידוֹת. They seem to be written more for the sake of entertaining and interesting the reader, (if I may so speak), than for his direct instruction. They are evidently designed to whet his curiosity, and set him on the alert, in order that he may educe from them something useful. Surely, such an object is not beneath the office of him who teaches youth, in a book like the present, which has not a few passages of witty and sarcastic irony. Why should this be entirely excluded? Did not Elijah use the most cutting irony, in speaking to the priests of Baal? A heathen moralist has said, that "ridicule sometimes cuts deeper than severity." And when the wise king has said, that "a sluggard, who dips his hand into the dish, will not so much as bring it to his mouth," in order that he may feed himself; and also that "the sluggard will not turn himself over in bed, but must be rolled over by others," has he not uttered sarcasm, and held up such a man to ridicule? Even so with Agur. When he says that "there is a generation, — O how lofty are their eyes, and their eyelids lifted up!" (v. 13), and again, when he says that "there are four things which the earth cannot endure," and counts among these "a servant who comes to bear rule," and "an ugly woman who comes to be married," does he not teach in the way of *sarcasm?* vs. 21—23. Verses 18—21 are indeed of a peculiar tenor; but the point to be illustrated, viz. concealed wicked doings, is vividly illustrated by the similes adduced; although in the last of them there is a boldness of illustration that seems somewhat hazardous, in the view of things as now regarded by us.

On the whole, this chapter has no parallel, and even no similar, in all the Bible. And still, the moral and religious tone of it is high. Look specially at 1—6, 8 and 9, 17, 32, 33. The language is vivid and poignant throughout. And if חִידוֹת comes within the plan of the whole collection of the book of Proverbs, as 1: 6 assures us it does, we cannot wonder that *the men of Hezekiah*, or the like men who came after them, added the piece before us to this book. In the narrower sense, hardly any of the verses in it are proverbs; but the instructions given assume the general costume of proverbs, i. e. they exhibit *metre* and *parallelism*, although in the laxer sense.

The tenor of this chapter seems to render it certain, that the general introduction in 1—7 was not written, until this was added, and probably chap. xxxi. also; for 1: 6 appears pointedly to recognize such a composition as this. That the compilers of Part IV., the men of Hezekiah, made this addition to the book, and wrote the general introduction, cannot indeed be positively proved; but it still remains quite probable, that the book was completed, and brought to its present form, by them. If so, then was it completed not far from 700 B. C. There is nothing in its diction or in the facts to which it adverts, that renders a junior age of this composition necessary, or even probable.

§ 10. *Characteristics of Part* VI. *chap.* xxxi.

The introduction, in v. 1, tells us that the sequel contains *The words of king Lemuel.* It tells us also, that he was *king of Massa;* and since 30: 1 presents us with a *queen of Massa*, and Lemuel is said (31: 1) to have been taught by his mother; and since the two compositions (in ch. xxx. xxxi.) are united together, as if they came from the same or a like source; we may reasonably conclude, that both originated in Massa, and at or near the same time. For this cause, it was natural to associate them together, as the compiler has done. In case this is conceded, then the time, place, and author, are sufficiently ascertained, if what has been said in § 9 is correct.

The part appropriate to Lemuel consists only of vs. 1—9. The king was warned, he says, by his sagacious mother, against wine, and women, and oppression in the judgment of causes. The *parallelisms* here are altogether regular, and unusually synonymous. The verses, indeed, are not all of the same length; but there is nothing specially notable in regard to them, in this respect. The composition is through and through *gnomic* in its cast, and the precepts given are not only excellent in a moral point of view, but highly important. Well might Agur exalt the excellence of a mother, who could teach thus; and in a filial and honorable manner did he behave, when, although a king, he attributed to her the honor of the composition which he wrote down.

CHAP. 31: 10—31.

I have not ranked this as a *seventh* Part of the book, (as might be done), because it seems to me probable, from the connection here, that the same mother who taught Lemuel, composed the eulogy that follows, of a virtuous, or rather of an energetic woman; or else the son, perhaps, may have composed it in honor of his mother. If it be objected that such occupations as are here described, could not well be attributed to the *queen-mother*, it should be called to mind, that the queens of small nations or tribes were not exempt, in those times, from labor, or rather from overseeing the affairs of their household. Every classical reader is familiar with the story of Penelope, the wife of Ulysses, and of the web which she daily wove. But it is not necessary, that this should apply personally to the queen herself of Massa;

it is sufficient that she, or whoever wrote the piece, had right views of the importance of industry and care in the mistress of a household, and has given us the outline of them.

As to the eulogy itself, it is in the highest style of parallelistic writing. In perfection of metre, scarcely any even of the Psalms exceed it. Nearly every verse is a synonymous parallelism, and the whole composition has an air of such simplicity, vivacity, and *naïveté*, that it is truly admirable. From whatever quarter the composition came, there is no discerning reader who would not regret its omission. The tenor of it is, indeed, not the same as that of the Proverbs in general; but as it inculcates, in a most attractive manner, both industry and frugality, it falls in entirely with the general spirit and design of the Proverbs.

One other circumstance should be noted. This is, that the song is *alphabetical*, like a number of the Psalms, and the book of Lamentations. This method of writing reminds one of our *acrostics*. Beyond all doubt, such a composition must be designedly *artistic*. Why this fashion of writing should be introduced, we may not be able to say with certainty, but there is much probability that the object in view was to make songs easy to be remembered. The *alphabetic* order of the verses would plainly aid recollection. Whether this method of writing belongs only to the later Hebrew, as Ewald, and after him Bertheau, asserts, is a question that does not concern the passage before us; for this was composed, as we have seen, in Hezekiah's time, or soon after, i. e. not far from 700 B. C. But in regard to Ewald's general assertion, it may be said, that violence must be done to the Hebrew text, in order to make it good; for Ps. xxv. xxxiv. xxxvii. are expressly ascribed to David, in the title. I know not how the genuineness of such titles can be disproved. If not, then David, the leader of all lyric poets among the Hebrews, practised this method of writing, and of course it did not originate with the later Hebrews.

§ 11. *Plan of the Book.*

Having thus gone through with the several parts of the book before us, and endeavored to show the manner and design of the composition, and the authorship of the various portions of it, it may be well to add some miscellaneous remarks on the general nature and design of the PLAN which appears to have been followed in the compilation of the book.

(1) The first thing which strikes us is, that all the proverbs are adapted to regulate our moral, religious, social, and civil demeanor. Some *principle* of conduct, some *rule* of life, some *cautions* adapted to produce sobriety and regularity, lie upon the face of the whole book. *Historical* allusions are scarcely found in it; and yet this mode of proverbializing was not unknown to the Hebrews, as one may see in Judg. 7: 13. 8: 2, 21. 1 Sam. 10: 11. 19: 24. Such we meet with, also, in the Arabic Proverbs of Meidani (edit. Schultens); e. g. "More profligate than Abu Lahab," (No. 113); "We have got Phalhas to sup," (111); "Making more gain than Agrab," (121); "More arrogant than the foolish Tha-(kis," 147); and so in a multitude of cases, but still intermingled, now and then, with cautionary and preceptive gnomes. So in the Proverbs of Abu Obaid. A collection of proverbs by the Caliph Ali, comes much nearer to the book before us, since it is mostly made up of *didactic* precepts. It is evident throughout the book of Proverbs, that the design is not to give that which can have only an *individual* application, but such maxims as are of general or universal use. The popular proverbs in mass doubtless comprised many which had an historical basis; for this is usual among all nations. But although the compilers of the book of Proverbs must have known this, their design was to select only such maxims as were of general import. Both the maxims of Solomon, and of other wise men, appear in our

book; but only that part of either of them which was adapted to general instruction. The like to this we find in the book of Psalms. A pure individual and historical basis none of them have; although historical facts are adverted to in some of them, and are often interwoven. But they are merely *subservient*, and not *predominant*. This, moreover, is of course the most instructive method in the propounding of proverbs, and one the most generally useful.

(2) A survey of the different parts of the book, as to *form* and *manner* of arrangement, is fraught with instruction in regard to the plan of the compilers. Evidently, Part I. was designed to comprise *the longer and more connected series of thoughts.* If it arose, as we have seen it to be probable in § 5, from combining several compositions of different writers, yet nothing was admitted which was contrary to the designed plan of Part I. Like compositions respecting wisdom and incontinence, and some other things, were brought together, because both matter and manner permitted them to be associated. The whole forms an appropriate introduction to the rest of the book.

On the other hand, Part II. consists wholly, as we have seen, of *proverbs completed in one sentence.* From whatever sources the proverbs were selected, only such were admitted as belonged to this category. Not even a mixture of long and short was allowed, as in the rest of the book. Solomon himself, or any other person who selected from him, adhered rigidly to this rule through the whole of Part II.

It was not because Solomon composed no other than simple and single proverbs, that no other are admitted into this Part for Part IV., selected from Solomon's works, exhibits every variety of proverb. It was plainly because the *plan* of selection rejected all the longer gnomes. On this ground, moreover, it becomes plain, why Part IV. is separated from Part II. by intervening matter, viz. *the words of the wise.* If the men of Hezekiah's time had not found Parts I—III.

already collected and united together, they doubtless would have joined Part IV. to Part II., still preserving the title. That they did not adopt this order, seems to be the consequence of possessing an older and an authoritative compilation already made and received, and current probably for a long time among the Hebrews. This they would not venture to disturb. They merely added other things, therefore, of like nature, although sometimes discrepant in respect to form. Consequently, the plan was completed, by adding Parts IV. V. and VI.; which are nearly all of the mixed kinds of composition.

In 22:20, the compiler, or he who added Part III. to the first two, in his introduction to Part III., speaks of the precepts which "*he had before written*" to instruct the reader. This helps, therefore, to distinguish Part III. from that which precedes. In all probability, he who added this third part, did not *compose* it, but transferred it from other collections of proverbs. But nothing hinders our supposing that this compiler was Solomon himself. Indeed, it is difficult to understand 22:20, in any other way, than to suppose this to be implied; for who else wrote the preceding Part II.?

Bertheau says, that the title in 10:1, *The Proverbs of Solomon*, necessarily implies that what precedes (c. i—ix.) was not regarded by the compiler as belonging to Solomon. I do not consider this criticism to be well grounded. The title in 10:1 is the result of a plan, which separates one kind of gnomes from another, since they differ in respect to form and length. Part II. stood by itself at first; and when inserted in the compilation, it was inserted entire, title and all. But this does not make, by any fair construction, any denial of Solomon's claim to authorship in respect to some, or even all, of Part I. For other reasons which have been stated above (§ 5), we conclude that there were several authors concerned with the writing of Part I.; but the reason in question, considering the nature of the case, can hardly be deemed valid.

(3) It has already been brought to view, that the general introduction in 1 : 1—7, must have been written *after* the compilation of the whole book was made. The ground of this is, that in 1 : 6, mention is made of *the words of the wise*, which are to be produced, as well as *the proverbs of Solomon*. This title, as we have seen, is found in 22 : 17, which begins Part III. of the book, and this Part includes 22 : 17—24 : 34, i. e. two and a half chapters. Then follows the selection from Solomon's writings, by *the men of Hezekiah*, xxv—xxix.; and after this the compositions of Agur and of Lemuel, together with the eulogy that closes the book. Bertheau classes under or among *the words of the wise*, these last compositions. This may be allowed, in one respect; for doubtless both of these authors are to be classed among the *wise*. But I apprehend that Bertheau, and all other critics whom I have seen, have failed to discover, in the general introduction (1 : 1—7), what is intended (I might say) to specificate the last part of the book. Chap. 1 : 6 runs thus : "So that he may understand a proverb, *and a dark saying*, — the words of the wise, *and their enigmas*." Whoever reads attentively chap. xxx., will see at once what *dark saying* and *enigmas* here mean. How exactly these words characterize this chapter, must be felt, indeed, by every discerning reader. When commentators of the present day have done their utmost, they are obliged to confess, as I have done, that they can see but darkly. There are parts of the chapter that yet remain in a measure unexplained, — not as to the language, perhaps, but as to the *design* of the writer. Nearly the whole chapter puts on veiled or enigmatical forms. The meaning of most can be made out by diligence; but it requires not a little both of diligence and of knowledge to make it out satisfactorily. In view of this, all seems to be plain in 1 : 6. Not only is

22: 17—24: 34 designated by *the words of the wise*, but the closing part of the book seems to be specifically designated by *dark sayings* and *enigmas*.

From this view of the matter, it appears quite certain, that *the general introduction in* 1: 1—7 *was designed to cover the whole ground*, and therefore must have been written when the collection or compilation was completed. Of course this introduction came from a later hand, from some one who lived at or after the time of Agur and Lemuel.

The whole order of the book in general reminds us of the order of the five parts of the Psalms. Passing by Prov. i—ix., as an appropriate introduction to the book in general, we have in Part II. the proverbs of Solomon; in Part III. the words of the wise; in Part IV. again the proverbs of Solomon; in Parts V. VI. the words of Agur and Lemuel. So with the book of Psalms; Part I. the Songs of David, ii—xli. Part II. songs of Davidic singers, xlii—l. Part III. David again, li—lxxii. Part IV. Davidic singers again. (Exceptions in these parts are few). So there comes David, his contemporary singers, and then David again, followed again by them. So in Proverbs; beginning with c. x., we have first Solomon, then his contemporaries; then Solomon again, followed at the close by Agur and Lemuel. The two last Parts, like the two last in the Psalms, were added to the book, before extant, a considerable time after the first two were in circulation.

There can be no doubt, that a book like that of the Proverbs, must have arisen *gradually*. These proverbs had many of them, doubtless, been long in circulation; and they were adopted by the compilers because of their truth, and of their moral, civil, social, and economical worth. But the book was not so long in being completed, as the book of Psalms. If we regard David as commencing this last book about the latter half of the eleventh century B. C., and call to mind that it was not closed until after the return from the Babylonish exile, it must have been receiving accessions for about five hundred years. In the case before us, we do not go down much beyond three hundred years from the commencement of the book, in order to find the probable completion of it.

§ 12. *Idioms and Peculiarities of the Book.*

(1) Those who have been disposed to find a late period for the composition of Proverbs, have ill succeeded in finding arguments to correspond with their wishes. From beginning to end, the Hebrew bears no special marks of the later dialect. Indeed one is astonished, considering the nature of the composition, to find how few of the words vary from the older Hebrew. It was to be expected, that a book which records the maxims and gnomes of the common people and every-day life, would exhibit many a word and phrase not elsewhere to be found; since the language of popular intercourse usually varies much from that of books. Yet seldom do we find much difficulty here in regard to this matter. We find indeed, of necessity, and from the very nature of the case, many expressions of sentiment nowhere else to be found; but the costume of this varies little from that of the common Hebrew.

In the *grammatical forms*, there are some traits which are noticeable. One of these is, the frequency with which the paragogic or demonstrative נ is employed, before the suffixes appended to verbs; e. g. in 2: 4, תְּבַקְשֶׁנָּה and תַּחְפְּשֶׂנָּה, and the like. I have not kept count of these paragogics thus employed, but I have an impression that they are the predominant usage of the book, in cases of a verbal-suffix to the Imperfect.

(2) Another particular deserves special notice, as it has an important bearing on the grammar, or rather on the exegesis, of the language. This is, that *the plural number*,

specially of the feminine, is very often employed in the way of *intensity*, and also as a method of constituting *abstract nouns*. E. g. in 1: 20. 9: 1, we find חָכְמוֹת plural, joined with a verb singular, because the idea is an abstract one, or because (more probably) the plural form merely denotes *wisdom par excellence*. Nowhere have I met with this usage so often as in this book; and many a passage would have gained much in our English version, had our translators well understood this. Besides, it saves much grammatical difficulty. Where a plural noun is joined with a verb singular, it has been often put to the score of *anomaly;* whereas, in many, if not most, of these cases, there is merely a concord *ad sensum*, in respect to the noun and the verb. For example, חָכְמוֹת, as above represented, is either an *abstract* noun, or a designation of *intensity ;* and in either case the *sense* is that of the singular. Hence the verb singular. — Just so with אֱלֹהִים elsewhere. It is a plural of intensity; *God par excellence*. Hence the singular verb joined to it. — It is impossible for any one to read the book of Proverbs, with these principles of construction in view, without a feeling that the usage in question widely pervades the Hebrew language. But it appears, as I believe, nowhere so often as here.

(3) In such a book as that before us, there must of necessity be some *peculiar words*, used as the names of things which are nowhere else mentioned. But still, the *ἅπαξ λεγόμενα* here are not numerous. In the cases which follow, some are peculiar as to *form ;* some peculiar as to meaning; and some occur in no other book. E. g. 1: 10, תֹּבֵא = תֹּאבֶה; 3: 26, לֶכֶד; 12: 27, יַחֲרֹךְ; 15: 4, סֶלֶף (bis); 17: 3. 27: 21, מַצְרֵף; 17: 14, הִתְגַּלַּע; 17: 22, גֵּהָה; 18: 8, מִתְלַהֲמִים; 22: 8, וָזָר; 22: 14, כָּפָה; 23: 7, שָׁעַר; 23: 21, נוּמָה; 23: 28, חֶתֶף; 23: 19, אֲבוֹי; 23: 34, חִבֵּל; 25: 11, דָּבֻר; 26: 8, מַרְגֵּמָה; 26: 18, מִתְלַהְלֵהַּ; 27: 15, סַגְרִיר; 29: 11, בְּאָחוֹר; 29: 21, מְפַנֵּק; 31: 19, כִּישׁוֹר; ib. פֶּלֶךְ. Probably

I may have overlooked some of the same nature. But this is a small list, considering the extent of the book, and also the great variety of subjects which it exhibits. Every book of any considerable length, has of course its ἅπαξ λεγόμενα; and a book which exhibits the language of popular intercourse, may be expected usually to have many words of this class. We can only say, that here are fewer peculiar words than one would naturally expect. Besides, the fact of some words being peculiar to this book, establishes nothing either as to the antiquity or the lateness of them. The *indicia* of later Hebrew, such as we find so frequently in Coheleth, are not to be met with here. The difference in style and diction between the two books, is a thing so palpable, that no one can help seeing and feeling it, who is familiar enough with Hebrew to judge of a difference in style.

§ 13. *Practical Importance of the Book.*

Gnomes, proverbs, comparisons, and even enigmas, have always been the storehouse of a nation's practical wisdom and ingenuity, in the earlier stages of its existence. A nation without any books, and unacquainted with the art of writing, could perpetuate the wisdom of its leaders, only in the way of handing down, traditionally and orally, the maxims and short sayings of wise men. These usually obtained so much currency and credit, that subsequent literary acquirements rarely expelled many of them from their wonted circulation. Few proverbs, perhaps, are originated, after a cultivated state begins; but the mass of any people are not dependent on books, for the modes of intercourse which prevail among them. In fact, the proverbs which are rife and continuous among any people, are always indicative of their manners, habits, and feelings. They contain a compendious history of a nation's mental exercises, in regard to all the various objects of thought and reflection. They are the result of experience, of sagacity, of a knowledge of men and things; and they serve an important purpose in stimulating as well as enlightening them.

It is no matter of wonder, then, that every nation which has made any figure on the world's stage, should abound in proverbs. The oldest gnome of the enigmatical kind, which we find on record, is that of Samson, in Judg. 14: 12—18, which takes the form of what we call a *riddle*. Doubtless the Hebrews must have had an almost inexhaustible store of proverbs, since we find that Solomon alone spoke three thousand of them, 1 K. 4: 32. If, as seems probable (§ 6. 5), Solomon added Part III. of the Proverbs to the other two preceding Parts, and selected it from the works of other wise men, it would seem that the Hebrews abounded in proverbial lore, at that period, beyond almost any other nation. The Arabians, however, who are a kindred people, and one of lively fancy, vivid imagination, and ready, poignant wit, have perhaps outdone the Hebrews in this respect. Lockman, an alleged contemporary of Solomon, the author of some beautiful Arabic Fables, exhibits many proverbial sayings in them; and in later writers, such as Meidani, Tsamahshari, Abu Obeid, and the Caliph Ali, appear a great multitude of gnomic sayings. Burckhardt made an immense collection, which has since been published. In Persia, Ferid Attar and Sadi have exhibited many select apothegms of their nation. The Scythians (Herod. iv. 31), the Hindoos, and the Chinese, possessed like stores. Even Odin, in northern Europe, had a proverbial system of ethics; (see Eddae Saemundianae Pars dicta Havamoal, edit. Resenii). Among the Greeks and Latins, also, are many gnomic productions. Proverbs have always been, with the mass of the people everywhere, the most favored kind of moral lore.

Imagine a people, like the ancient Hebrews, destitute of books and the art of printing, and then ask: What would be the *value* of such Proverbs as are contained in the book before us? It would be almost beyond estimation. Short, pithy, pointed, sensible sayings, imprint themselves deeply on the mind and memory; and by these, a people may become in a good measure instructed in their moral, civil, and social duties. One advantage is, that the mind comes to have within itself the stores to which it may resort for prudential counsel in time of need. It must not be supposed, that all the proverbs of Solomon were composed *de novo* by him. They came originally from many thinking minds, in different conditions of life, and with a great variety of experience. Solomon selected many, composed others, and put together those which he judged to be true, most striking, and most worthy to be preserved. No matter what their origin was, whether among men inspired or uninspired; for surely, inspiration or special divine suggestion, was not needed for the composition of many of the Proverbs. The natural wit, and discernment, and talent for observation, which many shrewd men possessed, was adequate to such a task. *Nec Deus intersit, nisi dignus vindice nodus* — may be applied in this case. *But all these proverbs had afterwards the sanction of an inspired man*, as to their truth and importance; and consequently they are of the same authority as if composed *de novo* by the compilers. The case is like that of the book of Genesis; which, as we can hardly doubt, originated from various sources, but passed through the hands of Moses, and received its present shape from him, and is, therefore, now stamped with his authority. It matters not, then, how much of the book of Proverbs Solomon actually composed; we only need his *sanction* to what it now contains.

In looking carefully through the whole book, there will be seen a collection of moral and prudential maxims, which attain a high elevation in the dominion of morality, industry, social kindness, and indeed of all the civil and social virtues. A people who originated these, and brought them into popular use, must needs have made great advances in civil and social life. A Caffre or a Tartar could hardly understand them, even if proposed in his own language ; and if he should, he would have little relish for them. To have received and retained them, then, and set so much value on them as the Hebrews did, shows a state of moral cultivation, in the time of Solomon and Hezekiah, by no means of an inferior grade. It cannot be denied that there is a high tone of religion, morals, social obligation, and even comity, pervading the whole book. Humility before God, reverence for him, the love of our neighbor, justice, kindness, temperance, gentleness of spirit and demeanor, prudence, economy, active diligence, chastity, purity of heart, modesty, and (in a word) all which makes men happy in themselves, and creates a happy state of society, are exhibited and urged in the most pointed manner in the book before us. And we, after all the light which Christianity has shed upon us, could not part with this book without a severe loss. Better by far to loose all that Socrates, and Plato, and Plutarch, and Epictetus, and Cicero, and Seneca, and their heathen compeers, ever left behind them, on subjects of this nature. Pity that the book is not more studied, and better understood, by Christians of the present day! A popular exhibition of the results of critical examination, with a plain and explicit statement of the real sentiment conveyed by each proverb where there is any obscurity, would be, as I cannot but hope, a favorite book for the people ; and at all events an exceedingly useful one. The book contains a striking exhibition of *practical wisdom*, so striking that it can never be antiquated.

§ 14. *Ancient Versions of the Book.*

I. THE SEPTUAGINT.

Eichhorn, after commending the Sept. translation of the Pentateuch above that of any other books of the Old Testament, proceeds thus : " The next place must be given to the translator of the Proverbs. His work proceeds not in the stiff gait of a dictionary; for he had both languages at his command. Often, he expresses merely the sense of the original; but when he misses that, you recognize his genius even in his mistakes," Einl. § 165.

I apprehend that one would get but an imperfect view of the Sept. version of Proverbs, from reading such a passage as this. *The stiff gait of a dictionary*, I suppose, means a literal translation made out by the help of a lexicon merely, — help in regard to the sense given to the words. And true enough it is, that the translator does not limit himself to any lexicographal bounds. Almost everywhere, and on all occasions, does he overleap them, more or less. Why he does so, Eichhorn does not go on to explain, excepting that he says of the translator, that "he had both languages at his command." One who has compared the version throughout with the original Hebrew, will be slow, I apprehend, to claim for the translator a thorough knowledge of the *Hebrew*, whatever he may affirm of his acquaintance with the Greek. Undoubtedly, he approaches nearer to a *classical* diction, than any other Septuagintal translator. He seems to have been conversant with the classic Greek, and to have taken great pains to make his version bear the stamp of it. There is no other book in all the Septuagint, which has so few *Hellenisms* as the book of Proverbs. If it be any praise, in a case like the present, to aim at and exhibit *classicity* of style, then has our Greek translator acquired a right to eulogy, so far as this is concerned. But alas for the reader of this version! He can surely acquire but a very imperfect view of the original by means of it. The liberties taken with the Hebrew are almost beyond calculation. A literal or exact rendering of it is indeed, one might almost say, the *exception* rather than the *rule*. But *classical Greek* is no compensation for this. We go to such a translation, rather *to find what the Hebrew original means*, than to find classical Greek; for this we can find, in a better form, in the classics themselves. Consequently, its unfaithfulness to the original is not compensated for, by any skill in selecting Greek words which are aesthetically good. I am aware that some critics have spoken of this Greek version of the Proverbs, as standing on a level with the golden verses of Pythagoras. For its moral and religious qualities, it is undoubtedly far above the verses of that celebrated sage. But this belongs to the original writer, and not to the translator.

In an introduction like the present, there is no room for an expanded view of the faults of the translation before us. All which I shall aim at will be, to give specimens of whole classes of *additions ;* of *omissions ;* of *strange and peculiar renderings,* which do no justice to the original, and for which we cannot well account; and also of cases where error was committed by *mistaking the proper vowels,* or *mistaking similar letters.*

(1) ADDITIONS. These are either a single clause, two clauses, three, four, etc., even up to several verses. Specimeas I shall now subjoin, presenting them in English, for the convenience of the reader. The literal translation of the Hebrew is printed in the usual type, while the Sept. version beneath it is thrown into small type.

Chap. 1: 18. But these lie in wait for their own blood; they lurk for their own lives.

For these are partakers of murder; they treasure up evil for themselves; but the destruction of transgressors is grievous.

We can account for *treasure up* here, because the Hebrew word צָפַן sometimes means to *lay up* or *conceal treasures ;* but the *concealing,* in the case before us, is *concealing themselves,* and not hiding treasures. The last clause is constructed of *de novo* material.

3: 15. More precious is she [wisdom] than pearls, and all thy jewels cannot compare with her.

More valuable is she than precious stones; nothing bad can compare with her; she is well known to all those who draw nigh to her, and no precious thing is comparable to her.

Here is a whole verse, or two clauses, without any voucher for it in the original.

4: 27. Turn not aside to the right or to the left; withdraw thy foot from evil.

Incline not to the right or to the left; turn away thy foot from the way of evil; for the ways which are on the right, God knoweth, and those on the left are perverted; but he will make thy paths straight, and lead on thy goings in peace.

Here are two short, yet entire, verses added.

6: 8. In summer she [the ant] prepareth her food; at harvest-time she hath gathered her provender.

She prepares her food in summer; and makes much store in harvest. Or, go to the bee, and learn how laborious she is, and how decorously she executes her task; the fruit of her labors kings and private persons make use of for health; she is desired by all, and is illustrious; and although weak in respect to strength, since she honors wisdom, she is promoted.

This is travelling out of the record, with a witness.

16: 5. An abomination of Jehovah is every man of a lofty mind; should hand be added to hand, he will not go unpunished.

Unclean before God is every one of a proud heart; thrusting hands into hand unrighteously, he shall not go unpunished. The beginning of a good way is doing righteously, and is acceptable to God, rather than slaying sacrifices; he who seeketh the Lord, shall find knowledge with righteousness, and they who seek him rightly shall find peace. All the works of the Lord are with righteousness; but the ungodly is reserved for the day of evil.

Such are some of the specimens of the boldness, with which the translator executed his task. But after 24: 22, follows a whole passage, inserted between vs. 22 and 23, together with 30:1—14 joined on to it, and transferred hither from its proper place. It runs thus:—

The son who keepeth the word, shall be free from destruction; and whoever has received it, let him utter to the king no falsehood from his tongue, and let nothing false go forth from his tongue. The tongue of a king is a sword, and not fleshly; and whomsoever he shall deliver up, shall be dashed in pieces; for if his anger be excited, he destroys men with chords, and devours the bones of men; yea, he consumes them as a flame, so that they cannot be eaten by the young of eagles. My son, fear my words; and receiving them, repent.

How tame, and spiritless, and incongruous, all this sheer interpolation is, will be felt by every intelligent reader. It is unnecessary to comment upon it. It is well that there are not many such passages as this, either as to extent or taste; for then the version, as such, with all its boasted *classic* Greek, could scarcely be redeemed from contempt.

Let not the reader imagine, however, that I have given him anything more than a mere prelibation. But my limits forbid extracting any more under this category. Instead of this, I would refer any one who wishes to pursue the subject of comparison for himself, to the texts cited in the margin.[1]

Among these more than fifty texts will be found very many which add a whole verse, and some which consist of two or more verses. And all these, be it noted, are only a moderate portion of the verses which have added something to the text, or at least inserted something which is not in it. Had I catalogued the whole, it would amount to some twenty or twenty-five per cent. of the whole book. As it is, we have here more than sixty verses, (including those produced at length above, and such additions as include two or more

[1] See 1:7, 14. 3:16, 18, 22, 28. 4:10. 5:2, 16. 6:11, 16, 25. 7:2. 8:21. 9:7, 10, 12, 18. 10:4. 11:16. 12:11, 13, 26. 13:9, 11, 13, 22. 15:5, 18, 27, 29, 30, 33. 16:17, 27, 28. 17:5, 6. 16:21. 18:22. 19:7. 22:9, 14, 30. 24:7. 25:10, 20. 26:11. 27:20, 21. 28:17. 29:7, 25. 31:3.

verses), which are made *de novo* by the translator, so that if no more were reckoned, we have a proportion of some sixty-five to the whole number of verses = 917. In other words, we make out fourteen per cent. of adulteration of text by direct interpolation. A formidable mass, indeed, in a professed copy of the original! But if to this, one should add all the minuter additions or variations, he must swell the account to the full amount above stated, or even more.

(2) OMISSIONS. First of a *clause*; e. g. 8: 29, where the Hebrew runs thus: "When he marked out for the sea its limit, so that the waters should not pass beyond its shore; when he defined the foundations of the earth." For all this the Sept. has only: "When he made strong the foundations of the earth." The like in 3: 3. 4: 5. 7: 25. 17: 19. 21: 18. In other cases a whole verse, and sometimes several verses, are omitted; e. g. 11: 4. After 15: 29, a new chapter begins, and then, after giving v. 1 of chap. xvi., vs. 30, 32, 33, of chap. xv. are inserted, while v. 31 is wholly omitted. After 16: 1, these three verses of chap. xv. are not only inserted, but vs. 2—4 belonging to chap. xvi. are wholly omitted. After 18: 22, vs. 23, 24 are omitted. In chap. xix., vs. 1, 2 are omitted, and v. 3 is tacked on to the end of chap. xviii., so that chap. xix. begins with v. 4. In chap. xx., after v. 9, comes vs. 20—22; and not only this, but vs. 14—19 are wholly omitted. After 22: 5, v. 6 is wholly omitted. Put all these together, and we have a serious defalcation and departure from the original Hebrew.

(3) PECULIAR DEPARTURES *from the original text.* These are so numerous that they cannot well be reckoned. I need to give but a few specimens to show the nature of them. Thus 1: 12, "Let us swallow them up alive as Hades; and let those in a sound condition be as those who go down to the pit." For the last clause, the Sept. has the following: "And let us take away their remembrance from the earth." In 2: 16, the Hebrew runs thus: "That

they may deliver thee from the strange woman; from the stranger who maketh smooth her words." The Sept. says: "To remove thee from the straight way, [to make thee] a stranger to righteous knowledge. My son, let not evil counsel take hold of thee." In 14: 9, the Hebrew stands thus: "Sin-offering mocketh fools; but with the upright, there is ready acceptance." Sept.: "The houses of transgressors need purification; but the houses of the righteous are acceptable."

Such are some of the specimens under the present category. Very many of those referred to in the Note, are equal to, and some surpass, the specimens produced. But beside all that I have marked, and which are submitted to the reader in the Note below,[1] there are smaller departures from the Hebrew quite beyond enumeration. No one who reads the Hebrew text intelligently, can fail of meeting them in every paragraph; I had almost said in every verse. One of two things is true; either the translator had no adequate knowledge of the Hebrew, and paraphrased in this way because he did not know his original well enough to render it more exactly; or he took unbounded and unwarrantable liberties with his text, and designed merely to fix up what he thought would be a readable book, in well-chosen Greek diction. In either case, he has very unfaithfully and inadequately performed his task. If the reader will spend one tenth part of the time in following and comparing the texts referred to in the Note, which it

---

[1] See and compare 1: 19. 2: 18. 4: 15, 25. 5: 19. 6: 14. 7: 7, 10, 22. 8: 2, 27. 9: 13. 10: 5, 10, 12, 24, 26. 11: 7, 9, 14, 24, 25, 26, 30, 31. 12: 2, 28. 13: 4, 15, 23. 14: 7, 15, 23, 24, 32, 35. 15: 1, 4, 15, 22, 23. 16: 21, 30, 33. 17: 1, 4, 7, 8, 9, 10, 11, 12, 14, 23. 18: 1, 8, 11, 14, 19. 19: 6, 13, 18. 20: 1, 4. 21: 8, 10, 14. 22: 11, 19, 26. 23: 2, 7, 15, 20, 21, 27, 28, 29. 24: 5, 9, 10, 11, 15, 30, 31. 25: 4, 9, 19, 20, 23, 27. 26: 6, 10, 11, 18, 23, 24. 27: 9, 13, 19, 22. 28: 2, 10, 26. 29: 9. 30: 1, 3, 15, 31, 32. 31: 1, 2, 3, 4, 21, 26, 29. Amount here = 116 verses.

has cost me to collect them, he will, by his own efforts, have the whole matter before him, and have it in such a way as descanting on the Sept. cannot give it to him. The amount of departures is indeed very great, and beyond all reasonable measure.

(4) DIFFERENT READING *of the Vowels, or mistaking similar letters.* In 3: 4, the Heb. words שֵׂכֶל טוֹב, *good discretion*, the Sept. has rendered προνοοῦ καλά, *consider things good*, reading the word שֵׂכֶל as a verb in Piel, viz. שַׂכֵּל. In 4: 21, the Heb. מֵעֵינֶיךָ, *from thine eyes*, the Sept. translates αἱ πηγαί σου, *thy fountains*, having read the Heb. as מַעְיְנֶיךָ, which means *fountains.* In 11: 3, we have תֻּמַּת יְשָׁרִים, *the integrity of the upright;* in the Sept., we find 'αποθανὼν δίκαιος, i. e. they read the first word as תָּמוּת. Even then the gender is anomalous. In 23: 28, the Heb. has תּוֹסִיף, *she shall add*, from יָסַף; but the Sept. derived the verb from אָסַף, *to take away*, and have rendered it 'αναλωθήσεται, *shall be destroyed.* In 19: 6, הָרֵעַ means *the friend;* but the Sept. has κακός, reading it הָרָע from רוּעַ, *to do evil.* In 19: 23, we have רָע *evil;* Sept. read דֵּעַ *knowledge*, from יָדַע. In 20: 4, Heb. מֵחֹרֶף, *during autumn;* in the Sept., 'ονειδιζόμενος, reading the word מְחָרֵף, Part. of the Piel of חָרַף, *to reproach.* And so of the rest.[1]

Such are the leading classes of additions, omissions, strange translations, and changes of proper vowels for wrong ones. Besides all this, there occurs not a little confusion in the *order* of verses, and the ending of chapters; e. g. see in 15: 29 and 16: 1, seq. See also 18: 22, seq., where four verses are omitted, and chap. xix. begins with v. 4. After 20: 9, seq., occur next vs. 20—22; then the regular order up to v. 13; after which vs. 14—19 are

[1] See also 7: 18. 8: 1. 1: 21. 2: 7. 11: 8, 18, 19, 28. 12: 23. 13: 17, 19. 15: 14, 15. 16: 16. 17: 3, 9. 18: 9. 20: 4, 6. 21: 6. 22: 11, 18. 23: 3, 4. 24: 7. 25: 2. 26: 10, 13. 28: 12, 15, 28. 29: 5, 14, 16. Sum = 34 cases.

wholly omitted. After 24: 22, follows an interpolation of some four entire verses, having nothing correspondent to it in the Hebrew, and being followed by chap. 30: 1—14. Then comes 24: 23—34; and after this, 30 : 15—33. This too is followed by chap. 31: 1—9; and then the regular order is resumed with 25: 1, seq. Once more; after the end of chap xxix., the rest of chap. xxxi., viz. vs. 10—31, is subjoined, and comes in, as in the Hebrew Bible, at the close of the book. Such is the oft-repeated *ὕστερον πρότερον* of the book before us, brought about by the carelessness of the translator, or of some copyist, or else by the ill arrangement of his Hebrew codex.

I find nothing, however, in all these changes and additions made by the Sept. version, which properly ranks under the Jewish מִדְרָשׁ, i. e. allegorical, spiritualizing, *double-sense* commentary. The passage in 6: 8, (produced above, p. 67), respecting the *bee*, comes the nearest to a מִדְרָשׁ of anything in the book. This interpolation does in fact approach somewhat near to the הַגָּדָה, which means *story*, *narration*, *anecdote*, and the like, added to the text, in order to give pleasure to the reader.

We meet with nothing which betrays, with certainty, the *where* and *when* of the translator. It would seem, however, from his conceded classical knowledge and style, that he was a *native Greek*, imperfectly acquainted with Hebrew. It would not be easy for a Jew to free himself from that kind of reverence for the Scriptures, which would restrain him from tampering with them as much as our translator does, unless the *Midrash* or the *Haggadoth* were designedly in view. Even these were not designed to change the text itself, but only to amuse and attract the reader. But throughout the Septuagint version reigns a spirit, which is entirely different from that which appears in the Targum of Job or Psalms. There, we have plenty both of the *Midrash* and *Haggadoth*. In fact, the levity (I had almost said) with which the book is treated, in the Septuagint version, indicates strongly that the author was a man embarrassed by none of the usual Jewish prejudices, in regard to the exterior of the Scriptures. Whoever he was, we are under no great obligations to him for a translation so interpolated, so full of omissions, so often abandoning the proper meaning of Hebrew words, and so frequently built on incorrect readings of the vowels and consonants. All these are high and substantial charges against it. But they are not made out, by any theory or desire of mine. They are forced upon our notice, by a careful attention to all the *minutiae* of the Septuagint; and they lie before the reader, not in the form of an *exparte* decision, made without a hearing of the party concerned, but in the form of direct and unequivocal testimony which cannot be called in question. The condemning evidence is stamped on the very face of the whole book.

Looking now deliberately on this mass of facts, is it not to be regarded as a stain upon the escutcheon of sacred criticism, that the Septuagint version before us has been so long and so much extolled? Long ago began the practice of praising it. Once commenced, it has become a kind of traditionary inheritance among critics. See, for example, at the beginning of this section, what Eichhorn has said respecting it. The like had been done before, and has since been often repeated. With how much reason, has been amply shown above. Even Hävernick and Bertheau seem to have taken mainly upon trust what they say of this version; although the latter has made some critical discriminations as to the characteristics of the Sept. But such indiscriminate eulogy as we find in most cases, leads one to see how many of such things are said merely upon trust, and without any rigid examination. The Septuagint is opened, perhaps, at a venture, and the critic lights, it may be, on this passage and that, which are translated into good Greek, and rendered in a spirited manner. Now and then, too, a lucky hit occurs. All this can be found, I well know, here and there in the version. But it is very unequal. Were it not for the *diction*, one might almost be led, in some cases, to suspect different translators. But as the diction forbids this, we can account for these inequalities only by recurring to an ancient criticism on Homer, one made by a master in this art: "Aliquando bonus dormitat Homerus." But our translator not only *nods*, but *dreams*, at times, and exhibits not a little of the perplexity and intricacies and claro-obscure of a dreamy state. It is high time that the indiscriminate eulogy of his performance were laid aside by critics, who examine, or ought to examine, for themselves.

All this serves to show, beyond any ground of reasonable doubt, that the Septuagint, *as a whole*, never came from one man, nor from the same body of men. There is such a wide diversity in the style of different books; such manifest tokens of different degrees of knowledge as to the Hebrew original, and with all (as in the present case) such a wide difference in the sense of obligation to keep close to the text, that it is really beyond all critical possibility to vindicate a oneness of authorship to the whole version.

Those who are prone, as many still seem to be, to set up the version of which we are treating, as a corrector of the Hebrew Scriptures, should look well before they leap. Those who make desperate endeavors to force upon us the Septuagint *chronology*, ante-diluvian and post-diluvian, would do well to read J. D. Michaelis on this subject, in his *Syntagma Dissertationum*. Nothing is plainer, than that the object of the Septuagint chronology is, to make out the supposed requisite period of five thousand years, before the birth of the Messiah. Hence, by various stratagems, six hundred out of the needed one thousand years, are made out before the flood; and the complement, after it.

Thus in the Heb. of Gen. 11: 10—13, we have the genealogy of Shem, the son of Noah, in this order: "Shem, Arphaxad, Salah, Eber," etc.; in the corresponding Sept., we have "Shem, Arphaxad, *Cainan*, Salah, Eber," etc. Unluckily for this apparent piece of pious fraud, we find in the Sept. itself, in 1 Chron. 1 : 17, 18, *the exact Hebrew order*, viz., "Shem, Arphaxad, Salah, Eber," etc., and *no Cainan.* The man who played this trick with the Septuagint, should have kept a better look-out for the genealogy in Chronicles, and have adapted this as well as the other list of names to his design. It is well, however, that imposture is not always on its guard. But as for those critics who would fain bring us to the Septuagint chronology, and thus exalt the Septuagint above the Hebrew, and at its expense, I would beg leave to commend to them 1 Chron. 1: 17, 18, compared with Gen. 11: 10—13, and also the Septuagint version of the book of Proverbs, as exhibited above.

II. THE PESHITO OR OLD SYRIAC VERSION.

When or where the name *Peshito* was first given, is uncertain. But as this word probably means THE SIMPLE, there seems to be little room for doubt, that the name was designed, whenever given, to distinguish it from the kind of metaphrastic versions, such as exist in the Targums; where not only the sense of the text is often given loosely, but the version is interlarded with *Midrash* and *Haggadoth.* In opposition to this stands the Syriac version, justly named *Simple,* inasmuch as it is the most literal and simple of all the ancient versions. The man or men who made it were undoubtedly persons whose vernacular was Syriac, but who studied the Hebrew so as to attain an intimate familiarity with it. The transition is easy from one language to the other. Our missionaries among the Arabians and Syrians find, that it takes but as it were a few days for an intelligent

Arabian or Syrian to learn to read fluently and understand the Hebrew. This might have been done, or rather, must have been done, by the Syriac translator of the Old Testament, and certainly by the translator of the book of Proverbs. Otherwise the translation could not have been so literal and exact as it is.

In the region called anciently *Adiabene*, which lay in eastern Syria, (or more anciently in western Assyria), between the Euphrates and the Tigris, and north of Mesopotamia, were located the ten tribes, who were carried away captive by Shalmaneser the king of Assyria, 2 K. 17 : 23. Josephus (Antiq. V. 2) says, that at the time of the return of the Jews from the Babylonish exile, only *two* tribes returned; but that "the ten tribes, consisting of immense myriads (μυριάδες ἄπειροι) of Jews beyond the Euphrates," did not return, because they liked their long-wonted habitations too well to quit them. King Agrippa, just before the Roman-Jewish war, in exhorting the Jews to submission, advises them "to place no confidence in the aid of their fellow tribes (ὁμοφύλους) of Adiabene;" Bell. Jud. II. c. 16, p. 808, edit. Col. There can be no question, that a vast number of Jews were at that time scattered over that country, then subjected to the Parthians. The same Josephus tells us, that Izates, king of Adiabene, sent (of course before the destruction of Jerusalem) "*five sons, who were young, to learn the language vernacular with the Jews, and to obtain accurate instruction*," Antiq. XX. c. 2, p. 687. This king was himself a zealous convert to Judaism, as was also his mother, Helena, who visited Jerusalem. When the Jewish priest Eleazar visited Izates, he found him reading the Pentateuch; ut sup. p. 685. The reign of this king was probably A. D. 40—60. It must then have been a Septuagint or Greek copy of the Old Testament; for probably no version had yet been made into the Syriac. Is there not then the highest probability, that this king, whose zeal for Judaism had induced him to send five sons to learn the Hebrew language and religion, did on their return, direct them to translate the Hebrew Scriptures into the Syriac language? A brother of Izates, viz. Monobazus, seems also to have been a zealous convert to the Hebrew religion; for the Talmud (Tract. Yoma, c. 3. 10) relates, that this individual, the son of Helena, consecrated golden vessels to the temple at Jerusalem. *Some time, then, during the latter half of the first century, it is probable that the Old Testament Peshito was made.* It is enough to render this probable, that Helena, the queen-mother of Adiabene, and Izates her successor, and his brother Monobazus, were zealous Judaizers; and Izates, moreover, had five sons, thoroughly instructed in Hebrew, by the master Rabbies in Jerusalem; (see a copious history of these personages in Jos. Antiq. XX. 2). It seems quite probable, at all events, that the O. Test. Peshito was made first, before the N. Test. Version, and separately from it. One reason for this is, the strong probability that Izates would promote such an object, since he could easily accomplish it by the aid of his sons. Then again, the N. Test. Syriac, when it cites passages from the O. Test., cites them not from the O. Test. Peshito, but makes a new version of its own. This shows that the N. Test. Syriac translator was a person different from the translator of the Old Testament; for the same person, making the entire version of both Testaments, would very naturally, in translating the N. Test., quote his O. Test. Version, where the O. Test. is cited; or if he first translated the N. Test., then he would have conformed passages of the O. Test., cited in the New, to the version which he had already made. Once more, the tradition among the Syrians themselves assigns both translations to the same period, but not to the same persons; see the excellent and recent Latin Essay on the Syriac Versions, by J. Wichelhaus, Halle, 1850, p. 119.

Of the N. Test. Peshito, it would be irrelevant to say much here. Suffice it to remark, that Adiabene was early filled with Christians, even before the end of the first century. In Acts 2: 7, seq. we read of men who were "Parthians, Medes, Elamites, *and the dwellers in Mesopotamia*," as being present to hear the sermon of Peter, on the day of Pentecost, and that three thousand of his audience were converted on that day. Must not some of these have been persons from Adiabene, who would of course carry back to their respective places the gospel of Christ? The Syrians have an ancient and apparently uniform tradition, that the N. Test. Peshito was made by the disciples of an apostle, or at least of one of the Seventy disciples, who first preached the gospel in East Syria. In all probability, then, this version was made near the close of Cent. I., or near the beginning of Cent. II. This shows a good reason, why some of the later books, viz. 2 Peter, 2 and 3 John, Jude, and the Apocalypse, are omitted in the N. Test. Peshito. They had not yet come, at so early a period, into circulation among the inhabitants of that distant region. But I can merely refer the reader to Wichelhaus, as cited above, where he will meet with more than he can elsewhere find, in regard to this deeply interesting version.

But to return: If we consider it quite probable that the five sons of Izates, who were taught at Jerusalem, made the Peshito version of the Old Testament, then we have in it a good mirror to reflect the forms of Hebrew criticism and exegesis, at that period, at least among a part of the Jewish literati. And certainly, when viewed in this light, we must feel disposed to give them much credit. Of all the ancient versions of the Old Testament, the Peshito is the truest and the best. It shows great skill in transferring the Hebrew idiom into the Syriac; although this was not a difficult task for a man skilled in both languages. Of course there would be some words in the Hebrew, which antiquity had rendered obscure, and the meaning of which the translator into Syriac has sometimes missed. But on the other hand, he has poured light on many an obscure word or phrase; which is of serious importance to the interpreter of the Hebrew Scriptures.

It has been objected to the position that the Old Testament Peshito was made directly from the Hebrew, that in some places it conforms to the Sept. The fact is in some few cases apparently so; but it is easy, since the passages are so few, to ascribe them to changes afterwards made in the copies of the Peshito, out of a superstitious regard to the Sept., which was supposed to be of divine origin. Besides, in some cases, the Sept. translator, and the Syriac one, may both have drawn from the same exegetical sources among the Jews.

So far as our present object is concerned, I can say, from actual comparison, that the Syriac is as remote from the Sept., as this is from a true representation of the Hebrew. No connection between the two translations is discernible, beyond very narrow limits. That the Peshito translator, however, was conversant with the Sept., can hardly be doubted. That he has followed its irregularities, its incorrectnesses, its additions, and its omissions, to any extent even worth naming, is certainly not true.

The Peshito of Proverbs is indeed a model as to manner. Where it becomes *exegetical,* it uses the fewest words possible. It indulges in no paraphrases. It exhibits no Midrashim or Haggadoth. Some things (small ones) have probably crept into it from marginal notes; such as might be taken from the Syriac commentary of Ephrem Syrus. Most of the departures from the Hebrew are confined to the book of Psalms; and these may be accounted for from the fact, that the Psalms were a *liturgic* book.

It is strong proof against the authenticity of the Apocryphal books, that no one of them ever belonged to this ancient version. Ephrem Syrus, indeed, cites them; but not as books canonical or authoritative.

In a few cases, we find additions made to the Hebrew; and who the person was that made them, is a point difficult to be settled. What I mean is, that these additions are so small, compared with the mass of the book, that it is more easy to suppose them to have come in from the margin, in process of time, than to account for them by supposing the translator himself to have made them, and in a manner so contrary to the general tenor of the version. This, however, Bertheau accounts for, by supposing that the Hebrew text, from which the translator made his version, differed from our present Masoretic text. He appeals to the fact, that several clauses, or even whole verses, are found here and there, which are added to our present text. The fact itself of *addition* cannot well be denied. Thus in 4: 4, there is added, at the close: "And my law, as the pupil of thine eyes." In the midst of 11 : 16 are inserted *two clauses*. In 13 : 13, the same; also in 14: 22 and 14 : 23, in the middle of the verse. In 22 : 21, there are some two words added. There may be a few other cases of this latter kind; but not enough to make out an amount worth reckoning. In some of these cases, it would seem to be not improbable, that the Hebrew text has suffered somewhat by the omission of one or more clauses; for the matter supplied in the Syriac seems to be quite congruous. But in others I should be inclined to believe, that they came in the way of having originally been marginal annotations. We surely can make but very little of so few additions as are here, if we compare them for a moment with those of the Septuagint.

Bertheau further remarks, that *considerable departures* from the Hebrew are to be found in the Peshito. He refers us to 7: 22, 23. 15: 4, 15. 19: 20. 21: 16. 22: 24. But most of these departures are so small, and of so little importance as to the sense, that they are scarcely worth our special notice. Some of them are evidently nothing more than a different manner of translating several Hebrew words.

The result of all this is, that the general character of the Peshito for fidelity, is by no means impeachable. The addition of some five verses in the whole book, would hardly serve as a good basis for an impeachment; and most of the alleged discrepancies hardly deserve our notice, except for some special purposes of criticism.

Thus much for this noble old version, which gives us a portion of the separate history of the Hebrew text; for this image of it, I mean the Peshito, has come down from the first century of our Christian era, through hands different from those of the Hebrews. It is doubly important to us, in consequence of its being a version of the Hebrew so close and literal. Of course, it casts light on many difficult Hebrew words, although not upon all; and it shows us, at all events, what ideas were attached to such Hebrew words by those who spoke one of the Semitic dialects. The reader of it will much advance and expand his knowledge of the Semitic languages, by a diligent and faithful study of it. Walton's Polyglot is the most convenient apparatus for the Syriac text, as it has the vowel-points. The comparative study of the sacred books in different languages, is greatly facilitated by this immortal work. Whoever reads the Peshito version of the Proverbs carefully, will be ready to bear witness to the directness, and plainness, and faithfulness of it. Never can he doubt that it is well worth special attention.

III. The Chaldee Targum.

That the Chaldee Targum, i. e. translation of the Old Testament Hebrew into the later Chaldee, arose from different authors, is agreed on all hands. Of the Pentateuch, Onkelos was the translator; and he rendered it into quite pure Chaldee. His version is generally close, faithful, and for the most part as it were *verbum verbo*. In the small poetic portions of the Pentateuch, however, interpolations have been made, which disclose themselves, and show that they came not from the hand of Onkelos. The work, as a whole, is the most perfect specimen of the later pure Chaldee which we have.

Of the prophets, both *former* and *latter* in the Hebrew sense, Jonathan ben Uzziel is supposed to have written a Targum. The *former prophets*, i. e. most of the historical books, are more literally translated than the second, prophetic, poetic part. In general, his version is less true and literal than that of Onkelos. He indulges himself at times in the introduction of *Midrash*, and even some brief *Haggadoth*. But he is well worth consulting in very many cases, where obscure and difficult Hebrew words occur.

The Jews generally assign the *Hagiographal Targum* to *Joseph the Blind*, a somewhat uncertain, if not a mythic personage. Nothing is more evident than that the Targums of this portion of Scripture came from different hands, at different times. Such is the diversity of style, manner, and even language, of the Targums, in different books, that any other supposition is altogether improbable. Compare, for example, the Targum on the Proverbs and on Canticles.

Among the Hagiographal Targums, those of Psalms, Job, and Proverbs, are distinguished for their qualities. These books constitute the only ones which are acknowledged by the Rabbins of older times to be *poetical*. The *symbolic name* of these, among the Jews, is the word אֱמֶת, which means *truth*. The letter א stands for אִיּוֹב, *Job;* מ stands for מִשְׁלֵים, *Proverbs;* and ת for תְּהִלִּים, *Psalms*. Because these three books constituted the *corpus* of Hebrew poets, (if we accede to the Masorites), and because they are better translated than the rest of the Hagiography, a confident opinion has arisen, and has often been expressed, that they came from one and the same hand; and not only so, but that they were executed as near to each other in point of time, as the nature of the case would permit. We must examine this matter a little, because the character of the Targum on the Proverbs is deeply concerned with it.

Le Long, in his Biblioth. Sac. (I. p. 91), is the first in whom I find the Targum on אמ״ת ascribed to one and the same person. Hävernick (Einl. § 82) says, that "The Targum on Proverbs stands so related to that on Job and Psalms, as to the manner of expression and comprehension, that all are rightly regarded as belonging to one and the same person." Zunz, a distinguished critical Rabbi of the present day, in his *Gottesdienstliche Vorträge* (p. 64), declares, that "the Targum on the Proverbs has the same *linguistic* character as that on the Psalms and Job." Bertheau concedes this, and says that we may deduce from it the conclusion, that all these Targums took their rise about the same time and in the same region, (Einl. in Comm. über Proverbien, § 6). He next puts the Targum on Proverbs down very low, in point of time, because he finds the name *Constantinople* in the Targum on the Psalms, and the word אַנְגְּלֵי (= *ἄγγελοι*) in the book of Job. If the assumption be true, then the reasoning is well; for surely it must be a *late* Targum, which could originally employ such words. Still, it is easy to suppose them to have once been mere glosses on the margin, which afterwards crept into the text since that text has been in circulation. Such words do indeed look very much like glosses explanatory.

With all the deference due to such authorities, I must beg the liberty of dissenting from this judgment. I am bound to state my reasons; and I shall now proceed to do it.

(1) There are several characteristics of usage as to the *forms* of words, which widely distinguish the Targ. on Prov., from those on Job and the Psalms. (a) In Prov. we find everywhere the letter נ used as the *formative prefix* to third pers. masc., sing. and plural, instead of the usual י. Examples are not needed, except merely to illustrate the nature of the case; e. g. 16 : 10, sing. נִדְגּוֹל = יִדְגּוֹל; so third plur.

נְסוּפוּן = יְסוּפוּן, in Prov. 2:22. Hundreds of cases occur of the same nature. So far as I have made out an estimate, at least one half of the Fut. forms, third masc. sing. and plur., are made out in this way, and about one half with the elsewhere usual and normal י formative. This is surely a very striking distinction, and one which shows that the Targumist of the Prov. was familiar with the Syriac dialect, so familiar, that the cases with נ formative of the third pers. Fut. which are there normal, were, either consciously or unconsciously, carried over into his Chaldee version. This goes to show that both person and country, in this case, are different from those in the other case. The Targums of Psalms and Job, never exhibit this peculiar dialect at all.

(b) In the later Targums it is a well-known practice occasionally to *clip* or *abridge* the plural formations of nouns, and instead of ־ִין to write and read ־ֵי, thus making the absolute and construct forms of a noun plur. to be the same. Now in the Targ. of Prov., this *abridged* form is the much more usual form of the plur. absolute, so that the regular forms are the exception, and not the rule. On the contrary, in Job and Psalms we meet indeed with the abridged nominal forms, but merely as the exception, and not as the rule. The difference in this usage between the two books in question and the Prov. is so palpable, that it cannot escape the notice of any attentive reader.

(c) There is a striking difference between the Targums in question, in respect to employing the word *Jehovah*. In the original Hebrew of Proverbs, we find the word *God* (אֱלֹהִים) only six times, while יְהוָה is employed seventy-six times. In translating יְהוָה, however, in the book of Proverbs, the word אֱלָהָא is nearly always employed; and very rarely can be found the word יָי, i. e. יְהוָה. How different in Psalms and Proverbs, where, in the latter, יָי is the rule, and אֱלָהָא the exception! This is another charasteristic difference, then, which is very striking. Nowhere in Proverbs is מֵימְרָא דַיְיָ employed as a periphrasis for *God;* while in Job and Psalms this is not unfrequent.

(2) The genius and style of the Targum on the Proverbs, is altogether different, in some highly important respects, from that in Job and Psalms. The former is preëminently literal and close, and, considering the nature of the book, not a whit behind the Targum of Onkelos. It stands side by side with the Peshito, and is very little, if any, inferior to it, so far as *this* book is concerned. In reading many chapters, I have scarcely found difference enough in the Targum from the Hebrew, to induce me to take a single note of it. In some very few cases, like those in the Syriac, there is a small addition, and sometimes the same which is made in the Syriac; e. g. in 7 : 22, 23. 14: 14. 15 : 4. But on the other hand, the Syr. and Chald. more often differ from each other, where either of them disagrees with the Hebrew, than they agree with each other. This shows that the Targum is not, as Bertheau and others suppose, a copy of the Syriac. Both offer incontestable evidence of having been made from the original Hebrew. There is not in all the ancient versions, any specimen of a more plain, direct, intelligible, and faithful translation than this Targum. Bertheau says, however, that there are *many departures* from the Hebrew in it; and he appeals to 7 : 22. 10 : 3. 14 : 14. 25 : 1, 20, etc. But whoever examines these passages, will find the departures too insignificant to make much impression upon him. Put all of them together, they will not amount to so much as may be found in a single chapter of the Sept. Instead of drawing from them an argument to prove that the Heb. text of the Targumist was different from our present one, we can deduce the conclusion with confidence, that in nearly all respects it must have been the same text which we now have. So literally and exactly does the Targum reproduce it in another language.

Let us now turn for a moment to the Targum of Job and

of the Psalms, and see what liberties they have given themselves, in regard to the original Hebrew.

Heb. Job 1: 3. His substance also was seven thousand sheep ; and three thousand camels ; and five hundred yoke of oxen ; and five hundred she-asses, and a very great household.

Chald. His substance was seven thousand sheep, *one thousand for each of his sons ;* and three thousand camels, *one thousand for each of his daughters ;* and five hundred yoke of oxen, *for himself ;* and five hundred she-asses, *for his wife ;* and service-labor exceedingly much.

Thus much at the outset ; which, however, is a prelibation quite congruous with the sequel.

1 : 6. Now there was a day, when the sons of God came to present themselves before Jehovah, and Satan came also among them.

Chald. And it came to pass, on the day *of judgment at the beginning of the year*, that there came *troops of angels*, that they might stand *in judgment* before Jehovah, and Satan also came in the midst of them.

1: 10. Hast thou not made an hedge about him and about his house, and about all that he hath on every side ? Thou hast blessed the work of his hands, and his substance is increased in the land.

Chald. Hast thou not *by thy Word* protected around him and around the men of his house, and around all which he hath round about him ? And the works of his hands hast thou blest, and his possessions are mightily increased in the earth.

3 : 5. Let darkness and death-shade pollute it ; let a cloud dwell upon it ; let the utmost bitternesses of the day terrify it.

Chald. Let darkness defile it, and the shadows of death ; let a cloud dwell upon it ; let as it were the bitternesses of the day terrify it, — even the grief which distressed Jeremiah, when the house of the sanctuary was destroyed, and Jonah, when he was precipitated into the sea of Tarshish.

4 : 10, 11. The roaring of the lion, the voice of the fierce lion, and the teeth of the young lions are broken. (11) The old lion perisheth, for lack of prey, and the stout lion's whelps are scattered abroad.

Chald. The roaring of Esau which is compared to a ravenous lion, and the voice of Edom which is compared to a lioness, they rage as bears over their prey ; and his princes (who are compared to the lioness) separate themselves that they may seize the prey. (11) As the lion perisheth, when he hath no prey, so will perish Ishmael, because he hath no merit ; and also his sons, the robbers, who separate themselves from the right way. (Another reading). Ishmael, who is compared to lions, shall perish because he has no merit ; and the sons of Lot, who is likened to the old lion, shall be separated from the congregation.

The like we find almost at every step of our way, through the whole book. But it is of no use to cite further ; *ἐξ ὄνυχος — λέοντα.*

Turn we now to the book of Psalms. Here is more moderation, indeed, but still a like spirit.

Ps. 19 : 12 (11). Moreover, by them is thy servant warned, and in keeping of them is great reward.

Chald. Truly by them is thy servant warned ; as their varieties were kept, so was the good of Israel accomplished.

45 : 18. I will celebrate thy name in every generation ; therefore shall the nations praise thee forever and ever.

Chald. At that time shall ye say : We will remember thy name in every generation ; therefore the people who shall sojourn, shall confess thy name forever and to ages of ages.

46 : 6. God is in the midst of her, she shall never be moved ; God shall help her, at the approach of the morning.

Chald. The Shechinah of Jehovah is in the midst of her, she shall not be moved ; Jehovah shall help her, because of the righteousness of Abraham, who prayed for her at early morning.

110: 1. Jehovah said unto my Lord: Sit thou at my right hand, until I make thine enemies thy footstool.

Chald. Jehovah hath declared by his Word, that he would make me Lord over all Israel; but he said to me again: Wait for Saul of the tribe of Benjamin, until he die, for there is no kingly dominion which will bring near an associate with it; and after this, I will make thine enemies thy footstool. [Another Targum]. God said by his Word, that he would give me rule, because I have sat as a learner of the instruction of the law, at his right hand. Wait thou until I shall make thine enemies thy footstool.

It must be noted, that these specimens by no means stand alone, as if they were singular or strange, in the Targums of these books. More or less which resembles them will be found on every side, if any one will take the pains to pursue an examination. Let it be noted also, that the Peshito has not the least spice of this *Midrash*, in any one of the passages above cited; and so generally, in regard to all the Midrashim and Haggadoth of the Targums. What then becomes of Bertheau's position, viz., that the Targums copied the Syriac version?

But as to the main point before us, nothing can be plainer, than that the judgment of Zunz, of Hävernick, and of others, as to *identity of authorship* in respect to the Targums of אמ״ת, is a hasty judgment, made up without much examination, and at all events without sufficient grounds. We deny the assertion, in its whole length and breadth; and we have produced witnesses on whose testimony we may rely.

As we have no certainty in respect to the individual who was the author of the Targum on Proverbs, so we may be allowed to indulge a little in *conjecture*, keeping all the while in mind that it is no more than conjecture. It is plain that the *Syriac* translator has nowhere exhibited either the Targumic paraphrases, or glosses, or Midrashim, or Haggadoth. Now as the Targum on Proverbs has the same character in all respects, as the version of the Syriac;

and specially as the author of the Syriac has more than half the time employed נ as a prefix formative of the third pers. sing. and plur. of the Fut., instead of the usual and normal י, (thus showing a strong bias to use Syriac forms, and showing thereby that he was probably a Syrian Jew); putting all these things, I say, together, and bringing into the account the strong resemblance between the two versions, viz., the Syr. and Chald., is it not quite probable, that the Chaldee version was made for such of the Mesopotamians as spoke Chaldee; or at least made by a Syrian Jew, who was conversant with the Peshito, and imitated its main features? I mean that he followed the general style and manner of the Peshito, not that he copied from it individually, or made it a basis of his version in this special respect. Too often does he differ from the Syriac, to render such a supposition allowable.

In this way we can account for what all acknowledge, viz., the resemblance between the Peshito and the Targum. The taste of the translator was formed by the Peshito; and, approving of this, he has translated simply, neatly, and accurately. Invaluable would the other Targums be, if they were all like this.

When this work was performed, is uncertain. I can find nothing which indicates a *late* period. On the other hand, the tenor and spirit of the Targum, would seem to render it probable, that it was made not much after that of Onkelos. There is the same simplicity; although the Chaldee is not so pure. But this depended more on *individuality* of character and talent, than on any particular *time*. The deepest Rabbinisms of the Talmud do not abound here. Neither the form nor the manner of any part of the work speaks of the Talmudical age. In such an age, it would hardly have been possible to make a version so true, simple, and literal as that of the Targum on the Proverbs. The universal remains of the later Rabbinical ages exhibit a different taste and style of writing. *Midrash* was a thing of course to be expected in them; and the later the version, the more does this, and also *Haggadoth*, abound. Hence the *mare magnum* of Rabbinism into which the Targums on Ecc. and Canticles plunge. Indeed, the general tenor of the Targums on the Hagiography, is widely diverse from that on the Proverbs; so widely, that an earlier age is the only probable period of the rise of the Targum before us.

IV. THE VULGATE.

Little need be said of this, as it is so easily accessible, and every one can compare for himself. In general, it is about as literal, simple, and faithful, as the Targum and the Peshito. Now and then, we meet with a case where Jerome read the text with different vowels from the present Masoretic ones; in some cases the similar letters are exchanged. These all, however, are not of any amount worth special reckoning. Jerome appears to have entered well into the spirit of the book, and in general to have understood it aright.

The perplexing title to chap xxx. he has rendered nearer to the Heb. text, than any of the ancient translators. Still, one part of it is a singularity: "Verba Congregantis filii Vomentis, visio, quam locutus est vir, cum quo est Deus, et qui Deo secum morante confortatus, ait." He renders אָגוּר as a Part. of אָגַר, *to collect*, and so makes out the Gen. *Congregantis*. But *Vomentis* seems to be a problem. He doubtless sought for the root of the strange word (יָקֶה) in קוֹא, *to vomit*, which he must have read in the Imperf. Hiphil, יָקֵיא = יָקֵי. Hence his *Vomentis*, (a *personal* name which is strange enough). For the rest, מַשָּׂא is *visio*, and נְאֻם is rendered participially, or rather as a verb deponent. *Cum quo est Deus*, is made out from לְאִיתִיאֵל, which he must have read לְאִיתוֹ אֵל, making אִית out of אֵת,

with, Yodh being used only as a *mater lectionis*. In the second case, this same word is rendered: *Et qui Deo secum morante*, which is merely a variation of phraseology. Then comes *confortatus*, for which we have no word left but אֻכָל, and which must have been regarded by Jerome as the Part. of Pual, omitting (as not unfrequently) the מְ formative. Jerome, therefore, probably attached to it the idea of *fed, supplied with food*, and so, tropically, *comforted*. He seems not to have conjectured, that there were any proper names in the last part of the verse.

The Sept. translator has shown that the verse in question baffled his knowledge of the Hebrew. He sums up the whole verse thus: *Τάδε λέγει ὁ ἀνὴρ τοῖς πιστεύουσι θεῷ, καὶ παύομαι*. The *τοῖς πιστεύουσι* it is somewhat difficult to make out, but still it may be done. They must have read לְאוֹתֵי אֵל, i. e. *to those who consent to* or *confide in God*. As to the last words, *καὶ παύομαι*,, they are the literal rendering of וָאֵכֶל, Fut. apoc. of כָּלָה. See Comm. on 30 : 1, where this hint is followed out, in the rendering and explanation of the verse.

The Targum here gives the lead to our common English version, and follows closely the present Hebrew vowels. The Peshito is in perplexity: "The words of Agur, the son of Jakeh, who obtained the prophetic gift, and acquired strength, and said to Ithiel." In *acquired strength*, we see the same idea which in Jerome is expressed by *confortatus est*, i. e. the Pual Part. אֻכָל, *fed, nourished*.

It is obvious that, in consequence of the various hints given in these versions, the recent exegesis of this passage has been aided not a little. At all events, we seem now to have obtained a version which is more congruous with perspicuity and with the context.

The difficult word אַלְקוּם, in 30 : 31, plainly perplexed Jerome. He has rendered the clause thus: *Nec est rex, qui resistat ei*. The *nec* is against the tenor of the sense, which demands *et* here. Had he rendered it thus: *Et rex cui nemo resistat*, he would have come very near to the meaning of the original.

On the whole, we could not well dispense with the Vulgate. It is so far literal and close, as to afford either new aid in interpreting the text, or else it helps to confirm the other and older versions.

§ 15. *Apocryphal Imitations of Proverbs.*

Of these we have two books, comprised in the so-called *Apocrypha*. This contains books written originally for the most part in Greek, and at a late period, i. e. during the second century B. C. The usual names of the two books in question, are *The Wisdom of Solomon*, and *The Wisdom of Jesus the son of Sirach*, which last is also named *Ecclesiasticus*, and thus distinguished from *Ecclesiastes* or *Coheleth*. We begin with the latter, because that, in all probability, it is the *older* of the two; and which, for convenience sake, we shall call simply *Sirach*.

I. SIRACH.

In the prologue to this book, the name of the original author is given, viz. *Jesus*, who was a Jew of Jerusalem, that devoted himself to sacred studies, and to "gathering the grave and short sentences of wise men who had been before him;" and not only this, but "he uttered some of his own, full of much understanding and wisdom," (Pref.). His book, "almost perfected," was bequeathed by him to his son; and the last bequeathed it to his own son, *Jesus*, named after his grandfather the author of the book.

It was written originally in *Hebrew;* but the original seems to have perished long ago, and we have no specimens of it left, excepting about some forty passages, preserved in the early Jewish Rabbinical writings. These show that it was written in pure Hebrew; as might be expected from the character and attainments of the author. The *Greek translation* of the book was made by the son of Sirach (and grandson of the author), about A. D. 131. It must therefore have been written about A. D. 180; at all events, before the bitter and bloody persecutions of Antiochus Epiphanes, since no express allusion to them seems anywhere to be made. Chap. xxxvi. may perhaps be construed as having relation to these; but I apprehend the meaning here to be more general, and it has too little of intensity. The Greek version which is before us, is doubtless a pretty faithful one; since the author appears to be a modest and sensible man, and one well skilled in both languages, if we may trust to his Prologue. Doubtless the Greek version became current abroad, at Alexandria, and elsewhere, where Greek was understood, and where there were but few who could read the Hebrew.

The whole work is plainly a *designed imitation of the Proverbs of Solomon.* But it is much more copious than the Proverbs, containing fifty-one chapters of about the ordinary length.

In *manner* and *form*, the resemblance to the work of the true Solomon is somewhat striking. By far the greater portion of the book consists of parallelisms completed in one and the same verse; like Part II. of the book of Proverbs. Yet there is nothing like the uniformity, in this respect, which reigns in Part II. It resembles much more Part IV. of Proverbs, where single couplets are often exchanged for double ones, or for treble, and even more. So in Sirach. It comprises some fourteen hundred and one verses in the whole; and of these, at least two hundred and sixteen are double couplets, and some are treble, and some even more. Then again, there are a few examples, as in the book of Proverbs, of sentences completed by *only one* member of the parallelism; e. g. 12:7. 17:10. 32:21, 22. 34:4, 5.

37 : 3, 17. It is unnecessary to refer to the *complex* verses individually, as they everywhere present themselves to the eye of the observer.

Besides these, however, are a large number of passages where the same subject is continued through several verses; e. g. 4 : 11—19, respecting *wisdom;* again the same subject, 6 : 18—33. So as to various subjects, in 9 : 1—9. 10 : 7—18. 14 : 20 to 15 : 5. 24 : 1—34. 25 : 17—26. 26 : 1—27. 30 : 1—13. 31 : 1—10 and 25—31. 33 : 25—31, al. Chaps. xliv—l. are a continuous and connected *eulogy* of the ancient worthies. Chap. li. is one *continuous prayer.* Besides these striking exhibitions of long-continued subjects, there are many more of a briefer kind, comprising two, three, four, or more verses.

As to the *poetry* of the book, it is, as might be supposed in regard to a period so late, of the looser kind, in respect to a very considerable part of it. Indeed, one might well say of a large portion: "Nisi pede differt, sermo merus." Take, at random, as a sample of much in the book, a passage in 37: 12—16.

(12) Be continually with the godly man, whom thou knowest to keep the commandments of the Lord; whose mind is according to thy mind, and who will sorrow with thee if thou shouldest miscarry; (13) And let the counsel of thine own heart stand, for there is no man more faithful unto thee than it; (14) For a man's mind is sometimes wont to tell him more than seven watchmen, who sit above in a high tower. (15) And above all this, pray to the Most High, that he will direct thy way in truth; (16) Let reason go before every enterprise, and counsel before every action.

Here, if we except v. 16, there is scarcely a vestige of poetical costume. Yet there is a kind of correspondence in the *length of clauses,* such as may be found in some of the latter part of Proverbs, and in Coheleth. All this is characteristic of the later form of Hebrew poetry.

The book contains a large number of excellent maxims; and almost or quite an equal number of sentences, which rather incline toward tame and common-place ethics. Eichhorn has characterized the work pretty justly. He says: "The book of Jesus Sirach is a rhapsody of moral declamations; of reflections both longer and shorter on the course of worldly things, on the modes of life and of wise living among men of all conditions, ranks, and age. It is a collection of various thoughts and sallies of the mind, sometimes separate and sometimes connected; of common and discriminating, of witty and pointed sayings, which have respect to a wise and prudent use of life. It is a fit companion for the Wisdom of Solomon," Einl. iv. p. 42.

This is not a proper place for pursuing critical characteristic into detail. We must therefore be content with a few hints more, which may give a general lead to our thoughts respecting the character of this book.

With not a little here and there that is either *flat* or *mediocre*, there are some sentiments, also, which are erroneous in a moral or religious point of view; e. g. 3: 30, "Alms maketh an atonement for sins." In 4: 5, 6, the author recognizes the ancient superstition, (still widely spread among the heathen), that cursing by an envious and malignant man, will have a sure fulfilment. Some singular ideas appear here and there. In 18: 9, he states the number of man's days, at most, to be a hundred years. In 20: 4, is a sentiment respecting eunuchs, that at least seems strange. In 25: 24, he says: "Of the woman came the beginning of sin," (adhering to the letter of the history in Genesis, like Paul, in 1 Tim. 2: 13—15). In 33: 25—31, is a singular paragraph respecting *servants*, which contains a strange mixture of severity and of kindness: "Bread, correction, and work, are for a servant; tortures and torments for him also, when he is idle or vicious. If he will not work, — put on more heavy fetters." This looks ominous; but it is softened somewhat and amended by what follows: "Be not excessive in demands on him; let him be unto thee as thyself; entreat him as a brother, for thou hast need of him." This shows at least, that, although among the Hebrews the punishment of servants was left at the discretion of the masters, yet the maxims of humanity were predominant, and all unnecessary severity was to be shunned. Singular, indeed, also, is 38 : 1—15, in respect to a *physician*, and the aid which he may render. More strange are some things in 38 : 16—23, in respect to mourning for the dead. The thoughts concerning the *leisure* necessary to a man who would become learned, although expressed in a manner *unique*, and even in such a way as to provoke a smile, will yet address themselves with force to the sympathies of every real student; see 38 : 24—34.

Some of the writer's *similes* are quite peculiar. Thus, speaking of himself as having many thoughts to communicate, he says: "I am filled as the moon at the full," 39 : 12. In the doctrine of evil spirits who inflict vengeance, he is a full believer, 39 : 28. Yet there are no special traits of superstition, or Pharisaic views respecting the worth of legal rights and ceremonies; indeed, the direct contrary seems to be taught, in 8 : 9.

Throughout the book, there is a high moral and religious tone. The great doctrine of *retribution* is everywhere advanced, as in the book of Proverbs and Coheleth. Yet the immortality of the soul, and future rewards and punishments, are rather implied, than expressly taught; plainly they are not taught as in Wisdom 2 : 23. 3 : 1—3, al. So far as the interests of religion are concerned, the book, with the exception of a very few verses, might be joined with our Canon of Scripture, without any serious injury. But with all the good which it contains, and the many prudential and excellent maxims which it inculcates, one cannot help the feeling, while reading it, that it is quite different from anything in the Old Testament or the New. Indeed, it is plainly a true copy of a pious Jew's feelings, at the time when the book was written. But we find in it no *Messianic* hopes, and no certain index to the then prevailing opinions of the Jews, in relation to this great subject. This seems strange; and the more so, as chaps. xliv—l. contain a eulogy of distinguished men, in the regular order, for the most part, of Jewish history. This last composition, by the way, is widely distinguished from all the rest of the book; not so much by mere style and manner, as by a long-protracted discourse or eulogy, which ends with the famous high-priest, Simon, one of the Maccabees, and drops the subject with him, without an attempt to look into the future condition of the Jewish people, or at any deliverer of them from their oppressions by the heathen.

That they were under such oppression, when the author wrote, is plain. Such passages as 36: 1—14. 51: 2—11. 50: 24—29, and others which might be adduced, clearly show this. But before the time of Antiochus Epiphanes, the Jews had been treated with more or less severity alternately by both the Egyptian and Syrian kings, and also by their neighbors, the Samaritans; see 50: 25, 26. Strong as 36: 1—14 seems to be, it would probably have been much stronger had it been written under Epiphanes. It should be noted, that *foreign* rulers are complained of, and not native Jewish rulers.

Nothing is clearer, than that the author was, through and through, a genuine Palestine Jew. His literature is all sacred; his circle of knowledge merely scriptural. He is familiar with all parts of the Hebrew Scriptures, and alludes to passages almost without number, in Prov., Job, Coheleth, the Pent., and also the Psalms and Prophets. Yet he has hardly ever quoted literally. He puts new costume on ancient personages, and so presents them to the reader, that the latter is sometimes at a loss to discover where they have been found or met with; comp. e. g. Prov. 17: 2 with Sir. 10: 25; Prov. 18: 12 with Sir. 10: 7. One thing is remarkable, considering that he lived at a time when Greek domination had been exercised for two centuries over all hither Asia, and of course Greek literature had been widely diffused, viz. that still, *Sirach never manifests any acquaintance with it;* — a matter in which he greatly differs from the author of the book of Wisdom, who was thoroughly a *Graecizing* Jew, as to extent of knowledge.

It is specially to be noted also, that there is, in this Jewish writer, not a spice of *Midrash* or *Haggadoth;* no curious, conceited, allegorical, or mystical interpretations of the Heb. Scriptures. This is the more remarkable, since Philo of Alexandria everywhere abounds so much in them. But such seems to have been the difference between the Alexandrine and the Palestine taste, about the commencement of the Christian era. The Targum on the Proverbs, and the early Peshito version of the same book, speak plainly as to the same point, and shows that the mystical and allegorical among the proper Jews, was an *exotic* of later growth, although, when once domesticated, it flourished among the Rabbins belonging to the dispersed Jews, beyond all example elsewhere.

Whoever wishes to make a comparison of this peculiar book of Sirach with the Proverbs, may select for a main topic that of *Wisdom.* Let him now compare Sir. chap. i. 4: 11—19. 6: 18—33. 14: 20—27; and most of all, let him compare 24: 1—25: 12, with Prov. viii. ix., the former being designed as a kind of counterpart of the latter. Sirach is, indeed, not destitute of some fine sentences and noble sentiments; but as a whole, how striking the difference between the imitation and the original! In the former, there are many things which might well be spared, because they are superfluous, and which one would rather wish to see stricken out, because they approach the declamatory, and almost border on the puerile. In point of real fact, the imitation, when placed beside the original, can hardly be said to be anything more than a *failure,* — pardonable, perhaps, but still rendering the picture unworthy of the high rank of that in the proper book of Proverbs.

Everywhere the well-informed reader will find material for comparison between Sir. and the O. Test. It would be useless to occupy room here with a list of such passages; for they occur on almost every page.

On the whole, as a specimen of Jewish thought, feeling, ethics, and religion; also of Jewish exegesis and theology; during the interval between the disappearance of the prophets and the coming of Christ, the book before us is well deserving of critical attention. It will richly repay the student, by the enlarged views it will give him of ancient Heb. customs, manners, and modes of thinking and writing. Had such a book come from the hand of a *heathen* Greek, it would probably have found ten commentators, where it now has obtained one; and long since it would have been made a part of a *classical* course of study. As it is, few now even read it; much fewer *study* it; and yet it has more sound, prudential, ethical, and religious precept in it, than the whole body of Greek and Roman moralizers, from Socrates down to Marcus Antoninus. I know of no good reason, why a Hebrew writer, who has higher eminence as a moralist and a religionist, should be put in a place below those to whom he is actually superior. It is true, that the Greek of Sirach is not as attractive as that of Plato and Xenophon; but to me it seems not much inferior to that of Epictetus or of Plutarch.

After all, as has already been said, the book does not, in spirit and manner, seem like to the books either of the New Testament or of the Old. There are some things in it, which are trivial and unimportant; there are many which are *mediocre;* while, at the same time, much of it would make no unworthy addition to the book of Proverbs itself. In animation, however, in graphic sketching, in energy, and in the power of making a deep impression, the latter book must ever be regarded as quite preëminent. This indeed, of itself, would not decide that Sirach should be excluded from the Canon. But inasmuch as some of the sentiments (e. g. that of alms making an *atonement*) are plainly wrong; since the author makes no claim to inspiration; and since the book was professedly compiled long after the succession of Heb. prophets had ceased, and accordingly has never been recognized by the Jews as an inspired book, or admitted to their Canon, although originally written (as Jerome testifies) in Hebrew; we cannot accede to the Romish arrangement, which includes it among the books of Scripture, even when this inclusion is qualified by naming the book *deutero-canonical.*

One thing, at least, is demonstrated by the existence of such a book, viz. that the proverbial literature of the Hebrews, if we may so speak, was exceedingly rich. The first Prologue, (from the hand of Pseudo-Athanasius, in Synopsis Scripturae Sac.), says that the author collected most of his book "from the grave and short sentences of wise men," and also "uttered some of his own." This, although no authentic declaration, at least shows what the opinion of the Christian fathers in the fourth century was, and in itself it looks quite probable. How many of these gnomes had come down traditionally from Solomon himself among the Hebrews, we cannot determine; but that many of them were ancient, and sanctioned by popular and long-continued use, seems quite probable. It would be difficult to find such copious *gnomic* stores among any other nation. The Arabians, indeed, are very rich in this particular, as has been noted above; but a large portion of their maxims and pointed sayings have an historical basis; like to our *rich as Croesus; cruel as Nero; ambitious as Alexander*, and the like. In moral and religious gnomes, we could not expect them to abound as the Hebrews do. The simple fact, that such a vast store of gnomes, moral, religious, and prudential, existed among the Hebrews, shows that their minds had been busy with subjects of this nature, beyond any of their heathen neighbors. In fine, the book before us, which displays the richness of these stores, has claims on the attention of all who read the Hebrew Scriptures, and wish to study the Hebrew character. Nor will a proper attention to it be without a due reward.

II. THE WISDOM OF SOLOMON.

Such is the current title of a book, belonging to the Apocrypha, and which seems to have been regarded by many as one of the genuine works of Solomon. It is useless, at this time, to refute at large an opinion which has so little in its favor. The question has long been regarded by most critics as settled, that the production is from a much later hand, — from some person who lived in Egypt and was a Jew, but who was extensively acquainted with the literature, the manners and customs, the superstitious and idolatrous rites, of Egypt and of all the countries in hither Asia. Two considerations suffice to show, that Solomon had no concern in the composition of this book. The first is, that the style is for the most part utterly discrepant from the plain and simple style of the Proverbs; the second, that references are everywhere made in it to Isaiah, Jeremiah, and other late sacred writers, who lived some centuries after Solomon was dead. To these arguments we might add others, scarcely less decisive, viz. that the book was originally written in *Greek* (no Hebrew original being ever mentioned as known); and also that it is filled with most demonstrative evidences of the knowledge of Alexandrine Platonism, as it existed at or near the time of Philo Judaeus, among the disciples of the later Platonism.

Hence, even in ancient times, the more discerning among the Christian fathers rejected it from the Canon. The Jews never admitted it. To Philo and Josephus it was unknown; at least, it is not mentioned by either of them. Athanasius, Cyrill Hieros., Gregory Nazianz., and Epiphanius, declare it to be *apocryphal;* and Origen omits it, in his catalogue of canonical writers. It is almost needless to add, that all enlightened modern and Protestant critics reject it from the Canon.

It is much easier to show that Solomon was not the author of the book before us, than to show who did write it. It has been attributed to Zerubbabel (J. M. Faber); also to Philo the elder (Drusius), a contemporary of Demetrius Phalereus, in the time of Ptolemy Philadelphus, and mentioned by Josephus, Cont. Apion. I. 23. For the former no good historical reason is alleged; for the latter, it is enough to say, that Philo the elder was a *heathen*, while the book of Wisdom discloses, in every page, the hand of a pious and zealous Jew, intimately acquainted with all parts of the Jewish Scriptures. Not a few have attributed the book to *Philo Judaeus;* and even in Jerome's time, there were some who were of this opinion, as he tells us in his Pref. ad Lib. Sap. Many things seem to favor this opinion. A large number of maxims, ideas, and hypotheses are found to be alike in both. The coloring of New Platonism is common to both. The like knowledge of Egypt, and of literature in general, is common to both; and so far as *time* is concerned, Philo may have been the author, for he was born some twenty or twenty-five years before the Christian era. But Eichhorn (Einl. iv. s. 166, seq.) has shown beyond all question, that the discrepancies between Philo and the book of Wisdom, are too numerous and too important to admit of sameness of authorship. The agreements are sufficiently accounted for, on the ground that the author, whoever he was, lived in the same country, and at or near the same time, as Philo. Two men, brought up in the same philosophico-religious school, and surrounded by the same people and the same objects, must needs hold many opinions, and have many views, in common. Nothing can be more certain, than that the theological views of the author of Wisdom, are different, in many respects very different, from those of Philo. The latter, in his views of the Godhead and of sin and holiness, was half a Platonic heathen, as Dorner has fully shown, comp. in Biblioth. Sac. 1850, p. 696, seq.; the former is true to his Jewish origin and his religion. A holy God, making retribution to sinners, and rewarding the just, stands out in high relief, from every page of the book of Wisdom. In Philo's hands, sin and holiness, in their appropriate scriptural sense, scarcely develop themselves in a prominent way.

There have not been wanting some of high name, who regard the book as of Christian origin. So Bunsen, in his book on the *Church of the Future*. Dr. Nitzsch, of Bonn, (Deuts. Zeitschrift, 1850, No. 47, seq.), has fully answered his allegations, and shown the utter improbability of such a supposition. Indeed, I know not how one can carefully read the whole book, and then cherish such an opinion. *There is not one word about a Christ, present or to come, in the whole book.* There is not even a Messianic longing or hope expressed in it. After a careful examination of those passages which are alleged to have their basis in the New Testament, I have found none which did not admit of another solution. E. g. Wisd. 15 : 3 is compared with John 17 : 3, but may easily be referred to Jer. 9 : 24; so Wisd. 15 : 7 is referred to Rom. 9 : 21, but may be easily traced to Jer. 18 : 6, or to Is. 64 : 8. Again, Wisd. 14 : 25—27 is referred to Rom. 1 : 28—32. But the two descriptions need not be so regarded, as if the one were dependent on the other, (for there is considerable dissimilitude), but viewed as springing from a like source, viz. a thorough knowledge of heathen character. And so of all the other cases, where similarity is said to exist, it either springs from a common source of quotation, i. e. the Old Testament, or else from a knowledge of facts common to both, or from traditionary exegesis. It was impossible for a real Christian to write a book so religious, and not once recognize the religion of Christ as already existing, or about to be introduced.

Of all the apocryphal books of the Old Testament, the one before us stands preëminent as to an express recognition of the immortality of the soul, and of a future retribution of the righteous and the wicked; see 1:15. 2:23. 3:1, 4. 4:7—10, 14, 19. The supremacy of the Godhead; his wise providence; his hatred of sin, specially of idolatry; his propensity to mercy; and his love to the obedient, are everywhere displayed and insisted on in such a way, as that the book, in respect to its main constituents, might very safely be admitted to at least a *deutero-canonical* rank. But hardly could we place it higher. In 11:17, we have a declaration which indeed is not altogether clear, but which seems somewhat plainly to recognize the Platonic doctrine, that God did not *create*, but only arranged and adorned *matter without form:* "Thy hand formed the world, ἐξ ἀμόρφου ὕλης;" (contrary to the spirit of Gen. 1: 1—3). Chap. 8:20 indicates plainly *the preëxistence of human souls*, before their union with bodies. Much coloring also is given to various parts of the book, by the Platonism of the writer; unconsciously developed, it may be, but still, as the book now is, this serves to distinguish the whole of it very widely from both the Old Testament and the New. In a word, since the Jews have never acknowledged the book as canonical, we may well accede to their judgment in the matter, at least if we regard a *prophetic* origin as necessary to make a book sacred; or, if we demand of a book that, in order to be ranked as canonical, it must present internal evidence of close resemblance to the admitted Hebrew Scriptures, that resemblance cannot be found here. That the book before us can claim neither the one nor the other of these characteristics, must be admitted by every discerning and candid reader.

Still, it is a highly distinguished and deeply religious book. Its author was extensively read in the learning of the times, and all Egypt and hither Asia are evidently before him, and his allusions extend even to some of the Parsi religious notions, as well as to the different modes of idolatry. It is a book which deserves much more attention than it has received; and one on which, I may add, we have no tolerable commentary in our language.

But our specific object is not a *critique* at large upon the book. We have said thus much, merely to give the reader a general view. Our more particular purpose of comparison with the Proverbs, must now be pursued.

Like the Proverbs, it exhibits a large number of gnomic precepts, couched in parallelisms; but these in general are of the looser kind, and savor somewhat of the prosaic. Still, the number of verses, which contain three, four, or more clauses, is quite large, and specially frequent in the middle and close of the book. Many of these are merely a kind of measured prose. There is also a very considerable number of verses, which contain only one clause. Indeed, such is the internal structure of the book, on the whole, that we can hardly suppose the writer to have designed to write *poetically*, — I mean as to *measure*. It stands out prominently and widely distinguished from the generality of the book of Proverbs in these respects.

But inasmuch as the writer personates Solomon, and represents him as speaking, we naturally expect that he would have his eye on the writings of the wise king, and in many respects aim at imitating them. This he has done; but how successfully, each one can decide for himself, who will take the pains to compare some of the topics which are common to both books. We must limit ourselves here, however, to one principal topic, which constitutes the leading similitude between the two books. As Solomon was counted the wisest of men, and as he has presented us with a sublime and striking picture of *Wisdom*, in Prov. i—ix., specially in chap. viii., so the writer of the book before us, has, directly or indirectly, pursued this topic throughout his book. In

Part I. (chap. i—vi.), which is addressed to magistrates and kings, he points out the counsel which Wisdom gives, in order that they may live uprightly and do good to others. In this counsel is included many a maxim, which is of a generic nature, and might well stand in the book of Proverbs.

These admonitions being completed, the writer next proceeds, in imitation of Prov. viii., to eulogize and personify Wisdom. Chaps. vii—ix. are occupied with this subject, and with the expression of the writer's earnest desire, to enjoy the teachings of Wisdom. Chaps. x—xix. are occupied with exhibiting the blessings conferred by wisdom on the good, and the severe penalties which she inflicts on the foolish or wicked; specially on those who are devoted to idol-worship. The example of punishment, taken from the plagues of Egypt, is repeatedly introduced, and the writer dwells upon these plagues, and adorns his style with much rhetorical diction, and by the accumulation of splendid, and many of them poetical, images. But alas! he has overdone the matter, and displayed not a little of erroneous taste and artificial rhetoric. Is this to be attributed to the wise king? No; a writer so artificially ornate, and showy, and sometimes all but declamatory, can never have been Solomon himself, nor even any one who had caught either his style, or his simple manner of thinking.

Yet with this occasionally swelling and pompous rhetoric, and the evident efforts to write finely, there is intermingled many a vivid image, and many a truly eloquent thought. The later Grecian rhetoric everywhere gleams through; but this does not wholly obscure or suppress what is highly worthy of perusal.

I have already mentioned, that WISDOM is the leading topic of the book, — Wisdom as she is in herself, and Wisdom as exhibited in the practical instruction and guidance of men. We must dwell for a moment on this subject.

I would premise here, that *σοφία* is the more usual word,

employed to designate that *wisdom* of God which is manifested in his word and in his works. It has two other names, which, as employed in this book, are of nearly or quite the same import. It is sometimes spoken of as πνεῦμα, and sometimes as λόγος. These are, indeed, too plainly of the same substantial import, to need any argument in the way of confirmation.

The Wisdom or Word of God is *personified* in the representation; and sometimes, as an energizing influence, it is said to be diffused over all creation, and to dwell in and guide the good and pious. A few expressions must be quoted to enable the reader to make a comparison with Wisdom, as exhibited in the book of Proverbs.

Wisd. 1: 6. Wisdom is a loving Spirit . . . (7) For the Spirit of the Lord filleth the world, and . . . containeth all things. 6 : 12. Wisdom is glorious, and never fadeth away.

In chap. vii. the writer goes on to show how ardently Solomon desired communion with Wisdom, and what universal knowledge of men and things she communicated to him, 7 : 1—21. Personifying her, the writer then proceeds as follows: —

V. 22. Wisdom, which is the worker of all things, taught me, for in her is an intelligent spirit; holy, one only, manifold, subtile, mobile, clear, undefiled, perspicuous, incapable of harm, loving good, quick, incapable of hindrance, prone to do good, (23) Philanthropic, steadfast, sure, free from care, all-powerful, overseeing all things, pervading all intelligent, pure, and most subtile spirits; (24) For Wisdom is more mobile than all motion; she passeth through and pervadeth all things by reason of pureness; (25) For she is the breath of the power of God, and a pure emanation of the glory of the Almighty; therefore no defiled thing can light upon her; (26) For she is the radiance of everlasting Light, the unspotted mirror of the power of God, and the image of his goodness; (27) And although but one, she is able to do all things, and remaining in herself she maketh all things anew; and in all ages, passing into pious souls, she maketh them friends and prophets of God. (28) For God loveth no one, except him who dwelleth in Wisdom; (29) For she is more beautiful than the sun, and above all the arrangement of the stars; compared with the light, she is found superior to it. (30) Night indeed will follow, but it will not prevail against Wisdom.

From this soaring and adventurous flight of fancy and philosophy, the writer descends, in order to relate the doings of Wisdom in Solomon and in others, in chap. viii. " God only can bestow Wisdom," he says at the close, " and she is to be obtained only by prayer." Chap. ix. exhibits a specimen of praying for her; and Solomon is alleged to have uttered such a prayer. The rest of the book exhibits the doings of Wisdom, in respect to the righteous and the wicked, by detailing a series of historical events recorded in, and drawn from, the O. Testament. Very much of it is occupied with inveighing against idolatry; and scarcely anywhere can be found more indignant sarcasm and cutting reproof in respect to this sin. Chaps. xvi—xviii. are occupied with a vivid, highly wrought, and in many respects poetic, picture of the plagues of Egypt; which is brought to a close by a description of that terrible night, in which all the first-born were stricken dead. The awful executioner, on this occasion, is thus described:—

18:15. Thine Almighty Word leaped down from heaven, out of thy royal throne, as a fierce man of war, into the midst of a land devoted to destruction; (16) And brought thine unfeigned commandment as a sharp sword, and standing up, filled all things with death. It touched the heaven, while it stood on the earth.

Such are the views of the writer before us, on the subject of the *Wisdom* or *Word of God;* views partly Platonic and partly Hebraistic. To deny that they are in some respects sublime, would be to do the author injustice. Not a few of his conceptions are indeed lofty, and morally pure, and highly spiritual. An immeasurable distinction between Wisdom and any corporeal personage, is everywhere kept up. Yet plainly the whole is *personification* merely, and Wisdom is not a hypostatic or personal substance.

A single look will tell the whole story of the difference between the picture before us, and the truly sublime and simple representation in Prov. viii. We turn away from the comparison, after making it, with almost a rising dislike of the picture by the later and factitious Solomon, when viewed in connection with that of the original and real one. Later Grecian philosophers and rhetoricians might applaud the book of Wisdom; for its style is adapted to their taste. We too may admire its lofty religious tone, its high and reverential regard for the God of the Bible, and its deep-toned abhorrence of heathen pollution and idolatry. We may well wonder, indeed, that there is so little in the book which will give any offence to a well-informed Christian mind. The author, beyond a doubt, was a person of uncommon piety and zeal for religion, so far as he knew what constituted true religion. We find in him neither Pharisaism nor Sadduceeism. He seems to have been a true and warm-hearted disciple of Moses; while he was, as it were, unconsciously a disciple of the later Platonism.

Hence the conclusion, that he was *not a Christian*. A man of feelings so ardent, must have spoken out plainly and fully concerning the Messiah. But not one word about such a personage, either as already come, or to come. The idea of a *spiritual* Messiah seems, indeed, to have been mostly given up among the Jews who lived at, or some time before, the beginning of the Christian era. A temporal deliverer was all they in general expected; at any rate, no other appears in the books of Wisdom and of the Son of Sirach. In fact, it is quite doubtful whether we can find even such an one, who is a *specific* person. I am aware, indeed, that some have referred Wisd. 2:12—22 to the persecution and death of Christ, because "*the just man*" who is persecuted, is called "*the son of God*," (v. 18). But this cannot prove anything important to the purpose in question, because, in the idiomatic language of the Jews, *all good men* were called *the children of God.* The passage is in its nature too general to admit of the specific application in question. The sequel to the text before us shows plainly, that *the just man* (in v. 18) is only a type or representative of the righteous in general; see specially 3 : 1—7. The passage in 3 : 8, is the only one that seems to be Messianic: "They [the just] shall judge the nations, and have dominion over the people; and their Lord shall reign forever." The context shows, that this designates merely the ultimate triumph of the righteous, and the establishment of a perpetual kingdom by him who is the Guardian and Guide of *just men.* It might be *Messianic,* if the context called for such a meaning; but as it is, the context does not seem to allow of this interpretation.

What is there, then, in all the book, to determine its age? Nothing, excepting that the want of any reference to Christ, as already come, or near at hand, shows that the writer was not a Christian. The address to judges and kings, in i—vi., gives strong evidence that oppression and violence were then and there rife. The severe reproaches of idolatry in x—xix. show, moreover, that the writer was much annoyed by idol-rites and worship. He could not, therefore, have lived in Palestine, where idolatry never flourished, after the return from the Babylonish exile; but, as the tenor of his work shows, he must have been a resident in Egypt. If he had lived at or near the time of the birth of Jesus Christ, then was there in Egypt, at that time, a mingled and motley throng of idol-worshippers, the old Egyptians or Copts, the Greeks, and the Romans, who had recently added Egypt to their domain. Doubtless these different nations had a rival spirit in the performance of their religious rites, and therefore exhibited much zeal in the prosecution of them. All of them were idolaters, although of different classes. This fact will well account for the phase of the last part of the book of Wisdom. The book may have been written in Philo's time, for he was born some twenty or twenty-five years B. C.; but clearly it was not written *by* him; at least if *diversity* in the style, and in the manner of treating subjects, can decide anything in respect to such a question. The probability is, therefore, that some pious Jew, whose name is not given, either not long before, or else a little after the birth of Christ, wrote the book of Wisdom. It is singular, indeed, that his book is so free from all expressions, which might help to determine the exact period in which he lived.

At all events, however, while we have abundance of manifest tokens that he meant to tread in the steps of Solomon, inasmuch as he had assumed his name, we yet see, in the most convincing manner, how insufficient Grecian art and philosophy are, to enable a writer to imitate the genuine Hebrew authors, who were under the leadings of divine inspiration. The deep conviction of all this, which the study of the book of Wisdom gives, is enough to repay the reader amply for the labor which that study costs.

§ 16. *General Remarks on the Proverbs of the Hebrews.*

We have now come to a position, in which we can survey to advantage the ground of *proverbial lore* among the Hebrews. We have seen how very extensive it was, even so early as the days of Solomon, "who spake three thousand proverbs," 1 Kings 5. 32. Nothing is plainer than that, when the book of Proverbs was written, or at any rate when it was finally completed, there were great multitudes of proverbs which had been originated by others, as well as by Solomon, and which were then current among the Hebrews. The work of Jesus Sirach shows us a very large number, which were current nearly two hundred years B. C. The author of the book of Wisdom has exhibited many more, which are incorporated with the body of his work. At a later period still, we have a large accession also in the *Pirqe Abhoth*, or *Maxims of the Fathers*, among the Mishnical Tracts. Had we the whole in one body, and if to these were added the many gnomes scattered up and down the Mishna and the Talmud, such a book would constitute a *Corpus Proverbiorum* not to be equalled, perhaps, by the proverbs of any other nation.

It is thus that the want of means to publish and circulate books, occasions an active and energetic people to embody the result of their experience and reflections in short and pithy sentences, which are easily impressed on the mind, and are easily remembered for a long time. In this way, traces of the mental energy of an unlearned people do not perish or wholly disappear, by the progress of time; for their character and their wisdom are enstamped on the gnomes and apothegms which are perpetuated by tradition.

There is a still more interesting point of view, in which we may contemplate this matter. The *proverbs* of a nation exhibit in reality, as has already been remarked, a *history* of its social, moral, and religious culture or condition. Maxims and gnomes are perpetuated among any people, only because they accord with their feelings, views, and reasonings. Of course, they are unmistakable intimations of its social, moral, and religious views or condition. No history of its external relations, of its wars and conquests, or even of its political revolutions, can give us such an insight into the character and genius of a nation, as the current maxims which regulate their every day life. In these are embodied the mental reasonings, the moral feelings, the social propensities, and (in a word) the whole character of the interior man. And hence we might confidently say: Place before us the whole store of popular proverbs among any people of ancient times, and we will tell you to what pitch of civilization, refinement, and moral culture they have arrived.

Highly important, then, in respect to a knowledge of that most distinguished people, the ancient Hebrews, is the gnomic lore, which has, through various channels, descended to us. Their *external* history, important as it is, makes them far less known to us, than this internal one. Consequently, as has been intimated before, he who intends to become extensively acquainted with their whole and true character, must study it as developed in their proverbs.

It has often been said: "Give me the privilege and power of composing the popular ballads of any people, and I will readily concede to you all other means of moulding and conforming them to your wishes." This may be true as to cherishing a military or a patriotic spirit; and perhaps it may reach even farther than this. But I would say with double emphasis: "Give me the power and privilege of composing all of a nation's proverbs, and of making them popular and current, and all you can do with books and treatises will have less influence upon the mass of them, than the homely maxims which are in every body's mouth and in every heart."

I would further remark, that, if we may judge of the ancient Hebrew nation by their *proverbial lore*, we must surely place them in an elevated rank among the nations of former times, as to their social, moral, and religious views. In vain do we go to Hindoostan, to Persia, to Arabia, to Greece, or to Rome, for any such body of popular maxims to regulate both the heart and life, as we find among the Hebrews. In all this, the elevating influence of the Old Testament religion on the national character becomes a plain and palpable fact. In *literary* cultivation the Greeks exceeded them; and in later times, the Romans. But this kind of cultivation seems to have produced but a partial influence on the moral and religious state of those heathen nations. And although bad men among the Hebrews were never wanting, in any age, yet that the mass of the nation should have chosen and retained the gnomic precepts that have been recorded in their books, is evidence not to be gainsayed of their superior moral culture, and of their general social and moral condition.

Having ventured on such an assertion, I must crave the liberty to offer some specimens of heathen proverbs in order to substantiate it. I can of course present here only a few of these ; and that few I shall confine to the nations of Arabia and of Greece, who bordered on Palestine. What I do select, will be limited, moreover, to those only which appear to be among the more important, and which are most worthy of the comparison in question. The great mass of them, (which are indeed not without significance, but are comparatively less important), I must of necessity omit.

§ 17. *Specimen of Arabic Proverbs.*

In the second edition of Erpenius's Arabic Grammar, with Notes by A. Schultens, is inserted, among other things, and in the way of helping to make out a Chrestomathy, a *Century of Arabic Proverbs*, i. e. a hundred proverbs, selected from the large mass of Arabic proverbial lore. The design of these is to present specimens of the best part of this species of composition. From these I shall select and translate as many as the present occasion will allow, in order that the reader may compare them with the Proverbs of Solomon. The *numbers* prefixed, correspond to those prefixed in Erpenius ; so that the original Arabic may be easily found and compared, by any one desirous of so doing.

(1) The beginning of wisdom is the fear of God.

(2) The learned man, in his own native land, is like gold in the mine.

(3) He who regards himself as a wise man, both God and man will regard him as an ignorant one.

(4) Whoever desireth to become powerful in wisdom, he must not let women rule over him.

(5) It is easier to withdraw a malicious man from his malice, than a melancholy one from his sadness.

(6) Beware of him, whom thou knowest not well.

(7) He who is borne onward in the chariot of hope, will have poverty for a companion.

(9) In the head of an orphan, the surgeon obtaineth knowledge for himself.

(11) It is better for thee to keep thine own secret, than that others should keep it for thee.

(15) A fool who is his own enemy, — how can he be the friend of another?

(18) Long experience is increase of knowledge.

(19) If all men should become wise, the world would be depopulated.

(20) Robbery taketh away much wealth.

(21) Sloth and much sleep remove from God, and bring on poverty.

(23) Do good, if you desire others to do good to you.

(24) Correct thyself that thou mayest correct others.

(25) The beginning of anger is madness, and its end is sorrow.

(27) The man whom concupiscence overcometh, will perish.

(28) Religious duty slayeth concupiscence.

(29) A wise enemy is better than a friend who is a fool.

(30) To abstain from coveting, is to be rich.

(32) Poverty is better than forbidden riches and unjust gain.

(33) The tongue of a mute is better than the tongue of him who uttereth falsehood.

(34) The worst of men, is a learned man who profiteth not by his learning.

(35) There are two who are never satisfied; he who seeketh after learning, and he who seeketh after wealth.

(36) A person without instruction is a body without a soul.

(39) He who multiplieth words, will slip up.

(41) A learned man in exile, is better than a pensioned fool.

(42) Hear and learn; keep silence and have peace.

(46) Patience is the key of joy, but haste is the key of penitence.

(48) He who justifieth himself without being blamed, will bring blame upon himself.

(50) Three are not profited by three, the noble by the ignoble, men of probity by those without probity, the wise man by the fool.

(52) He is the wisest man, who looketh at the end.

(53) Three things are unknown, except in three places; bravery is not known except in war, a wise man is not known except in anger, nor a friend except in time of need.

(54) He who cannot tell good from evil, must be joined with beasts.

(56) A wise man is not wise, until he has conquered all his lusts.

(57) He who maketh experiments, increaseth knowledge; he who taketh everything upon trust, increaseth error.

(59) When thou hast uttered a word, it hath the mastery over thee; when thou hast not uttered it, thou hast the mastery over it.

(61) Seek knowledge from the cradle to the grave.

(64) He who praiseth obscurity perpetuateth it.

(66) The love of the world and of riches is the source of all sin.

(69) Whatever is in the hands of a servant belongeth to his master.

(71) The world is a carcase, and they who seek it are dogs.

(74) Reckon not thyself with men, so long as anger getteth the better of thee.

(75) Be content with what God giveth, and thou shalt be rich.

(76) Abstinence is a tree, whose root is contentment and its fruit quietude.

(76) The visitor is in the grasp of him who is visited.

(79) A camel kneeleth down in the place of a camel.

(80) The world consisteth of a sufficiency, and not of an abundance.

(83) Rare visits increase love.

(86) Perfection consisteth in three things; devotion in religion, patience in adversity, and prudence in life.

(87) A ruler without justice is a river without water.

(89) Learning without action is like a cloud without rain.

(90) He who honoreth his father, prolongeth his days.

(91) A rich man without liberality is like a tree without fruit.

(92) A poor man without patience is like a lamp without oil.

(93) A youth without penitence is like a house without a roof.

(94) A woman without modesty is like meat without salt.

(95) One day of the learned man is worth the whole life of an unlearned one.

(98) Show not thine enmity to thine enemy, nor to him who envieth thee.

(99) Undertake nothing, until thou hast well considered it.

(100) Talk not with a fool, neither have any intercourse with him, for nothing will shame him.

Very few of these maxims need any explanation. Respecting those which may seem doubtful, I will add a word for the sake of the reader.

In No. 9, the chirurgeon or surgeon is represented as choosing the *orphan's head* for the purpose of dissection, i. e. of examination. The gist of the proverb lies not in the assertion that knowledge is acquired by dissecting a head, but in the assertion that an *orphan's* head is selected as the subject of operation. He has no parents to prevent the profanation of his dead body, and to rescue it from a treatment to which the bodies of criminals only were subjected. The surgeon, desirous of knowledge, ventures on obtaining it by dissection in such a case, without the fear of being brought to punishment. The *moral* of the gnome seems to be, that men, under pretence of accomplishing something useful, will invade the rights of others who cannot avenge themselves, in order to secure some advantage.

No. 19 is a sarcasm on women. The somewhat occult meaning is, that if all men were *wise*, they would abstain from marriage and from sexual intercourse, and so the world would soon become depopulated. In reality, the gnome is the outpouring of bitter irony, against the woes of an unlucky union in marriage.

No. 79 is of partial application, being used only in reference to such things as, being alike, usually follow one another in succession. We say: "Like begets like," to the same purpose. The original imagery is taken from a spring or watering-place, where camels successively kneel to drink, each taking the same attitude and the same place which its predecessor occupied. The general meaning of all the rest of the proverbs here, will be obvious to every intelligent reader.

In No. 39, *will slip up* is the literal meaning of the Arabic; we might give the secondary meaning of the Arabic verb, viz., *will err*. But the other is more graphic. This corresponds well in sentiment with Ecc. 5 : 3, "A fool's voice is known by the multitude of words;" and also to 5 : 7, "Many words are vanities." It is evident at first sight, that the same sentiment for substance is common to all these declarations.

It will not escape the notice of the considerate reader, how often the Oriental proneness to comparison and metaphor, manifests itself in these very brief maxims. Let him cast his eye over Nos. 7, 36, 46, 76, 87, 89, 91, 92, 93, 94. No. 71 is very striking: "The world is a carcase; and they who seek it, are dogs." There is a kind of playful but cutting sarcasm in this; and above all, when we consider the full tropical import of the word *dogs*. The like says Paul: "Beware of *dogs*," Phil. 3 : 2; and also John, Rev. 22 : 15, "Without are *dogs*."

Every one must be struck, moreover, with some surprise, at the numerous maxims that are here found, which correspond altogether in *spirit*, and some of them even in *diction*, with what is said in the Scriptures. Let him compare Nos. 1, 20, 21, 23, 24, 25, 32, 39, 42, 54, 66, 75, 83, 87, 90, 98, 99, 100, with corresponding declarations of the Bible, which he may easily find; for in this way he may learn, how well the *morale* of the Scriptures corresponds with the conclusions of sober reason and conscience in the breasts of even the heathen, when somewhat enlightened. He may also learn in this way, that Solomon probably adopted many of the maxims of social life as true, and gave them his sanction, not because he composed them *de novo*, but because they were true.

In regard to the *parallelism*, (which we find everywhere prevalent in the proverbial lore of the Hebrews), we find it in Arabic but seldom; and even then it seems rather to be accidental than expressly designed. Most of the Arabic proverbs, moreover, are very *short*, as well as pithy. Yet we now and then meet with a protracted one, like some of the long ones in the latter part of the book of Proverbs; No. 53 above affords an example. In No. 70 of Erpenius, we have another specimen: "A fool is known by six properties; that he is angry without reason; that he speaks useless things; that he trusts every and any one; that he changes when there is no reason for change; that he seeks what does not belong to him; and that he does not distinguish his friend from his enemy." But the like to these, as to length, very seldom occurs.

One other circumstance will cast some light on the frequent occurrence of *two things*, *three things*, and *four things*, (which seem at first view so strange), in Prov. xxx. In the *Centuria* of Erpenius, Nos. 35, 44, give us specimens of *twos;* Nos. 50, 53, 86, of *threes;* and No. 70 above, of *six*. Both these and Proverbs xxx., taken together, and compared with Amos i. ii., will show how deeply such modes of expression have been engraved on the Oriental mind and discourse.

Finally, I cannot refrain from the remark that, in a mere aesthetical point of view, the Hebrew proverbs are, for the most part, altogether superior to the Arabic. There is more point, vivacity, and energy in most of them. Yet some of the Arabic gnomes are very striking. But if we go from the aesthetical ground to the moral and religious one, comparison can hardly be made between them. The social *morale* of the Arabic is good; but the higher considerations of accountability to God and retribution, of our relations to God, and of our duties which grow out of these, stand in high relief on the Hebrew picture, and only in the background in the Arabic one. Others may impute this to what natural causes they see fit; but my persuasion is, that it comes by reason of special divine illumination upon the minds of the Hebrews.

For the rest; the proverbs of the Arabians are exceedingly numerous. The *Extracts (Pars)* from Meidani, by H. A.

Schultens (Lug. Bat. 1795), consist of four hundred and fifty-four proverbs; and there are several other and much larger collections besides this. Most of these have an *historical basis,* instead of a generic and abstract meaning. The like of this we sometimes find in the Hebrew Scriptures; e. g. "Is Saul also among the prophets?" 1 Sam. 10: 11. 19: 24, and the like in other places. We find, in Meidani, that the great mass is of the following type: "More avaricious than Madara;" "More pious than Amallas;" "Colder than the north wind — than ice — than hail — than the day after the rain;" "Farther off than the vulture's eggs — than the stars — than the Pleiades;" "More odious than the visage of sellers in a dull market;" "More arrogant than Thakis;" "More liberal than Hatem." With these and the like are intermingled now and then a *preceptive* or *didactic* gnome which is of a generic tenor.

Every one sees at once, therefore, that the gist of the great mass of Arabic proverbs, can be gathered only by a knowledge of particular persons, things, and places. Not so with the Hebrews. Doubtless, however, the Hebrew people had in general circulation many such proverbs as the Arabic presents; yet only a few of these have been committed to writing in the Sacred Records.

§ 18. *Specimens of Greek Proverbs.*

These might be found in their highest perfection, in the writings of Plato and Xenophon which exhibit the conversations of Socrates, who abounded in maxims. They might be found, in great abundance, in a didactico-poetic form in the *choruses* of the Greek Tragedies, i. e. in the works of Aeschylus, Euripides, and Sophocles. Above all, is Aeschylus the distinguished religious and moral poet of the Greeks. The lofty form given to moral maxims, in the exquisite choruses which display the highest talent of the poets, would, in an *aesthetic* point of view, make them to compete with the Hebrew poetic gnomes. From Plutarch, from Epictetus, and others, a large accession to these stores might be selected. But it would lead me too far away, should I pursue this method of illustration; and it would also detain the reader longer than he would wish, should we attempt to travel over this ground. I shall content myself, therefore, with a brief selection, from the sayings of some of the Greek poets, who are styled *Gnomici Poetae Graeci.* I use the edition of Brunck, 18mo. 1784.

Theognis (fl. 549 B. C.) thus expresses himself:—

(1) The sun looks down on no man now living, who is entirely good and temperate.

(2) All things do not take place in accordance with the earnest wishes of men, for the immortals are much better than mortals, (ib.)

(3) Every one honoreth the rich, and dishonoreth the poor; yet there is the same mind in all. [All men have the same or the like intelligent spirit; and so, in this respect, all men are equal.]

(4) There are all kinds of bad dispositions in men, and all kinds of virtuous ones, and of contrivances for livelihood.

(5) It is a base thing, that a drunken man should consort with sober ones; and a base thing, if a sober man abide with drunkards, p. 27.

(6) Youth and early life render a man light-minded; yea, they rob many of their minds even to distraction, (ib.)

(7) Take counsel twice and thrice, as to whatever may come into thy mind, for a hasty man is a doomed one.

(8) Knowledge and modesty follow the good; not indeed the multitude, but certainly the few.

(9) Hope and danger among men are alike, for they are both troublesome demons.

(10) Swear not that this thing shall not be, for the gods will control, to whom belongeth the end, (p. 26, seq.)

My next extract is from the remains of *Solon,* (a contemporary of Theognis), the famous Athenian legislator; Brunck, ut sup. p. 73.

(11) He is a happy man, who hath beloved children, horses whose hoofs are uncloven, and hounds of the chase, and a stranger-guest.

(12) No mortal is entirely happy, but all are subject to distress, even all the mortals on whom the sun looks down, p. 76.

(13) In great doings, it is difficult to chime in with all.

(14) I am becoming old, but I am always learning many things.

(15) The mind of the immortals is always hidden from men.

(16) Satiety breedeth contempt, even when much pleasure followeth. [Things luscious speedily produce disgust].

(17) By the help of the gods I have accomplished things unhoped for; and at the same time, no work is in vain, p. 84.

The next following extracts are from Simonides, a contemporary of both the preceding writers, Brunck, ut sup. p. 99, seq.

(18) A man can obtain nothing better than a good wife, and nothing more horrible than a bad one.

(19) No one is altogether faultless or harmless, p. 100.

(20) We should not think of one who is dead, (if we think at all), more than one day. [It is useless to protract grief, when there is no remedy for the evil suffered].

(21) Death overtakes him who shuns the contest.

(22) Being but a man, say not what shall be; nor, seeing a man, how long he shall be; for swifter than the swift-winged fly, is our change of condition.

(23) Our season of living is short; but when a mortal man is once laid under the ground, he lieth forever.

(24) Zeus only hath a cure for all things.

From the *Works and Days*, usually attributed to Hesiod, a contemporary of Homer, are selected the following maxims: —

(25) Whoever ventureth to strive with rulers, wanteth understanding, and undergoeth reproach and sufferings without the hope of victory.

(26) Jupiter hath given this law to mortals: for a beast becometh food for beast, and a fish for fishes, and a bird for birds, because they are restrained by no sense of right; but the better light of justice is given to men.

(27) He deserveth the wrath of the gods and the hatred of men, who liveth without activity; like a stingless drone, the sluggard consumeth what hath been gathered by the labor [of others], p. 180.

(28) Shamefacedness often maketh men poor; confidence rendereth them rich; that which is given of the gods, and is not acquired by plunder, is the better possession.

(29) When prepared, do not put off a thing until to-morrow and to-morrow; he who procrastinateth provoketh losses to his sorrow.

(30) Silver is a second life to some pitiable mortals.

(31) Time is to a man sometimes a mother, and sometimes a step-mother, p. 182.

The next extracts are taken from relics of the Greek comic poet, Menander, p. 191; (fl. 300 B. C.)

(32) Peace nourisheth well the husbandman, although among the rocks; but war badly, even in the plain.

(33) A daughter marriageable, if she say nothing, by her very silence saith much respecting herself.

(34) I have never envied the dead, who is expensively buried; for he cometh to a house which is the same as that of him who is buried without expense.

(35) Do not find fault if I speak, although I am young; specially do not blame me, if I speak the words of reflecting men.

(36) He who is severe toward his son in the way of admonition, is bitter indeed in his words, but paternal in his deeds.

(37) It is not easy to check a weighty stone hurled from the hand; and so, with a word from the tongue.

(38) He is the most powerful man, who best knoweth how to do most wrong to his fellow-men.

(39) He whose body is diseased hath need of a physician; but he who is diseased in soul needeth a friend; for a kindly word is an expert in relieving sorrow.

(40) When one deems himself to have a mind in love, he will appear to another as having no mind.

(41) He who condemneth before hearing openly, the same is a bad man, nurturing an evil credulity.

It would be easy to make many remarks, in view of these proverbs, on the state of society which they disclose, and on the difference between them and the Arabian gnomes. But this is not the appropriate place for commentary at large. I advert only to a few particulars which are of the more striking kind.

In general, the *morale*, so far as it goes, is good. Even some measure of *religiosity* is developed, in several of the maxims. But let it be noted, that only the *supremacy* or *sovereignty* of the Deity is specially brought to view. How could a Greek, who in any measure believed in the popular mythology, regard the gods as either holy, or just, or good? With him we find, indeed, a disposition toward fear and submission; but where, in heathen proverbial lore, is the precept to *love God*, and *hope for his salvation?* And inasmuch as *God is love*, and should *be loved*, all the wisdom of Greece falls short of teaching the main thing in religion. To teach this belongs only to revelation. Nos. 2, 10, 15, and indirectly 22, afford a specimen of the Greek theosophy. The want of perfection in all men, is exhibited in Nos. 1, 19. The substantial equality of men is taught, in Nos. 3, 33. Solon's idea of a happy Athenian *gentleman* (sit venia!) is strikingly exhibited in No. 11. One portion of the English gentry would like such *legislation* right well.

The precepts concerning temperance, sober consideration, industry, slander, self-conceit, and the like, are in the main pungent and much to the point. If the reader will look back to Nos. 9, 31, 32, 37, 39, he will see, that a striking acuteness of observation and power of expression are very manifest. No. 37 vividly illustrates the *heroism* of ancient, and alas! of modern times also. No. 39 may appear somewhat obscure, at first view. In reality it expresses only this idea, viz., that a man desperately in love often acts like a fool; which, we may well believe, is as true now as it was in Menander's time.

On the whole, if we compare these proverbs with our present book of Proverbs, where the same subjects (at least in part) are touched upon, we shall see, that the Hebrew gnomes are graver, and withal have a stronger grasp. Above all, *religious principle*, the love of God and the love of man, and the doctrine of accountability and of future retribution, are manifestly lacking in the Greek proverbs. And although some of these topics are touched upon in the Memorabilia of Socrates, for example, and some good things are said there, and also by Plutarch, yet the God of the Bible is so immeasurably different from the gods of the Greeks, (even their speculative ones), that it were irrational to expect from them a *Hebrew* theology. As *Jehovah* was not known to the Greeks, so they could form no appropriate precepts respecting his worship.

In the mean time, if any one will compare the proverbs of the Greeks with those of the Arabians, he will easily see, that each class is stamped with peculiar national characteristics. We can only refer here to one example. No. 19 of the Arabic gnomes says, that "if all men were *wise*, the world would be depopulated," i. e. all *wise* men will abstain from sexual connections; while No. 18 of the Greek proverbs says, that "a man can obtain nothing better than a good wife, and nothing worse than a bad one." The Arabians have always held females in comparative contempt, except just at that season of life which is appropriate for writing love-songs. Accordingly, Mohammed, as most have understood him, excludes women from heaven; for he supplies a new genus of women, viz., the *Houris*, for the use of his followers in Paradise. The Greeks divided their divinities, higher and lower, into male and female, — an idea which partakes of the impracticable to an inhabitant of hither Asia, tinctured with Asiatic notions. Hence the Arabian readily utters sarcasms in earnest on women, where the Greek would only playfully utter them. Culture made a great difference between the two nations; *Disciplina emollit mores.*

How different are the views disclosed by the Hebrew Proverbs! Father and mother are put on the same level in relation to their children. Eternal Wisdom is personified by a *female*, in order to represent her as attractive and persuasive. The marriage vow must be sacredly kept, Prov. 5 : 15—23. Wise women build up their houses, 14 : 1. A good wife is a great treasure, 18 : 22. Yet the vices of women are not overlooked, 2 : 16, seq. 5 : 3, seq. 6 : 24, seq. 7: 5, seq. The book, moreover, concludes with a delightful song, in praise of virtuous and energetic women. All this shows a state of society, and of moral and social feeling, far in advance of that which existed among the Arabians and the Greeks.

One striking feature in the style of the Greek proverbs is, that there is nothing more than merely accidental, but never designed, *parallelism* in them. Even in poetry, (and I have quoted only such), this characteristic is wanting. The Greek poetry demanded not *parallelism*, but *measure*, i. e. artificial arrangement of long and short syllables ; the Hebrew demanded no regular measure of syllables long and short, but *parallelism* and *a kind of rythm* among the clauses thereof. So much do education, state of society, country, and different occupations and usages, affect the tenor of any nation's thoughts and their modes of expression.

§ 19. *Use of the Book of Proverbs.*

We do not resort, at the present day, to this book, with the expectation of finding *Christian* instruction in it, which is of a higher and peculiar evangelical nature. Its homilies, if we may so speak, are not on points of doctrine, but on those of moral, social, and industrial virtues. Religion, or reverencing and obeying God, is indeed often and everywhere a subject of regard. It is intermingled with all our social, relative, and personal duties. But the precepts here are generic. They are such as we might expect under the old Covenant, and are not entirely in the manner of the new. Still, although in one sense the Proverbs are not a part of the Gospel, (in its limited and appropriate sense), yet they prescribe in morals, manners, and social and relative duties, the same things for substance which the Gospel, in its fuller and enlarged sense, requires. We may now employ them for a highly important purpose, viz. to inculcate justice, prudence, temperance, chastity, industry, and in a word, all the duties usually denominated either moral, social, or industrial; and also reverence for God, and for his commandments.

It may in truth be said of the book of Proverbs, that it contains the essence of what might be expanded into hundreds of discourses, on things religiously, socially, and morally important. The advantage it possesses over homilies on the virtues, is this, viz., that what is widely expanded in the latter, is concentrated in the former, and only the essence of the thing in question is expressed. Consequently, it makes a deep impression; and this causes the impression to be lasting. A brief and pithy aphorism is remembered easier and longer than an expanded discourse. It is on this ground, that the book before us holds a high place among didactic books. It is a *general regulative* of every one's active life and social demeanor. And it contains matter far more grave and important, than any or all of the books on morals, which have ever been composed by those who were destitute of the light of revelation.

We have many and excellent moral and religious precepts in the New Testament; and most of them in a form which is not to be bettered. But the book of Proverbs touches many points not fully developed in the New Testament, and assists greatly in guiding the simple into the way of wisdom. Besides, it is pleasing to find, that so much of the book of Proverbs is available for us at the present time. As the gnomes here are never dependent on individual facts, or individual history, it is very plain that they must convey general precepts and doctrines, which are not dependent on specific time or mere individuality. Now as man is essentially the same being in all times and countries, there are certain rules or principles, which have respect to his conduct, that are always applicable. From the very nature of the book of Proverbs, its use is not limited to any age or nation. In reading the Pent., we find many laws and prescriptions, which were designed to be temporary and local; and which, therefore, have now only an indirect relation to us. Not so in the book before us. There is very little in it, which does not apply to us at present, as really and truly as to the Hebrews. Of course, we can avail ourselves of it as a practical *Vade mecum*, in all the various conditions and circumstances of life, because we can draw from it that practical advice which we need.

The value of such a book, couched in such brief, and pithy, and pungent language, and containing so much sound wisdom and practical judgment respecting the various affairs of life, is, and must ever continue to be, very great. Its usefulness will cease, only when men cease to live and act as men, in all their mutual relations and dependencies.

§ 20. *Peculiarities of Exegesis appropriate to the Book.*

On this subject, much cannot be said here. As a book on *Hermeneutics* is no part of our present task or design, we shall take for granted all the great principles of historico-philological exegesis, and merely make a few remarks, on some peculiarity in the application of them to the present book.

This peculiarity arises from the fact, that the language of the book is so compressed, brief, pointed, and strong. There is scarcely any book which calls upon us so often to apply the golden mean between literality on the one hand, and flimsy and diffuse generality on the other. A multitude of the gnomes would be absurd, in case they were to be literally interpreted. Some of them would be contradictory; e. g. "Answer a fool according to his folly;" and again,

"Answer not a fool according to his folly." Both of these are right and proper advice, in their connections, and for reasons which the context brings to view. And so of other gnomes. But the principal thing in the present case is, that the strong and pointed language, so often employed in order to make the sentiment impressive, demands almost everywhere a degree of modification or tempering. So is it with most of the proverbs, which we employ in every-day life. Strong and pointed expression must often be put to the account of a design to make a deep impression; but precision and exactness of sentiment must be made out by aid of the context, (if there be any which stands connected, for often there is none, i. e. the gnome is entirely independent), by reasoning from the nature of the case, and by comparison with similar declarations.

Sometimes the modification in question has respect to the *intensity* of the language, and sometimes to its *tropical nature.* For example: "When a man's ways please the Lord, he maketh even his enemies to be at peace with him," Prov. 16: 7. Is this a *universal* truth? It stands in the form of one; yet apostles, martyrs, eminent Christians in all ages, have often found their enemies very far from being peaceful toward them.

So 16: 10. "A divine sentence is in the lips of the king; his mouth transgresseth not in judgment." And do all kings pass sentence in this way? Do kings' mouths never transgress in judgment? In this case, plainly, that which ought to be is described, rather than that which actually is, although the form of the sentence is a simple and seemingly universal assertion.

So 16: 13. "Righteous lips are the delight of kings, and they love him who speaketh right." And are there no kings, then, who love flattery, and therefore love lying lips? And do all kings love those who speak that which is right? So when the writer says: "Pleasant words are ... sweet to the soul, and health to the bones," (Prov. 16 : 24) ; can there be any other valuable meaning here than a *tropical* one? Again, Prov. 16 : 27, " An ungodly man diggeth up evil, and in his lips is a burning fire." This is plainly *tropical.* But since *didactic* poetry does not admit of the figurative, in like manner and measure as that which is descriptive and devotional, we seldom find any difficulty in Proverbs on the score of *tropical* language; or if we do, the solution is usually at hand. What is generally true elsewhere, in regard to tropical language, may be so considered here. The usual rules which are prescribed, are adequate for the occasion.

In respect, however, to *intensity* of affirmation, it is obvious that we must often meet with it in this book. The bare attempt to explain the meaning of many gnomes, without any modification of the language exhibited in the assertion, would be wholly fruitless. The result indeed of a *literal* exegesis would, in many cases, be a downright untruth.

When I speak, as in the title to this Section, of *peculiarities* in the exegesis of the Proverbs, I wish to be understood that this pertains only to the *frequency* of the modifications to be made, and not to the mere fact itself of modification. There is scarcely any part of the Bible which is doctrinal and didactic, where the very same phenomena are not found, and where the same solution is not called for. But it must be obvious to every intelligent reader, that when sentiment is to be conveyed in the briefest, the most compressed, and the most animated and energetic method possible, it must assume many prominent and (so to speak) sharp corners and edges, which will cut even too deep, unless the interpreter understands how to mediate between the *form* of expression and the *real sentiment* of it.

Indeed, of all the books in the world, I should say the Bible is preëminently the one, which appeals most often to *common sense* and *sound judgment,* in order to be interpreted.

To the common sense and reason of mankind is it all addressed; and were it not for these, the great mass of mankind would in reality have no Bible. Any rule of exegesis at war with these, is *ipso facto* repealed. Set common sense, moreover, to judge of the meaning of Scripture, the single words being once explained, and it will rarely miss the mark. When our Saviour says, in his Sermon on the Mount: "Whosoever shall smite thee on thy right cheek, turn to him the other also; And if any man will sue thee at the law and take away thy coat, let him have thy cloak also; And whosoever shall compel thee to go a mile, go with him twain;" does good common sense ever misinterpret this? Matt. 5:39—41. These sayings of our Lord are unquestionably *proverbial* ones; and they are to be so modified in expounding them, that the *true design* of the speaker may be brought out of them. Just so in the book of Proverbs; for there are many proverbs in that book, which are uttered in like manner, and demand the same application of the common-sense rules of interpretation.

If it be asked: "How can we know what common sense dictates as to interpretation?" The answer is, that common sense, and that only, can judge for itself; and if we are possessed of that, we need not be much at a loss what to do. Without it, all the technical rules in books of hermeneutics will be of little or no avail. And if any one aver, moreover, that "this judge is *fallible*, and may deceive us," our answer is, so is man, man universal, fallible. But still, he can trust many of the judgments which he makes. And so, for the most part, he can confide in his common sense, respecting this or that method of interpretation.

In fact, fallible or infallible, it is the highest court to which we can make an appeal; for enlightened and religious common sense constitutes that court. If these fail us, then we shall not be able to find any higher tribunal, nor any further resort, in times of deep perplexity. No mechanical or technical rules will of themselves make a good interpreter. The idea that this is an art, learned like one of the arts manual, and that one can obtain a knowledge of it in the same way as the arts in general are learned, is a visionary idea, that never can be realized. The study and knowledge of rules may ward off many errors, and correct faults, in the interpreter; but the positive part of his duty must be evermore under the guidance of common sense and sound judgment. All the acuteness imaginable in philology, and all the antiquarian lore which any one may possess or acquire, will not of themselves make a good interpreter. They may very much assist him. They may be the sails even, or the steam-moved wheels of the ship, but it depends after all on the mind of the man who steers that ship, whither she shall go, and where she shall land. John Calvin, with a moderate skill in the Hebrew, and no very distinct and accurate perception of the Hellenistic idiom of the New Testament, was, on the whole, one of the most able commentators we have hitherto had. Sound judgment, perspicacity, and simplicity, are predicable of him in an unusual degree.

It needs such qualities as have been described, to interpret well the book of Proverbs. If Calvin has sometimes failed in interpretation, as doubtless he has, it is owing more to the general lack of information in philology and sacred antiquities, at the period in which he lived, than to any deficiency in his own powers of exegesis. An interpreter of the present day has many helps, of which he was destitute.

On the whole, no one should object to the book of Proverbs, that its language often needs much modification. Nor can he well doubt, whether common sense should be applied to the interpretation of proverbs. The very fact, that most of proverbial lore is the result of strong conviction and concentrated feeling, expressed in language that corresponds, is of itself significant of the manner in which we are to interpret. Proverbs are to be regarded *as proverbs*, i. e. as short, pithy, animated sayings, which of course are to be interpreted as such. Let the interpreter of them beware, and not mistake costume for person. If he can dexterously avoid this, he may hope to gain a satisfactory knowledge of the book before us.

§ 21. *Exegetical Helps.*

It would be to no valuable purpose to make out a complete catalogue of these. I shall mention only those, which appear to me to be of the more valuable class.

P. Melancthonis Explicatio Prov., 1535. It is needless to say, that Melancthon was both a scholar and a Christian.

J. Merceri Comm. in Prov. Solomonis, 1651, edit. 2. Mercier seldom makes trifling or irrelevant remarks.

Prov. Salom. a M. Geiero, 1725, ed. 2, a specimen of the older commentary, and of the manner of Geier.

C. B. Michaelis, Annott. in Prov., in his Uberior Annott. in Hagiographa, 1720, 4to. A sound interpreter, and well skilled in the Oriental languages.

Prov. Salom., edit. A. Schultens, 1748, in compend., ed. G. I. L. Vogel et Teller, 1769, (the best edition). Schultens has everywhere brought *Arabic* to bear upon the language of Proverbs; and, while he has carried this to great and unwarrantable excess, he has still furnished many important hints to the interpreter.

Umbreit, Commentar ü. d. Sprüche, 1826; a book which has many good illustrations, and exhibits much diligence and a good degree of learning.

Besides these, Ziegler, a man of some note, has given a translation of the book, with Remarks (in German), 1791. And the like has Müntinghe done, in Dutch, which has been translated into German by Scholl, one vol. 8vo. 1800. Both of these writers are deserving of consultation; specially the latter, who was an eminent critic and theologian.

There are some essays on the *ancient versions* of Prov., which deserve attention, in I. G. Jäger, Observatt. in Prov. Salom., 1788; also in Dahler, on the Sept. version of the book.

The most critical and thorough work on Proverbs, although very brief, is that of Bertheau, 1847, in vol. vii. of the recent Exeget. Handbuch zum Alt. Test. There is more of true philology and criticism in it, than in all the commentaries which preceded. The Neology of the writer is scarcely apparent. He has shown in general much candor and great acuteness, in his work; and I acknowledge myself specially indebted to him for many good hints. I have sometimes differed from him in opinion; but I have assigned my reasons for differing.

There is also a recent work on Proverbs, by C. Bridges, of England; but, as I have not seen it, I cannot characterize it. The older work of Hodgson on the Proverbs seems not to have excited any permanent attention.

The leading writers of an *homiletic* cast, it is easy for the student to consult, if he desires. Henry, Scott, Adam Clarke, and others, have in substance preached very many sermons on the book of Proverbs, and not a few good ones. The aim of the Commentary which follows, is simply to develop the meaning of the Hebrew text. This once attained, every preacher of the Gospel ought, at least, to be able to make out his own deductions, and to construct his own homilies. If he needs aid of this sort, any of the commentaries just mentioned above will supply it.

COMMENTARY.

PART I. CHAP. I. 1—7.

[The first seven verses are a *general introduction* to the whole book. Yet the whole book came not originally from one and the same hand. As is shown in the Introduction to this work, other writers besides Solomon composed some minor parts of it, viz. 22 : 17—24 : 34, and xxx. xxxi. The original authorship of a part of the first nine chapters is, as the Introduction shows, not quite certain. There is no specific assertion, to say the least, of Solomon's authorship, in regard to these chapters. The title in 1: 1 belongs, as a general *characteristic designation*, to the whole book; and this professedly contains not only Solomon's writings, but also "*the words of the wise*," v. 6. Because the book consists mainly of Solomon's Proverbs, it is significantly named after him; just as we often speak of *the Psalms of David*, when we intend to designate in a generic way the whole collection. Of course, then, if this be conceded, we have no other means of deciding the question of authorship, in respect to chaps. i—ix., than the comparison of the style with that of x—xxii. 16, which we know to have been written by Solomon; see 10: 1. But the two compositions are so very different in their tenor, that a real comparison becomes difficult, and but little, if any, satisfaction is to be gained from it, because the subjects are so unlike. So much can be said, however, in favor of the position that Solomon wrote the first part of the book, viz. that if the compiler of the book, in its present form, did not mean that we should attribute it to that king, why did he not prefix some special title, in order to guard against it, as he has done in 22 : 17. 25 : 1. 30 : 1. 31 : 1? But let the authorship of chaps. i—ix. be assigned to whomsoever it may, it alters not the contents of the piece itself, nor the nature of the general introduction in 1: 1—7, which evidently is appropriate not only to the first part of the book, but to all the other parts.

V. 1 simply gives the general title. V. 2 indicates, in a general way, the object or design of the book, which is to communicate instruction as to wisdom, and to teach the intelligent discernment of instructive discourse. In vs. 3, 4, more particular specifications are made, in order more completely to unfold the general ideas of v. 2. The simple and inexperienced may learn, by what this book contains, sober considerateness, justice, equity, uprightness, and sagacity, as well as acquire skill in devising plans of action. In vs. 5, 6, the attention of even the wise is invited, in order that they may add to their knowledge and their dexterity, even so as to understand proverbial and pointed sayings, and discern the true meaning of what the wise utter in an enigmatical way. V. 7 admonishes the reader that wisdom cannot even commence, (much less be completed), without *the fear of God;* and that only fools will despise the instructions of wisdom.

The order of thought stands thus: (1) The general object of the book, v. 2. (2) The particular things to be taught, and the persons who are to be instructed (vs. 3—6), viz. first, the young and unwary, and then, secondly, even the wise may, by the things developed here, become more wise, and dexterous, and acute in discerning. (3) To profit by the book, without a reverence for God at the outset, will be expected in vain; and none but fools will despise such an admonition.]

(1) The Proverbs of Solomon, son of David, king of Jerusalem.

The Hebrew word מָשָׁל is of wide extent. Its original meaning is *similitude;* and hence it is often employed to designate compositions which abound in comparisons and similitudes, whether they be prophecies, or consist of didactic matter, or of pointed irony; (see Lex.) The name is appropriated mostly to discourse written in *parallelisms*, i. e. in the forms of poetry; for in such discourse, similitudes are most frequent. *Parable* the word מָשָׁל may and does also designate, as Ezek. 17: 2. 24: 3. But more often is the word applied, as in the present case, to *sententious sayings, gnomes*, or *pointed apothegms*, where these (as usual) are composed in parallelisms or couplets; for this last circumstance shows, that the idea of *comparison* is not wholly dismissed even in this particular use of the word. The running *Hebrew title* of the book before us is taken from the word now under consideration, מִשְׁלֵי (the plur. const. form) being retained, while, for the sake of brevity, the word שְׁלֹמֹה in the

Gen. is omitted. It is unnecessary, however, to interpret this generic title-word very strictly or narrowly, as if all the book consisted merely of gnomes; for it is plain, from the latitude of meaning which the word has, as explained above, that it will cover all the ground occupied by this book. *Solomon* is, at all events, the principal, if not the only author; and the book may, therefore, be well and appropriately named after him.

מֶלֶךְ in this case refers to *Solomon*, and not to David. The two last words are in apposition with the two preceding ones; and each of these two clauses, in and by itself, serves to designate Solomon more specifically. — *Israel* is here the *generic* appellation (as often) of all the descendants of Israel or Jacob, i. e. of the nation *en masse.*

(2) In order that one may know wisdom and instruction that one may understand the words of the intelligent.

לָדַעַת, for לָ, see § 100. 1. *c*. For Inf. דַּעַת (from יָדַע), see § 68. 3. n. 1. — *Wisdom* usually means here, not mere *sagacity*, but *a considerate and discerning state of mind* in regard to the whole circle of duty, moral, religious, and prudential. — *Instruction*, מוּסָר, is that which is communicated by teachers to the younger and inexperienced. The first meaning of the word is *chastisement;* then *discipline*, which is administered in this way; and finally (as here) *instruction* as the result; for such a meaning is appropriate here, since it is descriptive of the nature of the good to be obtained, and of the method of obtaining it. The implication is, that the young are here designated as one class, or rather as the leading class, to be taught; and this corresponds well with v. 4. Specially in chaps. i—ix. are the *young* addressed.

That one may understand, is a secondary meaning of הָבִין, which originally designates the idea of *separating, distinguishing;* and from this comes the secondary meaning, viz. *to gain accurate knowledge.* The *Hiphil* form of the verb seems to indicate the necessity of translating thus: *to cause one to understand.* But the Hiph. of בִּין often has a Kal sense, (see Lex. Hiph. 2); and moreover דַּעַת, in the first clause, is in Kal, and the parallelism, therefore, demands the Kal sense of הָבִין, if feasible, as in fact it is.—I have rendered בִּינָה by *intelligent,* putting the concrete, i. e. *intelligent person,* for the abstract *intelligence.* That I have given the meaning truly is plain from the fact, that *words* must be spoken or written by *persons,* and not by an abstraction. Such cases of abstract for concrete, occur too often to need any argument for defence, or even for explanation; see under § 104. 2. e. g. By the *intelligent,* is here meant persons of superior capacity and education, to understand whose writings, a good degree of intelligence in the reader is necessary. The design of the book before us is to assist in the acquisition of such intelligence.

(3) That one may receive the instruction of discreetness, righteousness and justice, and uprightness.

הַשְׂכֵּל, a noun of Inf. Hiph. form, (Ewald, Gramm. § 156. *c.*); meaning *considerate and discreet counsel* or *action.* What youth most of all need, is discretion or sobriety; for they are prone to act with much ardor and precipitation.—*Righteousness and justice and uprightness* are so near to each other in respect to meaning, that they may be regarded as particulars of the same genus. The design in accumulating words of a meaning so kindred, is not to urge any nice distinctions between these virtues which are to be made by the mind of the reader, but simply to bring before him the whole domain (so to speak) of moral propriety and fitness. Strictly considered, צֶדֶק means *that which is right* = *righteousness;* and then it branches off into *what is lawful, what is due, probity, integrity;* and finally, it designates the result of these, viz., *liberation, salus,* and also *happiness* or *prosperity* in general—מִשְׁפָּט has its basis in the idea of *judgment*, viz., of a court, and then (by consequence) it comes to mean *law*, or supreme authority. It naturally, in this way, designates *statute, ordinance, decree;* and finally, whatever is in accordance with these = *just, lawful.* In accordance with the last meaning, I have translated it by *justice.* This does not mean simply justice in our dealings between man and man; for it designates a wider sense of *jus, justum, legitimum.* — מֵשָׁרִים, *uprightness,* the plur. form being used, as in many other cases, to denote the abstract noun, § 106. 2. *a.* The three nouns comprise whatever is right and proper, conformed to law, and agreeable to integrity. They cover the whole ground of moral action, both as it regards the mutual rights of men, and also in regard to probity of mind. These virtues lie at the basis of a great portion of the book of Proverbs. Some of the commentators (Ewald, de Wette, et al.) join the three last nouns of the verse with הַשְׂכֵּל (in the Gen.), and make all the four nouns to be *Genitives* dependent on מוּסַר, and then translate thus: *the instruction of discreetness, of righteousness,* etc. But evidently, the verse has two (and but two) parallel members, and the last three nouns are therefore in the Acc., being governed by לָקַחַת implied in the sense of *acquiring,* and mentally transferred from the beginning of the verse. The first clause the Sept. translates thus: δέξασθαί τε στροφὰς λόγων, νοῆσαί τε δικαιοσύνην, in which they make הַשְׂכֵּל an Inf. *verb,* and separate it from its proper connection. Of course, they must have read מוּסָר, i. e. they took the noun to be of the abs. form, and not of the construct, as our text makes it. Not so the Chald., Vulg., and Syriac, which all take the word in question as a verbal noun.

(4) That they may impart sagacity to the simple; to the young, knowledge and reflection.

לָתֵת, Inf. of נָתַן with לְ, § 65. 2. *n.* 3. I take it to be coördinate with לָדַעַת in v. 2, and to stand connected with מִשְׁלֵי of v. 1; and thus we have: *Proverbs ... in order to know*, etc. ... *in order to impart* or *that they may impart*, etc. — לִפְתָאיִם, *the simple*, lit. *to those who are open* (root פָּתָה *to open)*, i. e. open to every kind of impression from without, and so, not being wary (עָרוּם), they are easily misled. It is also written פְּתָיִים in 23: 3, and פְּתָיִם in 1: 22, the sing. being פֶּתִי; as to the א in the first form, in the place of the י radical, see § 91. vi. 6. — עָרְמָה, *cunning*, either in the good or bad sense of the word. In Gen. 3: 1, the serpent is called עָרוּם, *subtle*. In our text, the *cunning* is taken in the sense of *sagacity*, i. e. a shrewdness which leads to the apprehension of approaching dangers and temptations, and suggests the means of escaping them. This is what the פְּתָאיִם have not. — To this latter word נַעַר of the second clause corresponds. It means a *youngling*, one who of course has not yet come to the period of עָרְמָה. — מְזִמָּה comes from a root (זָמַם) which means literally *to bind* or *tie together;* then figuratively, to *meditate*, e. g. *a plot* or *plan*. In the first case, viz., the meaning of *plot*, it is taken *in malam partem;* and more usually the noun מְזִמָּה means *wicked device*, *mischievous plot*. But a *plan* may be either for good or bad; and it is in the first of these senses, that מְזִמָּה is here used. I have translated by *reflection*, because I can find no word that comes nearer to designate the thing here intended; for reflection indicates a continued meditation on a subject, and carries with it the idea of *sober and wary determination*. This is just what the *youngling* needs. *Knowledge and reflection* are important ends to be brought about by reading the book before us. Sept., very well: ἔννοια.

(5) Let the wise man listen, and he will add to his learning, and the intelligent one will acquire skill in management.

The Imperf. form, יִשְׁמַע is optative or voluntative here, § 125. 3. *b*. — וְיוֹסֶף, is to be taken as a proper or ordinary

Fut. here, for the Vau is not *consecutive*, (comp. 48. *b*. 2), and the accent is thrown on the penult merely because the ultimate is followed by a tone-syllable in the next word. Of course the סֵף — of the ordinary form, by losing the accent becomes סֶף —, § 29. 3. *b*. — לֶקַח is *what one receives*, viz., from a teacher, and so means *doctrine*, *learning*, *knowledge*, root לָקַח *to take* or *receive*. — נָבוֹן, Niph. Part. adjective, *intelligent*, i. e. one endowed with the power of discrimination, from בִּין *to discriminate*. — תַּחְבֻּלוֹת, (בֻּ for בוּ), from חֶבֶל *rope*, especially the *anchor-rope* or the *helm-rope;* so that *guidance*, *management*, is a derived or secondary sense; and the shade of the idea is expressed in the version. It is the plur. of abstraction, § 106. 2. *a*. Sentiment: 'Even wise men may increase their knowledge and their skill, as to controlling various matters, by the reading of the *Proverbs*.'

(6) So that he may understand a proverb, and a dark saying, — the words of the wise, and their enigmas.

לְהָבִין is not a continuance or resumption of the Infinitives in vs. 2—4, but it connects with the preceding verse, in the way of exhibiting the consequences of attending to the Proverbs. The reader of this book may be able, by due attention, not only to understand a מָשָׁל, i. e. figurative or parabolic speech, but even such words as constitute a מְלִיצָה, which word the Seventy have well translated by σκοτεινὸς λόγος, i. e. a *dark saying*, one that needs interpretation, (from the Hiph. הֵלִיץ, *to interpret*). — Not only so, but he may also come to understand even *the enigmatical words of the wise*. חִידָה comes from חוּד, which in Arabic means *to make knots*. *A knotty saying* (our usage admits this expression) is one that is difficult of solution or interpretation; a saying that is pointed and shrewd, but wrapped in such an envelop as demands a discriminating intellect to develop and understand it. In both clauses I take the וְ to be that of mere *accession*, § 152. B. 2. The noun following the וְ

qualifies the preceding noun, by characterizing specifically the nature of its meaning. Sentiment: 'The study of the Proverbs will render a wise man more capable of understanding the apparently obscure, or singular, or pointed sayings of the wise.'

(7) The fear of the Lord is the beginning of knowledge; wisdom and instruction fools despise.

As to sentiment, comp. 9 : 10. Ps. 111: 10. Sir. 1: 16, 25. The first Arabic proverb, in the collection of one hundred proverbs by Erpenius (in his Arab. Gramm.) runs thus: "The beginning of wisdom is the fear of God." The preceding verses (2—6) having shown the design of the book, the introduction is now concluded by v. 7, which shows what temper of mind must be possessed by him, who means to be profited through the reading of the Proverbs.—*Fear of God* means: *Paying him reverential awe;* it does not designate *terror.* The verse declares, that not even a *beginning* of true knowledge can be made, without the reverence in question; much less then can a full knowledge be gained without it. It is God who gives wisdom and knowledge; as is declared in 2 : 6 below. Wisdom and reverence for God are inseparably linked together, and this is the constant doctrine of the Old Testament. That wisdom (so called), which is without the fear of God, is no wisdom; for he who has no knowledge of God, cannot be wise, but is a *fool,* comp. Job 5 : 3. Strikingly does the verse before us accŏrd in spirit with the words of the Saviour: "If any man will do his will, he shall know of the doctrine, whether it be of God," John 7: 17.

Wisdom and instruction fools despise, i. e. none but fools will despise such wisdom and instruction as are here proffered. All *who fear God* will avoid such a course. *The fool,* then, as here characterized, is one who is chargeable with impiety.—אֱוִילִים comes from אָוַל *to be foolish,* the root having a ו movable.

[Thus ends the compiler's introduction to the book of Proverbs. It exhibits, (1) The title. (2) The design of the work, vs. 2, 3. (3) The persons are specified for whom it is designed, and the benefit pointed out which they may receive, vs. 4—6. (4) The subjective qualification of the reader, in order to be profited, is then explicitly disclosed. Every verse consists of two parts — parallelisms; and nearly all of these contain *three* words. Once, in v. 5, we have *four* words; and twice, in v. 7. It is evident, that this rigid adherence to even measure has occasioned several *ellipses* of verbs, as has been hinted above, but these are not such as to obscure the sense.]

CHAP. I. 8—IX. 18.

Admonition to love wisdom in all circumstances and conditions, to strive for the acquisition of it, and to shun everything which is opposed to it.

As to the *characteristics* of this part of the book of Proverbs, both in respect to style and sentiment, the reader is referred to the discussion concerning them in the critical Introduction.

CHAP. I. 8—33.

[This may be separated into *three* divisions; (1) vs. 8, 9. (2) Vs. 10—19. (3) Vs. 20—33. The first two verses here exhibit the relation of the person addressed to his monitor, and make an earnest appeal to him, urging him readily to receive the proffered instruction. To induce him so to do, it holds forth the beautiful ornaments of character, which such a readiness will confer upon him.]

(8) Hear, my son, the instruction of thy father, and forsake not the teaching of thy mother.

My son is the usual address of a teacher to a learner, and is common in Persia and Arabia, as well as in Palestine. The learner is usually a *young person ;* but the term *son,* in this case, is merely indicative of *affection,* and not of descent. In other words, the writer assumes the attitude of a parent addressing his children. — תִּטֹּשׁ, Imperf. Kal, second pers. of

נָחָשׁ. אַל designates a *negative*, in a hortative or imperative clause. — תּוֹרַת *doctrine, teaching*, which is the original sense of the word, since it comes from יָרָה, *to instruct.* It passes over, very naturally, to the sense of *law, precept.* But in Prov. it is often used as above; e. g. 3 : 1. 4 : 2. 7: 2. 28 : 7, 9. 29 : 18, al. Specially does it designate parental instruction, which has in it something of the nature of law.

(9) For a graceful wreath shall they be to thy head, and a collar to thy neck.

The moral beauty which will become conspicuous by following the advice given in the preceding verse, is here symbolized by objects of conspicuous adornment to the person. — *Graceful wreath*, means a *beautiful* one, for חֵן, like the Greek χάρις, means both *beauty* and *grace* or *favor.* The second noun supplies the place of an adjective, § 104. 1. — הֵם, *are they*, § 119. 2. The simple meaning is, that 'obedience to parental precepts will be as a beautiful diadem on the head of him who yields it.' — *Collar to thy neck*, comp. Dan. 5 : 29, which relates that Belshazzar, in order to honor Daniel, commanded "a chain of gold to be put around his neck." The *insignia* of office and honor were usually displayed by some conspicuous ornament on the neck. — עֲנָקִים is plur. probably because the chain or collar consisted of many composite parts; but we may express the idea substantially by the singular — *collar* — which is preferable in our language to the plural form. The meaning of the whole is plain: 'Obedience to paternal precepts will be to thy character and reputation, what diadems and necklaces of honor are to the person.' In other words: It will render thee conspicuous and admired for thy virtues.

Second division; vs. 10—19.

[This contains an earnest dissuasive from associating with those, who seek for gain in robbery and murder. The warning thus placed at the head of all others, betokens a state of society much like that which now exists in Italy. It would seem that *Banditti* were not only frequent, but that the attractions which such a mode of life offered to young, idle, and profligate persons, were great and dangerous. The civil police must of course have been unskilful or inefficient. Such a mode of life was not only utter ruin to character, but it was fraught with the most imminent danger of destruction. Those who lived in this way, as it would seem, employed all the arts of persuasion to entice the young to join their corps, and thus to strengthen them in their warfare against the peaceful possessors of property. They promised them abundance of shining gold and houses filled with spoil, vs. 10—14. The youth is cautioned to keep himself far from them, and is assured that their wicked course will speedily end in a dreadful doom.]

(10) My son, if sinners entice thee, consent thou not.

יְפַתּוּ, Imperf. Piel of פָּתָה. — תֹּבֵא, for תֹּאבֵא, from אָבָא = אָבָה, *to consent*, being a weaker form of the common verb as last given. The omission of א in writing, when it quiesces, is too common to need particular illustration, § 8. 4. The Piel form of יְפַתּוּ designates *repeated attempts at persuasion, continued efforts to persuade.*

(11) If they shall say: Come now with us, let us lay wait for blood, let us lurk for him who in vain is innocent.

The actions of banditti are here accurately described. *They lie in wait*, in order to destroy the unsuspecting. *They lurk*, so as to cause no alarm to him, who, confiding in his innocence or harmlessness, goes forth in security. But his innocence is חִנָּם *fruitless*, or *in vain.* His imagined security exposes him the more to the assassins, inasmuch as he goes unarmed. That חִנָּם qualifies or modifies נָקִי, is plain from its position. The meaning is, that even innocence is *fruitless*, as to exempting from the attack of such assassins; comp. Ps. 35: 19. 69: 5. Lam. 3: 52. At the same time, this greatly aggravates the crime of the robbers. The sing. נָקִי is generic, comprehending that class of persons. The sequel shows this, where they are spoken of in the plural number. — לְכָה, i. e. the Imper. לֵךְ (root יָלַךְ), with ה paragogic or hortative, § 48. 3. The like is the case with the other two verbs, only that they are Imperf. first pers. plur., which tense often follows the Imp. mode.

(12) Let us swallow them up alive, like the under-world; even those in full strength shall be as those who go down to the pit.

Swallow them (plur. pron.) *up*, means to devour in a sudden and fearful manner. — *Like the under-world*, i. e. *Sheōl, Hades*, which swallows up the race of man. — *Alive*, חַיִּים, the same in Ps. 55 : 16. 124 : 3. Usually, the grave devours or swallows up only the dead; but the depredators, in this case, propose to do to the *living*, what the grave does to the dead in consuming them, yet not literally, but figuratively. The idea is that of sudden and unexpected destruction in the midst of life, and in the *full state of health*, as the subsequent תְמִימִים plainly indicates. Gesenius has mistaken the meaning of this word here. He gives *incolumis, salvus*, as the sense. But plainly the meaning is kindred to and connected with חַיִּים. The two words indicate *life* and *good health*. Comp. as to *swallowing up*, Num. 16 : 30, 31. Sentiment: 'Let us destroy those suddenly and unexpectedly, who are not only among the living, but in sound health. This shall be no protection to them. We can as easily devour them as the grave devours the unresisting dead.' — יוֹרְדֵי בוֹר, *pit-descenders*, i. e. the buried dead. Comp. for this phrase, Ps. 88 : 5. Ezek. 26 : 20. 31: 14. The essence of the comparison lies in this, viz. that living persons, who are of sound health, may be as easily and surely devoured, as the grave devours dead ones. No resistance or danger from them need be anticipated.

(13) All precious wealth shall we find; our houses shall we fill with spoil.

This verse begins the *persuasive* part of the address to the youth. The *hortative* is dropped here, as the form of the verb (without ָה paragogic) indicates, and the plunderers venture to predict the consequence of their foray. — יָקָר denotes what is *precious* or *rare*, referring probably to jewels, and the like. — בָּתֵּינוּ, irreg. plur. of בַּיִת, with suff. — שָׁלָל, a second Acc., governed by the verb of *filling*, § 135. 3. *b.* § 136. 1.

(14) Thy lot shalt thou cast in the midst of us; one purse shall be for us all.

In other words: 'Thou shalt be a partner with us, and entitled to thy full proportion of the spoil.' *One and the same purse shall be for all,* repeats the same idea in a different form, viz. 'We will have one common purse.' Thus far the exhortation of the plunderers. The teacher's advice comes next.

(15) My son, go not in the way with them; keep back thy foot from their paths.

This is in direct opposition to the counsel of the plunderers, and is as much as to say: 'Do not associate with them, but refrain from all intercourse.'— אִתָּם, compounded of ָם suff. pron., and אֵת preposition = *with.*

(16) For their feet run to evil; and they hasten to shed blood.

In other words: 'They are eager to do evil, and hasten swiftly to scenes of bloodshed.'—לִשְׁפָּךְ, with short ŏ in the final syllable, because of the Maqqeph which follows.

(17) Surely in vain is the net spread in the sight of any bird.

כִּי cannot be *causal* here, for this verse assigns no reason or ground of the preceding one. This particle not unfrequently has an intensive meaning, (like the Latin *imo*, or the German *ya, truly, indeed*), in the beginning of a sentence; e. g. Is. 28: 28. 8: 23. 32: 13. Ps. 77: 12. 71: 23. Ex. 22: 22. Job 8: 6; see Ewald's Gramm. § 320. *b.*, Ges. Lex. כִּי, 5. *c*, who, however, has given but a narrow view of this not unfrequent usage. The writer means to say: 'It is indeed true that the net, etc.'—מְזֹרָה, Part. of Pual, from זָרָה. The ו is merely a *fulcrum* for the vowel Hholem, which is substituted for the regular Qibbutz, because the Dagh. is excluded from the ר.—הָרָשֶׁת, with the article, an appropriate kind of net being meant.—בַּעַל כָּנָף, lit. *possessor of a wing*, i. e. winged creature = *bird*; see Lex. In other words: 'Birds which see the net spread for them fly away, as we well know, and escape.' The comparison intended is completed by the next verse.

(18) But these lie in wait for their own blood; they lurk for their own lives.

The וְ is here adversative, § 152. B. *b.*—*For their own blood* . . . *for their own lives*, not to protect and save them, but they act as if they were bent upon destroying them. They use their cunning and their efforts in the like way, as if they were laboring to bring themselves into ruin. The implication is, that while they spread the net for others, they, like the birds, will take cognizance thereof and escape. But not merely this; those who spread the net will be resisted and attacked, and will lose their own lifeblood. Their confident boast of easy conquest will not be realized. Instead of spoiling others, they will be despoiled; for others will have their eyes open to see the net, and thus they will escape it, and moreover inflict vengeance on those who laid it. The *but* at the beginning of the verse, seems to indicate that the plunderers are less wary than the birds, and rush on to a destruction which might easily be avoided, if they would but open their eyes to see its indications.

(19) Such are the ways of every one greedy of plunder; it taketh away the life of its master.

Such is the conclusion of this second division, viz., vs. 10—19.—בֹּצֵעַ בָּצַע, lit. *plundering plunder*, is a usual Hebraism to make out a strong expression. The shade of meaning is truly given in the version. — בְּעָלָיו, plur. form with suff., but with the meaning of the singular; see Lex. — יִקָּח in pause, Imperf. of לָקַח, in the sense of *taking away;* see Lex. *b.*

Such is the solemn warning of paternal admonition, addressed to all the young who are tempted to embark in unlawful doings for the sake of gain. It escapes them after all, and they, by their wicked course, bring on themselves destruction.

Third Division, vs. 20—33.

[In the preceding paragraph, the invitations and allurements of wicked depredators addressed to youth are presented. The fatal consequences of listening to them are also brought to view. The section now before us presents a call or invitation of a character entirely opposite. *Heavenly wisdom,* (here *personified* in the oriental manner), utters a louder, more distinct, and more earnest call, urging upon the young the fear of God. The importance and necessity of this are proclaimed in all conspicuous places, where the people throng, — in the streets and bustling market-places, at the openings of the gates, and throughout the city. She rebukes men for loving and cleaving to folly and hating knowledge, and exhorts them to listen to her admonitions, vs. 20—23. She presents the consequences of not listening to them, and of rejecting them; and declares, that at a future period she will remain unmoved by their outcries, when calamities invade them, vs. 24—27. Finally, when their sorrows become insupportable, she predicts that they will earnestly call upon her to interpose; but she assures them that she will remain quiet and inactive, as they did, when she called unto them. Their hatred of true knowledge and their impious rejection of all admonition, suffice to justify the course which she will take, vs. 28—31. From this particular view of their actions and their consequent doom, the writer deduces an important general sentiment, viz. that the aversion of fools to wisdom, and their spiritual sloth, must at last bring about their utter ruin; while those, who timely hearken to admonition, shall dwell in safety and quietude, without any fear of evil, vs. 32, 33.]

(20) Wisdom crieth aloud without; in the broad streets she uttereth her voice.

חָכְמוֹת, of the plur. form, but sing. in meaning. The

ground of this is, either that the plur. is a favorite form for *abstract* nouns, or else (as usual) the plural form denotes *intensity;* see the same in 9 : 1. So Hitzig, and so Ewald (Gramm. edit. 5. § 165. *c.*), both inclining to the first solution. Hence תָּרֹנָּה, as Ewald supposes, is prob. sing. (see בָּנְתָה in 9 : 1), the fem. ending נָה — being added to distinguish the third pers. fem. from the second masc.; see the like in 8 : 3. Judg. 5 : 26. Ex. 1: 10. Is. 27: 11. 28 : 3. Job 17: 16; see Ew. Gramm. § 191. *c*, who fully notices this peculiarity. If any one prefers the *plur.* of the verb here, in accordance with the *form* of the noun, he is at liberty to do so, although this principle does not apply to most of the parallel cases which are referred to, where the verb is plainly singular. — בָּרְחֹבוֹת, lit. *in the wide places*, but the word commonly designates *the streets,* which are usually *wide openings.* — תִּתֵּן, *gives out, utters,* where the verb is third fem. sing.; as is also the suff. pron. in קוֹלָהּ; and these sing. forms render probable the conclusion above made respecting the sing. of תָּרֹנָּה.

(21) At the head of the bustling places she makes proclamation, in the openings of the gates; in the city, she utters her words.

הֹמִיּוֹת, plur. fem. Part. of Kal, from הָמָה, and meaning *noisy places*, i. e. places where the busy and bustling throng are met together, probably = *market-places.* — *Openings of the gates,* the place where tribunals were held, and consultations carried on, because of the broad space around the opening. The punctators, by a pause-accent, have joined this clause with the last part of the verse, since they have separated the first στίχος at תִּקְרָא; but the pause-accent ought to stand on שְׁעָרִים. The word בָּעִיר is not to be joined with this as an accession to it, for then it would have a וְ before it. But it needs no *Vav* if we translate as above. In the *openings of the gates* and *in the city* are two different phrases; but the latter is coördinate with the former, and is designed to be an enlargement of it. All the places of usual concourse are first mentioned, and then comes the generic word, comprising both these and all others not yet mentioned, viz., בָּעִיר. It would seem from the manifold and wide-spread action here described, that under the appellation of *wisdom* are here comprised all the wise men and teachers and prophets, who, in various ways and in different places, taught and proclaimed to men their duty.

(22) How long, ye simple, will ye love simplicity, and scorners delight themselves in scorning, and fools hate knowledge?

פְּתָיִם, for the form, see under v. 4 above. — תְּאֵהֲבוּ, Imperf. Piel, with Tseri under א, because the following Gutt. (ה) excludes the Daghesh. — As to פְּתִי, *simplicity* is the first meaning of this root, which is indeed an abstract meaning, but then such abstracts are often employed as concretes; e. g. *folly* for *fools*, *simplicity* for *simple persons*, and the like. — לֵצִים, plur. Part. of לוּץ, like מֵתִים from מוּת. — חָמְדוּ לָהֶם, *delight themselves*, seems to present a *Dat. commodi* in לָהֶם. But we may also translate, *desire for themselves*, with a Dat. of the person *for whom*. — לָצוֹן is here an abstract noun, from לוּץ, although this ending more usually is concrete, § 85. 2. 4. In the second clause, חָמְדוּ is in the *Perf.*, which is somewhat unusual in such a case of habitual action. The other two clauses present the Imperfect, as usual in such cases. There are, however, many cases of designating past action which still continues and will continue, where the Perf. is employed; for this tense is used to designate general truths, which have by experience already been established and definitely settled; e. g. comp. Ps. 10: 3. 33: 13, seq. 39: 12. 84: 4. Prov. 11: 2, 8. 22: 12, etc. 1 Sam. 2: 3—5. Ewald has most fully treated of this, in § 135. *b*. In several of the examples above cited, the Perf. and Imperf. precede and follow each other, in the same train of narration; which shows that, by usage, they often occupy nearly the same ground. Still, we may say in general, that the Imperf. looks more to what is going on and will go on, but the Perf. more to what has past and still continues. — *The knowledge which is hated*, is that knowledge which is equivalent to *wisdom*, viz., the knowledge of what is good and true and pious.

(23) Turn ye at my reproof; behold! I will pour out my spirit upon you, I will make you to know my words.

תָּשׁוּבוּ, Imperf. for Imper. hortative, § 125. 3. *c.* The לְ which follows, points out the direction toward which they are to turn, quasi: *turn ye toward my reproof*, i. e. put yourselves in such a posture, as to notice it and take warning; or לְ may mean here *on account of*, *because of*, Lex A. 6. — אַבִּיעָה (Hiph. of נָבַע), lit. *I will cause to gush forth my spirit unto you*, or *upon you*. — *My spirit*, i. e. my animating and energizing influence. This influence is here plainly of a moral and sanctifying nature; and those who hearken to *wisdom* will have experience of it. The transition from the primitive meaning of רוּחַ (*wind*) is easy and natural. The wind is an invisible and mysterious, yet powerful agent. Even so the divine רוּחַ is the invisible and yet powerful agent, in moving and quickening the minds of men to obedience. — *I will make you to know;* the pronoun אֶתְכֶם is in the Acc. and is governed by the verb (the Hiph. of יָדַע with ה ָ paragogic) ; which also governs דְּבָרַי a second Acc., § 136. 1. The אֵת is merely the Acc. partic. — All here promised will follow from *turning*, i. e. from true repentance and the forsaking of sin. But the next verse shows the great contumacy of those who will not hearken, and also the earnestness with which they have been admonished and warned.

(24) Because I have called, and ye have refused, I have stretched forth my hand, and no one hath listened;

Our *pres.* tense might be employed in rendering all the verbs here, since the Perfect often designates *enduring action*, just as our present tense also does. But, although adopted by Bertheau (Comm.), I prefer the Perfect; for the speaker seems to take his stand at the close of probation, when final trial and retribution are about to ensue. *I have called* is therefore appropriate. — *Called*, i. e. proclaimed the truth, and given you repeated invitations to listen to it. — *Stretching forth the hand*, is the gesture of one earnestly beseeching. — *Listened*, viz. to my call.

(25) But ye have rejected all my counsel, and have not desired my reproof.

וַתִּפְרְעוּ, = the Praeter sense, by reason of the וַ consecutive; which is not frequent in such a book as the present, but is common in narrations. However, the discourse assumes here somewhat of the form of narration.

(26) Even I will laugh at your calamity, and mock when your fear cometh.

Even I, not *I also*, for who are the others that laugh and mock? *Even I*, is emphatic, — *I*, who have warned you so often, so tenderly, and so earnestly, — *even I*, shall henceforth treat you as enemies, who deserve contempt. — בְּבֹא, Inf. const. before a noun which is its subject. Lit. *in the coming of your fear*, i. e. of that which was your fear, or which you feared. The intensity of the tropical language here makes the expression exceedingly strong. *Laughing at* and *mocking*, are expressions of the highest and most contemptuous indignation. Comp. Ps. 2 : 5, where, as applicable to God, this same bold language is employed.

(27) When your fear cometh as a destructive tempest, and your calamity advances as a sweeping whirlwind, when distress and anguish come upon you.

The word שׁאוה, in the text, if retained, should be pointed thus: שַׁאֲוָה. The Masorites, however, have adjusted the vowels to the marginal reading שֹׁאָה; unnecessarily, for the text-form is normal, and probably legitimate. This verse exhibits one of the usages, in respect to the Inf. construct, which deserves special notice, viz., the fact that a word qualifying the action of the verb, or designating the object of its action, may be placed between the Inf. const. and the noun which is its proper subject. Thus to the first belong כְּשַׁאֲוָה and כְּסוּפָה, both placed between the Inf. and its subject, and qualifying the action of the verb; to the latter belongs עֲלֵיכֶם, designating the object of the verb's action. — יֶאֱתֶה, Imperf., is a change of construction; but this tense frequently is a continuative of the Inf. mode; and this usage serves the purpose of variety. — The imagery employed here is vivid and awful. It is partly obscured in our common version. Umbreit translates שֹׁאָה and סוּפָה, by *Donnerwetter* and *Sturmwind*, which come near the force of the original words.

(28) Then shall they call upon me, but I will not answer; they shall earnestly seek me, but they shall not find me.

Here, in the version, *shall* implies confident prediction, *will* both predicts and expresses determination. In all three of the plur. verbs, the ו final of the normal forms is omitted, and it is written in each case by a *vicarious Qibbuts* (§ 9. 1. *b.*), — a very common usage in writing; (read *ū-nᵉni*); see also § 47. 3. n. 4. This ending (נִ-ֻ) differs somewhat in development from the *Nun epenthetic*, as described in § 57. 4; for that takes the vowels (ַ) and (ֶ) before it, and is usually written by a Daghesh. The effect, however, of both seems to be nearly the same, see Note in § 57. 4. This development of the Imperf. with נ suff., as here, is confined to poetry, and is frequent in this book; see Note, *ib.* — The verb שָׁחַר means *to burst* or *break forth;* and so שַׁחַר comes to mean *morning.* So we say, *break of day;* and the like did the Hebrews. But while the idea of *early* does not belong to the verb of itself, still, the nature of the action designated implies *intensity, earnestness.* I have so translated. The verb comes to designate *seeking earnestly,* as its secondary sense, by reason of the impetuosity usually exhibited by those who are anxious seekers. The Piel form in the text gives additional intensity to the meaning.—Sentiment: 'When danger is imminent and punishment has begun, then, sinners who have refused to listen unto warnings, and have despised admonition until their probation has ended, will seek anxiously, but in vain, for deliverance from further punishment.'

(29) Because they have hated knowledge, and have not chosen the fear of God.

The word תַּחַת, *because*, is introductory to the four following clauses, each and all of which belong to the *protasis* of a long sentence; the *apodosis* follows, being introduced by וְ *apodotic* in v. 31. The arrangement stands thus: 'Because they have done so and so ... therefore they shall be punished so and so.'—בָּחָרוּ (חָ in Pause) might be translated: *delighted in* or *desired*. But the word *choose* is better here, because it indicates the giving of preference to one thing over another. They *did not give preference* to piety over disobedience.

(30) They desired not my counsel; they despised all my reproof.

The preceding verse gives the *positive* part of their wickedness; this, the *negative* one, i. e. they refused counsel, they despised reproof.

(31) Therefore shall they eat of the fruit of their own way, they shall be satiated with their own counsels.

The וְ here, at the beginning, marks the commencement of the *apodosis*, and consequently may be rendered *therefore*.—*Their way*, means their conduct.—*Their counsels* (root יָעַץ) means here *devices* or *plans*. The מִ stands for מִן, the quiescent being omitted, as oftentimes, in writing.—Our version translates יִשְׂבָּעוּ by *filled*. The Heb. verb is of a stronger signification; which is given in the version above. I should prefer a Saxon word to the Latin derivate *satiated;* but where is it to be found?

Such is the fearful doom of the contumacious opposers of heavenly wisdom. The two following verses develop the general ground or principle, on which this sentence is founded.

(32) Surely, the turning away of the simple shall slay them, and the slothful quietude of fools shall destroy them.

Turning away, viz., from proffered admonition. — שַׁלְוַת, *quietude*, here designates unfeeling apathy under all remonstrances and exhortations to rouse up to dutiful action. Amid all these the simple remain unmoved and indifferent. *Quietude* cannot be meant here, in the way of peaceful enjoyment.

(33) But he who hearkeneth to me shall dwell in confidence; he shall be tranquil, without fear of evil.

Lastly comes, to crown all, the *promises* of reward to the obedient. The second clause explains the first. *Dwelling* בֶּטַח, *in confidence*, (Acc. of manner), means, that he will have no reason to apprehend evil, and therefore will not anticipate it. — וְשַׁאֲנַן (made Fut. by וְ) is the Pilel form of שָׁאַן. — I take the מִ in מִפַּחַד to mean *without*, Lat. *sine;* so in Job 11: 15. 21: 9. Gen. 27: 39. Is. 14: 19. Jer. 48: 45. Like בֶּטַח in the preceding clause, it denotes the manner of the tranquillity. Our version — *quiet from fear* — can hardly afford a tolerable meaning. We say *free from* fear, *delivered from fear*, and the like; but *quiet from fear* would seem to mean: *quiet through* or *by reason of fear;* which is far from the true idea. The accents divide, as in the version above. The last two words need no וְ before them, because they merely qualify the verb.

CHAP. II. 1—22.

Exhortation to seek after wisdom; many and important benefits will ensue from finding it.

[Continued, constant, and earnest seeking after wisdom will lead to the fear and the knowledge of God, vs. 1—5. Jehovah will impart wisdom to such seekers, and sound discretion; he will protect them and keep them in the right path, vs. 6—8. Consequently, the sincere seeker will be led to understand the good and the true; and such knowledge shall give pleasure to his soul, and discretion shall preserve him, vs. 9—11. These will save him from the evil and perverse man, who forsakes uprightness and walks in darkness; who rejoices in evil doing and perverseness; whose ways are crooked and perverted, vs. 12—15. He shall be delivered from the strange woman who flatters; who forsakes the guide of her youth, and forgets the covenant of her God; whose house goes down to death, and her paths to the land of ghosts; and all who go in unto her, return no more to the paths of the living, vs. 16—19. We must watchfully observe and walk in the paths of the good; for the upright shall have a safe and permanent habitation in the land, while wicked traitors shall be cut off from it, vs. 20—22.

Properly speaking, this whole chapter has not only one theme, but it virtually consists of only one prolonged and composite sentence. There is nowhere any sign of the commencement of a new theme or sentence; nor any palpable marks of separate strophes. Yet the structure, in another respect, is somewhat artistic. Analysis will show that there is a peculiar arrangement. If we divide the chapter into two parts, each has in it a series of connected verses of four, four, and three, making eleven verses in each part. The first four verses in the chapter constitute a protasis; the second four, an apodosis; and then the three which follow (vs. 9—11), are a second apodosis; both the apodoses commence alike with אָז תָּבִין. In the second part of the chapter (vs. 12—22), which describes the divine protection, the two first groups of four begin each with לְהַצִּילְךָ, and the last group of three begins with לְמַעַן, which is equivalent to the לְ that stands before the verb at the head of the two other groups. Besides this peculiarity of numerical arrangement and harmony, every verse has only two parts or parallelisms, and for the most part, these have the same number of words in them, which is usually *three*. In a few cases we find *four*, where the words are short, and *two* where they are long. This shows that some kind of rhythm is aimed at, although we cannot successfully decipher it. The whole chapter is, in one respect, a monogram by itself; but still, it is here intimately connected with, and allied to, the main subject. The tenor of the style, in this chapter, is like that in the surrounding context.]

(1) My son, if thou wilt receive my words, and treasure up my commands with thee;

To *receive*, is the first thing in a sincere disciple. *To treasure up* or *carefully keep*, designatès another and higher degree of readiness to obey, inasmuch as it shows the value put upon the instructions. This is the beginning of the *protasis*, which is continued, by coördinate conditional clauses, throughout the three following verses.

(2) So as to make thine ear attentive to wisdom, and incline thine heart to understanding.

הַקְשִׁיב אֹזֶן means *to erect* (or *prick up*, as we say) *the ear*, i. e. to put it in a listening attitude. So the Germans: *Die Ohren spitzen*. When the ear of any animal is flexible, it is *erected* in listening, in order to catch any sound more easily. The version above gives the meaning for substance; it would hardly do to translate *prick up thine ears*, for with us this borders on the vulgar style. — The Inf. mode here seems alien from the other forms of verbs in the paragraph. But it is not unfrequent to substitute this, with a לְ prefix (as here) in the room of an *Imperf.* tense. It serves to vary the construction. — The form תַּטֶּה (r. נָטָה) exhibits the normal Imperf. here. Both *wisdom* and *understanding* are abstracts, and so have the article (as is more usual) before them, § 107. 3. *c.* — לִבְּךָ, from לֵב = לֵבָב; hence the Dagh. forte.

(3) Yea, if thou wilt call for discrimination, and utter aloud thy voice for understanding.

The כִּי here is simply an intensive; see under 1: 17 above.

— בִּינָה, from בִּין *to distinguish, to discriminate*, may be well rendered as it is above. — תְּבוּנָה is indeed of the same root, but by usage it rather designates the consequences of discrimination, i. e. *intelligence* or *knowledge*. — תִּתֵּן, *to give forth*, and here *(ab exigentia loci) to utter aloud.* — The design of the verse is to exhibit *earnest request for wisdom;* for such earnestness of course would be uttered with a loud voice.

(4) If thou wilt seek for her as silver, and search her out as hidden treasures.

As silver, i. e. as men usually seek for silver, viz., with eagerness or earnestness. — תַּחְפְּשֶׂנָּה, for ־ֶנָּה, see p. 289, in col. B; תַּחְ (and not תִּחְ) because of the Guttural; the verb is in Kal. — *As hidden treasures*, i. e. (as before) with such eagerness as men usually exhibit in search of such treasures.

The protasis ends here, and now comes the *apodosis*, ushered in by אָז תָּבִין.

(5) Then shalt thou understand the fear of Jehovah, and acquire a knowledge of God.

יִרְאַת יְהוָֹה is the usual Hebrew designation of *true piety;* not *fear* in the sense of *terror*, but in that of *reverence*. *To find knowledge* means to acquire it, to get possession of it. *The fear of Jehovah* is a *treasure*, Is. 33 : 6; it is also a refuge in times of danger and trouble, Prov. 14 : 26, comp. also Ps. 19 : 10. 115 : 11. All true wisdom leads to a knowledge of God.

(6) For Jehovah will communicate wisdom; from his mouth is knowledge and understanding.

The ground of the preceding assurance is here given. The connection is thus: 'Wonder not at the promises made, *for* [כִּי causal] Jehovah gives wisdom, and from his mouth cometh knowledge.' מִפִּיו means *what his mouth utters*, viz. his words. These are the sources of all true wisdom.

(7) He keeps in store help for the upright, — a shield for those who walk blamelessly.

The Kethibh would be normally pointed thus: וְצָפַן; but the Qeri bids us read יִצְפֹּן, which is right, because this verb is a continuation of יִתֵּן in v. 6, which is in the Imperfect. — מָגֵן, *a shield*, is governed by יִצְפֹּן mentally carried forward. This clause might perhaps be translated thus: *a shield is he*, etc. But if this was the shape of the sentiment designed to be communicated by the writer, he would of course have said: מָגֵן הוּא. — תֹּם is used adverbially.

(8) He will protect the paths of justice; he will watch over the way of his saints.

לִנְצֹר is another example of the Inf. in continuation of the Imperf.; see the remarks on the same construction under v. 2. above. — חֲסִידָו for חֲסִידָיו, as the Qeri informs us. If the Kethibh is retained as a singular, then it must be pointed חֲסִידוֹ, which, generically taken, would amount to the same as the Qeri. The *Yodh* before such a ו suffix is sometimes omitted in writing. This verse merely enlarges upon and enforces the preceding one.

The three following verses are a second apodosis, beginning, like the preceding group of four, with אָז תָּבִין.

(9) Then shalt thou understand right and justice and uprightness, — every good path.

The accents throw וּמֵישָׁרִים into the second clause. But if it belongs there, we should expect the וּ before it to be omitted; as it in fact is, before the next and final clause. The whole verse is, first, an accumulation of the particular things to be sought after; and then follows a generic clause, which comprises everything besides which is good. The word *path* or *track* is here = דֶּרֶךְ, i. e. it signifies manner of life, pursuit, and so the meaning is: 'Every pursuit in which good may be found.'

(10) For wisdom shall come into thy heart, and knowledge shall be pleasant to thy soul.

כִּי, *for*, causal. It is implied also before the following three clauses, just as in vs. 6, 7. The masc. יִנְעָם (in pause) is noticeable; for דַּעַת seems to be unequivocally *fem.* We might translate thus: *As to knowledge — there shall be pleasure to thy soul.* This seems to have been the mode of conception in the mind of the writer, who appears to have used the verb in an impersonal way. However, the anomaly in question stands not alone; see the like discrepancy in gender, in the Chron. 2 : 48. Gen. 4 : 7. Is. 21: 2. Lev. 2 : 8. 13 : 14, and many more examples in Ges. Lehrgeb. p. 716. The strictness of concord is not rigidly carried out in Hebrew, either as to gender or number. See Ges. ut supra.

(11) Reflection shall watch over thee; understanding shall preserve thee.

מְזִמָּה is here used in the good sense, indicating repeated thinking or reflection on a subject. — The last verb (a verb פ״ן) preserves the נ in the Imperf.; which is not frequent, except Gutturals follow it. Examples, however, are not wanting, § 65. 2. n. 1. The ־ֶכָּה has an assimilated נ in it, and ךָ is written (and so not unfrequently) with the parag. ־ָה. — As to the course of sentiment, there is first a promise of benefit, and then a promise that this shall be rendered stable by protection. The same order appears in vs. 6, 7, above.

In the second half of the chapter, the discourse takes a new direction The blessings of wisdom and knowledge, of guidance and protection, have already been set before those addressed, and also deliverance from evil. But there is one special evil, that has not yet been brought particularly into view, in this address. It is that of *incontinence.* True wisdom will be certain to deliver those who possess it, from all defiling and destructive intercourse with the unchaste. This constitutes the closing theme of warning; and the writer is so much in earnest, that he exhibits more than usual fervor, and more of poetic energy. This shows that the times were fraught with danger as to the vice in question, and that there was urgent need of guarding the young against it. Something like to this is also true, in respect to men of *deception* and *falsehood*, whom vs. 12—15 have brought into view, and have also warned the youth to shun them. But when the writer comes to his last theme, which has been described above, he shows that he had adopted an arrangement in his discourse designedly climactic. His greatest energy, therefore, is developed at the close.]

(12) That they may deliver thee from the way of evil, from the man who speaketh perversely.

The preceding verse speaks of safe keeping by reflection and understanding. Here the object of such a guardianship is set forth. So we have a לְ before the Inf., designed to express the idea, *in order that*. The subject of הַצִּיל (Hiph. Inf. of נָצַל) is *reflection* and *understanding*. — רָע, *evil*, a noun here, but still qualifying דֶּרֶךְ. — תַּהְפֻּכוֹת (from הָפַךְ), lit. *perversities*. It is an abstract plur. here, used adverbially, (so rendered in the version), or it may be rendered *perverse things*, i. e. deceptive, mendacious, fraudulent things.

(13) Who forsake the paths of uprightness, to walk in the ways of darkness.

In v. 12, אִישׁ is generic; accordingly we here find the *plural*, the subject being the same as before. — לָלֶכֶת (see on 1: 2 for לָ) *in order that they may walk*. That is, in other words: "They choose darkness rather than light, because their deeds are evil."

(14) Who rejoice to do evil, who exult in evil perversions.

This verse adds to the description, by showing that they do evil with a strong feeling of gratification. — יָגִילוּ (in Kal) has no subject expressed, (if there were one, it would be אֲשֶׁר), because the relative הַ in the Part. (= אֲשֶׁר) is carried forward mentally, and supplies the true subject. — The רָע at the end of the verse, serves to strengthen the preceding noun, and to make it more intensive.

(15) Whose ways are distorted, and in their paths they are perverse.

Distorted or *tortuous ways* means deceitful and fraudulent conduct. — *Perverse* means substantially the same thing, viz., first, literally, that which is *bent*, *crooked;* and therefore, secondly, its tropical meaning is *fraudulent*. The Part. comes from לוּז, *flectere*.

Thus much for the first four verses of this second division. The next four are occupied with the subject of the *strange woman*.

(16) That they may deliver thee from the strange woman, from the stranger who maketh smooth her words.

לְהַצִּיל stands in the same connection as in v. 12, i. e. reflection and understanding (v. 11) will so guard thee, *as to deliver*, etc. — זָרָה, participial noun, from זוּר, lit. *one who turns aside*, *deflects*, i. e. from the paths of rectitude, and usually applied to a *foreigner* as an *enemy*. But the idea of a *foreign* origin is not essential (indeed it is not admissible) here, if we compare the remaining verses. The *woman* in question acts as foreign women were wont to do; and hence the name of *stranger* is applied to her. — נָכְרִי lit. designates *one of foreign origin;* but as the next verse speaks of the woman in question as *forgetting the covenant of her God*, she must of course be a *Hebrew*, and merely one who acts like a *heathen*. We often speak of *heathen men* as living in our midst, meaning merely to designate those who act like heathen. So the writer before us. — The pron. אֲשֶׁר is omitted before אֲמָרֶיהָ, as it very often is in poetry, and not unfrequently even in prose, § 121. 3. — *To make smooth her words* means *to speak enticing and flattering words*.

(17) Who forsaketh the friend of her youth, and forgetteth the covenant of her God.

נְעוּרֶיהָ, plur. form, in order to express the idea of *extended* time, § 106. 2. *a*. — שָׁכֵחָה, (in Pause which makes the ֵ), the *Perf.* being used in order to designate a continuing or abiding period = *has forgotten and is forgetting.* — *The covenant of her God*, shows that, in the ceremony of marriage at that time, appeal was made to God, who was called to witness the vows and promises made. The adulterous woman (and such is the one meant here) breaks these vows, or this covenant. She has a double load of guilt, that which respects her husband, and that which has respect to God. All this refers to some custom at weddings, in regard to vows and promises, which the Pent. has not enjoined or described, but which the times and the exigencies of the case had rendered necessary.

(18) For her house sinketh down to the dead, and her paths to the shades.

As שָׁחָה now stands accented (on the penult), it must come from שׁוּחַ, and is third pers. fem. But its subject, בַּיִת, is nearly always masc. There can be little difficulty in the case, however, if any one consults the list of *common gender* nouns in Ewald's Gramm. § 174. *d*, which expressly includes בַּיִת; and so decides Bertheau, in his *Comm.* on this verse. — I have rendered מוּת *(death)* by *dead*, the abstract being used for the concrete; and so this first clause of the verse is like the last. — *To the shades*, or *ghosts*, i. e. the *manes* or *umbrae* of the Latins; for *shades* has often this sense in English. — רְפָאִים means *ghosts*, *spectres*, inasmuch as it signifies *debiles*, *flaccidi*, i. e. weak, withered, having neither blood nor energetic vitality. The popular belief among the Hebrews was, that the region of the dead (שְׁאוֹל *the under world)* was peopled by such *umbrae.* — Sentiment: 'Her habitation will sink into certain destruction and ruin.' There is plainly a reference to the earth as swallowing up Korah and his company; this is, therefore, a loud note of warning to the imprudent and unsuspecting youth, who may be enticed by the adulteress. It is still more fully developed in the next verse.

(19) All who go in unto her, return not; they do not attain to the paths of life.

In יְשׁוּבוּן, the accent is drawn down on the ultimate, by the נ paragogic, and therefore (ָ) under the Yodh of the first syllable is dropped. — יַשִּׂיגוּ, *Hiph.* of נָשַׂג, because the Kal form is not in use. — Sentiment: 'The destruction of all who visit her is certain and irremediable.'

(20) So that thou shouldst go in the way of the good, and keep the paths of the righteous.

That is, all these warnings are uttered *that, in order that,* etc., לְמַעַן; which is like to the לְ at the beginning of vs. 12, 16. — *The way of the good,* or *path of the righteous,* is the only way of peace and safety.

(21) For the upright shall inhabit the land, and men of integrity shall remain therein.

Men of integrity, תְמִימִים, are those who do not walk in the crooked and perverted ways mentioned in v. 15; comp. Matt. 5:5. — יִוָּתְרוּ, Niph. Imperf. of יָתַר, lit. *shall be left,* or *be remaining.* The meaning is, that while the wicked are cut off from the land, the upright shall remain or be left therein.

(22) But the wicked shall be cut off from the land, and the treacherous be swept away from it.

This accords with the usual tenor of threatenings in the Old Testament. "The wicked shall not live out half their days." Premature and violent death will come upon them. — יִסְּחוּ makes some little difficulty, being, as it would seem, from נָסַח, and in the Imperf. Kal. Lit. *they will sweep themselves away,* i. e. *tear themselves away,* from the land. I should prefer a root סָחַח (like שָׁחַח), and point it in Niphal, יִסַּחוּ, which would give of course a *passive* sense. There is another way, however, of solving the difficulty. Render thus: *And the treacherous shall they sweep from the land,* i. e. the people or magistracy will sweep away the בֹּגְדִים, the verb having (as often) an indef. subject which is not expressed. This is the most simple construction, as the text now stands; and this amounts to the use of a *passive* voice, Ewald, § 272. *b.* See Roedig. Gramm. § 134. 3. *b.*

CHAP. III. 1—35.

[This chapter has a triplex division, viz. (*a*) vs. 1—10. (*b*) vs. 11—20. (*c*) vs. 21—35. Each of these divisions is introduced by the compellative, בְּנִי. The first division has artistic marks about it. It is subdivided into five couplets, each of which consists of two verses. In every one, the second verse of the couplet exhibits a promise of good, consequent on obedience to what is prescribed.

A summary of contents is rather a difficult task, since there is so much of the gnomic stamp in the chapter. In some cases several verses are connected; but there is no long-continued series respecting the same subject. The first division (vs. 1—10) comprises summarily this: My son, attend diligently to my instruction; for long life and peace will be the consequence, vs. 1, 2. Never neglect kindness and faithfulness, for these will render thee an object of favor to God and man, vs. 3, 4. Trust implicitly in God, and he will direct thy ways, vs. 5, 6. Be not wise in thine own conceit, but fear God, who will keep thee from evil, and make thy condition safe and salutary, vs. 7, 8. Honor Jehovah with thy substance, and he will make abundant provision for thy support and comfort, vs. 9, 10.]

(1) My son, forget not my instruction; let thy heart keep my commandments.

The original sense of תּוֹרָה is here retained, viz., *instruction*, from יָרָה *to teach.*—מִצְוֹתַי (read *mĭts-vō-thī*) is from צָוָה, with a ו movable consonant.—יִצֹּר, with נ radical assimilated, while in 2: 11. 5: 2, it is retained in full, in the same tense. This shows an oscillation of usage, in regard to the Imperf. of verbs פ״ן. The Imperf. here, as is very common, is *hortative.*

(2) For length of days, and years of life, and also peace, shall be added to thee.

This is of like tenor with the fifth commandment, which has the same promise. *Long life* is a very frequent promise to the obedient; comp. Prov. 9 : 11. 10 : 27. On the contrary, the impious are soon cut off; see 2 : 22.—*And also peace*, since this commences the second clause, it needs some note of distinction. By rendering וְ *and also*, we make a distinction, and one quite within the province of this particle. That the wicked shall not have peace is clear; see Is. 48 : 22. 57: 21.—*Will they add*—who or what will add? Apparently the Nom. or subject is the *instruction* and *commands* of v. 1. But the verb is *masc.*, the nouns both *fem.*; of course the Nom. indefinite must be supposed = *they shall add*, which is equivalent to a *passive*; and so I have translated it (see § 134. 3) by the passive.—יוֹסִיפוּ might be rendered, *cause to increase;* but Kal has no Imperf. in use, and Hiphil is its substitute; and so we may render simply by *add;* but this means here *increase*.

(3) Let not kindness and faithfulness forsake thee; bind them on thy neck, inscribe them on the tablet of thy heart.

That is, demean not thyself so as to compel them to forsake thee, or, treat them not with neglect so as to alienate them,—חֶסֶד means *kindness* of disposition toward others, *love* of a friend, or the *love* of God for us.—אֱמֶת (apoc. form of אֱמֶנֶת) means *faithfulness* or *truthfulness*, properly *that which can be relied on, that which is stable.*—*Bind them on thy neck*, i. e. wear them as a conspicuous ornament of honor, (see on 1: 9); for such were chains about the neck, set with rubies.—*Inscribe on the tablet of the heart*, i. e. inscribe them on a tablet which will be always present with thee, and always reminding thee of thy duty; comp. Jer. 31: 33. The ָם plur. suff. after each Imper. verb, refers to *kindness and faithfulness* in v. 3; and not, as C. B. Michaelis and others say, to instruction and command in v. 1, for these are both *fem.*, while the suff. is masculine.

(4) And thou shalt find favor and good success in the sight of God and man.

וּמְצָא follows another Imper. which contains a monition, and therefore, although Imp. in form, it here designates a *promise* of what is consequent upon obedience, § 127. 2.—שֵׂכֶל is somewhat difficult here. If (with Bertheau) we render it *understanding*, (as in 13 : 15. Ps. 111: 10), it hardly seems appropriate; for the fact of having *obeyed*, shows of itself that the obedient is already in the possession of שֵׂכֶל. One meaning of הִשְׂכִּיל, however, is *successum habuit* or *dedit.* As kindred to this I have given the meaning of שֵׂכֶל in the version; and then we have something that corresponds with a gift now bestowed, and not before possessed. Ges. renders it by *felicitas*, in his Lex., which = our *good luck.* —*In the sight*, etc., i. e. in the view, judgment, or opinion, of both God and man. In other words: 'Thou shalt find favor and be truly prospered, God and man both bearing witness to thy well-directed efforts.'

(5) Trust in Jehovah with all thine heart, and lean not upon thine own understanding.

This inculcates humility, and stands opposed to pride and self-confidence.—אֶל, *to, toward;* so the Heb., but in our own idiom we say: *lean upon.*

(6) In all thy ways acknowledge him, and he will make straight thy paths.

This verse connects intimately with the preceding one, and presents a good reason for following the advice there given. —דַּע with the suff. becomes דָּעֵהוּ.—הוּא has an emphatic sense, and it is inserted for this reason. The meaning is, *he and none else.*—יְיַשֵּׁר is reg. Piel Imperfect.

(7) Be not wise in thine own view; fear Jehovah, and turn away from evil.

That is, instead of confiding in your own sagacity and ability to secure your peace and welfare, fear God and avoid doing evil. This is the safer and wiser course; for the fear of God will guard you against the doing of evil.

(8) It shall be healing to thy body, and refreshment to thy bones.

תְּהִי, of the optative or voluntative form, but as it has no וְ to mark an *apodosis*, it must be taken as indicating *promise;* comp. 5: 18. 7: 9. — לְשָׁרֶּךָ, from שֹׁר with suff., with Hholem shortened by its standing in a mixed syllable, lit. *thy navel.* Being the central point of the body, it is virtually taken as the representative of the whole. — שִׁקּוּי, lit. *irrigation,* figuratively *refreshment.* Sentiment: 'The fear of God will give healing in sickness, and refreshment in a time of need.' — *Bones* represent the substantial parts of the human frame, which, when wearied or exhausted, needs rest and refreshment.

(9) Honor Jehovah with thy substance, and with the first fruits of all thy produce.

This refers to the precepts of the Law, which direct that of all the first fruits an offering shall be made to God, Ex. 23: 19. Lev. 2: 12, 26. 19: 23. Deut. 18: 4, 11. comp. Gen. 28: 22. Sentiment: 'To show gratitude to God for his blessings, is one of our leading duties.'

(10) Then shall thy granaries be filled abundantly, and thy presses shall burst forth with new wine.

The blessings of plenty shall be copiously bestowed on the obedient. The corn and the wine shall abound and overflow.— שָׂבָע, used adverbially. — וְתִירוֹשׁ, placed first emphatically. The shape of the Hebrew seems to be thus: '*And as to new wine,* thy presses shall pour it forth.' So the accents indicate.

Second Division, vs. 11—20.

[It is difficult to make out a connected plan here. Vs. 11, 12, enjoin diligent attention to the chastisements which Providence inflicts. Vs.

13, seq. relapse into the praises of Wisdom, and the precious rewards that she bestows: which are better than silver, gold, rubies, and all choice things, vs. 13—15. Length of days, riches, honor, pleasure, and peace, are all within her gift, vs. 16, 17. She is a tree of life, which makes those blessed who lay hold of her, v. 18. Jehovah founded the earth by her assistance, and established the heavens; he clave the abysses, and made the clouds to distil rain, vs. 19, 20.

It is apparent, therefore, that there is no visible connection between vs. 11, 12, and the sequel. But vs. 13—20 are closely united in one theme.]

(11) My son, despise not the chastening of the Lord, nor loath his reproof.

This comes appropriately after a promise of blessings; for it is as much as to say: 'You must not expect that all will be prosperity. Adversity will come; God's chastening hand will smite; but do thou not shrink from it, nor repine, for it is the hand of fatherly discipline, smiting for your spiritual good — smiting in order to keep you humble, and to teach you how dependent you are on him.' —תָּקוֹץ is stronger than the preceding verb, and the verse is climactic. Our English version *(weary)* does not give the true sense of this word, since it is too weak to express the Hebrew.

(12) For whom Jehovah loveth he chasteneth, even as a father the son in whom he delighteth.

Chastisement, in the way of discipline, is only a fruit of kindness; see Deut. 8:5. Ps. 118:18. Prov. 13:24.— יִרְצֶה demands אֲשֶׁר to be supplied before it, since it constitutes a *relative clause.* It is singular that the Sept. should here have read יַכְאִב, and rendered it *μαστιγοῖ, chastens,* instead of reading the text וּכְאָב, *and as a father.* In Heb. 12:6, this version is followed. This shows that the Seventy had no vowel-points to guide them. — The verb יוֹכִיחַ is to be mentally supplied before אֶת־בֵּן, from the preceding clause. The word כְּאָב, *as a father*, merely qualifies the manner of the chastisement. In other words: 'If promised prosperity should be interrupted, and suffering come, remember still, that when God chastens the obedient, it is not from want of love for them, but only with a design to try and to purify them. Remember, moreover, that, such being the case, he will chastise in measure and in mercy, even as an affectionate father does.'

(13) Blessed is the man who hath found wisdom, even the man who draweth forth understanding.

Here the two tenses (in a kind of contrast) have a special significance. מָצָא, Perf., *has found and still finds;* יָפִיק (Imperf. Hiph. of פּוּק), lit. *makes to come forth*, i. e. *habitually draws forth* from its fountain. The Targum well renders here by מַבִּיעַ, *causes to gush forth;* see Ps. 144: 13. Is. 58: 10. The Imperf. designates that the wise man does this habitually, or that he is doing and will do this. The two clauses stand related almost as *past habitual obtaining* does to *future acquiring* which will be continual. In the second case, *the causing wisdom to come forth*, implies that he will *obtain* it from God, the source of all good; comp. Prov. 8: 35. 18: 22, for the like sentiment.

(14) For the gain thereof is better than the gain of silver; and the produce thereof than fine gold.

סַחַר means lit. *gain resulting from traffic.*—חָרוּץ is a word whose etymology has perplexed the critics. Ges. says, that "it designates *gold*, sive a colore acuto dictum est, sive quod avide appetitur ab hominibus." Certainly not a very satisfactory etymology. Pure gold is rather dull of color than acute or sharp; and the *avide appetitur* in this word, must be referred to the Arabic for any support. There is a more easy solution. The ancient mines in hither Asia, as well as those now in California, doubtless yielded gold, more or less of which was like the pure lumps now found in the latter region. This was of course in the highest repute;

for what was *native*, could not have been alloyed by any fraud. Now as one sense of חָרַץ is *to dig, fodere*, so חָרוּץ lit. means, *that which is dug out;* and this appellation seems to be applied to *gold κατ᾽ ἐξόχην*, as being the most valuable of all which is dug out of the earth. All the ancient versions understand the word as meaning *the better sort of gold.* Sentiment: 'Wisdom is better than the most splendid wealth.'

(15) More precious is it than pearls; and all thy jewels cannot compare with it.

The tenor of the discourse is climactic. *Pearls* and *jewels* are valued as the highest kind of riches. — פְּנִיִּים is elsewhere always written פְּנִינִים, (see Job 28 : 18. Prov. 8 : 11); and so we have it in the *Qeri* of the margin. One cannot well doubt, that the second נ has fallen out in the Kethibh here. *Jewels* are figuratively named חֲפָצֶיךָ *thy desirable things*, because they are things so much desired and sought after in the East, for the adornment of both sexes. See a like comparison in order to show the worth of *wisdom*, in Job 28 : 12 —28, truly a most splendid description. — יִשְׁווּ *(yĭsh-vū)* from שָׁוָה with ו medial consonant.

(16) Length of days is in her right hand; in her left are riches and honor.

As to *long life*, compare 9 : 11; also vs. 7—10 above, and v. 2. As to *riches and honor*, comp. 8 : 18. 22 : 4. — *In her right hand, and in her left*, i. e. she dispenses her blessings *with both hands*, or, in other words, *abundantly*.

(17) Her ways are ways of pleasantness, and all her paths are peace.

Her ways means the ways which she points out and recommends. — נֹעַם, *whatever is lovely, pleasant, agreeable.* — *Peace* is a word expressive of the opposite not only of all disquietude, but also of all alarm from fear of evil.

(18) A tree of life is she to those who lay hold upon her; and those who grasp her, shall each be blessed.

A *tree of life* is a tree whose fruit imparts or preserves life; with reference, perhaps, to *the tree of life* in the garden of Eden. — מְאֻשָּׁר, sing. number, while the subject apparently is plural. But this word here is what grammarians call an *individualizing* predicate. In other words, when the subject is plural and comprehends a mass, the predicate, by being simply put in the *singular*, makes the declaration contained in it applicable to *each and every individual* of the mass. I have therefore so rendered it in the version. Comp. for like usage, Ex. 31: 14. Gen. 27: 29 (bis), comp. 12 : 3. Zach. 11: 5; see Ewald, § 309. *a.* On the other hand, the sing. often goes over, in a continued construction, into the plural, when it has a generic and therefore comprehensive meaning; see Ew. ib. and comp. Rödig. § 143. 4. § 143. 1.

(19) Jehovah hath founded the earth by wisdom; he hath established the heavens by understanding.

This is the highest testimony to the excellence of wisdom which can be given. To the Most High she is as it were a counsellor. How invaluable, then, to erring men, who so much need counsel! The words חָכְמָה, דַּעַת, and תְּבוּנָה, are so often interchanged with each other, that we may safely conclude *variety of diction* merely to be the object in view, and not the expression of ideas substantially different from each other. In v. 19, the first and last of these three words are obviously of the same import. The next verse gives us the other variation, which is plainly equivalent in signification.

(20) By his knowledge the abysses were cleft; and the clouds which distil the dew.

In Gen. 1: 6, *the waters* (= תְּהוֹמוֹת) are separated, and a part are congregated above the firmament and a part below; see v. 7 in the sequel there. It is this *dividing* to which the נִבְקָעוּ of the text refers. It needed great skill and wisdom to make this separation, so as to promote the most beneficial ends. To the upper תְּהוֹם belong the clouds with their aqueous contents. These distil the waters of the upper region upon the earth, and fructify it. — The clouds יִרְעֲפוּ, *distil*, i. e. gently drop or let fall, viz. the dew. This is effected by his *wisdom* (here called דַּעַת), which is strikingly manifested in this arrangement of the two abysses. Without the vapory תְּהוֹם above, there could be no dew.

Such is the impassioned and sublime eulogy of Wisdom. Well may the writer urge all his readers, to strive for the attainment of it.

Third Division, vs. 21—35.

[The monitor now resumes his hortatory address to his pupil, to persuade him to cleave to the pursuit of wisdom. It will keep him in safety; he may lie down in security and sleep sweetly, for no fear of destruction will disturb him, since Jehovah is his keeper, vs. 21—26. The next five verses all begin with אַל, which stands before clauses designed to be *prohibitions*. One must not withhold any feasible good from his neighbor; he must not put off a favor to him, which he can now do; he must not slander him; he must not causelessly contend with him; he must not be emulous of him, vs. 27—31. All this must not be done, for Jehovah hates the perverse, while he is the friend of the righteous; his curse is on the house of the wicked, while the habitation of the just is blessed, vs. 32, 33. Inasmuch as he mocks scorners, and shows favor to the righteous, the wise shall inherit glory, but shame shall take away fools, vs. 34, 35.]

(21) My son, let them not depart from thy sight; hold fast counsel and reflection.

One difficulty here is, to find the plur. masc. subject of יָלֻזוּ. Some choose the two nouns in the second clause, and say that they are here anticipated, (as it sometimes happens). But both of these nouns are *feminine*. If we fall back, as does Bertheau, on v. 1 of the chapter, then there is the same objection. It is easier, therefore, to make יַלֻזוּ refer to the various דְּבָרִים, i. e. *things said*, or *matters treated of* in the context preceding, and thus give to the verb a comprehensive aspect. Meaning: 'Do not lose sight of any of these precepts or things inculcated.'— נְצֹר, *to keep* or *guard with care, to hold fast* or *firmly*. — תּוּשִׁיָּה (from יָשָׁה) *counsel*, viz. such as had now been given. — מְזִמָּה, here in a good sense again, *reflection*, or rather here, *the result of thought and reflection*, viz. such a result as had been communicated; not = *devote yourself to reflection*, for this would be expressed by שׂוּם אֶל־לֵב. The reward follows: —

(22) And they shall be life to thy soul, and grace to thy neck.

What shall be so? The verb is masc., and therefore the subject cannot be the two nouns that immediately precede. The reference, then, must be regarded as the same as that implied in the case of יַלֻזוּ. But all difficulty may be avoided by making חַיִּים (plur.) the subject, and translating thus: *Life shall be to thy soul*, i. e. long life, life *par excellence*. But neither Umbreit nor Bertheau notice this. — *Grace to thy neck*, i. e. they shall adorn thy neck with a collet of honor; comp. v. 3, and specially 1: 9. If the first clause be rendered as just proposed, then the second must run thus: *Grace shall be to thy neck.*

(23) Then shalt thou go on thy way in confidence; and thy foot shall not stumble.

לָבֶטַח, the ל of condition, see Lex. B. 3. — תִּגּוֹף (from נָגַף), *to hit or strike against* anything, and thence to *stumble*. In other words: 'The journey of life shall be safe and smooth.'

(24) When thou liest down, thou shalt not be afraid; yea, when thou liest down, thy sleep shall be sweet.

When danger is feared, sleep is apt to be light and interrupted. *Sweet sleep* accompanies quietude and a sense of security. The shape of the Hebrew in the last clause stands thus: *And shouldest thou lie down, then thy sleep shall be sweet.* But the version above expresses well the sense.

(25) Fear not any sudden terror, nor the destructive tempest of the wicked when it shall come.

פִּתְאֹם, lit. *suddenly*, as an adverb. But very often an adverb is employed in the place of an adjective. — *Tempest of the wicked* may mean *that tempest which the wicked raise;* but the *passive* meaning is better here, viz. that tempest which comes, sudden and furious, to sweep away the wicked.

(26) For Jehovah will be thy confidence; yea, he will keep thy foot from the snare.

בְּכִסְלֶךָ, lit. *in thy confidence.* But this English version would not give the true meaning. The ב here is the *Beth essentiae* or *Beth predicate*, and merely gives intensity to the expression, comp. Ex. 18: 4; see § 151. 3. *a. γ.* — לֶכֶד, *snare*, found only in this book. Sentiment: 'Jehovah will impart to thee strong confidence, and keep thee from concealed dangers.' — For similar declarations, see Ps. 78: 7. Job. 8: 14. 31: 24.

(27) Withhold not good from those to whom it belongs, when it is in the power of thy hand to do [it.]

Good is here favor of any kind — *a favor*, as we say. — לִבְעָלָיו, lit. *to the owners of it*, i. e. those to whom it belongs or is due. — בִּהְיוֹת לְ, *when it appertains to.* — אֵל, *might, strength, power*, probably the remoter root of אֱלוֹהַּ, *God*, quasi *the Mighty One.* For the same expression as here, see Gen. 31: 29. Mic. 2: 1. Deut. 28: 32. Neh. 5: 5. — יָדֶיךָ has the vowels of יָדְךָ (Qeri) in the sing.; but this is useless, for we may just as well read יָדֶיךָ. — לַעֲשׂוֹת omits, through brevity, the pronoun which I have supplied in the version above. The next verse shows more exactly what the present one means.

(28) Say not to thy friend: Go, and return, and to-morrow I will give, when it is with thee.

לְרֵעֶ֫יךָ, with vowels for the sing. לְרֵעֲךָ, which is correct here (so Qeri), as the verbs which follow are in the singular. —אֶתֵּן (Imperf. of נָתַן), here used absolutely without any object, simply designating *the act of giving.* — וְיֵשׁ, *and yet it is* or *there is*, § 152. B. *b.*, which I have expressed for substance in the version. The Nom. to יֵשׁ may be טוֹב (of v. 27); but it may also be rendered *impersonally* by *there is.* The other, however, is rather preferable.

(29) Devise not evil against thy neighbor, when he dwelleth securely with thee.

תַּחֲרֹשׁ, lit. *fabricate, machinate,* but trop. as above; see Ezek. 21: 36. — *Dwelleth securely with thee,* probably refers here to the sojourning traveller, who seeks a friendly lodge, and feels secure in it, in accordance with the laws of hospitality nearly universal in hither Asia. The host is not to lay a plan for robbing his guest, who has entrusted himself to his care and protection. Doubtless there were men enough who practised such breaches of good faith and kindness; and hence the necessity of a warning. Such a crime was a very aggravated one. — וְהוּא, plainly = *when he,* and it is designed to be emphatic.

(30) Strive not with a man without cause, when he has done thee no harm.

תָּרוֹב, the Kethibh should be pointed; but the Qeri is also well.—The חִנָּם here is explained by the next clause. There is no proper *cause* or *ground* of striving, where no wrong has been done. — גְּמָלְךָ, lit. *rendered thee.* The Hebrews often said: *Render good* or *evil* to a person, where we say: *Do good* or *evil* to him. The Nom. subject is comprised in the verb גָּמַל.

(31) Be not envious toward the man of violence; and choose none of his ways.

תְקַנֵּא, means a *jealous love* or *desire*, and indicates a high degree of affection or desire toward any person or thing, which brings with it anxious wishes to obtain or retain it. Sentiment: 'Do not anxiously covet the booty which men of violence acquire; do not desire any connection with them.' — *None of his ways*, i. e. none of those ways in which he develops the character of a depredator.

(32) For the perverse is an abomination to Jehovah; but with the upright is his secret.

כִּי is employed here as in 2 : 26, i. e. to introduce a new shade of thought. It may, however, be regarded here (as also there) as *causal*, introducing a reason for the preceding declaration. — סוֹדוֹ = *secret* or *confidential intercourse*. Only friends, i. e. the upright, enjoy this privilege; comp. Job 19 : 19. Ps. 55 : 15, where a like sense of the word occurs.

(33) The curse of Jehovah is on the house of the wicked; but the habitation of the righteous he will bless.

The curse of Jehovah, when it falls on the house of the wicked, destroys and eradicates it; comp. in Zach. 5 : 3, seq. Mal. 2 : 2.

(34) When he mocketh the scorners, and giveth grace to the humble;

A *protasis*, of which the following verse is the *apodosis*. Emphasis rests on הוּא here, and for this purpose, indeed, it is inserted. Meaning: 'When he (God) himself mocks, etc.;' here the verb is followed by לְ before the object. It may be employed either with or without it; but most usual is the latter construction, Ps. 119 : 51. Prov. 14 : 9. — עֲנִיִּים, Qeri עֲנָוִים, both forms, however, are used and are normal.

(35) The wise shall inherit glory, but as to fools — shame shall sweep [them] away.

Glory means here *honor*, or *an exalted station*. — מֵרִים קָלוֹן has been differently rendered: *Shame shall elevate* or *ennoble fools*, spoken sarcastically; so Ziegler, Ewald. But Chald., Syr. C. B. Mich., and others: *Shall receive shame*, making מֵרִים = *take up*, with the adjunct notion of *carrying away*. I prefer the meaning sanctioned by Ezek. 21: 31. Is. 57: 14, viz., *to take off*, *to sweep away*, like as the dust which is elevated by the wind and is swept off, as may be seen in Is. 17: 13. comp. Is. 29: 5. Ps. 35: 5. At least the image, understood in this way, is very vivid. It stands thus: 'Fools are elevated like the light dust, and then are *swept away* in the same manner. Their shameful conduct brings this upon them.' But the following sense is not a bad one: *Shame is the exalter of fools;* said, of course, ironically. It is at least literal, and very significant, and is not without parallels. Müntinghe significantly: *Shame is the nobility conferred on fools.* קָלוֹן, lit. *lightness*, rather favors, however, the idea of being *elevated and swept away*, as light bodies are wont to be, by the storm, i. e. by the divine indignation.

CHAP. IV. 1—27.

[This chapter also has three divisions, made by *My son*, at the beginning of each. In the first portion, vs. 1, 2, the *children* are exhorted to listen to wise and good instruction. The writer goes on to state, that when he was a child, he received instruction from parental affection, with counsel to observe it diligently, vs. 3, 4. The advice given was, above all things to acquire *wisdom*, and never to swerve from it; for this would keep him in safety, vs. 5, 6. Wisdom is there fore the first or principal thing, and should be obtained at all events. She will exalt and honor him, who attains her. She will also adorn him with a beautiful wreath and diadem, vs. 7—9.

The corresponding clauses here, and throughout the chapter, are very exact, with the single exception of v. 4, which alone has *three* clauses. The Syriac has a clause after v. 4, omitted in the present Hebrew text, which runs thus: *Let my law be as the apple of thine eye.* If this were admitted, it would make v. 4 into four clauses, i. e. into two verses, and would restore regularity to the whole chapter. The Sept. is so perplexed here, that we cannot well make out from it what its Heb. text was.]

(1) Hear, ye children, the admonition of a father, and listen to knowledge and understanding.

The *plural*, בָּנִים, is employed here in the room of the usual singular. Comp. 1: 8, as to the tenor of the command.

(2) For good doctrine have I given to you; forsake not my instruction.

For לֶקַח, see 1: 5. 9: 9. The Perf. נָתַתִּי has what is called the *continuing* or *permanent* sense, *have given and still give.* — תּוֹרָתִי, here in its primary sense.

(3) For a son was I to my father, a tender and only [child] in the view of my mother.

The design is to refer to a *tender* age (רַךְ) or early childhood, and also to the fact that he either was, or was treated as, an *only son;* of course, as one much beloved. In this condition he received, in early life, the paternal instruction thus timely given. In other words, he had been taught from childhood the lessons of wisdom which he was going now to teach. — *Son to my father* denotes something more than physical origin. The writer means, that he was *treated as a son* by his affectionate father; who, as the next verse shows, was his instructor. The second clause shows in what light his mother regarded him, treating him as *a tender and only child.* — יָחִיד, *only*, means more than simply *beloved;* for *special* affection is usually the lot of the *only child.* In the New Testament, μονογενής has just the same meaning.

(4) And he taught me, and said to me: Let thine heart take fast hold of my words; keep my commands and thou shalt live.

וַיֹּרֵנִי, Hiph. of יָרָה; in Kal the meaning *to teach* is wanting. — וֶחְיֵה, (for וֶ with Seghol, see § 102. 2. *c.*), lit. *and live.* But being a second Imper., it implies a promise, § 127 2, and is equivalent to the Imperf. second person.

(5) Get wisdom, get understanding; forget not, and decline not from the words of my mouth.

Each clause here is bi-membral. — *Forget not,* has no Acc. after it expressed; but אֲמָרַי is a proper one, and may be gathered or supplied from the next member of the clause.

(6) Forsake her not, and she will keep thee; love her, and she will preserve thee.

אֱהָבֶהָ, *love her,* the Imp. with Pattah, אֱהַב, makes the form in the text, before the suff. ־ֶהָ is appended. For the repeated ־ֶךָ, suff. to two of the verbs, see Gramm. p. 289, B. on the left.

(7) The principal thing is wisdom, get wisdom; even with all thy property, procure understanding.

That is, if it cost thee all thy wealth, still obtain wisdom. It is worth more than all which can be given for it. Therefore at all events obtain it, if it be possible. — בְּ before the noun which expresses the price paid for a thing, is common, Lex. בְּ, B. 9.

(8) Exalt her, and she will elevate thee; she will honor thee, when thou shalt embrace her.

סַלְסְלֶהָ, Pilpel of סָלַל. In other words: 'Hold her in the highest estimation, and thou thyself shalt be exalted and honored.' — *Embrace her,* is indicative of, or designed to express, affectionate attachment.

(9) She will give to thine head a graceful wreath; a beautiful diadem will she bestow on thee.

For sentiment and mode of expression, see 1: 9. — תְּמַגְּנֶךָּ, an unfrequent verb, and used only in Piel; so here, and in Gen. 14: 20. Hos. 11: 8. It governs two Accusatives here, as Piel often does, § 136. 1. The second division of the chapter now follows, and urges still further the acquiring of wisdom, and holds up the many advantages that are secured by it.

Part Second, vs. 10—19.

[In different forms are presented the ideas of the writer with respect to the importance of wisdom. His *earnestness* on the subject appears from his repeated exhortations to acquire the possession of it, and the promises of many blessings to be derived from it. Long life, safety, and deliverance from danger, are the reward, vs. 10—12. One should therefore grasp it firmly, and hold it fast; and in order to do this, he must never frequent the path of the wicked, vs. 13, 14. That path he must firmly reject; he must turn from it, and go on in another direction, v. 15. The wicked are sleepless, unless they can do evil. They feed on the bread of wickedness, and drink the wine of violence, vs. 16, 17. Truly the path of the just is like the rising light of the dawn, shining more and more unto perfect day; but the path of the wicked is dark, they know not on what they stumble, vs. 18, 19.]

(10) Listen, my son, and receive my words, that they may increase for thee years of life.

Comp. the same sentiment in 3 : 2, and see the remarks there. For the meaning of וְ before יִרְבּוּ, see § 152. B. *e.*

(11) I have instructed thee in the way of wisdom, I have made thee to tread in the paths of uprightness.

הֹרֵתִי for הוֹרֵתִי, Hiph. of יָרָה. To teach the disciple wisdom, is to prepare him of course to walk uprightly.

(12) When thou goest, thy step shall not be straitened; and if thou runnest, thou shalt not stumble.

The verse is climactic. *Running* increases the danger of stumbling; but even the higher danger shall be warded off. — For יֵצַר, Imperf. Kal of יָצַר, see Lex. No. ii. The Pattah belongs to the intrans. verb as such here; but without this reason, the ר final would well account for it.

(13) Take fast hold of instruction, and do not let go; keep her, for she is thy life.

תֶּרֶף, apoc. second person of Imperf. Hiph. of רָפָה, instead of the normal apoc. תֶּרֶף, § 74. Note 14. This form is *hortative*. — נִצְּרֶהָ, keep *her* — who? Doubtless *wisdom* (the great object before the writer's mind) is implied here; for the preceding מוּסָר, its equivalent, is masc. The Daghesh in צּ is *Dagh. euphonic*, § 20. 2. 2; also called *dirimens*, i. e. separating. It makes the preceding short syllable and the Sheva half-syllable to be heard more distinctly, and is in itself a mere arbitrary sign of one of the niceties in pronouncing certain words. Ewald has treated more fully of it than other grammarians, in § 92. *c*. — הִיא fem. in reference to wisdom implied. — *Let not go*, without an Acc. after it, renders it necessary to make out a supply mentally, either thus: *Remit not thy hold*, or else: *Remit not instruction*. Either is good.

(14) In the path of the wicked do thou not go, nor travel in the way of evil men.

תְּאַשֵּׁר, a new verb, for the sake of variety in the diction; lit. *take* [*no*] *steps*. The אַל before the two verbs shows that they are *voluntative* or *hortative*, rather than peremptory. Absolute prohibition would require לֹא.

(15) Reject it, pass not upon it; turn from it, and pass away.

The Imp. with suff. here, פְּרָעֵהוּ, in the simple state would be פְּרַע. The *Pattah* under the ר is made a *Qamets*, by being placed in an open syllable. — תַּעֲבָר־, with final short ŏ because of the Maqqeph. — וַעֲבֹר, and *pass away*, i. e. from the path of the wicked, not *pass on* it, i. e. on the road of the wicked. In other words: 'When in thine own right path, avoid the ways of the wicked; turn from them, and go forward as you were before going.'

(16) For they sleep not unless they have done evil; and are robbed of their sleep, if they have caused none to stumble.

The three Imperfs. here denote habitual and customary action, i. e. they express an enduring Present, which of course must comprise a future sense. — יָרֵעוּ, from יָרֵעַ, Imperf. Hiph.; רוּעַ, as a root, would also give the same form. The verb is intrans. and abs., and therefore has no object after it. — *Are robbed of their sleep*, lit. *their sleep is taken away* or *robbed.* I have preferred our familiar English idiom here. — The ו in the last verb is manifestly wrong. Hiphil does not allow this. The Qeri puts *Yodh* for it; and to this letter the vowel that precedes is adapted. The Kethibh would be pointed יִכְשׁוֹלוּ, in Kal, and would then give an irrelevant sense.

(17) For they feed on the bread of wickedness, and the wine of violence do they drink.

That is, they feed on the bread which wickedness has obtained, and drink the wine which they have procured by their violence.

(18) But the path of the righteous is as the dawning light; which goes on and shines until the full completion of the day.

נֹגַהּ, *splendor*, but here evidently *the dawning light.* — וָאוֹר הוֹלֵךְ, Inf. abs. and Part., (see § 128. 3. *b.* n. 3), which indicate a constant progression in giving out light. — נְכוֹן, Part. Niph. in the const. state, meaning *that which is established* or *completed.* I have translated it by *full completion*, meaning thereby the highest point of the light's progress, which of course is at mid-day. After this, the light decreases; and the second part of the day belongs not to the imagery here presented. Sentiment: 'The path of the just will ever become plainer, clearer, and more certain, until they come to the consummation of their journey.' But *then* — what follows? This question is not answered here; but may we not suppose the same feeling to have pervaded the mind of the writer, as that which the Psalmist entertained, when he said: *In thy light shall we see light*, i. e. in thy presence is true and eternal light, *light* in the highest sense? Ps. 36: 10 (9). This is indeed the *perfect day.*

Indirectly, this verse seems to confirm the idea of *perseverance* in the way of righteousness. The path grows brighter constantly, even until the consummation of the journey. This would not exclude the idea, that clouds and darkness might occasionally eclipse the light; but it seems to establish the position, that, although eclipsed, it is not quenched, it will surely return.

(19) The way of the wicked is as thick darkness; they know not on what they shall stumble.

Here, *thick darkness* is contrasted with the *light* of the preceding verse. Of course, in such a darkness no one can know on what he may stumble. In other words: 'They are surrounded with darkness which exposes them to continual danger of stumbling to their ruin.'

Third Division, vs. 20—27.

[This begins like the other divisions, with exhortation to listen diligently, and keep the precepts given carefully in mind, because they will secure life and prosperity, vs. 20—25. The heart must above all be guarded, for the issues of life are from this, v. 26. One must turn away from those who speak perversity and deceit, and look only on the path which is straight and direct, vs. 24, 25. He must well consider his goings, and then his way will be steadfast, v. 26. From this way he must never turn, either to the right or to the left.]

(20) My son, listen to my words; incline thine ear to my sayings.

הַט, apoc. Imper. of נָטָה, in Hiph., instead of the normal הַטֵּה. The final ה with its vowel is dropped. in order to form the apoc. word; and by reason of this, the Dagh. of course falls out of the ט, because it cannot stand in a letter now become final.

(21) Let them not recede from thy sight; keep them in the midst of thy heart.

יַלִּיזוּ, Imperf. Hiph. of לוּז, *more Chaldaeorum*, with a

Dagh. in the ל. The normal form would be יַלִּיזוּ. The peculiar Hiph. signification hardly obtains here. So we have יַלִּינוּ from לוּן, in the same way of conformity to the Chaldee. Sentiment: 'Always keep them before thee, and let them ever be in thy mind.'

(22) For they are life to those who find them; and to the whole body are they healing.

They are life, viz., his *words* or *precepts*, see v. 20. — *Find* is *to obtain.* — בְּשָׂרוֹ, lit. *his flesh* = his body. The וֹ suff. is sing., and is an *individualizing* of the plural לְמֹצְאֵיהֶם; see on 3: 18 for explanation of the idiom. — מַרְפֵּא is a simple *Hiphilic* noun, *healing.*

(23) Above all [other] watching, guard well thy heart, for out of it are the issues of life.

I take מ before כל here to be comparative = *more than, rather than.* — מִשְׁמָר, *that which is kept*, or *custodia*, i. e. *keeping* or *watching over.* I have varied the shade of meaning in the version, in order to make it more expressive. — *Issues of life*, because the heart is the fountain, where, if good precepts are laid up and kept, they flow out, as it were, and become the occasion of virtuous conduct which tends to life.

(24) Turn away from thee perverseness of mouth; and craftiness of lips remove far from thee.

Both of the Acc. nouns are *abstracts*, and therefore strongly significant. — עִקְּשׁוּת designates *perversion*, lit. *contortion;* while לְזוּת (const. of לָזוּת from לוּז) means the same thing called by another name. Lit. the last means *deflection*, i. e. from the right way, or *a winding and turning course* instead of one straight forward. The *moral* idea designated by both, is *crafty deception*, whether by words or actions.

(25) Let thine eyes look straight forward, and thine eyelids keep a direct course before thee.

This is said in opposition to the obliquity and perverseness mentioned in the preceding verse. One must not turn aside from the plain way of integrity, nor even look wishfully at any other course. — *Eyelids* is of course, here, only another designation of the *eye* — i. e. a part for the whole.

(26) Ponder well the path of thy foot, that all thy ways may be steadfast.

פַּלֵּס, lit. *to weigh in a balance;* fig. as in the version. — *That all thy ways may be steadfast*, i. e. may be such as will never incline to go with the perverse, now in this direction and then in that. In other words: 'If the way is well chosen, there will be no occasion for deflection from it. The course will be a straight and steady one.'

(27) Turn not aside, to the right or to the left; withdraw thy foot from evil.

In v. 20 occurs הַט, Imp. of נָטָה, and an apoc. in Hiph.; here is תֵּט (of the same root) second pers. sing. apoc. of Imperf. in Kal, instead of the full form תִּטֶּה. In the apoc. form, the short *Hhireq* goes over into the long vowel *Tseri;* see Lex. In Hiphil it would be תַּט. The formation is somewhat irregular. This verse presents, in another form, the sentiment of the preceding one. The last clause gives a general and summary direction.

CHAP. V. VS. 1—23.

[This is one connected discourse, devoted to warning against adultery. It begins, as usual before, with summoning the disciple to hear attentively, that he may learn discretion, vs. 1, 2. The strange woman beguiles by flattery; but the sequel is bitter and destructive, vs. 3, 4. Her steps go down to Sheol; and she conceals and renders doubtful the path of life, vs. 5, 6. Again a careful listening is demanded; the disciple is urged to keep far from the way of the strange woman, and from her habitation, lest he should be robbed of his property, and he himself become a prey to the cruel, and all the fruits of his toil be seized by them, vs. 7—10. Bitter sorrow will follow his ruin, and much self-reproach will be uttered for not listening to teachers, and thus running into the greatest dangers, vs. 11—14. The young man is counselled to confine his enjoyments to their lawful and proper bounds; within them he may find all needful satisfaction. And these enjoyments should be exclusively his; while he should take pleasure, on his part, in rendering happy the wife of his youth. Her love alone should allure him, vs. 15—19. He must not seek strangers; for God looketh on all his doings, and will duly weigh them, vs. 20, 21. The iniquities of the wicked will surely overtake them, and they shall die through their great folly in rejecting instructions, vs. 22, 23.

The subject of this chapter has already been strikingly introduced, in 2: 16—22. The line of thought in both compositions must of course be for substance the same, inasmuch as both treat of one specific vice. But the *costume* of each is different. Even the construction of the parallelisms is varied, the present chapter being much less confined by strict adherence to rythm than the second. Indeed, there are several long-continued and closely-connected descriptions here, e. g. vs. 3—6, 8—14, 15—19, which are somewhat unusual in this book. Again, some of the verses here exhibit a scanty measure of words, e. g. vs. 14, 17. On the other hand, some verses are trimembral, as v. 19. So far as we can judge of Hebrew rythm, it is much less strictly regarded here, than is usual in the book of Proverbs.]

(1) My son, listen to wisdom, incline thine ear to understanding.

הַט, Hiph. Imper. Apoc., see in 4: 20, 27, what is said on הַט and הֵט. The form of this verse is the same as before, on like occasions. The mode of address amounts to an almost established formula of compellation, in consequence of its frequent repetition. By a Maqqeph after הַט, the punctators have contrived to make this and the following word into a kind of compound word = הַקְשִׁיבָה, and corresponding to it.

(2) In order to preserve thoughtfulness, and that thy lips may keep knowledge.

The לְ before the Inf. indicates design or object. — מְזִמּוֹת, (in the good sense), *thoughtfulness* or *reflection*. This may exist for purposes of either good or evil; the context will usually show which is meant. — Instead of another Inf. with לְ, we have now an Imperf. preceded by וְ, which is equivalent, and is often employed in a continued representation. See the same usage in 2 : 8, and the remarks there made upon it. — וְדַעַת, the וְ here = the conj. *that, and that,* § 152. B. *e.* — One other difficulty occurs, noticed neither by Umbreit nor Bertheau. The last verb is *plur.* masc., while שְׂפָתֶיךָ is apparently *feminine.* The true solution, as I apprehend it, lies in the fact, that the members of the human body, although usually *fem.,* are most of them employed occasionally as *masculine;* e. g. such is the case with the *hand, foot, finger, eye, arm, ear, tooth, beard,* etc.; see Ewald, § 174. *d.* The נ radical is also retained in the Imperf. here; a usage uncommonly frequent in this book. — Sentiment: 'The object of listening is to preserve thoughtfulness of mind, and to acquire the power of communicating knowledge.' The indication of this lies in the noun *lips,* which are the instrument of communication.

(3) For the lips of the strange woman distil honey, and her palate is smoother than oil.

נֹפֶת comes from נוּף. — תִּטֹּפְנָה, third plur. fem. of Imperf. Kal, from נָטַף. Here נ (as more usual) is assimilated, and a plur. *fem.* is joined with *lips;* directly the reverse of the usage in the preceding clause. This shows, of course, the *common* gender of the noun in usage. — *Palate* is only another name for *lips* or *tongue,* as we see in 8 : 7, where it is presented as *uttering* truth. Both of these words (*lips* and *palate*), have a tropical meaning here, i. e. they are equivalent to *speech, words.* So *honeyed words,* and *words smoother than oil,* are highly descriptive of persuasive and delusive flattery.

(4) But her end is bitter as wormwood, sharp as a two-edged sword.

Her end = the ultimate consequences brought about by her, or we might briefly say: *at last.* — מָרָה, *bitter*, in contrast with the *sweet* or *honey* of the preceding verse. — *Sharp* or *cutting* stands in contrast with *smooth*, in the verse before. — *Two-edged sword*, lit. *a sword of edges* or *mouths.* — Here are exhibited both usages in respect to the *article* after כְּ of similitude; the first noun has the article, the second omits it. Both usages are normal; see § 107. 3. *a.* When any word is added, that designates some attribute which defines the word that has the כְּ, then the article is generally omitted, because the thing is already made definite. Under this category falls the word כְּחֶרֶב, which is defined by פִּיּוֹת.

(5) Her feet go down to the grave, her steps take hold of the world beneath.

מָוֶת, as the context shows, plainly means here *the place of the dead*, i. e. the grave. So *Sheol* is parallel with it, having the meaning which is assigned to it in the version. — Sentiment: 'Her ways lead to certain and irremediable ruin.' — שְׁאוֹל is put at the beginning of the clause for the sake of emphasis.

(6) That she may not ponder the path of life, her ways are become unsteady, while she regards it not.

The latter part of this verse is somewhat obscure, and it has been variously rendered by different critics, some taking both verbs as second pers. sing.; others take both as the third pers. fem. — *Ways are unsteady*, נָעוּ, *vacillate.* This creates the danger; for how can she be certain, in such a case, of choosing safety? — It is moreover added, that she is regardless of this vacillation, and therefore is in the greater danger still. In other words: 'She is so busied and perplexed with her vacillating course, that she fails to ponder the path of life.' — תֵּדַע (from יָדַע), *to care for, to take knowledge of*, see Lex.

(7) And now, children, hearken to me; and turn not away from the words of my mouth.

Another formula employed in calling attention; only we have the plural here, viz., *sons*, and not *my son*. In פִי, the *Yodh* suff. (= *of me*) coalesces with the Yodh of the noun, and so one Yodh falls out, as is usual in such cases.

(8) Remove thy way far from her; and come not near the door of her house.

The second clause repeats the sentiment of the first, but gives to it a more graphic shape.

(9) That thou mayest not give to others thy bloom, nor thy years to a cruel [master.]

For הוֹד, as designating *youthful bloom* or *splendor*, see Dan. 10: 8. Hos. 14: 7. The idea here expressed I take to be this, viz., that the adulterer was of course exposed to a punishment for his crime, and this punishment usually terminated in his being sold into slavery; and sold, probably, to some hard master, in the way of punishment. The Levitical law inflicted death for adultery, Deut. 22: 22, seq. If the injured person prosecuted him who did the injury, he might insist on this penalty; but if he chose to act more mildly, he might sell the offender into bondage, while the price obtained was accepted in part as a mulct for the crime. The idea of *bondage through life* seems to be suggested by the word שְׁנוֹת *(years)* of the text.— *Cruel* [*master*], was such an one as the injured man would be very likely to choose, in the way of retribution.

(10) That strangers may not be replenished with thy wealth; nor thy painful toil be in the house of a stranger.

What a slave earns, of course goes to his master, and becomes his כֹּחַ.— Or, in the present case, it may be that forfeiture of the goods of the offender to the injured, as a part of the penalty. — *Painful toil* is service performed in bondage, the avails of which are stored in the house of the master.

(11) For thou wilt moan in thy latter end, when thy body and thy flesh are consumed.

בְּשָׂרְךָ, *body*, originally *the whole body* in distinction from נֶפֶשׁ. — שְׁאֵר belongs mostly to poetry, but is limited in its meaning to *flesh*. Both together, as here, comprise the complete whole or entirety of the human physical system. Meaning: 'When total ruin comes, as it will at last come, then thou wilt bemoan thyself.'

(12) Then shalt thou say: How have I hated instruction, and my heart despised reproof!

Then shalt thou say, for וְ and the Perf., see § 124. 6. *a.* — *How have I hated*, etc., that is: 'Very much have I hated, etc.'

(13) And I have not hearkened to the voice of my teachers, and to my instructors I have not inclined mine ear.

The force of אֵיךְ, in the preceding verse, may extend also to this, and we may translate: *And how have I refused to hearken*, etc.! — מוֹרָי (Qamets by reason of the pause), Part. noun of Hiph., root יָרָה, מוֹרָי has a suff. pronoun (ְי–), and is in the plural.

(14) I was well-nigh in all evil, in the midst of the assembly and of the congregation.

כִּמְעַט, *almost*, *prope*, or (as above) *well-nigh*. — *In all evil*, i. e. evil of every kind, or rather, *the worst evil*. — *In the midst of the assembly*, etc., who are here supposed to surround him, and to condemn and punish him by stoning him to death; for so were adulterers dealt with, Ezek. 16 : 40.— עֵדָה, *counselling assembly*, who had judicial power. — Here ends the lamentation. It is followed by counsel and caution, such as, if obeyed, would save the repetition of the like evils and dangers.

(15) Drink waters from thine own cistern, and flowing streams from thine own well.

Figurative language is here employed to designate the demeanor of the young married man, who desires to live chastely and innocently. He must confine himself to his own lawful sources of enjoyment, and not go abroad in quest of other sources. — נוֹזְלִים, Part. noun, designating *flowing streams*. The imagery is drawn from a well with a living spring, which sends forth streams of water.

(16) Let [not] thy fountains issue forth abroad, thy water-brooks in the streets.

The meaning of this, as it stands in the Heb. text, seems to be simply, that his water-sources are not to be confined to himself, but others also may have the enjoyment of them. Yet the very next verse *contradicts* this view. There seems to be no feasible way of solution left, except we adopt the reading of the Sept. and Aquila, who both prefix אַל before יָפֻצוּ, e. g. μὴ ὑπερεκχείσθω. I have inserted this negative in brackets in the version. So De Dieu, Umbreit, and Bertheau. Sentiment: 'Guard well thy house against the approach of seductive persons.'

(17) Let them be for thee alone, and not for strangers with thee.

This confirms what has been said above. This *cistern* and these *well-streams* are to be *his alone*. — *With thee*, i. e. in common or in company with thee.

(18) Let thy fountain be blessed, that thou mayest have joy from the wife of thy youth;

Blessed, viz., with children or offspring, so much the object of desire and joy in the East. — So the sequel: *mayest have joy*. The wife of his youth brings him children, which makes him a *joyful* father. This would not take place, in case the husband sought after harlots.

(19) A lovely hind and a graceful doe — let her breasts satiate thee at all times, with her love do thou continually inebriate thyself.

The *hind* and *doe* are a continued description of the *wife of youth*, and in apposition with the latter. Or we may supply תְּהִי from 6 : 18. — *Intoxicated with love* is a common expression among us; and so with the Hebrews. The meaning is, that the chaste husband should find ample scope to satisfy his desires, when confining himself to the wife of his youth. It is not an exhortation to excessive venery, but merely a declaration, that in a chaste conjugal union there is ample means for the full satisfaction of reasonable conjugal desires. — תִּשְׁגֶּה means to *stagger* or *reel* as a man intoxicated, and is to be taken figuratively of course here, as designating ample enjoyment of love.

(20) And why shouldest thou intoxicate thyself, my son, with a strange woman; and embrace the bosom of a stranger?

The latter clause of the verse explains the former. The intoxicating passion of unlimited sexual desire, is what the writer means to describe. What need of this, when he has ample sources of enjoyment at home?

(21) For directly before the eyes of Jehovah are the ways of man; yea, all his ways doth he ponder.

נֹכַח, *coram, directly before;* of course, *in full and plain view.* This verse gives the reason why the remonstrative question of the preceding verse was asked: 'Why shouldest thou do so, when Jehovah's eyes are upon thee, and he will bring thee to judgment?'

(22) His iniquities shall ensnare him — the wicked; and by the cords of transgression he shall be held fast.

In יִלְכְּדֻנוֹ, נ is a demonstrative ending before the ו, and the latter is a pronoun *anticipative* or *pleonastic*, which is explained by the noun that follows, § 119. 6. n. 3. — Sentiment: 'His wicked deeds will involve him in toils, and hold him fast for punishment.'

(23) He shall die without instruction, and through the abundance of his folly shall he reel.

The pronoun הוּא prefixed to the verb is emphatic. — *Without instruction*, i. e. because he refused to receive any, and through lack of it he now perishes. — יִשְׁגֶּה refers back to vs. 19, 20. There the husband has ample enjoyment of love, or is *inebriated* with it; here the transgressor *reels* by reason of the fulness of the cup of retribution which he is compelled, like criminals about to die, to drink to the dregs.

Vs. 15—23 are remarkable, in this book, for a continued series of tropical language. The delicate subject introduced is purposely clothed with this costume, in order to avoid anything which is unseemly in expression.

CHAP. VI. vs. 1—19.

[Only vs. 1—19 of this chapter stand in mutual connection. Vs. 20—35 belong to a theme which seems to comprehend the whole of 6: 20—9: 18; consequently, this part should have been joined to chap. vii. Here, vs. 1—19 are subdivided into four parts, viz. (*a*) Vs. 1—5. (*b*) 6—11. (*c*) 12—15. (*d*) 16—19. The first treats of becoming surety for the debts of others; the second, of idleness or sloth; the third, of crafty deceit; the fourth, of seven things which Jehovah hates.

In (*a*), comprising 1—5, warning is given against becoming ensnared by pledges of surety, and advice to hasten an accommodation in relation to them, by earnest efforts, in order that the person pledged may escape being sold into slavery, when he has no ability to redeem the pledge.]

(1) My son, if thou art pledged for thy friend — hast shaken hands for a stranger;

The sentence is unfinished, and is completed in the next verse, only so far as the *protasis* is concerned. The אִם, the sign of conditionality, is to be mentally carried forward through all the four clauses of vs. 1, 2. — עָרַבְתָּ, *given pledge, become surety*, i. e. for the payment of another's debt; and this, whether he be friend, רֵעַ, or enemy, זָר. The latter word has the article, because it distinguishes a specific class; the former would have it, if the suffix did not prevent it, § 108. 2. — *To shake hands* is both our gesture and expression, in making unwritten contracts, even at the present time. The Hebrews said: *Strike hands*, i. e. bring them together with force. Both actions mean the same thing. Those who *strike hands*, upon a contract offered and accepted, agree mutually to abide by it.

(2) [If] thou hast become ensnared by the words of thy mouth; art caught by the words of thy mouth;

Both of these are plainly a part of the conditional *protasis*. For brevity's sake, neither אִם nor וְ is repeated before the three last clauses. This adds to the energy and force of the description.

(3) Do this then, my son, and free thyself, for thou hast come into the power of thy friend; go cast thyself down as a suppliant, and strongly urge thy friend.

הִנָּצֵל, Niph. *reflexive*, as often. — *Come into the power of thy friend*, i. e. hast given him a right to enforce payment of the debt ensured, even by reducing thee to bondage. — רֵעֶךָ here is not the same as in v. 1, but the friend *to whom* (not *for whom)* the pledge is given. — הִתְרַפֵּס, lit. *give up thyself to be trodden upon*, i. e. *prostrate thyself;* and here, plainly, in the way of supplication. — רֵעֶיךָ is not plur., but sing. with suff. The original form of this is רֵעֶה, and many nouns from roots ל״ה, preserve in the sing., before a suff., the original *Yodh* of the root, and thus take apparently the form of the plural. See § 91. 9; and also a full illustration in Ewald, § 256. *b*. The two phases of the same word result merely from a difference in orthography.

(4) Give not sleep to thine eyes, nor slumber to thine eyelids; (5) Free thyself as a hind from the hand — even as a bird from the hand of the fowler.

V. 4 warns against all inactivity and delay; v. 5 presents the danger as such, that it should be speedily escaped. Of course, *from the hand*, in the first instance, is elliptical, *of the hunter* being spontaneously implied, according to the suggestion made by the next clause. Bertheau changes the reading, and puts in מִפַּח, *from the net*, instead of מִיָּד; and so Sept., Syr., and Targum. The sense is good; but the change is unnecessary.

(*b*) *Verses* 6—11.

[Exhortation to diligence. The slothful man should go to the ant for instruction, who timely provides for herself, vs. 6—8. If he will not rouse up to action, then poverty and want will speedily destroy him, vs. 9—11.]

(6) Go to the ant, thou sluggard, consider her ways, and be wise. (7) To her is no leader, overseer, or ruler.

רְאֵה, *see* mentally, i. e. consider. — *No overseer*, etc., that is, the ant is not compelled by superiors to labor, but, from the love of diligent employment, she engages in it. Whether, as a matter of fact, the ants, like the bees, have their leaders, does not seem to be apprehended by the writer. He assumes the common opinion, viz. that they have none.

(8) In summer, she prepares her food; at harvest-time, she has gathered her provender.

In the early part of the summer, קַיִץ, she begins her work; and when *the harvest is cut down*, בַּקָּצִיר, she has already collected her store. Hence the second verb is in the Perf., to denote that the collection has been made antecedently to the harvesting.

(9) How long, O sluggard, wilt thou lie down? When wilt thou rise up from thy sleep?

עַד־מָתַי, *until when*, in reference to the time when sleeping shall end. In the second clause stands simply מָתַי, in reference to the beginning of waking up. This and the following verse constitute a *protasis*, to which v. 11 is the *apodosis*.

(10) A little sleep, a little slumber, a little folding of the hands to lie down.

This presents the anticipated answer of the sluggard to the preceding questions. He begs longer quietude; at least that he may have indulgence for a short period more. Both of the nouns, *sleep* and *slumber*, are in the *plural*, in order to denote the continuance or expansion of such a state, — plur. intensive. — *Folding of the hands* is the putting them into a state of inaction or of rest, and is preparatory to the quiet here desired.— Such is the anticipated answer of the sluggard. The consequences follow:

(11) And then shall thy poverty come like a traveller, and thy want like a man of the shield.

וּבָא, *and so shall come*, § 152. B. *a*. 3, i. e. the וּ is *consecutive* or *consequential*. — כִּמְהַלֵּךְ, not simply as one who walks leisurely, for the Piel form denotes intensity; therefore, *as a courier, runner*, etc., who moves rapidly. If a *robber-traveller* be meant, as many assert, then we might translate by *highwayman*. — *Man of the shield*, i. e. one who is armed with a shield, and therefore a soldier or invading enemy. — Two things are denoted by this imagery; *(a)* That idleness will *quickly* bring poverty; *(b)* That it will come as a *destroyer*.

(c) Verses 12—15.

[The vices here enumerated, are such as will bring sudden and irremediable destruction.]

(12) A worthless man, a man of wickedness, goeth forth with a perverse mouth.

Perhaps the true shape of the first clause is thus: *A worthless man is a bad man,* i. e. being *useless* (בְּלִיַּעַל) is being *wicked.* But on the whole, I rather incline to the climactic sense, as given in the version. Then the meaning of the verse stands thus: 'A very bad man is he, whose mouth habitually speaks perverse things or deceits.' — עִקְּשׁוּת is the Acc. of manner, and may be regarded as qualifying the noun that follows, § 104. 1. n. 1.

(13) He winketh with his eyes, he talketh with his feet, he maketh signs with his fingers.

Here (as often in this book) the י of plurality before the suff. ו in nouns, is left out in two cases. The Qeri has noted and corrected them. This, however, is a matter of indifference, as it changes not the manner of reading. All the modes of communication here described are characteristic of plotters and sly intriguers, who deal secretly in this way, in order that their *words* may not be adduced in testimony against them. — *Maketh signs,* is the original meaning of מֹרֶה, Part. Hiph. of יָרָה, the ו after מ being omitted, because it is quiescent. Every one's recollection will supply him with examples of like doings among intriguers.

(14) Perversions are in the heart of him who deviseth evil, who is ever stirring up contentions.

That is, *he is very perverse,* etc., the plural of intensity being here plainly and significantly employed. — *Stirring up contentions,* viz. between neighbors and friends. — מְדָנִים belongs, as to its vowels, to the Qeri מִדְיָנִים. The Kethibh should be pointed מְדָנִים, hardly a form that needs correction, perhaps, for it reappears in v. 19, and is not there corrected. Here, the Imperf. follows (as often) in the sequel of a preceding participle. Both denote *habitual* action.

(15) Therefore shall his calamity come suddenly; he shall be dashed in pieces, and there will be no remedy.

Such is the consequence of perverse and fraudulent dealing, which rouses up strife. A remediless evil awaits it, which will come suddenly, and of course unexpectedly.

(d) Verses 16—19.

Seven evils are next specified, this being a favorite number, indicative of completion or fulness. They are not climactic, for some of the worse stand near the beginning.

(16) These six things Jehovah hateth; yea, seven are the abomination of his soul.

It is not unfrequent among the Hebrews to begin with one less than the full sum intended, and then to add that one as the sign of completion; comp. Amos. 1: 3, 6, 9, 11, 13. 2: 1, 4, 6.—I prefer the Kethibh תּוֹעֲבוֹת, because the plural is *intensive;* which is altogether apposite here. The enumeration follows:

(17) Lofty eyes; a lying tongue; and hands shedding innocent blood; (18) A heart devising plans of evil; feet swift to run unto evil.

Here, in לָרוּץ, the לְ defines the purpose for which the feet are made *swift.* In לָרָעָה, the לְ shows for what object this is done. The article, implied in לָ of the last word (= *the evil*), refers back to the preceding אָוֶן, which is synonymous, so that this is virtually a case of *repetition*, § 107. pref. remarks.

(19) Who breatheth forth falsehood—a lying witness—and stirreth up strife between brethren.

יָפִיחַ, Imperf. Hiph. of פּוּחַ, here in a clause in which אֲשֶׁר (*he who*) must of course be implied. We have a like expression: 'He utters falsehood with every breath.'—עֵד שָׁקֶר is in apposition with this implied אֲשֶׁר, and explanatory of it. The *dash* in the version is designed to indicate this.—מְשַׁלֵּחַ, Part. after the Imperf.; often is such a sequency to be met with; more often, however, the Part comes first, and then the Imperf. follows. Both denote *customary* action.

CHAP. VI. 20—35.

[As stated above, this belongs to a theme, which, in its full extent, occupies 6 : 20—9 : 18. This large portion, however, is subdivided into three parts: (1) Chap. 6 : 20—35. (2) Chap. vii. viii. (3) Chap. ix. — As usual, the writer begins with an exhortation to hearken; and then he adds promises of good in case of obedience, vs. 1—3. Lay hold of, and make thyself familiar with, parental admonition, saith he, and then it will guide and watch over thee, and be thy light, vs. 20—23. It will keep thee from temptations to defilement, v. 24. Lust not after beauty, for unchastity will impoverish thee, and adultery expose thee to the loss of life, vs. 25, 26. If a man takes fire into his bosom, his clothes will be burned; and burning coals will scorch the feet, vs. 27, 28. So with the adulterer, v. 29. Even a thief, who steals to satisfy hunger, although he may not be despised, yet, if caught, will have to make ample retribution, vs. 30, 31. An adulterer is destitute of reason, and suicidal; he will incur disgrace not to be wiped away, vs. 32, 33. Jealousy is an outrageous passion, and will not be propitiated by any bribes, vs. 34, 35.

Here the subject of 2 : 16—22 and 5 : 3—14 is again resumed, but it is presented in an attitude somewhat different. The whole being taken together, (and chap. vii. must also be specially joined with the present section), it seems to betoken compositions originally different, which were given out at different times. But here they are collected into one *fasciculus*. So far as we can judge from the style and manner of the pieces, they appear to come, at least they might come, from one and the same hand. They are not expressly ascribed to Solomon; but the eulogics of wisdom, so often repeated in this part of the book, naturally turn our thoughts to him. And surely he had good reason to understand, and could well describe, the mischiefs of lascivious gratification. Possibly the pieces were written by other hands, and *compiled* by Solomon. In that case, it would be natural to speak of them as his. When we compare 10. 1—22. 16, expressly ascribed to Solomon, the kinds of composition, or subject (so to speak) is so different, that there is hardly room to find analogies of style with any success. But, whoever wrote that portion of the book now before us, wrote what is palpably true; and this is sufficient for our purpose.]

(20) Keep, my son, the commandment of thy father, and forsake not the instruction of thy mother.

Comp. 1: 8, where in substance the same formula is found.

(21) Bind them upon thy heart continually; fasten them around thy neck.

Comp. 3:3. Here the idea seems to be, that the commands are inscribed upon the ornaments, or the vestments, of the breast and throat. Meaning: 'Keep them carefully, and always make them conspicuous.'

(22) When thou goest forth, it shall lead thee; when thou liest down, it shall watch over thee; and when thou awakest, it shall commune with thee.

The sing. here, *it*, refers to מִצְוָה of v. 20. — תְּשִׂיחֶךָ, governing the Acc. of the object which it affects, like יְגוּרְךָ, *dwell with thee*, as we must translate Ps. 5:5. The meaning is, that it will suggest to him themes of meditation in respect to a course of safe conduct.

(23) For a torch is the command, and instruction a light, and a way of life is instructive admonitions.

Torch and *light* are symbols of the clear and lucid teaching of parental care. — *Instructive admonitions* are called *a way of life*, because they point out the way and means of life. — A special design of these comes next into view.

(24) To keep thee from the base woman, the stranger of flattering tongue.

This seems, at first, to refer to a *foreign* prostitute. The latter part of the verse is so marked by the accents, that it should be rendered thus: *from the flattery of the stranger tongue.* But as we have *woman*, a *concrete* noun, in the first clause, it is hardly probable, that an *abstract* noun would correspond to it in the second. We may render חֶלְקַת, then, as the const. fem. adj., from חָלָק, put in construction with לָשׁוֹן. In this case we may carry forward מֵ to נָכְרִיָּה; or (with the accentuators) we may dispose of it, by making it an adjective agreeing with לָשׁוֹן (fem.) and translate thus: *flattering with a foreign tongue.*

(25) Lust not after her beauty in thy heart; let her not captivate thee with her eyelids.

יַפְעַף makes with a suff., יַפְעַפֶּיהָ. — *Eyelids* here means the *lashes of the eyelids*, which the Hebrew women and others in the East adorned by coloring them with a dye, (פּוּךְ or *stibium),* and making them more dark and strikingly defined. Great stress is laid on this, among female adornments in the East, even down to the present time. The eyebrow also is stained with it. Its aid in creating artificial and alluring beauty, is here plainly alluded to.

(26) For by reason of a woman who playeth the harlot, [one cometh] to a piece of bread; and [another] man's wife hunts after the precious [life].

A verse of some difficulty, because it is elliptical. — *To a piece of bread,* is brachylogy, such as belongs to popular apothegms — like the Greek *εἰς κόρακας!* Of course תָּבוֹא, or some such word, is implied before this phrase; as in the Greek above, *βάλλε* is implied. — זוֹנָה, a Participial, and translated above so as to retain its *verbal* sense. Meaning: 'A man comes to abject poverty by lavishing his money on harlots.' But a still greater evil is the concomitant of *adultery.* In this case, a man's *life* was forfeited, according to the Mosaic law, Deut. 22:22, comp. Ezek. 16:40. — Meaning: 'An adulteress allures to that which may cost a man his life, the price of his life.' I have inserted *another* in the version, merely to guard against mistake of the meaning.

In this simple way, the crimes of fornication and adultery are compared, as to the respective evils which ensue. The first impoverishes, by demanding money as the purchase of her favors; the second destroys what is far more valuable than money, viz., *life.* This makes the whole very significant. Bertheau and some others render thus: *Since for a harlot, even a piece of bread,* i. e. this is enough, or she will be satisfied with this; *but the wife of a man will ensnare the precious* [life]. But this is making the writer merely to say, that harlot-hire is very cheap, and the price of adultery very high. But against this is the fact, that the latter is not usually venal for money; and also, that the moral tone of the verse is much lowered in this way. The writer sets himself against every kind of illicit intercourse, (see 5:15, seq.), and dissuades from it. The shape given to the text by Bertheau, would seem to imply no more than that a man can gratify his passions, at a much cheaper rate than adultery will cost. Is this to the writer's purpose?—יְקָרָה fem. of יָקָר, like יְחִידָה and כָּבוֹד, is a tropical and affectionate designation or qualification of the *soul* or *life*.

(27) Can a man take up fire in his bosom, and his clothes not be burned? (28) Can a man walk on burning coals, and his feet not be scorched?

בֶּגֶד, in the plur., is here employed as *fem.;* as it sometimes is, Ewald, § 174. *d.* *β.*—תִּכָּוֶינָה, Imperf. Niph. third plur. fem., from כָּוָה. These questions are too plain to need any answer. The close of the comparison follows therefore immediately:

(29) So whoever approacheth the wife of his friend, shall not be innocent, not any one who toucheth her.

If the last clause, (which now is brachylogy), were filled out, it would run thus: *Every one who toucheth her* [*shall not be innocent.*] This I have briefly but virtually expressed in the version.

(30) Men do not despise a thief, when he stealeth to satisfy his appetite, because he is hungry.

יָבוּזוּ, Imperf., marking *customary* action. Men have regard to the temptation of such a man, and look on his fault with a feeling of pity. Here the first כִּי = *when;* the second = *because.*

(31) But when caught, he must render a recompense seven-fold; all the wealth of his house shall he give.

In Ex. 22 : 1, a *five-fold* restitution is enjoined. The *seven* here designated has therefore the usual figurative meaning of *seven*, i. e. ample, complete. In aggravated cases, doubtless the *mulct* would extend to all his little property.

(32) He that committeth adultery with a woman, lacketh understanding; he who will destroy his own life, even he doeth this.

Both participles here, as often elsewhere, imply their own subjects or Nom. cases, viz., *he who* or *whoever*. — הוּא is emphatic, and is so translated. — יַעֲשֶׂנָּה, *will do it*, viz., the adulterous deed. It implies, that only such as lack understanding will act in this suicidal manner.

(33) Stripes and shame shall he meet with, and his reproach shall not be blotted out.

This presents the least punishment that can follow the crime in question; but even this at best is but a sad alternative of the other.

(34) For jealousy makes an enraged man; and he will not spare in the day of revenge.

חֲמַת־גָּבֶר, lit. *is the rage of a man;* the version gives the substance of the idea, in conformity with our own idiom. The adulterer may count upon the vengeance of the injured and enraged husband.

(35) He will accept of no ransom; he will not yield, when thou shalt make large the bribe.

יִשָּׂא פְּנֵי, lit. *lift up the face*, i. e. to make one to look up with courage and hope. The contrary is: *His countenance fell*, i. e. he looked sad and stern. Here it is tropically used for *accepting*. No ransom will cause him to pass by the offence. — שֹׁחַד is *the bribe* offered for propitiation; but in vain, for *he will not yield* to the offer, *will not consent* to it.

CHAP. VII. INTRODUCTION.

This is surely a vivid picture of the evils connected with the crime in question. Especially does the writer bear hard upon the *adulterer;* whom he considers as much the most guilty. The punishment of death by the magistrate, when the crime is fully detected, or the vengeance inflicted by jealousy, is set forth in colors adapted to deter men devoted to illicit enjoyments from their pursuit, if they would but duly contemplate the consequences.

CHAP. VII. 1—27.

[The great danger to which the crime of adultery exposes one, has been set forth in strong colors. The writer now proceeds, in the way of forewarning, to set forth the alluring and deceitful arts practised by the adulteress (see vs. 19, 20), in order to inveigle and mislead the unwary youth. Forewarned, forearmed. If he gives diligent heed to the words of the faithful monitor, he may learn to shun the ways of crime and destruction. As usual, at the outset he is exhorted to hearken, and to impress deeply on his heart what is said, vs. 1—5. The remainder of the chapter is occupied with graphically describing the demeanor and wanton actions of the enticing adulteress.]

(1) My son, keep my sayings, treasure up my commands with thee. (2) Keep my commands, and thou shalt live; and let my instruction be as the pupil of thine eye.

וֶחְיֵה, Imper. in the sequel after another Imper. = Imperf. 2d person, § 127. 2, comp. in 4:4.—אִישׁוֹן, lit. *little man* of the eye, has reference to the reflected image of a man, seen in the pupil of that organ. The Greeks called it *κόρη* or *κοράσιον, damsel* or *little damsel;* the Latins, *pupa* or *pupilla,* of the same meaning; and so our English word *pupil* means of course the same, for it is merely the Latin word *pupilla* abridged.—As to the last clause, *keep* (from the first clause) might be mentally inserted before *instruction;* and this would be normal exegesis. Equally well here, however, does the implied copula-verb answer the purpose, as in the version. In either case, the meaning is: 'Let my instruction be watchfully guarded, or kept, as one guards the sight of his eyes.' Comp. 3:3. 6:21.

(3) Bind them on thy fingers; inscribe them on the tablet of thine heart.

קָשְׁרֵם, *bind them*, masc. pronoun, referring to אֲמָרַי in v. 1; and so of the next verb and suffix. — *On thy fingers*, refers to rings with large signets, on which were inscribed some weighty sentences or maxims; as in later days, and more at large, on the phylacteries. — *Transcribe them on the tablet of thine heart*, expresses the deep and abiding characters in which the precepts should be written, so that they can neither be lost nor erased.

(4) Say to wisdom: My sister art thou; and call understanding a familiar acquaintance.

That is, cultivate habits of the most endearing intimacy with, and friendship for, wisdom and understanding. — אָתְּ in Pause, for אַתְּ, second pers. fem. pronoun. The *Dagh.* in תּ final is a compensative sign of the נ which is assimilated; for the full form would be אַנְתְּ. When the word is written in the abridged form, (as in our text), the תְּ still remains, because the Dagh. virtually represents another letter before this תְּ, as the full form shows. — מֹדָע (= מוֹדָע) is a Hoph. Part., here used as a noun concrete; for *acquaintance* here designates a person, as in our English usage. — The true meaning is given above in the version.

Next comes a cogent reason why so much attention and care should be given to the acquisition of wisdom and understanding.

(5) In order to keep thee from the strange woman, from the stranger who flattereth with her words.

The last clause being a *relative* one, אֲשֶׁר is implied before the verb הֶחֱלִיקָה in Hiphil. — אֲמָרֶיהָ in the Acc.; lit. *who maketh smooth her words.*— That there is good reason for such *keeping* or *restraint*, is now shown, in the sequel. It begins therefore with a כִּי *causal.*

(6) For through the window of my house, through the lattice-work, I looked.

אֶשְׁנַבִּי, *window-slats*, like our Venitian blinds, made to keep out the sun and rain, and let in the air. The word is a formative of Pilel., Dec. viii. — נִשְׁקָפְתִּי, Niph., (in Pause), because Kal is not in use ; lit. *I stooped myself*, i. e. took the attitude of *stooping*, in order to look attentively.

(7) That I might see among the simple, and observe among the sons, a lad destitute of understanding.

וָאֵרֶא, voluntative, (not *and I saw*, but *that I might see)*, as shown by the following אָבִינָה, whose paragogic ־ָה denotes the *voluntative*, § 48. 3. For the Qamets in וָ, see § 102. 2. *d.* אֵרֶא, first pers. of Imperf. Kal, from רָאָה, in the apoc. form, where short Hhireq of the praeformative goes over into Tseri ; see § 74. Note 3. *b.* In this class of verbs, what is effected by ־ָה paragogic elsewhere, is here effected by *apocope.* Hence the *voluntative* meaning. If the simple idea — *I saw* — were here meant, then we should have וָאֶרְאֶה. — אָבִינָה, Imperf. voluntative, without the ו conj. being written, although it is mentally carried forward from the preceding verb, and makes the verb *voluntative.*

(8) He was passing in the street near her corner, and treading the way to her house.

Her corner, i. e. a corner of the streets where she was wont to go, that she might meet with and decoy paramours. — פִּנָּה appears to have פָּנַן for its root. In Arabic, this root means to *divide.* — *The way to her house* may be rendered *the way of her house.* Our idiom gives preference to the first mode of expression.

(9) In the twilight — at evening — of the day, in the midst of the night, even the thick darkness.

נֶשֶׁף, lit. *in the breeze* of the night, i. e. the time when the cool wind begins to blow; comp. Gen. 3: 8. — עֶרֶב is the *evening* after the sun has set. — אִישׁוֹן (as in v. 2) is lit. *pupil of the eye;* but as that is in the centre or middle of the eye, so it designates here the *middle* of the night, i. e. midnight, when the darkness was greatest; but as the mode of expression is unusual, its meaning is made plain, by the epexegetical clause וַאֲפֵלָה.

(10) And lo! a woman — in order to meet him, in the attire of a harlot, and wary of mind.

שִׁית, in the sense of *attire,* is not common; but it is found also in Ps. 73: 6. Bertheau puts שִׁית זוֹנָה in apposition with אִשָּׁה, = *a woman — a harlot-dress;* meaning, by the last two words, to designate the woman herself. But this is not an easy or inviting construction. I take it to be simply the *Acc. of manner;* as rendered in the version — נְצֻרַת, fem. Part. in const. state, has been much controverted. But without any good reason; for *watchful, wary, guarded of mind,* appropriately describes such a wily personage.

(11) Noisy is she, and refractory; her feet abide not in her own house.

הֹמִיָּה, Part. Pres. fem of הָמָה, *noisy, bustling about,* instead of staying quietly at home. — סֹרָרֶת, Part. fem. in Pause, *refractory* or *contumacious,* as to the rules of order and decorum in her husband's house. Hence the sequel: *Her feet abide not at home,* the place for modest women.

(12) Now abroad, and then in the wide streets; and near to every corner she lurketh.

This is descriptive of her conduct, while she is hunting for her prey. Finding it not in one place, she goes to another.

(13) And she caught hold of him, and kissed him; she made up an impudent face, and said to him:

The description being finished, the narrative recommences. — הֵעֵזָה, Hiph. from עָזַז. We should expect to find a Dagh. form in the ז. Normally this would be so. But when the final syllable, in such a case, is toneless, (as here, the accent being on the penult), the doubling is in a goodly number of cases omitted; see § 66. n. 11, and also Ewald, § 193. *b.* § 63. *b.* Lit. it runs thus: *made strong her face;* which however has the meaning given above. — What she said, in order to lure her prey, now follows; and the address is dexterously managed.

(14) Peace-sacrifices are due from me; to-day I fulfil my vows.

עָלָי, lit. *on me*, i. e. they are on me as a duty to be performed, or the obligation lies *on me* to make the offerings; a sense frequently conveyed by עַל, Lex. A. 1. *a.* *γ.* The *offerings* here named are those of thanksgiving and joy, on account of blessings received. Of such offerings the guests partook in part; so that a rich feast is here virtually set before the simpleton, under the garb of a religious usage. The pretence is, that she had before bound herself by vows, to make the offerings in question. This therefore is represented to be a lucky day for the invited guest. Umbreit thinks there is no good evidence of a feast-meal on such occasions; but see Lev. 7: 13—17. For the *peace-offerings* themselves, see Lev. 3: 1, seq. For *vow-offerings*, see Deut. 23: 22. Ps. 50: 14. Ecc. 5: 3, 4.

(15) Therefore have I come forth to meet thee; to seek diligently thy face, that I might find thee.

לְשַׁחֵר, in Piel, and therefore with an augmented force, which is expressed in the version above. The Guttural ח excludes the Daghesh. For וָ before the last word, see § 152. B. *e.*

(16) With coverlets have I strowed my couch, with tapestry of Egyptian thread.

מַרְבַדִּים means the *coverlet*, and רָבַדְתִּי *the action of spreading it on the couch*. The ב of the noun should normally have a Dagh. lene; but it seems to be left *Raphe* or soft here, seemingly in order to imitate the sound of the verb רָפַד = רָבַד, and having the same meaning. It is written in the same way (Raphe) in Prov. 31: 22. It indicates, in this case, merely a softening of the ב so as to resemble the פ. *Why?* is a question which only the Masorites of ancient times could well answer. At all events, the orthography is abnormal.— חֲטֻבוֹת, *striped stuffs;* i. e. *tapestry*, which was usually figured or striped by the aid of needlework. The corresponding Arabic verb (חטב) means: *to be particolored.* —*Egyptian thread*, doubtless means *fine thread* or *yarn*, either of cotton or flax. To speak of the *tapestry* in this way, conveyed a meaning of like import with our phraseology, when we speak of a *Turkish carpet*, meaning the *best* of carpeting.

(17) I have sprinkled my bed with myrrh, aloes, and cinnamon.

The last three nouns are in the second Acc., which indicates here the means employed, or the instrument, etc. The spices named were costly and favorite ones in the East; comp. Ps. 45: 8.—נַפְתִּי from נוּף. Of course, the liquid *extract* from these spices is meant; for the substances themselves would hardly be commodious for *sprinkling*.

(18) Come, then, let us take our fill of love until the morning, let us enjoy ourselves in amorous delight.

לְכָה, from לֵךְ Imp. of יָלַךְ, the *hortative* form. The plur. דֹּדִים and also אֳהָבִים, are plur. *intensive*, i. e. they augment the force of the words. Plainly the plur. here is not one of *abstraction*.—נִתְעַלְּסָה, Hithp. of עָלַס and hortatory; the word is a weakened form of עָלַץ. The verb having here a reflective sense, a preposition (בְּ) is inserted after it, in order to govern the noun and express more fully the instrumentality. The article (involved in בַּ) is employed in the way of speciality, i. e. delights appropriate to the nature of the case.

(19) For the man is not at home, he has gone a long journey.

בְּבֵיתוֹ, lit. *in his house*—the Heb. mode of saying: *at home.*—הָאִישׁ, *the man*, i. e. the master of the house.—דֶּרֶךְ, *way*, and trop. *journey.*—מֵרָחוֹק, *distant*, lit. *of* or *belonging to distance, of far away.* It might mean *from a distance*, but then a verb of *returning*, or the like, must precede it.

(20) A purse of money hath he taken in his hand; on the day of the full moon he will return home.

Return home, lit. *enter his house.*—The *purse of money* intimates a long delay, one which he expects will be attended with expense.

(21) She turneth him aside by the abundance of her speech; she forceth him along by her smooth talk.

הִטַּתּוּ = הִטַּתְהוּ, fem. Perf. Hiph. of נָטָה, with suff.—לֶקַח usually means *doctrine*, but here it is = *taking* or *persuasive words.*—*Smooth talk*, lit. *smoothness of her lips.*' *Lips* is to be taken tropically, as designating *what the lips utter*, i. e. *talk.*

(22) He that goeth after her, will speedily go as an ox to the slaughter, yea, as to a foot-chain for the chastisement of a fool.

הוֹלֵךְ here does not seem to refer specifically to the individual נַעַר of v. 7, but to any and every one, who is led away. The Part. involves its own indefinite Nom., i. e. *whoever.* Speedy mischief ensues; and evil that is unavoidable and disgraceful; for the ox cannot escape his fate, and the chain disgraces and renders powerless the fool. I have, in my version, carried forward אַל before טֶבַח, to the noun עֶכֶס.

(23) (Until an arrow shall pierce through his liver); even as a bird hasteneth to the snare, and knoweth not that it is for his life.

וְלֹא יָדַע, *knoweth not*, may be applied to the *bird* rushing heedlessly into the snare. — The last two verses are, as they strike us, somewhat involved and apparently defective. V. 23 has three clauses, the first of which seems to belong to something which should precede, i. e. either to the last clause of v. 22, or to something dropped from the text. There are three comparisons of the simpleton here; (1) To an ox going to the slaughter-bench. (2) To a criminal chained by the feet in order to punish him and to prevent escape. (3) To a bird hastening heedlessly into a snare. The simpleton, like the latter, knows not that his life is in danger, and therefore rushes on. Interpreters disagree about the detail of the passage; and, in like manner, the ancient versions, Sept., Syr., Chald., give involved and difficult meanings; which shows, either that they had a text before them different from the present, or else that they assigned to the text, vowels different from the present Masoretic ones. That the text has in some way been disturbed, seems quite probable from the fact of its present *abnormal* condition. But I shall make no attempt to amend it, for this must be done by mere conjecture. The general meaning of the two verses is quite plain: ‘Unexpected evils will speedily come upon the adulterer.’

(24) And now, children, hearken to me; listen to the words of my mouth. (25) Let not thine heart turn aside to her ways; do not wander in her paths.

יֵשְׂטְ hortative form of שָׂטָה, Kal. Imperf.; see § 74. n. 3. *c.* — תֵּתַע, same form (but of 2d person) from תָּעָה, § 74. n. 3. *b. c.* — This is a general conclusion and deduction, in respect to the whole matter as already represented.

(26) For many are the slain which she hath cast down; even mighty men are all her *slain*.

I take the exact shape of the Hebrew to be as in the version, because רַבִּים is placed first, and therefore becomes (as usual) a *predicate* of the sentence. The sense is at all events virtually given in the version. — הִפִּילָה, Hiph. of נָפַל. — In the second clause, the Hebrew runs thus: *even the mighty are all her slain*, i. e. she slays all of them who go in unto her, but not all the mighty among men. The appeal is on this wise: 'If even the *mighty* are destroyed by her, how can the mere *youngling* expect to come off with impunity?'

(27) Her house is the way to the under-world, going down to the chambers of death.

Lit. *the ways of Sheol*, i. e. the way *par excellence*, the plur. of intensity. 'He who goes to her house, goes assuredly in the way to Sheol,' — is the meaning. — יוֹרְדוֹת, Part. Pres. plur., and fem.; for דַּרְכֵי (with which it agrees) is of the *common* gender, and so may have a fem. participle, as here. — *Chambers of death*, (i. e. of *the dead*, abstract for concrete), has reference to lodging-places built in under-ground tombs, for the reception of the dead.

Thus concludes this grave and earnest warning against adulterous intercourse. To see its full force, one must reflect that, by the Mosaic law, the adulterer could be put to death, John 8:5. Deut. 22:22. Ezek. 16:40. Hence the propriety of holding up the terrors of death before the person inclined to commit the offence in question. Punishment in a *future* world is rarely brought directly before our view, in the Old Testament.

CHAP. VIII. 1—36.

[A course directly the opposite to that of the adulterous woman, does *Wisdom* pursue, in order to gain her adherents. She seeks no covert in darkness, but makes her invitations in a public manner, and in the most frequented places, v. 1—3. She addresses men, even the simple and foolish, and entreats them to hear the excellent truths which she proclaims, because they are all just and plain and upright, vs. 4—9. Her instruction is worth more than silver or gold, or precious stones, vs. 10, 11. She has sagacity and knowledge, and declares the fear of God to be hatred of evil, and that she abhors pride and perverseness of heart, vs. 12, 13. She has at her disposal such counsel and skill, that kings and princes rule through her assistance, vs. 14—16. She loves those who seek her, and bestows on them enduring wealth and honor, vs. 17, 18. Better than all wealth is her fruit; for she walks in the way of justice and of right. She will fill their coffers with her treasures, v. 21. As to her exceeding excellence and worth, and her claims to be heard, they are exhibited by showing, that she is employed by Jehovah himself as his agent. Even before the earth was founded, from the very beginning; when there were no depths or fountains of water; before the mountains and hills; before the earth was made, and its elevations; when the heavens were established and the abyss limited; when the clouds were stationed above, and the fountains of the abyss below were made firm; when the bounds of the waters were established, and the foundations of the earth; even then wisdom was with God and near him; she was his delight, and always rejoiced before him; and she has continued to rejoice in the last and best work of creation, the world of mankind, vs. 19—31. Finally, she exhorts men to listen to her, because all who seek earnestly after her will be made happy, and obtain favor from God. But those who sin against her, destroy their own life, vs. 32—36.

Thus ends this splendid piece of composition. The *personification* of Wisdom; the giving to her a place in the divine counsels and operations; and the description of her aid in constructing the manifold and magnificent structures of the natural world, afford a beautiful specimen of sublime and impassioned allegory, similar in many respects, (but not in all), to the sublime description of the Logos in John 1 : 1—18.

It is well known, that nearly all the ancient and most of the modern expositors, have found here the same personage as the Logos in John i. They supposed that John took this chapter as the basis and model of his description of the Logos; and they seem not to hesitate in declaring, that the divine Logos is in reality here designated by Solomon. And yet the two cases are in some respects widely different. The Logos was not only *with God*, but *was God;* by him all things without exception were created; not by him as a mere *instrument*, but in his proper capacity as God. He became *incarnate*, also, and lived and acted among men. He was therefore a proper person, a real *ens per se*, and not a mere attribute or quality. But nothing like this is here said of Wisdom. Being *personified*, she must of course be spoken of in a *personal way*. But we must see what is ascribed to her, before we can determine whether she is a *concrete agent*, or only an *attribute personified*. The task of distinguishing is not difficult. Wisdom is not asserted to be *God*. She is something which Jehovah *possessed*, or rather *created*, (which קָנָה primarily means, v. 22); she is not Jehovah himself. Tropically of course is קָנָה to be understood; for, as a *divine attribute*, she was not literally created. But the manner of expression shows, that she cannot be God himself, or the eternal Logos who is God. When all his creative acts and his arrangements of the universe were performed and made (vs. 24—29), even before these began (v. 23), she was anointed to her office of counsellor (v. 23); she was *near him* in all his creative doings (אֶצְלוֹ, v. 30), i. e. she stood by, as his ready counsellor and instrumentality. She was his special delight, and his faithful confidant (אָמוֹן), v. 30. Here the allegory, which *personifies*, represents her as a counsellor and instrumental aider in the work of creation, installed in that high office before the world began, vs. 22 23, 30. The obvious meaning is: 'In wisdom has God made all his works;'—like what the Psalmist says, in Ps. 104: 24. *Omnipotence* without wisdom, would be an object of unspeakable terror. But *wisdom*, whose every essence it is *to choose the best ends and the best means of accomplishing them*, is the leading development of a benignant creative power. Hence the importance here attached to wisdom, in her highest manifestations. Of unspeakable dignity and worth she must be; and therefore ought highly to be regarded by men. But as to a *real personality*, there is nothing here that leads us properly to the belief of this. Indeed, the representation is incompatible with this, when considered in its true light, viz., that of allegorical poetry. *Wisdom* is not *God*, but that which God possesses, and in which he greatly delights, v. 30.

One beautiful touch finishes this admirable picture. It is, that *wisdom*, from the beginning, looked forward with joyful anticipation to the world of mankind, made in the image of God, and capable of enjoying him forever. No wonder the ancient Fathers of the church found here that Wisdom, which pitied and saved our perishing race. But the Logos, as *God*, had that wisdom, and those joyful anticipations. Because both the Logos and Wisdom concur, in regard to the matter before us, in the same end or object, it is not necessary to conceive of them simply as one and the same. The Logos is plainly not an *attribute* but a *person*. Wisdom did not, like him, become incarnate. Plainly, therefore, Wisdom is not a real *person*, but an *attribute* poetically personified.]

(1) Doth not wisdom call? Doth not understanding utter her voice?

A question asked by הֲלֹא implies, that an *affirmative* answer is certain: like the interrog. οὐ in Greek.—תִּתֵּן, *give forth* = *utter*.

(2) On the summit of the high places by the way-side, in the midst of the highways, she takes her stand.

מְרֹמִים, *lofty eminences* of any kind, which of course are conspicuous.—עֲלֵי, lit. *over against*, i. e. *by the side of* the way.—בֵּית, *within* or *in the midst of*, Lex. בַּיִת, No. 6. Some, (and so Umbreit), render בֵּית by *house;* then, *house of the paths*, they say, means a house on the corner, where the highways meet and cross each other. But Wisdom here is represented as going into *public* places, in order to give out her invitations; of course, we should not put her *into a house*. The idea of the first clause is, that of *high eminences on the side of the way;* of the second, that she not only makes proclamation there, but also among the throng, i. e. *in the midst of the highway*.—נִצָּבָה, Niph. reflex., *stations herself*.

(3) Near the gates, at the opening of the city, at the entrance of the avenues, she makes proclamation.

These different descriptions are not synonymous, for they distinguish different locations at the city-gates = *within them, and on each side of them*. Of course, crowded places are designated.—תָּרֹנָּה, prob. third fem. sing. Imperf.; see on 1: 20, where this anomalous form is accounted for; it being the same in appearance as the third fem. plural.

(4) Unto you, O men, I call, and my voice is unto the sons of men. (5) Ye simple, understand sagacity; and ye fools, understand discretion.

עָרְמָה, *sagacity;* but the word has here a good sense = *prudent foresight;* it may, when the context demands, have a bad one = *artful cunning.* — לֵב, tropically *wisdom, cautious prudence;* for שׂוּם אֶל-לֵב means to *consider, ponder.*

(6) Hear, for I will speak plain things; and the opening of my lips shall be uprightness.

The root of נְגִידִים (נָגַד) means *to be conspicuous* or *manifest.* Wisdom declares, that what she utters is *manifest,* i. e. that it is *plain* and *intelligible.* — *The opening of my lips* = my words. — *Uprightness,* i. e. without any duplicity, in honest sincerity.

(7) For my palate meditateth truth, and the abomination of my lips is falsehood.

Palate meditateth means, that the palate, which is employed in speaking, carefully weighs and considers what it is about to utter. Of course, the mode of expression is tropical. — As רֶשַׁע here stands opposed to אֱמֶת, it must mean specifically *falsehood;* and so I have translated, i. e. *ad sensum.*

(8) All the words of my mouth are uprightness; there is in them nothing deceitful or perverse.

In בְּצֶדֶק we have a *Beth essentiae;* therefore it is = *uprightness;* see on this בְּ, the remarks on 3: 26.

(9) All of them are easy to understand, and plain are they to those who possess understanding.

I understand נְכֹחִים here in a sense like to that of נְגִידִים in v. 6. נָכַח means *to be before one's eyes,* of course to be *visible,* or *plainly to be seen.* So יָשָׁר (יְשָׁרִים) is sometimes joined with דֶּרֶךְ, in order to denote *a way straight and plain;*

Lex. יָשָׁר, No. 2. The writer had just said, that his words were not *tortuous* or *perverted;* for if so, they would mislead, and could not be easily understood. Here he says, that all of them are made plain and straight. But the two plural nouns may be rendered *upright* and *just.* This rendering is adopted by Bertheau, because, as he says, there is a contrast with the *deceitful and perverse* of the preceding context. But this contrast is equally conspicuous in the version above. The ideas which Bertheau and others suggest, have already been often repeated in the preceding context. Either method of interpreting, however, can be made out grammatically.

(10) Receive my instruction and not silver; and knowledge rather than choice gold. (11) For wisdom is better than pearls, and all precious things will not compare with her.

חֲפָצִר, *things desirable κατ᾽ ἐξόχην,* therefore *precious.* — יִשְׁווּ, Imperf. of שָׁוָה with ו consonant. Comp. v. 19 and 3 : 14, for the sentiment.

(12) I, wisdom, dwell with prudence, and a knowledge of skilful plans do I obtain.

עָרְמָה, *prudential sagacity* here. — *Dwell with prudence* — the Heb. is stronger, viz. *inhabit prudence,* i. e. *prudent sagacity* is her dwelling-place; which signifies, that in all things she stands intimately connected with it, and has her stable abode and defence in it. — מְזִמּוֹת is something which is *often thought upon* or *revolved in the mind,* which stands connected with the formation of well-considered plans. It may have a bad sense, viz. *plots, devices.* But here, it is clearly employed in a good sense. אֶמְצָא, *obtain,* as often. The first verb and the second, although in different tenses, both convey the idea of *an enduring present.* So they are often employed, § 124, 3. § 125, 2. The object of the writer is not to make wisdom and prudence *co-equals;* but to show that wisdom ever exercises a prudential and preserving care, that she never forsakes the society of prudence. The latter is here presented, as if it were the dwelling in which wisdom lives. It is a somewhat singular, but a strong metaphor, to express the idea of constant and intimate connection.

(13) The fear of Jehovah is hatred of evil — of pride, and haughtiness, and the way of evil; and a mouth which is perverse do I hate.

שְׂנֹאת, Inf. const. as a noun, the ו being omitted, see Lex Several verbs ל״א form their Inf. with ־וֹת, like verbs ל״ה, § 73. n. 2. — גֵּאָה וגו״, in the Gen. after the same Inf. noun implied, the three nouns being in apposition with the preceding רָע. So I have translated. — *Perverse mouth*, lit. *a mouth of perversities*, intensive plur. = very perverse, or habitually perverse.

(14) Mine is counsel and sound discretion; as for me, my might is understanding.

What is here affirmed of wisdom, is preparatory to what follows. These are the qualities which are necessary in order to rule well. Bertheau inclines to make אֲנִי a virtual Dat. = לִי, and so to render as follows: *Mine is understanding, mine power.* The sense is good, and perhaps it is the true one; but the Heb. text, as it now is, will hardly bear this, since the pronoun stands first. The version above seems to give a more exact shape of the text. For the sentiment which it gives, comp. Ecc. 9 : 16: "*Wisdom is better than strength.*" So our text: "Wisdom is true strength."

(15) By me kings reign, and princes decree justice. (16) By me princes rule, and nobles — all the magistrates of the earth.

By me, i. e. by my aid. The different classes of rulers are here exhibited, in order to show that all are, or should be under the guidance of wisdom; at any rate, are under her control. — שֹׁפְטִים is generic here, and embraces *all magistrates*. Of course, by *reigning*, etc., is meant, that the governing is as it should be, i. e. a proper method of ruling, which, without wisdom, is impracticable.

(17) I love those who love me; and those who earnestly seek me, shall find me.

אֲנִי is emphatic, and so placed first. — The Kethibh should be pointed thus, אֹהֲבֶיהָ, i. e. *those who love her;* but the Qeri reads, אֹהֲבַי, *those who love me,* which best accords with the fashion of the sequel. אֵהָב, contract form of אֶאֱהָב, § 67, 2. § 23. 2. *a*; for the first pers. of the Imperf., in verbs פּ״א, drops the א of the root. *Qamets,* because of the pause. — מְשַׁחֲרַי Part. plur. of Piel, with suff. — ־ָנְנִי written fully, without the usual *Dagh. forte* in the last נ, § 57. 4. This mode of writing happens seldom out of this book.

(18) Riches and honor are with me; enduring wealth and prosperity.

With me, i e. in my possession and at my disposal. — *Enduring wealth,* in opposition to the usual, fleeting worldly riches. — צְדָקָה here means the fruits of righteousness, i. e. *prosperity, happiness, salus,* see Lex. No. 4. The context renders this shade of meaning the most probable.

(19) My fruit is better than native gold — than purified gold; and my revenue, than choice silver.

Gold and fine gold, in our English version, fail to give the shade of the ideas communicated by חָרוּץ and פָּז.

(20) I walk in the way of righteousness, in the midst of the paths of equity.

אֲהַלֵּךְ, Piel, which, in this verb, has sometimes the same meaning as Kal, but here Piel denotes *habitual walking.* This declaration is here introduced for the purpose that follows:

(21) To cause those who love me to inherit substance; yea, their treasuries will I fill.

As the Inf. לְהַנְחִיל here stands between two Imperfects of the first pers., it may be translated: *I will cause,* etc., in conformity with the Hebrew idiom; see on 2 : 2, 8. Some difficulty has been made about יֵשׁ, by those who make a *verb* of it. They join it with אֹהֲבַי, and translate thus: *who are my lovers.* But then יֵשׁ must *precede*, in such a case, and not follow; and again, the verb הַנְחִיל would be left without an object, when one is demanded. The noun יֵשׁ here means *substantial good*, i. e. that which endures.

Here, all the promises, as usual in the Old Testament, seem to be like those in the Pentateuch, viz. promises of temporal good. Yet this good is to be rendered more secure and lasting, than is usual.

We now come to the animated and noble *personification* of *Wisdom.* From the beginning, she has been the counsellor and confidant (so to speak) of the Creator of heaven and earth; and like him, she rejoices evermore in the happiness of man, made in his image. The language is exceedingly bold, and almost adventurous. But still, we must remember that we are reading animated and glowing poetry, and not simple didactic prose.

(22) Jehovah created me, the firstling of his way, before his works, long ago.

Assuming that *Wisdom*, in this chapter, is the same as the *Logos* of John, many ancient and modern expositors have contended strongly here for rendering the clause with קָנָנִי by *Jehovah possessed me.* So the Vulgate, Luther, and many others. But the Sept. gives ἔκτισε, *created;* and so the Chald. and Syriac. Recent commentators, generally, I believe, side with the latter. The theological disputes of Arian times called into action all possible effort to defend the same interpretation which is given in the Vulgate version, *possedit me*, on the part of the Trinitarians; for they believed Wisdom and the Logos to be one and the same. If Wisdom, (allowing this last position of theirs), *was created*, then, thought the Orthodox, a decisive advantage is given to Arius, who maintained the *creation* of the Logos or Son of God. Therefore *possessed me* was the meaning given by the anti-Arians. It is plain that this would help their cause, since it would show, that before the mundane creation began, Jehovah already possessed the Wisdom in question, and therefore it must, as they averred, be *eternal.* But as the assumption of a *proper person* here, such as the Logos was, is clearly against the tenor of the whole piece, we need not be bound by any of their scruples or fears. *Philology*, at all events, must have its proper place, independent of party views. — קָנָה, then, means originally, *to erect* any thing, *to set it up* or *make it steadfast.* As naturally flowing from this, come the meanings: *to create, to found*, exemplified in Deut. 32: 6. Psalms 139: 13. Gen. 14: 19, 22. Moreover, the Arabic (קנה) means *to create.* Then come the derived meanings: *prepare, acquire;* and lastly, *to acquire by purchase*, i. e. *to buy.* But the simple sense of *possedit*, as given by the Vulgate, has no footing in the Hebrew. We feel compelled, therefore, to relinquish it. In so doing, no *theological* question is in reality affected thereby. The anti-Arians, indeed, lose their assumed foothold, viz. that of *eternal possession* of Wisdom; which they compare with the *Logos*, and with John's assertion that he was *πρὸς τὸν Θεόν.* The Arians, on the other hand, gain nothing by the proposed exegesis; for, to make it of any avail to them, they must show that Wisdom and the Logos are not only *persons*, but are *one and the same person.* As such an assumption is demonstrably groundless, so they cannot prove *the creation of the Logos*, by the clause in question. The writer means to say that the first of God's creation was the *wisdom*, which guided all subsequent measures. Only *poetically*, of course, can this be said; and it is said only because the poet converts Wisdom into an allegorical personage, and makes her as it were a distinct agent. In and by Wisdom, God made all things. Of course, if Wisdom be *personified*, then she, considered as a personage, must have had a beginning, (for God only is self-existent); and her rise must have been antecedent to the works which were performed by her aid. Comp. vs. 24, 25, which again assert her *rise* or *birth.*

Accordingly, she is said to be רֵאשִׁית דַּרְכּוֹ, the *firstling* or *first creation* of his *active formative power* or *doing,* דֶּרֶךְ being equivalent here to *action* or *doing.* The idea of this compound phrase stands in apposition with the preceding נִי–, *me.* To supply בְּ before רֵאשִׁית, and then translate: *in the beginning,* is manifestly a departure from the text. *Before his works* means his *creative works* here; elsewhere it means *doings* of any sort.—מֵאָז is again another epexegetical clause, added to the preceding one. It here means *long ago,* in its most extensive sense, i. e. before the creation of the world. Nothing is clearer than that *wisdom* must have *preceded* all the works mentioned in the sequel, in which she aided. One must *be,* before he can *act.*

On the whole, I do not see how we can translate קָנָנִי by any of the secondary meanings of קָנָה. For what sense would it make to say: *Jehovah acquired, procured, obtained,* or *purchased* me, etc.? From whom did he obtain or procure Wisdom? Who *possessed* it, before he *acquired* or *procured* it? These questions preclude this secondary exegesis, and cast us upon the first, viz. 'Jehovah *set up* or *established* Wisdom first of all, and employed her aid in devising the plan and order of the creation.' Poetically, indeed, but very strikingly is this expressed.

(23) Of old was I anointed; from the beginning, from the earliest period of the earth.

The personification is carried on consistently. When wisdom has been raised up, she is inducted into her august office by *anointing* or *consecration.* The other sense of נָסַךְ here, i. e. *poured forth,* has no tolerable meaning, as it applies in this way only to the *pouring out of libations* or *of melted metal.*—קַדְמֵי, plur. of קֶדֶם, means of course *the commencing period* of the earth. The whole verse repeats, in another form, the views of the preceding verse. The ancient versions are all at fault here, not understanding נִסַּכְתִּי. — The main idea, viz. that of *antiquity*, is greatly expanded in the sequel.

(24) While there were no depths I was born, when there were no fountains laden with water.

If there be difficulty about קָנָנִי, as to the meaning given above, this verse would seem to solve it. Here, *wisdom* is said *to be born*. חוֹלָלְתִּי, Poal of חוּל. — *Laden* or *heavy with water*, Gesenius takes no notice of the Dagh. forte in ד of נִכְבַּדֵּי, but puts the word down merely as a Part. Niph. But surely it belongs not there. It is an intensive adjective, formed from the Niph. Part., and agrees with the masc. form מַעְיָנִים implied. *Laden* means *containing ponderous masses*. — *The deep* here, תְּהוֹמוֹת, refers to the great abyss beneath the earth; see Gen. 1: 2.

(25) Before the mountains were sunk down, before the hills, was I born.

Sunk down, i. e. sunk into the earth. — *Before the hills* [*were sunk*], *I was born;* again repeating the leading idea of the former verse, i. e. her very ancient birth.

(26) When he had not formed the land and the deserts, nor the mass of the dust of the earth.

Probably *land* here means *terra culta*, to which the word *deserts* stands opposed. — רֹאשׁ seems here to mean *sum, mass;* comp. Ps. 139 : 17. — Inasmuch as עַפְרוֹת is plur., it probably means *clods of dust;* or the plur. may designate the widely extended and multitudinous dust.

(27) When he established the heavens, I was there; when he marked out the circle on the face of the waters.

The heavens, i. e. the welkin, or (in other words) the concave set with stars. — חֻקּוֹ, Inf. of חָקַק, the usual חֹק goes of course into the short vowel, *Qibbuts*, when it takes a suff.

The suff. designates the *agent: when he defined,* i. e. *described, marked out.* — חוּג is the *circle* or *concave* of the arched heavens. — *On the face of the waters,* i. e. on the ocean, which, in the view of the Hebrews, surrounded the whole earth, and the edges of the *welkin* or *vault of heaven,* were supposed by them to rest upon the face of it. Here חוּג = רָקִיעַ in Gen. 1: 6. The idea is: 'When he defined or circumscribed the vault of heaven, which rests on the face of the great ocean.'

(28) When he fixed the clouds on high; when the fountains of the abyss were made firm.

Fixed the clouds, means that he firmly established the location or sustentation of them; and מִמָּעַל defines where this was. Lit. this word means: *on the part of the upper region,* i. e. above the חוּג or *welkin.* — The *fountains of the abyss* are the reservoirs of water above the firmament, Gen. 1: 7. 11: 7. How *the fountains are made firm,* may be seen in Job. 26: 8. *Firm* or *strong* they must be, in the view of the Hebrew, who knew nothing of the true formation of rain-showers, in order to retain the abysses of water above. For the *breaking up,* or rather *cleaving* of these abysses, at the time of the deluge, see Gen. 7: 11, and comp. נִבְקַע in Job 26: 8, where the same imagery is presented. — עֲזוֹז, Inf. Kal, is intrans., and does not mean actively *to strengthen,* but *to be* or *become firm* or *strong.* Hence I have rendered it as intransitive.

(29) When he marked out for the sea its limit, so that the waters should not pass beyond its shore; when he defined the foundations of the earth.

חֻקּוֹ, from the noun חֹק, root חָקַק. — פִּיו, not *mouth* here, but *lip* tropically understood, = *edge, margin, shore.* — חוּקוֹ, Inf. of חָקַק, = חֻקּוֹ, but taking the form of a verb ע״ו, i. e. as if it were from חוּק. See for this usage, § 66. n. 9. Umbreit says, that *foundations* here means *pillars,* and refers to Job 9 : 6 for proof. It is clear, in this passage of Job, that *pillars* are *supporters;* but they are not therefore exactly equivalent to *foundations.*

(30) Then was I near him as a confidant; I was a delight continually, rejoicing before him at all times.

Vs. 24—29 all belong virtually to a *protasis*, of which v. 30 is a part of the *apodosis*. The וָ before the first verb is *continuative*, and is so rendered. The verb (used as a Praeter) connects with the implied Perf. *(was)* before אֲנִי in v. 27. — *Near him*, i. e. in his immediate presence. — אָמוֹן, as a noun, may mean *artificer* (see Lex.), or, as it seems to me, it more probably means here, *one confided in* as faithful and true. This agrees better with the tenor of the latter part of the verse. — שַׁעֲשֻׁעִים, reduplicate form from שָׁעַע, plur. of intensity, like the Latin *deliciae*, i. e. *a source of much delight.* Bertheau: *ergötzliche Spielerei* = *a delightful sport.* This hardly consists with the root; and Jer. 31 : 20, to which he appeals, surely does not satisfactorily confirm this meaning. — *Rejoicing*, מְשַׂחֶקֶת, lit. *laughing, sporting*, e. g. as an innocent and joyful child sports. The imagery is vivid; but the dignity of the agent seems to prohibit a literal version. Indeed, the verb שָׂחַק is only a weakened form of צָחַק, and would rather import *smiling.* I have given a meaning *ad sensum* in the version, although it does not present the exact light and shade of the original. Our mode of expression, in relation to such a subject, is grave and respectful, and will hardly permit us to translate by *laughing* or *sporting*, much less *dancing* (as some translate) here.

(31) Rejoicing in the habitable world — his earth; and my delight was with the children of men.

Umbreit wrongly: *and I am the delight of mankind.* The writer tells us here, that Wisdom did not confine her presence merely to the heavenly world. When the inhabited earth appeared, she descended and abode upon it, mingling with men, and taking delight in counselling and guiding them. — Truly an exquisitely fine thought, and a very attractive turn of the discourse. If Wisdom has acted thus, with what gratitude and readiness ought men to listen to her! This is the obvious deduction from the text, and it prepares the way for the closing exhortation. — תֵּבֵל is a poetic word = the Greek γῆ οἰκουμένη. — *His earth,* i. e. this same earth which he created by Wisdom. — *With the sons of men,* i. e. associating with them, mixing with them, going among them.

After this sublime description of the excellence and dignity of Wisdom, with great effect does the writer return to his persuasive exhortations.

(32) And now, ye children, hearken to me; for blessed are they who keep my ways.

אַשְׁרֵי, has the form of plur. const., but always is employed in this way only, and virtually therefore an interjection. Before the verb יִשְׁמֹרוּ an אֲשֶׁר is implied. — *My ways* means: those which I prescribe.

(33) Hear instruction, and be wise, and reject it not.

After תִּפְרָעוּ (Qamets in Pause), the noun מוּסָר is of course implied. This verb occurs often in this book, viz., 1: 25. 13: 18. 15: 32.

(34) Blessed is the man who hearkeneth to me, so as to watch at my doors continually, so as to keep watch at the posts of my gates.

The לִ before the two Infinitives is designed to mark the verbs as limiting and explaining שֹׁמֵעַ, by showing what such *hearkening* consists in. Wisdom is here conceived of as dwelling in her temple, (see 9: 1), and the anxious inquirer for her, as watching and waiting for the opening of her doors.

(35) For he who findeth me; findeth life; and he shall obtain favor from Jehovah.

מָצָאִי has the vowels of the Qeri, which drops the Yodh final. This is the most simple reading. But the Kethibh would answer well, if pointed מֹצְאַי, *finders*, and the preceding word also pointed thus, מֹצְאַי, *the finders of me*. The sense is the same in both ways.—וַיָּפֶק, Imperf. Hiph. of פּוּק, with retracted accent, and therefore shortened final syllable, § 97. n. 7.

(36) But whosoever misseth me, injureth himself; all who hate me, love death.

חֹטְאִי is here used in its original sense, viz., that of *missing* a mark. In this way it stands contrasted with the מֹצְאִי *(finding)* of the preceding verse. The *missing*, however, is here taken as voluntary, because it takes place through neglect and indifference.—*Love death*, i. e. inasmuch as they are shunning my counsel and refusing my reproof, they show that they love "the way that leads to *Sheol*, going down to the chambers of death;" for this is the way to which the adulteress invites them.

In this allegorical and truly poetic description of the dignity and excellence of wisdom, we may see the high import attached to the word, where the writer employs it as designating moral and religious attainments or conduct. Of course, *folly*, which is the antithesis, becomes in his writings also a very significant word. The design of the chapter is to exhibit the claims which Wisdom has to be heard, on the ground of her antiquity, her excellence, and her sympathy with men. Being *personified*, she must be spoken of in accordance with this, for the sake of congruity. Not being God himself, who is eternal and *self-existent*, she must of course be conceived of as *originated*. But it was before time began, i. e. before the creation. Her *origination* (so called) consists in her active development. She was the רֵאשִׁית *(firstling)* of the creation. If any one still insists, that *the real Logos* is to be found here, i. e. a *real* and not a poetical personage; and also that קָנָנִי of v. 22 means *possessed*, (as many have said and still say); then let him reperuse vs. 24, 25, and consider what חוֹלָלְתִּי means. It is never applied to *begetting* as an act of the *father*, but only to *bringing forth*, as the act of the mother; then passively it designates the effects of that act, viz., *the being born*, in relation to the child. It is quite a different word from יָלַד, *to beget*, which applies both to *father* and *mother*, like the Greek γεννάω and τίκτειν, and the Latin *parere*. If, then, the interpreter will honestly follow out his Logos-scheme here, he must come at last to such a position, that the question may well be asked: Who then was the *mother* of Wisdom, and *brought her forth?* The verb cannot be attached to the action of a *father*. And if we are obliged to answer such a question as the word חוֹלָלְתִּי naturally raises, we must go I know not where to find an answer. In fact, this course of proceeding, if followed out, leads at last to a downright absurdity. The Logos (as hypostatically such) had no *mother;* nor, *as self-existent and independent God*, could he have in a proper sense a father. If the doctrine of real *eternal generation* be applied to vs. 22—31, then, to be impartial, we must find an *eternal mother*, as well as father. *Self-existence* and *independence*, in their true sense, are essential attributes of *Godhead;* and *derivation*, in any way or manner, known or unknown, obvious or mysterious, is still *derivation*, and therefore it is directly opposed to *self-existence* and *independence*. A *derived supreme* God is, at least to my own mind, a contradiction in substance if not in terms. The eighth chapter of Proverbs, therefore, should cease from being appealed to, in order to show the generation of the Logos — *who was God — God over all — the true God and eternal life*, John 1: 1. Rom. 9 : 5. 1 John 5 : 20 ; and therefore underived and self-existent.

CHAP. IX. 1—18.

[This is the closing part of the large discourse which reaches from 6 : 20 to 9 : 18. It is a kind of summary of the whole, not closely connected and rigidly continuous, but passing from one subject rapidly to another, in order to touch upon the leading points of the discourse. The nature of the case neither calls for, nor admits, the poetic fire and animation of the preceding chapter. The flow of speech seems less animated. The abruptness of the sentences, however, and the frequent transitions, to which allusion has already been made, occasion little or no obscurity, because of their obvious relation to the preceding context. It ends, as we might expect such a discourse to do, with a most solemn warning against the crime in question, by setting the fearful and inevitable consequences of it before the reader.

The chapter begins with the declaration, that Wisdom has provided herself a house or temple, where all due preparation is made for the feast, to which she invites her chosen guests, vs. 1, 2. She sends forth her criers to summon these guests; yet not any one and every one is invited, but the simple who lack information, vs. 3, 4. The scorner and the vile transgressor are not fitted for the instructions of wisdom, and would not receive them or profit by them. Her guests are invited to an excellent repast, not of physical luxuries, but (what is much better) of exhortations to walk in the way of life, vs. 5, 6. Scorners refuse reproof; and to administer it only brings contempt and contumely on the reprover, vs. 7, 8. Not so with the *wise*, v. 9. Wisdom is the fear of God, which secures long life; for this receives a recompense which is meet, as scorning also does, vs. 9—12. But that enemy of all true wisdom, the adulteress, who watches for her prey, and gives out her invitations, addresses the simple, and tells them that "stolen waters are sweet," vs. 13—17. It is an unwary youth, who does not see that her ways lead, as they surely do, to destruction, v. 18.]

(1) Wisdom hath built her house, she hath hewed out the seven pillars thereof.

The writer had just spoken of watching and waiting at the *doors* of wisdom. Here he assigns to her a dwelling, — a goodly structure, well supported and magnificently adorned, in the manner of a temple. The apparent plur. חָכְמוֹת is virtually an *abstract* noun, and *ad sensum* may have a predicate in the sing., as here; see 1: 20. — *Seven pillars* is a *sufficient* or *complete number;* a meaning that *seven* often tropically designates. The suff. in עַמּוּדֶיהָ may apply to בַּיִת (for this is sometimes fem.), and so I have applied it in the version. Berth., and others, refer it to *wisdom;* which, however, seems to be less appropriate.

(2) She hath killed her slaughter-beasts, she hath mingled her wine, she hath set in order her table.

Some refer טֶבַח to *an animal slaughtered for sacrifice;* but זֶבַח designates this. The *feast* here does not appear to be a sacrificial one. The meaning is, that she has prepared meat for the feast, to which she invites her guests. So of *the wine, which she has mingled,* i. e. mixed with water, or it may be with milk (Is. 55 : 1) ; for the temperate ancients never drank wine undiluted. All the predicates and suffixes here are *singular;* which shows that חָכְמוֹת above is regarded in that light.

(3) She hath sent forth her maidens, she maketh proclamation on the ridges of the high places of the city.

Females were the usual heralds of good tidings among the Hebrews; see Ps. 68 : 12. Is. 40 : 9. Here it is appropriate, that Wisdom should send her *female* servants, in order to give the invitation to the feast. — The accents join תִקְרָא to the first clause of the verse; wrongly, for it leads the second clause. — *She makes proclamation,* viz., by her messengers. To this Berth. assents. — גַּפֵּי, *back, ridges,* i. e. the *summits* of elevated places, from which proclamation might most extensively be made and heard.

(4) Whosoever is simple, let him turn aside hither; as to him that lacketh understanding, she saith to him:

יָסֻר would normally be יָסֹר, as a hortative Imperf.; but sometimes the same hortative tense occurs in the shape presented by the text, § 71, n. 4. *Turn aside,* viz., from the path of the simple, and repair to the house of Wisdom. — חֲסַר־לֵב may be taken as in the Nom. abs., and is so taken in the version; or we may bring forward the מִי of the preceding clause, and translate thus: *whoever lacketh understanding.* The sentence is left unfinished by the verse. The first clause exhibits the words of Wisdom; the second, those of the writer.

(5) Come ye, feed on my viands, and drink the wine which I have mingled.

The plural is here used, because the address is to many individuals, to each and every simpleton. — לָחַם means generally *to eat;* and לֶחֶם means first, *food* in general, and then *bread.*

(6) Forsake simplicity, and ye shall live; and walk in the way of understanding.

פְּתָאִים, abstract plural here, lit. *simplicities.* — *Ye shall live,* because the Imper. is here used in the sense of promise, § 127. 2. — אִשְׁרוּ, Kal Imper., more usually in Piel.

(7) He who reproveth a scorner, getteth shame for himself; and he who rebuketh the wicked, it is a blot to him.

That is, he meets with shameful and reproachful treatment; not that what he does is shameful, but that the man reproved acts shamefully toward him. — מוּמוֹ, lit. *his blot,* or *reproach,* i. e. his reproof becomes the ground of reproach. Hence the caution in v. 8:

(8) Reprove not a scorner, lest he hate thee; reprove a wise man, and he will love thee.

This verse gives the ground of the preceding assertion. The hatred of the scorner is roused by reproof, and so he will manifest it in reproaches. For suff. ֶךָּ (= ֶנְךָ), see p. 289 Gramm., for the forms. Exactly the reverse will be the wise man's conduct. He will be grateful, and will love thee for fidelity.

(9) Give to a wise man, and he will be still more wise; communicate knowledge to the righteous man, and he will add to his learning.

The *giving* in this case implies *admonitory counsel.* Sentiment: 'The good man will duly appreciate this, and so will add to his stock of instruction.'

(10) The beginning of wisdom is the fear of Jehovah; and a knowledge of the Most Holy, is understanding.

רֵאשִׁית may indicate here the *first* or *leading advantage;* but the main object seems to be to assert that even a beginning in wisdom cannot be made without the fear of God.— קְדֹשִׁים, (like אֱלֹהִים), plural of intensity, the meaning of which is given in the version. The same in 30 : 3. Scorners and fools, therefore, who have no fear of God, cannot attain true wisdom.

(11) By me thy days shall increase, and years of life shall be added to thee. (12) If thou becomest wise, thou art wise for thyself; and shouldest thou scorn, thou alone shalt bear it.

V. 11 makes the usual promise of *long life*. V. 12 shows the advantage to be gained for one's self, by becoming wise. — *Wise for thyself*, i. e. to thine own advantage.— וְלַצְתָּ may be translated, *if thou scornest*, by bringing forward the אִם of the preceding clause. The same thing is attained by the rendering in the version. תִּשָּׂא (from נָשָׂא) *shalt bear*, viz. the consequences of scorning, the penalty affixed to it, for this is of course implied.

(13) A foolish woman is noisy, she is silly, and knows nothing.

כְּסִילוּת, lit. *of folly*, an abstract noun, but used here as an adjective.—*Noisy*, comp. 7 : 11, i. e. is bustling about and talking much. The *adulteress* is of course here aimed at.— פְּתַיּוּת, with אֵשֶׁת implied before it, from the preceding clause, i. e. *a woman of simplicities*, or *a very silly woman.*—מָּה, *anything*. The Dagh. is merely euphonic, and inserted because of the Maqqeph, so as to make a kind of short syllable with the preceding vowel.

(14) She sitteth at the door of her house—on a seat in the high places of the city.

כִּסֵּא, *seat, lofty seat*, but not *throne* here, unless we say, that she takes her seat as if enthroned, i. e. haughtily, and also in a splendid dress. The idea is—makes herself conspicuous to public gaze, and challenges attention.—Next follows the design in view:

(15) In order to call to passengers on the way, to those who are going straight forward in their paths.

That is, in order to allure such way-passengers as were going directly on in pursuit of their proper business, and who were not hunting for by-paths. Of course, such are here considered as unwary and unguarded.

(16) Whosoever is simple let him turn aside hither; and as to him that lacketh understanding, she saith to him: (17) Stolen waters are sweet, and bread in secret places is pleasant.

In v. 16 the same thing is repeated, which is said of Wisdom in v. 4. But the tenor of the address that follows, is of course opposite to that in v. 5, seq. Bertheau represents v. 17 as the words of the writer, and not of the woman; but Umbreit assigns the words to the woman. Rightly; for they are more apposite to her than to the writer; who, if he speaks them, must be supposed to speak ironically. The contents of v. 17 are undoubtedly a common *proverb*. But this proverb the woman dexterously uses, in order to persuade the simpleton. *Bread* סְתָרִים, *of secret places,* means bread eaten in secret places, i. e. in the retired haunts of pleasure, whither the woman will conduct her guests.

(18) And he knoweth not that the Shades are there — her guests in the depths of the under-world.

רְפָאִים *ghosts, umbrae,* the dwellers in the under-world. — *Her guests,* lit. *those invited by her* and accepting the invitation, go down to certain destruction.

Such is the unhappy end of him, who listens to the invitations of the adulteress. The opposite of this, (see v. 11), is many days of life, or long life. Neither the promise nor the threatening, so far as the language here employed is concerned, goes beyond the retributions of the present world. How much was at that time supposed to be implied, however, by such language, beyond its first and obvious meaning, i. e. whether the language is tropically or literally employed, is a question which it would be difficult to answer. It may have depended much on subjective knowledge and feeling, in particular cases.

PART II. CHAP. X. 1—32.

[A summary of this is out of the question; inasmach as scarcely any two verses are connected together, and never more than two. Each verse is, almost without exception, complete in itself. The whole composition is strictly and invariably apothegmatic; and in a large proportion of the cases, the second στίχος is in *contrast* with the first. The regular arrangement of all this, shows great care and skill in the selection. Of course, in such a composition, the only connection which one verse has with another, is that of similarity of construction and rhythm, there being usually the same number of words in each verse. Brevity, energy, and vivacity of expression, characterize the whole. For particulars, see Introduction, § 6.]

(1) THE PROVERBS OF SOLOMON. A wise son maketh a glad father; but a foolish son is the grief of his mother.

Wise and *foolish* have now become very significant words, by reason of what has already been said concerning *wisdom* and *folly*.—The Hebrews said: *the grief of his mother*, as in our text; we should more readily say: *A grief to his mother.*

(2) The treasures of wickedness do not profit; but righteousness delivereth from death.

In these contrasts, a וְ almost everywhere stands at the head of the second clause, and in the sense of *but*, § 152. B. *b.*—*Do not profit*, because they cannot deliver from death the possessors of them; on the contrary, righteousness does deliver. Not from *natural* death, (for all die), but from that death which is a punishment for crime, or (in other words) from sudden death.

(3) Jehovah will not suffer the soul of the righteous to hunger; but the greedy desire of the wicked will he repel.

The Hiph. form, יַרְעִיב, has here the modified sense of *permitting to be hungry*, or *letting one go hungry*, not that of *making hungry.* Sentiment: 'The Lord will provide all needed good for the righteous; but the cravings of the wicked he will refuse to satisfy.'

(4) Poor is he, who worketh with a slack hand; but the hand of the diligent maketh rich.

רָאשׁ, more usually written רָשׁ. — עֹשֶׂה, *doeth, worketh,* with אֲשֶׁר implied, or rather, the Part. itself of course implies an indefinite Nom., when it is not expressed. — *Slack hand,* lit. *deceitful hand,* the Acc. of instrument, § 135. n. 3. — רְמִיָּה, which lit. means *deceitful,* is here rendered *slack,* i. e. *sluggish,* because such a hand frustrates all reasonable expectation of accomplishing the end desired. Besides, it is opposed to *the hand of the diligent,* which of course implies activity and energy.

(5) He who gathereth in summer is a wise son; he who sleepeth in harvest-time, is a base son.

The two participles here, as usual, supply their own indef. Nom., viz. *whoever,* or *he who, is qui.* — נִרְדָּם is Part. Niph., because Kal is not used, and is employed in the simple intrans. sense, as Kal might be. — מֵבִישׁ, lit. *causing shame;* which is equivalent to *base.*

(6) Blessings are on the head of the righteous; but the mouth of the wicked concealeth injury.

That is, blessings will come upon the righteous, because of the good they do; but the wicked conceal or keep secret a meditated injury, i. e. the mouth speaks not concerning it, in order that, by secrecy, they may strike the surer blow. The injured, in such a case, will bestow no blessings on them. This last thought is implied, but not expressed. — בְּרָכוֹת, plural of intensity, i. e. abundant blessing.

(7) The memory of the just shall be blessed; but the name of the wicked shall rot.

לִבְרָכָה, lit. *for a blessing*, which means, that every one who recalls the memory of the just, shall do it with invoking a blessing on him, (the usual custom of the East, down to the present hour); so this = *blessed*. — רָקַב, spoken of wood, means *to be worm-eaten*, or as we say: *powder-posted;* consequently, in a fragile and perishable condition. Tropically taken, it means *shall be loathsome.*

(8) The wise of heart will receive commands; but he who is foolish with his lips, shall rush headlong.

Commands are those of God, or of wisdom. — *Foolish with his lips* = speaks foolishly. — שְׂפָתַיִם may be a Gen. after the adjective before it; or it may be taken as the *Acc. of manner*. — יִלָּבֵט, in Niph. as intrans. Kal, because Kal is not here employed.

(9) He who walketh in integrity, walketh safely; but he who perverteth his ways, shall be discovered.

יֵ֫לֶךְ, Imperf. of יָלַךְ, accent retracted, and therefore the normal Tseri final is shortened; and all this, because a tone-syllable immediately follows, § 29. 3. *b*. — *The deceiver* (מְעַקֵּשׁ דְּרָכָיו) *shall be made known* = shall be discovered.

(10) He who winketh with the eye shall give pain; and he who is foolish with his lips, shall rush headlong.

Eye and *lips*, Acc. of instrument, and so we supply *with* in English. — עַצָּבֶת, a Piel form, intensive; Qamets in pause. Meaning: 'He who is trickish and deceitful, shall be duly punished.'

(11) A fountain of life is the mouth of the righteous; but the mouth of the wicked concealeth injury.

The righteous speaks words adapted to preserve life, he gives saving or salutary counsel; the wicked use deceit, in order to perpetrate injuries.

(12) Hatred stirreth up strifes; but love covereth over all transgressions.

תְּעֹרֵר, Imperf. Polel of עוּר, ו after ע being omitted.—מְדָנִים, from מְדָן, root דִּין.—Meaning: 'The spirit of true *love* is ever ready to pity and forgive transgressions.'

(13) In the lips of the intelligent, wisdom is found; but a rod is for the back of him who lacketh understanding.

Wisdom utters not that which will be injurious; but a fool says that which will be likely to provide a rod for him.

(14) The wise treasure up knowledge; but the mouth of a fool is destruction near at hand.

יִצְפְּנוּ may mean *lay up*, in the sense of a prudent holding back of communications, on some occasions where they might do harm = " Cast not your pearls before swine." The other clause shows, that the words of a fool are such as often occasion his speedy destruction. — קְרֹבָה here means *imminent*, for what is *close by* is ready to act.

(15) The wealth of the rich man is his strong city; the destruction of the poor is their poverty.

This is of course to be qualified. The simple meaning is: 'There are times when the wealth of the rich will avert danger and suffering; and at such a time the poor may perish for want of money.'

(16) The work of the righteous is unto life; the earnings of the wicked are unto sin.

Bertheau and Umbreit render פְּעֻלַּת by *Lohn, reward.* So indeed the word may mean. But its primary meaning, given above, is well; and so the ancient Versions. The meaning is, that the promise to *righteous doing* is *life*, i. e. *long life;* hence the tendency of the doing is *unto life*. On the other hand, the *fruits of wicked doing*, i. e. the earnings of the wicked, *tend to sin.* In other words: 'They so appropriate their earnings as to lead them into sin; or, their earnings are acquired by sinful practices,' and so bring on them the evils of sin.

(17) A way of life is he who keepeth instruction; but he who forsaketh reproof, leadeth astray.

In other words, the well-instructed man gives discreet counsel, which points out the *way of life.* So Christ, as teacher, is called *the way,* John 14 : 6. — מַתְעֶה, *causeth to wander*, or *leadeth astray*, namely, from the path of life. As the righteous points to this path, by instruction, and by his own example in following it, so the wicked lead astray by precept and by example.

(18) He who concealeth hatred is of lying lips; and he who uttereth slander, is a very fool.

שִׂפְתֵי שָׁקֶר is preceded, no doubt, by אִישׁ implied, i. e. *a man of lying lips.* But the version gives the idea sufficiently well.— מוֹצִא, Hiph. Part. of יָצָא, lit. *causes to go forth*, which, applied to *slander*, means *uttering* it. — הוּא, *he is*, (§ 119. 2). The design of it here is to give intensity to the expression; which I have imitated in the version.

(19) In multiplying words there will be no lack of transgression; but he who restraineth his lips is prudent.

רֹב is the Inf. const. of רָבַב. If it were a noun, it would shorten its vowel, and read רָב־, *rŏbh.* Sentiment: 'Much speaking exposes one to say things that will be injurious; (see the graphic passage relative to this, in Ecc. 5 : 1—7); and therefore a prudent man will guard well his lips.'

(20) Choice silver is the tongue of the righteous; the heart of the wicked is worthless.

The *tongue* utters words; the *heart* conceives them; so that *tongue* and *heart* have, in this passage, substantially the same thing in view. It is assumed here, that the righteous utters that which is accordant with his character, and then his words are of much worth. But the conceptions of the wicked are כִּמְעָט, lit. *as a very little thing = worthless*, as expressed in the version.

(21) The lips of the righteous feed many; but fools die for lack of understanding.

Feeding with the lips, of course means *imparting instruction*. *A teacher* was called רֹעֶה, i. e. *a feeder*, by the Hebrews; and so the New Testament *ποιμήν*; comp. vs. 11, 17. — חֲסַר may be, and probably is, the Inf. const. *nominascens* of the verb חָסֵר. 'Fools, who will not receive the food (the instruction) which the righteous impart, perish for lack of knowledge.' Perhaps חֲסַר is const. of חָסֵר adj.; if so, then we must translate thus: *through him that lacketh understanding;* the meaning then is, that fools die by the influence over them of foolish men.

(22) The blessing of Jehovah — that maketh rich; nor will he increase sorrow therewith.

הִיא, *that*, is intensive; as much as to say: *this is that which*, i. e. *this* and nothing else. — יוֹסִף, Imperf. Hiph. with ה formative omitted. The Nom. to this verb seems to be *Jehovah*, taken from the first clause: *Jehovah will not increase*, etc. Sentiment: 'God's blessing enriches, and that without increasing sorrow.' The meaning is not, that he who is *enriched* shall have no sorrows in the present life; but that sorrows are not of necessity increased by riches, when it is Jehovah who bestows them. The prosperity of the mere worldling, procured by unlawful means, brings many sorrows with it; comp. the vivid picture of this, in Ecc. 2: 21—23. 5: 10, 11. 6: 1, 2. — עִמָּהּ, *with it*, viz., with the bestowment of the blessing.

(23) It is like sport to a fool to do mischief; but wisdom belongeth to the man of understanding.

שְׂחוֹק, Inf. nominasc. — *To do mischief*, lit. *to execute an evil device*, evil because *mischievous*. Of course, a man of understanding will not regard *doing mischief* as sport or a joke, but as a very serious matter.

(24) The terror of the wicked — that shall come upon him; but the desire of the righteous he will grant.

Terror here means *that which is feared*, i. e. *the ground of terror*. — תְּבוֹאֶנּוּ, Imperf. third fem. of בּוֹא, with the suff. ־ֶנּוּ. — יִתֵּן has doubtless *Jehovah* implied for its Nom.; see v. 22. The nature of the case also implies thus much; for we may ask: Who punishes the wicked? Who blesses the righteous? And the answer is spontaneous.

(25) When the whirlwind passeth over, the wicked is no more; but as to the righteous — there is an eternal foundation.

The כ before the Inf. is here expressive of *time*, i. e. *when;* and so oftentimes. — וְאֵין רָשָׁע, lit. *then is not the wicked*. I have conformed it more closely to our own idiom. — But the whirlwind produces no effect on the established righteous, because he stands on a foundation that is never to be moved, or which is *eternal*.

(26) As vinegar to the teeth, and as smoke to the eyes, so is a sluggard to those who send him.

Every one's experience readily explains this. *Vinegar* sets the teeth on edge, as we express it; *smoke* causes painful excitement to the eyes; and a vexation like to these is a sluggard who is commissioned on an errand that requires haste. The article follows the כְּ of comparison here throughout; § 107. n. 1. *a*. — שֹׁלְחָיו, Part. plur. with suffix.

(27) The fear of Jehovah will increase days; but the years of the wicked shall be curtailed.

A sentiment very often repeated, and one on which much

stress is laid. — *Days* of course means *time.* — תִּקְצֹרְנָה, in Kal, but being intrans. here, it may be rendered passively.

(28) The expectation of the righteous is joyful; but the hope of the wicked shall perish.

Joyful, lit. *joy;* and it is so, because he believes that his expectation will be realized. *The hopes of the wicked,* on the other hand, will be frustrated.

(29) A strong hold for uprightness is the way of Jehovah; but destruction is for the workers of iniquity.

The way of Jehovah, is the way in which he acts; so that the sentiment stands thus: 'The upright will find protection, in the doings or providential arrangements of Jehovah.' This same *way* of his will bring destruction upon the wicked.

(30) The righteous shall never be moved; but the wicked shall not inhabit the land.

Heb. *not forever* = *never.* — יִמּוֹט, Niph. Imperf. of מוֹט. The threatening here is equivalent to other threatenings, which declare that *the wicked shall be cut off — shall not live out half their days,* etc. — *The land* here means the promised land, i. e. Palestine. But under this promise, a more general truth may lie.

(31) The mouth of the just bringeth forth wisdom; but the tongue of perversity shall be cut out.

יָנוּב, lit. *germinates, shoots forth in buds,* and thence, more generally, *produces* or *brings forth.* — תַּהְפֻּכוֹת, plur. of intensity, or else the fem. plur. simply for an abstract noun. We say of the tongue, *cut out,* rather than *cut,* or *cut off.* This shows the difference between the language and thoughts of the righteous and the wicked; the one inculcates wisdom, the other speaks that which condemns him to the loss of his tongue.

(32) The lips of the righteous know what is well-pleasing; but the mouth of the wicked is perverse.

רָצוֹן, lit. *approbation, pleasure;* used as an adjective, *well-pleasing,* viz., to Jehovah. Hence his blessing on the righteous. But the wicked utter only *perversities,* i. e. a series of falsehood and deceit,—the plur. being intensive; which of course cannot be well-pleasing to God.

CHAP. XI. 1—31.

(1) Balances of deceit are the abomination of Jehovah; but a complete weight is his delight.

The balances here mentioned are such as are provided with false weights, for the purposes of fraud.—What we call *full weight,* is in Hebrew lit. *a stone of completeness.* The *weights* were *stones;* and they were *complete* when they were *full* or *exact.*

(2) Does pride come, then shame will come; but with the humble is wisdom.

The וַ before יָבֹא is the *Vav consequential;* and so have I translated.—צְנוּעִים is an unusual word in poetry, but the meaning here is plain. זָדוֹן characterizes lofty assuming demeanor, while צָנַח means *to carry one's self meekly and lowly.*

(3) The integrity of the upright shall lead them; but the perverseness of the treacherous shall destroy them.

תַּנְחֵם, Hiph. Imperf. of נָחָה, with plur. suff.—יְשָׁדֵּם, should be read as in the Qeri with י prefix, and then it is the Imperf. of שָׁדַד with a suff., and this calls forth the Dagh. in the ד.—*Lead them,* e. g. as a shepherd leads his sheep, and therefore in the path of safety and peace.—*Destroy them* has here an intensive word in the Heb., quasi *lay hold on them with violent force.*

(4) Wealth will not profit in the day of wrath; but righteousness will deliver from death.

יוֹעִיל, Hiph. of יָעַל. — *Wrath* here means *divine indignation;* see Ezek. 7: 19.

(5) The righteousness of the upright shall make even his way; but the wicked shall fall by his wickedness. (6) The righteousness of the upright shall deliver them; but by their own greedy desire the treacherous shall be ensnared.

An even way is one on which the righteous will not stumble. — *Deliver them,* viz., from punishment or evil. — *Greedy desire* will strongly tempt men to sin, and so they will be ensnared.

(7) When a wicked man dieth, his hope shall perish; and the expectation of the afflicted perisheth.

His hope of riches or pleasures perishes at death. — אוֹנִים, is however a doubtful word. Most have taken it as a noun plur. from אָוֶן, *baseness.* But it may be regarded as a Part. here; see Hos. 9: 4, and Hitzig in loc. If a Part. from אוֹן = Chald. אֲנַן, then it signifies *afflicted.* The meaning of the verse then would be, that 'when the wicked die, all their hopes perish; and when they are sick and afflicted, their expectation of recovery or alleviation will be frustrated.' So Bertheau, and so the Vulg.; and the sense thus given is striking. There is indeed no antithesis here, but the representation is climactic. The truth of the first clause is plain to all; the second will strike with the more force, because it shows the extent of the mischief which wickedness occasions. However, the other interpretation is not a bad one: *The expectation of baseness* [*of the base*] *shall perish.* The plur. אוֹנִים is, when thus understood, a plur. of *intensity.* But the first method is somewhat more specific.

(8) The righteous shall be rescued from distress; and the wicked shall come in his stead.

Safety is here pledged to the righteous; while the wicked is doomed to the suffering of that which was before urgent on the righteous.

(9) By the mouth, a vile person destroys his neighbor; but by the knowledge of the righteous shall he be delivered.

By the mouth, i. e. by what the mouth speaks.—יֵחָלֵצוּ, Niph. Imperf. *plural,* although *neighbor* (sing.) is the subject. But then, this word is here virtually a noun of multitude, meaning *every and any neighbor.* A plur. verb in such case is very common.

(10) When it goeth well with the righteous, the city rejoiceth; but when the wicked perish, there is shouting.

Here are two Infinitives const. with בּ before them, both governing the Gen. as Inf. *nominascens.* Here are also two *rejoicings.* The first is the *joy* which men usually feel, when the righteous are prospered; the second is the *shout of exultation,* when base transgressors fall.

(11) By the blessing of the upright, the city shall be exalted; but by the mouth of the wicked, it shall be razed.

Exalted, תָּרוּם, seems here to mean, *put in a condition of safety,* or out of the reach of assault; like שָׂגַב, which means first *to exalt,* and then *to render safe.* The ground of the figure is a high wall, or a munition of rocks, the loftiness of which secures the safety of the enclosed city.—*The mouth of the wicked* is here supposed to utter curses or falsehoods, so as to bring vengeance on the city, or, so to speak, as to betray it by traitorous communications.

(12) He that useth despitefully his neighbor, is one who lacketh understanding; but the man of intelligence will keep silence.

בָּז, Part. of בּוּז, seems here to mean the utterance of contemptuous and slanderous language, which is despiteful usage; for, as opposed to this (in the next clause) stands *keep silence,* i. e. will not utter reproaches; either he will be silent where others reproach; or, he will be silent in respect to that, which the fool treats and speaks of contemptuously.

(13) He who goeth about as a slanderer, revealeth secrets; but he who is of a faithful spirit, concealeth a matter.

In other words: A slanderer will even reveal secrets, in order to gratify his propensity for prating; but a man of a trusty spirit will conceal what is committed to him in confidence. — נֶאֱמַן in const. state, so that the final Qamets of the Part. form is shortened, § 110. 2.

(14) Where there is no guidance the people fall; but by an increase of counsellors there is safety.

תַּחְבֻּלוֹת, plur. abstract, lit. *pilotage, steersmanship,* from חֶבֶל, *rope,* or חֹבֵל, *sailor = rope-man;* like our English *Salt* for *sailor.* All these meanings are secondary and tropical, for the root seems rather diverse from them. — רֹב, Inf. of רָבַב. — יוֹעֵץ, Part. used as a noun; and as it is here used in a *generic* sense, it may therefore be regarded and rendered as a plural. So I have given it in the version.

(15) An evil man showeth himself as evil, when he giveth pledge for a stranger; but he who hateth the striking of hands, shall be safe.

יֵרוֹעַ, Niph. Imperf. of רוּעַ, and in its reflexive sense; as in the version. *He shows himself as evil,* by hastily pledging himself, and then not redeeming his pledge as promised. — תוֹקְעִים means lit. *those who strike hands,* being to appearance a participle. The translation, however, I have made so as to refer rather to the *action* than to the *agents.* — Much difficulty has been made with this verse, by taking רַע as Inf. abs. in Kal, from רוּעַ. Erroneously, for this would be רוֹעַ, and not רַע. But the method of explanation, proposed in the version, is easy and obvious.

(16) A beautiful woman taketh fast hold of honor; even as the mighty grasp at riches.

כָּבוֹד, *honor*, in opposition to *shame*. A woman truly lovely will be eager to maintain strict propriety of conduct, instead of subjecting herself to reproach and shame.—עָרִיצִים, generally *violent*, *terrible*, but also *very powerful*, as here; see Lex. The meaning of the whole is, that a lovely woman will be as solicitous to maintain her honor, as the mighty usually are in quest of spoil or riches. Here comparison is signified by the וְ before the second clause, and therefore we may translate it—*and so*, or *even as*, § 152. B. 3.

(17) He who doeth good to himself, is a man of kindness; but he who troubleth his own flesh, is cruel.

The design of this is not to recommend *selfishness*, in the proper sense of that word, but a wise and prudent care and solicitude for one's own real good. This is *kindness*, i. e. kindness to himself. On the contrary, he who vexes himself by an improper course of conduct, is cruel to himself.

(18) The wicked acquireth deceitful gain; but he that soweth righteousness—a sure reward.

פְּעֻלַּת, is not only work, but also the *fruits of it*, i. e. *reward* or *gain*. To *deceitful gain* stands opposed *sure reward*. Before שֶׂכֶר, one may supply, if he chooses, עֹשָׂה from the preceding clause.

(19) As is righteousness in respect to life, even so is he that pursueth evil in respect to death.

That is, righteousness will gain the *sure reward* (before mentioned), and wickedness will meet with its recompense, viz. *death*. Some take כֵּן as a noun = *steadfastness*, and some as an adjective, *firm*, *fixed*. But this is unnecessary. The usual sense, as above, is well. The Sept. and Syr. read בֵּן, *son*. The text, from the seeming imperfection of its present construction, appears to have been disturbed; or, at least, it was *misread*, by some of the translators in ancient times.

(20) The perverse of heart are the abomination of Jehovah; but those who are upright in their way, are his delight. (21) Hand to hand, the evil man shall not go free; but the seed of the righteous shall be delivered.

In v. 21, we have two adjectives in the const. state, before the nouns which modify them; which construction is very frequent in this book, and common elsewhere. — יָד לְיָד, is an expression *sui generis*. Different meanings have been assigned to it; (*a*) *Hand against hand*, i. e. one man's hand against his neighbor's = the injurious man. (*b*) *From one hand to another* = from one generation to another. (*c*) *Joining hand to hand*, in the way or as a token of assurance = *truly, verily*. All these are little better than *guesses*. The phrase is evidently a proverbial one, and, like other brief gnomes, it is doubtless abridged or compressed. The most simple interpretation is that of J. H. Michaelis: '*Hand joined to hand*, will not protect the guilty, or get him clear.' In other words: 'Let the evil man struggle with all his might, he will not escape.' This is a good sense, and, in my view, the most easy and natural of all. The same is repeated in 16:5.

(22) A ring of gold in the snout of a swine, is a beautiful woman who departs from sound discretion.

In other words: Her beauty is like a gold ring in the snout of a swine, in case she departs from sound propriety in her conduct. A homely proverb, but very expressive. — סָרַת, Part. fem. const. of סוּר, lit. *a receder from.*

(23) The desire of the righteous is good only; the expectation of the wicked is indignation.

That is, the desire of the righteous will end in good or blessing; for God blesses the obedient. The wicked, too, have desire or expectations; but they will end in *indignation*, i. e. in bringing upon them the wrath of God, or punishment.

(24) There is who scattereth, and yet addition is made; and he who holdeth back more than is right, [it will be] only to poverty.

That is, there are those who give liberally, and yet grow rich. — נוֹסָף, *addition is made*, Part. Niphal. There is a different class, *who keep back* מִיֹּשֶׁר *beyond rectitude*, i. e. more than what is just and proper, and yet they grow poor in spite of their parsimony. Schultens and Bertheau take יֹשֶׁר here in the Arabic sense of the word, viz. *riches*. But this is against the rule which binds us to the Hebrew alone, so long as the word in question is sufficiently used to make it plain; which is the case here. 'Mean parsimony tends only to poverty,' is the sentiment of the last clause; and this is so significant, that we need not forsake the usual meaning of the Hebrew.

(25) The soul of blessing shall be well nourished; and he who waters, even the same shall be watered.

Soul of blessing, designates here, a man who cheerfully imparts blessings. — תְּדֻשָּׁן, lit. *shall be made fat;* the real idea is given in the version. — מַרְוֶה, Part. Hiph. of רָוָה; but the following יוֹרֶא comes from יָרָה, and is Imperf. Hiph., the final א being put for the ה, as the vowel-points show, § 74. n. 22. That is: 'The liberal man shall be liberally treated.'

(26) He who keepeth back corn — the people shall curse him; but blessings shall be on the head of him who procureth grain.

This refers to those, who, in a time of famine, hoard up their stores of corn in order to sell at a very advanced price, and thus take advantage of the poor and starving. — *Blessings on the head*, because, in the act of blessing, the hands of him who blessed were laid on the head of the object of blessing. — מַשְׁבִּיר, Hiph. Part. of the *denominative* verb הִשְׁבִּיר, constructed from שֶׁבֶר, *grain*. Hence the Hiph. verb, *to procure grain*. The verb, in other conjugations and cases, has a very different sense.

(27) He who earnestly seeks after good, will seek for [God's] good pleasure; but as to him who seeketh for evil, it shall come upon him.

The highest good is the *good will* of the Lord; so that a seeker for it will make it his object to obtain this. — The two first words of the second clause are in the Nom. independent, and are so translated.

(28) He who trusteth in his riches, he shall fall; but as a leaf shall the righteous blossom. (29) He who troubleth his own house shall inherit the wind; and a servant shall the fool be to him who is of a wise mind.

For v. 28, see Is. 66: 14. Ps. 92: 13. — V. 29, *He that troubleth*, etc., seems to refer to mismanagement, or the want of proper industry and economy. Such a man will acquire nothing valuable, but live as it were *upon the wind.* Nor is this all; such a negligent and slothful manager shall be reduced, even to becoming a servant to him who is wise enough to be active and economical.

(30) The fruit of the righteous is a tree of life; and he who winneth souls is wise.

The fruit of the righteous man, is the results which he produces by his words and actions. These, like a tree of life, impart to others a living and animating principle. — *Winneth souls*, lit. *taketh souls*, but the real meaning here is given in the version. It is only a *wise man* who can do this; and to do it is true wisdom, and one of its noblest works.

(31) If the righteous shall be recompensed in the earth; surely then the wicked and the sinner.

The question is not, whether *all* the reward of the righteous, or of the wicked, shall be dispensed in the present world; but the text says, first, that here the righteous shall receive blessings; and then, secondly, that the wicked shall surely have some retribution, viz. by sudden and premature death, and by the various evils which they must here suffer. If God's *mercy* bestows the one, his *justice* will inflict the other. — Bertheau makes אַף כִּי to mean *but not. How*, I am unable to see, (consult the Lex.), unless by making the last clause a negative *interrogatory*, so that אַף כִּי must be regarded as = *Is it truly so that?* which would imply a negative; see in Gen. 3 : 1. Of course, if we adopt this, we must render הֵן, at the beginning of the verse by *if;* as it sometimes clearly means. Indeed, with views differing from his, I have so translated it in my version. But if Bertheau is in the right, (and he may be *salva fide*), then the latter clause must be rendered thus: *Is it so indeed, that the wicked and the sinner* [*will be recompensed?*] If this be the sentiment, it looks like denying that adequate recompense will be made in the present world to the wicked. This certainly is true in one sense; for impenitent sinners do not here suffer all which they deserve. But is this truth revealed in such a shape, in the Old Testament? All along we have had, continually occurring, the threats of evil to the wicked, such as being prematurely cut down, having their hopes frustrated, etc. And can we safely build a different mode of speaking — one so widely different — on a doubtful grammatical construction? I have not ventured on this, in my version. And if Bertheau be in the right, then I apprehend הֵן should be taken *interrogatively*, as אִם often is. We must then render thus: *Will the righteous be recompensed in the earth? Is it indeed so, then, that the wicked* [*will be recompensed?*] But if these are real questions, we should expect some answer. And yet there is none. We must then regard the first clause as an *assumption*, viz. *If the righteous shall be rewarded in the earth*, (as all concede), *then*, etc. In this case, the sentiment runs thus: 'Since the righteous receive a recompense in such a world of suffering and sorrow as this, then doubtless the wicked will also receive a retribution.' In other words: 'The providential government of God is one of moral retribution; for both the righteous and the wicked have their appropriate recompense under it, even in the present world.' There is no necessity of straining these words, so as to make them mean, that *all* the reward of either class is here given and received. When the apostle says, that "Godliness is profitable unto all things, having promise of the life that now is," (1 Tim. 4: 8), this does not hinder him from adding: "and of that which is to come." But an addition like this is rare in the Old Testament; indeed, it cannot be found in such a shape. I draw, therefore, from our text this simple sentiment: 'The retributive government of God is exercised over both the righteous and the wicked, in the present world, assigning to each their appropriate reward.' If the writer reasoned analogically in his own mind, he was doubtless ready to say: 'The like retributive government must extend to the *other world*, as well as to this.' But that *other world* is not explicitly brought to view, in the book of Proverbs.

I cannot see how a *negative* form can well be given to this last clause. Not that grammar stands absolutely in the way, but because the whole book everywhere discloses the punishment or chastisement of sinners in the present life. This lies on the very face of it. This does not, as has already been said, deny chastisement in a future world; for of this the writer does not here treat. How then can we fairly make out of the last clause a denial of retribution in the present world, which is not only everywhere threatened, but is also everywhere in the Old Testament historically exhibited as matter of fact? I must therefore abide by the sentiment of the version. It will not be in point for Bertheau to refer to such texts as Ecc. 9 : 1, 2, 11, 12. 8 : 14, and the like; for these are merely sentiments of an objector. Such an attitude the author of the book and chapter before us does not assume.

CHAP. XII. 1—28.

(1) He who loveth instruction, loveth knowledge; and he who hateth admonition is brutish.

Instruction and *admonition* are nearly equivalent here. The first, however, is more general; the second somewhat specific. — בַּעַר might be rendered, in our vulgar tongue, *is a boor;* for this English word looks very much like a derivate from the Hebrew root.

(2) The good man shall obtain good will from Jehovah; but the man of evil devices will he punish.

Rare is the use of טוֹב, as here, for *moral good.* The usual words are צַדִּיק, or חָסִיד, or תָּמִים, to designate what we usually name a *good* man in the moral sense. — מְזִמּוֹת, in the bad sense here, which is the more common one. — יַרְשִׁיעַ, lit. *shall make guilty,* i. e. *shall treat as guilty,* which of course means *shall punish.* But who does this? *Jehovah,* as the preceding clause shows.

(3) A man shall not be established by wickedness; but the root of the righteous shall never be moved.

Wickedness cannot secure enduring prosperity; but *the root of the righteous,* (who is here tacitly compared to a tree), cannot move hither and thither. In this last case, viz. supposing the root to be moving hither and thither, the standing of the tree would then be unstable.

(4) A virtuous woman is the diadem of her husband; but like rottenness in the bones, is she who causeth shame.

חַיִל, like the Latin *virtus,* has two meanings, viz., that of *strength* or *fortitude,* and also that of *probity;* see Heb. Lex. No. 4. — *Rottenness in the bones,* would cause the whole fabric of the body to crumble and fall. — מְבִישָׁה, *causing shame,* viz. by her base conduct.

(5) The purposes of the righteous are justice; but the counsellings of the wicked are deceit.

Purposes are justice, i. e. not his outward actions and words merely, but even his *internal thoughts* and intentions. תַּחְבֻּלוֹת = κυβερνήσεις, *controllings, directions*, equivalent to *counsel* in respect to conduct. These are connected with fraud. The Hebrew is stronger (— *are justice* — *are deceit)* than the corresponding adjectives.

(6) The words of the wicked are a lying in wait for blood; but the mouth of the upright will deliver them.

The wicked concert plans for lying in wait to shed the blood of the innocent; for that such persons are implied, seems to result from יַצִּילֵם, where the plur. suff. to the verb refers to the *upright* who are in danger, who must be the same persons that the wicked wish to destroy. — אֱרָב־, with short ŏ, because of the Maqqeph. It is the Inf. *nominascens* of Kal.

(7) When the wicked are overturned, they are no more; but the house of the righteous shall stand.

הָפוֹךְ, Inf. abs., which is of all numbers, genders, and persons, and so may be translated as above. Or we may render thus: *Is there an overturning of the wicked*, or *are the wicked overturned, then are they no more*, i. e. final destruction shall succeed their overthrow. The lot of the righteous is the reverse of this. They are not overthrown, but remain steadfast.

(8) According to his discretion shall a man be praised; but he who is perverse of heart, shall be despised.

לְפִי is used as a particle = *pro ratione secundum*, root פֶּה. — נַעֲוֵה in reg. becomes נַעֲוֵה as in the text, and is a Niph. Part. adjective, *r.* עָוָה. לָבוּז, lit. *for contempt*, i. e. shall be exposed to it.

(9) Better is he who is despised, yet has a servant, than he who honoreth himself and lacketh bread.

Better, not in a moral sense, but as we say, *more lucky*, or *better off.* — To make עֶבֶד לוֹ mean *serve himself* (with Umbreit), can be done only by shifting the vowels and pointing thus: עֹבֵד לוֹ. But this adds nothing to show the *betterment*, which consists in the fact, that the despised person has one to aid his labors in the field, and thus procure sufficiency of bread, while he who boasts of honors lacks even the necessaries of life. Sentiment: 'Better is the condition of a poor man, who has the means under his control of aiding his exertions for sustenance, than the nobleman, real or fancied, who is in a state of starvation.'

(10) The righteous careth for the life of his beast; but the tender mercies of the wicked are cruelty.

יוֹדֵעַ, *taketh knowledge of, careth for;* and so, frequently. — בְּהֶמְתּוֹ, suff. state of בְּהֵמָה. — אַכְזָרִי, prop. adj., but here used as a noun — *cruelty.* 'While the righteous care even for the enjoyment of the brutes, the wicked disregard both man and beast.'

(11) He who tilleth his land shall have plenty of bread; but he who followeth after vain persons, lacketh understanding.

יִשְׂבַּע, lit. *shall be satiated with,* לָחֶם after it being the Acc. of the means; *Qamets* in pause. The sense is given in the version. — רֵיקִים, comp. Judg. 9 : 2. 2 Kings 4 : 3, for the meaning here given to the word. — It might mean *vanities;* but this would not alter the general sense of the clause. *Vain persons* here means *idle and profligate men,* who will not labor in order to till their land.

(12) The wicked desireth an evil net; but the root of the righteous shall be firm.

Ewald has changed the text until it yields this meaning: *The desire of the wicked is an evil net; but the root of the righteous endures*, i. e. the wicked wish to ensnare the good, but they are frustrated. Others have varied the meaning in several ways. All this is unnecessary. *The wicked desires an evil net*, i. e. destruction, in the same sense as when Wisdom says: "All who hate me, *love death*," 8: 36; and also like to 11: 27, "*He who seeketh after evil*, it shall come upon him." Where a false course is preferred to a true one, the Hebrews spoke of the man who exhibits such a preference, as *loving*, *seeking after* the false course, regardless of consequences; and so here. — As to the *root of the righteous*, see under v. 3. — יִתֵּן is an uncertain word. It comes apparently from נָתַן, which often means *put*, *place*, *constitute*, with an object after it. That object may be שֹׁרֶשׁ here, provided we make the word *God* a Nom. to יִתֵּן. Still, *putting* or *placing* does not give a sense altogether appropriate here. But there is another verbal root, יָתַן, from which אֵיתָן, *strong*, *firm*, comes; and this seems to me to be the probable root of יִתֵּן here. If so, it is to be placed with the third class of verbs פ״י, whose Yodh radical in the Imperf. assimilates with the letter that follows, as in the case of verbs פ״ן; see § 70. Then we have a good sense. The verb so understood is intrans., and שֹׁרֶשׁ is the Nom. to it. Thus we obtain the following version: *The root of the righteous shall be firm.* It is no more strange, to say the least, that Tseri should be the last vowel here, than that it should be in the case of יִתֵּן from נָתַן. Irregular verbs sometimes form the Imperf. in this way, § 47. 3. n. 2. This, moreover, makes the sense quite plain and easy. — Sentiment: 'The wicked desire that which will destroy them; but the righteous that which will give them firmness and safety.'

(13) In the transgression of the lips is a snare of the evil man; but the righteous shall escape from distress.

The evil which a man utters, often ensnares him, and causes him distress; but the righteous, who refrains from sinning thus, escapes the distress consequent upon sin.

(14) By the fruit of a man's mouth, he shall abound in good; and the reward of a man's hands he shall return to him.

Fruit of the mouth is what the mouth speaks. The supposition is here, that a righteous man speaks in harmony with his character. This shall bring him abundant good. — Also what he *does*, as well as *says*, will not be useless. *The reward of his hands*, i. e. the reward of what his hands have done, *he* [Jehovah] *will return to him*. If גְּמוּל were Nom. to the verb, as some make it, we should expect יָשׁוּב, as the Kethibh has it. But adopting יָשִׁיב in Hiph. (the better reading), we must then make *Jehovah* the Nominative. Often elsewhere is this word implied. This gives a good sense.

(15) The way of a fool is right in his own eyes; but he who hearkeneth to counsel is wise.

The fool, being self-conceited, feels that he needs no counsel; but a man truly wise will cautiously seek for counsel, when perplexities arise.

(16) The fool—his vexation is made known at once; but he who concealeth what is shameful is wary.

בַּיּוֹם, lit. *on the day*, i. e. at the very time when his vexation arises, he immediately and imprudently discloses it. More *wary* or *sagacious* (עָרוּם) is he, *who conceals shameful things*. The meaning of this last clause is: 'Who keeps back from bruiting abroad every shameful slander;' or perhaps (here), 'who refrains from immediately manifesting his indignation at contumelious treatment, or at shameful conduct towards himself.' A fool talks loudly about such matters, and takes ready and high offence; the wise man more prudently passes them by in silence.

(17) He who breatheth forth truth, uttereth that which is right; but a false witness — deceit.

יָפִיחַ, Hiph. of פּוּחַ *breathes out* or *forth*, seems to indicate the natural habit (so to speak) of truth-telling, i. e. he utters it as habitually and readily as he breathes. The case here in view, seems to be that of *giving testimony;* for so the עֵד *(witness)* of the next clause indicates. — *Deceit,* i. e. *uttereth deceit,* for the verb יַגִּיד is to be carried forward mentally, from the first clause, and supplied here. I have imitated the brevity of the original, in the version, which, by a discriminative punctuation, still makes the idea of the writer plain. Sentiment: 'A lover of truth will testify truly, while a lying witness speaks only to deceive.'

(18) There are who prate, like the stabbings of a sword; but the tongue of the wise is healing.

בּוֹטֶה is sing.; but since it is *generic* here, I have assigned to it a plur. number in the version, because this agrees better with our idiom in such a case. Deep and deadly wounds does a בּוֹטֶה make, like those of a sword. But the *wise* speak in order to soothe or allay wounded feelings, not to aggravate them. — מַרְפֵּא is a noun here, a formative of Hiphil, which gives it the additional shade of being *causal of healing.*

(19) The lip of truth shall stand fast forever; but the tongue of falsehood, only for the twinkling of an eye.

The lip of truth shall be rewarded by steadfastness of safe condition. — Lit. עַד־אַרְגִּיעָה, *until I shall make a wink;* for the verb is a Hiph. *denominative,* derived from רֶגַע, *a wink;* and so the Hiph. verb means *to make a wink.* But in our text, the word is employed as a Hiphilic noun with a Prep. before it. — Sentiment: 'A lying tongue shall suddenly be destroyed — the very reverse of the safe condition of those who speak truth.'

(20) Deceit is in the heart of those who devise evil; but to the counsellors of peace — joy.

The meaning of the first clause must be developed by the

aid of the second. *Deceit*, then, is the object to be accomplished by *devisers of evil*, when they give counsel. — But *peace-counsellors* instead of contriving *deceit* so as to injure others, have in their hearts the purpose of making their neighbors *glad*. It may, however, be rendered subjectively thus: *peace-counsellors shall have joy*. But *joy* seems to be the counter-part here of *deceit;* and of this evil-devisers are not the *recipients*, but the *authors*. So of *peace-counsellors*, their object is to become authors of the *satisfaction* or *joy* of others.

(21) No calamity shall befall the righteous; but the wicked shall be filled with evil.

יְאֻנֶּה, lit. *shall be caused to happen*, in Hoph. The version gives the true sense. — רָע, Acc., governed by a verb of *filling*, § 135. 3. *b*. — מָלְאוּ is made a virtual Imperf. by the *Vav* prefixed to the clause with which it is connected. If the verb stood first, the case would be plain; but since the Nom. here precedes, only for the sake of emphasis, the Vav before it exercises its usual power over the verb. This is demanded by the connection with יְאֻנֶּה in the Imperfect.

(22) An abomination of Jehovah are lying lips; but those who practice truth are his delight. (23) A wary man concealeth knowledge; but the heart of fools proclaims folly.

V. 22, the *doers of truth* means those who adhere to it in word and work; comp. the Greek *ποιεῖν τὴν ἀλήθειαν*, John 3 : 21. V. 23, *concealeth knowledge*, means that he modestly forbears to obtrude his knowledge upon others, or is somewhat shy of displaying it. — On the other hand, the fool has so much self-conceit that he cannot forbear displaying his folly. *Display* he will make, at all events; and if so, it must of course be one of *folly*.

(24) The hand of the diligent shall bear rule; but a slothful [hand] shall be tributary.

The diligent, by his activity, attains to power and influence. רְמִיָּה fem. adj. or Part., means lit. *deceitful*, but as it stands opposed here to the hand of the *diligent*, it here virtually means *slothful;* for such a hand *deceives* the hopes of those who depend upon its earnings. — לָמַס, lit. *for tribute*, i. e. it is obliged to become a tributary or a servant to the diligent. Sentiment: 'Idleness brings poverty and dependence.'

(25) Sorrow in the heart of a man will bow it down; but a goodly word will gladden it.

יַשְׁחֶנָּה, Hiph. Imperf. of שָׁחַח, exhibits two apparent anomalies; first, the verb is masc., while the Nom. דְּאָגָה is fem.; secondly, the suff. ־ֶנָּה is fem., while it relates to לֶב־. As to the first, real analogies are quite rare. If the verb *preceded*, the case could be solved on the ground of a kind of impersonal use of the verb; but here the *noun precedes*, and the case is therefore one which is wholly abnormal. Still the sense is plain, and unavoidable. As to the two fem. suffixes appended to the two verbs, there is little of serious difficulty. Nearly all the names of parts of the human body are, or may be, treated as nouns *feminine*. So with לֵב, which is plainly treated as fem. here; see a large list of these in Ewald, § 174. *d.* — *Goodly word* means either good tidings, i. e. an announcement that things are going on well, or a word of comfort and encouragement.

(26) The righteous showeth the way to his friend; but the way of the wicked will mislead them.

יָתֵר, Hiph. Imperf. of תּוּר, or its equivalent תָּרַר, lit. *to lead one round*, i. e. so as to take a survey. — מֵרֵעֵהוּ, a peculiar formation = רֵעַ, *friend*. It seems to be made up of מִן, *from* or *of*, and רֵעַ; which is of unfrequent occurrence. If the word were a *participial* of רָעָה, it must be written מַרְעֶה. Still, the meaning is plain. — תַּתְעֵם, Imperf. Hiph. of תָּעָה, with plur. suffix.

(27) The indolent man shall not roast his game; but a precious treasure of any man is a diligent person.

רְמִיָּה, here *indolence;* but as it means *the indolent man,* the verb is masc., i. e. it is a case of concord *ad sensum.* The most probable meaning seems to be, that indolence will prevent the slothful from catching the game, and so he will have none to roast. But perhaps the sentiment is still more pointed, viz., he is too lazy to cook his game when caught. The text will bear either explanation. — The חָרוּץ, on the other hand, will be sure to obtain game for his employer, and so is a treasure to him.

(28) In the way of righteousness is life; and [in] her path-way is no death.

The Masorites have removed the Mappiq from the ה in נְתִיבָה; wrongly, as it necessarily refers to צְדָקָה. — אַל־מָוֶת I take to be a compound word, in which the אַל is a negative like our *un* in *un-do*, etc. Comp. Prov. 30 : 31, where we find אַלְקוּם, i. e. אַל *not,* and קוּם *people,* meaning, in a kind of tropical way, *obedient subjects,* literally, *such as do not rise up,* i. e. in rebellion, = *non-resistants.* — *Death* by itself is the *opposite* of *life;* but as no opposition is here admissible, a negative is put in, which gives the meaning *no-death,* and this is equivalent to חַיִּים. Generally לֹא is employed in such cases; e. g. לֹא־עֵץ, *no-wood,* i. e. something different from, and opposite to, wood. So לֹא־אֵל, לֹא־אִישׁ, לֹא־אָדָם, etc. All such combinations approach to our negative use of *un.*

CHAP. XIII. 1—25.

(1) A wise son is instructed of his father; but a scorner hearkeneth not to rebuke.

מוּסַר, as pointed, is a noun in the const. state, so that lit. it means *instruction,* i. e. we have the abstract for concrete;

and as *concrete*, it is rendered in the version above. I prefer, with Ewald, to assign it to the Part. in Hophal, for then we have *he who is instructed.* Sentiment: 'In order to be wise, a father's admonitions must be received; but scorners will not submit to this.'

(2) Of the fruit of a man's mouth he shall eat good; but the soul of the treacherous — violence.

That is, in case a man speaks what is right and proper, he shall eat the good fruit of so doing; while the soul of him who speaks treacherously [shall eat] violence; i. e. such an one will be *violently dealt with* or treated, by those whom he has betrayed.

(3) He who guardeth well his mouth, preserveth his life; he who openeth wide his lips — destruction to him.

Not unfrequently, anger and slanderous words provoke to murderous deeds. To guard well against these, is therefore to preserve life. — *Openeth wide*, speaks, loudly and much, such things as provoke assault. — *Destruction to him;* may be taken as an exclamation optative; or simply thus: *destruction will be to him.* The latter is more probable. *Wishes of evil* do not appear in this book.

(4) His soul — the sluggard's — strongly craves, and there is nothing; but the soul of the diligent shall be abundantly fed.

The pronoun in נַפְשׁוֹ is anticipative, and refers to עָצֵל, *more Syrorum*, § 119. 6. n. 3. — *There is nothing*, because the sluggard will do nothing to provide. — תְּדֻשָּׁן, lit. *shall be made fat.* The real sense is given in the version. In the one case, there is starvation; in the other, plenty.

(5) A false report the righteous will hate; but the wicked causeth shame and putteth to the blush.

The wicked man, instead of loathing slander, will so speak as to cause others to be ashamed and to blush for him. Possibly the last clause may mean: *acteth shamefully and scandalously;* in which case we must give to Hiphil a Kal meaning.

(6) Righteousness will preserve the innocent in his way; but wickedness casts headlong the sinful.

תָּם, *tŏm*, short ŏ, because it is in regimen; ground-form תֹּם. — חַטָּאת (for חַטַּאת), lit. *sin;* but it is a plain case of abstract for concrete; and so it means *sinners.*

(7) There is who showeth himself as rich, and yet hath nothing at all; there is who showeth himself as poor, and yet there is much wealth.

In both cases the Hithp. Part. retain that peculiar meaning of the conjugation which designates *pretence, show,* § 53. 3. *a.* Both classes of such men are hypocrites and deceivers; the one for pretending to possess what he does not possess, the other for pretending to be worth nothing, (in order to cheat his creditors), when in fact he is rich. Sentiment: 'Men will often play the hypocrite for the sake of gain.'

(8) The ransom of a man's life is his riches; and yet the poor heareth not rebuke.

'Riches will frequently buy off a man from punishment,' is the meaning of the first clause. That of the second is somewhat obscure. To me it appears thus: 'Notwithstanding this obvious advantage of wealth, yet the poor man will not listen to those who rebuke him for sloth and wastefulness, which have made him poor.' The supposition on this ground is, that the man is poor by his own fault. Or it is thus: 'The rich are inculpated by oppressive magistrates, in order to exact money from them in the way of ransom; the poor escape such accusations, because they have nothing to give as a ransom.' This is a *possible* sense; but hardly the more *probable* one.

(9) The light of the righteous is joyful; but the lamp of the wicked shall be put out.

Is joyful, tropically understood, i. e. burns brightly and cheerfully, as if rejoicing. The reverse is true of the lamp of the wicked.

(10) Only by pride is strife produced; but with those who take counsel is wisdom.

We may translate the first clause thus: *Only by pride one produces or occasions strife.* The sense is the same as that in the version. — נוֹעָצִים, Part. Niph. of יָעַץ, denoting mutual or reciprocal action, as Niph. often does, § 50. 2. *b*. Of course, *taking counsel* denotes mutual communication. Those who act thus modestly, and do not proudly follow their own opinion, will walk in the path of wisdom, and produce no strife.

(11) Wealth gotten without effort will grow small; but he who gathereth into the hand increaseth [it].

הֶבֶל, *vanity, nothingness*, is a peculiar word for *slight effort*, or *no effort*. Yet the other clause seems to make this necessary. The meaning is: 'Wealth which is in any way obtained without industry or effort.' Nothing is more true, than that this is often squandered in a little time. But that which is gathered by industry, which is collected by *handfuls*, is commonly of that stable character, which secures increase.

(12) Hope deferred maketh the heart sick; but a tree of life is the desire which is accomplished.

"We live by hope." When the realization of it is long deferred, the heart sinks with discouragement. — *Tree of life* is a vivid image of the *animating power* of hope when it is fulfilled. — בָּאָה, spoken of desire, of prophecy, or of a sign of something future, means *happeneth*, or *is accomplished*, see Lex. בּוֹא. 2. *e*.

(13) He who despiseth the word, shall bring destruction on himself; but he who feareth the commandment, is he who shall be at peace.

23

Word, viz., of warning and reproof. — יֵחָבֶל־לוֹ, Niphal reflexive, with the pronoun of object expressed. The true sense is given in the version. — יְשֻׁלָּם, lit. *shall be made to have peace.*

(14) The instruction of the wise man is a fountain of life, that one may turn away from the snares of death.

תּוֹרָה in its original sense here, *instruction*; as is quite usual in this book. It not only gives life, but it operates so as to turn away the unwary from the snares of death. — לָסוּר, is here equivalent to תָּסוּר (third fem.) with תּוֹרָה for its Nom. Frequently is the Inf. with לְ employed in such a way; § 129. 3. n. 1. Comp. v. 25 below.

(15) Kindly discretion procureth favor; but the way of the treacherous is stony.

טוֹב, *kindness*, must be associated with *discretion* or *intelligence*, in order to secure favor. — *Way of the treacherous is* אֵיתָן, which last word means, first, *lasting*, then *firm* or *hard*, and finally (in poetry) *a rock*, from its hardness; see Lex. No. 4. *A stony way*, is one which it is hard to travel. — *Hard*, in our English version, is equivocal. A *way* literally *hard*, would be easy of travel; but *hard* in the sense of *difficult*, gives us what the Heb. aims at, yet not exactly what it expresses. The Heb. figuratively presents the ground of the way as being *hard* or *difficult*, viz., because it is *stony*. *Treachery* will of course render a man's way through life very difficult; for resentment will follow, and many of its consequences. It leads into a *stony* way, and makes rough travelling.

(16) Every wary man will act with foresight; but the fool diffuseth abroad folly.

דַּעַת means here that kind of *knowledge*, which has respect to what a man is about to do, and therefore = *foresight*. — *Spreadeth abroad his folly*, namely, by acting *without foresight*. All men see, in such a case, what folly he commits.

(17) A wicked messenger falleth into trouble; but a faithful ambassador is healing.

Wicked here means one who acts deceitfully through sloth; comp. 10: 26, which expresses the idea fully. *A wicked man*, in the common sense of this phrase, may be, and often is, a *swift* messenger. But *wicked as a messenger*, is what the proverb means; and this of course means *slothful*, *inactive*, and therefore disappointing those who send him. — He *falls into evil*, because he is punished by those who sent him, for his negligence. — On the other hand, *a faithful messenger*, (צִיר, from the root צִיר *to go round)*, is מַרְפֵּא, lit. *healing*, and here *soothing* or *alleviation*, i. e. relief from anxiety to hear something, respecting the matter of the embassy or mission; comp. this last word in 12: 18.

(18) Poor and despised is he who rejecteth instruction; but he who watchfully observeth admonition shall be honored.

רֵישׁ וְקָלוֹן, lit. *poverty and contempt*, both abstracts, which, in the version, I have turned into *concretes*, because such is the real meaning of the words. — שֹׁמֵר, is here used in the frequent sense of *watchfully observing* or *attending to*.

(19) Desire accomplished, is sweet to the soul; but it is an abomination of fools to turn from evil.

The contrast here implies, that the first clause has respect to the *desire of the wise*. This, it is taken for granted, is for good; and when that good is attained, then is it grateful to the spirit of a good man. — On the other hand, fools cling with such tenacity to evil, that they will not quit it so as to cherish such desires.

(20) He who walketh with the wise shall be wise; but he who delighteth in fools, showeth himself as evil.

The Kethibh of two verbs should be thus pointed: הָלוֹךְ . . . וַחֲכַם, i. e. first the Inf. abs. as a command, and then the

Imper. as declaring the sequel; a common construction, and equally good as the Qeri, § 128. 4. *b. c.* § 127. 2. — In the Qeri, וְחָכָם of the Kethibh is of course read יֶחְכָּם. — רֹעֶה has here the secondary sense of the word, in which it = רָצָה, and is merely a softened form of it. Such a sense of *the word is frequent in this book;* see 15: 14. 28: 7. 29: 3, and comp. Lex. — יֵרוֹעַ, Imperf. Niph. of רוּעַ, and reflexive like Hithp., § 50. 2. *c.*

(21) Evil will pursue sinners; but the righteous will he reward with good.

The Nom. to יְשַׁלֶּם, (ֶ because of Maqqeph), is *Jehovah;* which word is very often omitted in these apothegms, for the sake of brevity; but only in cases where it is readily supplied. The Piel verb here governs, as usual, two Accusatives, § 136. 1.

(22) The good man makes heirs of children's children; but the wealth of the sinner is laid up for the just.

We cannot exactly imitate the Heb. יַנְחִיל as to form, since it governs the Acc. directly. But the version comes near to this. — *Laid up for the just,* the wealth which the sinner lays up, is speedily dissipated, or by his premature death it soon goes to others. God regards it as treasured up for the just, and often appropriates it in this way.

(23) The fallow-ground of the poor [yields] an abundance of food; and there are, who are taken away by reason of injustice.

The Hebrew implies *is* where I have inserted *yields,* because this word is more accordant with our idiom. The second clause, by its contrast, leads us to understand *poor* here, as meaning *the righteous poor;* for unless they are righteous, this promise does not enure to them. — בְּלֹא מִשְׁפָּט, see what is said of such combinations in Heb., under 12: 28. Maqqeph should be inserted here between the words, as it is there. Lit. *by not-justice,* i. e. by injustice, as in the version. — נִסְפֶּה refers to the violent death which is threatened and frequently ensues, after flagrant acts of injustice. Sentiment: 'The righteous poor have their wants supplied; the unjust perish because of their wickedness or oppression.'

(24) He who withholdeth the rod hateth his son; but he who loveth him, earnestly seeketh his instruction.

Hateth his son, i. e. treats him as real hatred might well dictate. So it is said: "Those who hate me, *love death;*" If any man come to me, *and hate not his father*, etc." A common idiom, in Hebrew, and a very energic one. — שִׁחֲרוֹ, Piel with suff.; and this suff. is anticipative of מוּסָר, and related to it. This mode of phraseology is designed for intensity, although our Grammars call it *pleonasm;* § 119. 6. n. 3. But it may be, that the Acc. וֹ- is for the Dat., and means *for him,* § 119. 4. We are not obliged to understand *rod* here in the mere literal sense; but it means at least *correction in some way for faults.*

(25) The righteous eateth to the satisfying of his appetite; but the stomach of the wicked shall be empty.

For the first clause, comp. 10 : 3.— בֶּטֶן, lit. *belly;* and then, any of the principal *viscera* contained in it, e. g. the *stomach,* the *womb,* etc. — תֶּחְסָר (Qamets in pause), lit. *shall be lacking.*

CHAP. XIV. 1—35.

(1) A woman's wisdom buildeth up her house; but folly teareth it down with her own hands.

חָכְמוֹת, plur. for the simple abstract noun, which therefore may take a verb singular, (concord *ad sensum*); see on 1: 20. — נָשִׁים, plur., of *women,* i. e. such wisdom as belongs to women, or such as becomes them. The version is a shade more specific. — *Her house,* if referred to wisdom, (as the grammar seems to require), must mean *the house where she dwells.* — *Teareth it down with her own hands*, viz., the hands of folly. The ־ֶנָּה refers to בֵּית, which is usually masc.

(2) He who walketh in his integrity, feareth God; but he who is perverse as to his ways, despiseth him. (3) In the mouth of a fool, haughtiness is a rod; but as to the lips of the wise, they shall preserve them.

V. 2. יְרֵא const. state. — The same is true of נְלוֹז, Part. Niph. — בּוֹזֵהוּ, Part. of בָּזָה with suff. — V. 3, *Haughtiness is a rod,* i. e. he speaks so haughtily as to bring chastisement — *a rod* — upon himself. On the other hand, what the wise utter will conduce to their safety. — תִּשְׁמוּרֵם, Imperf. third plur. fem., with וּ in order to prolong the sound before a pause, (as in § 47. 3. n. 1). Still there is an *anomaly* here, which nearly or quite all of the critics have failed to explain, and most of them even to notice. The full third fem. plur. Imperf., without suffix, would be תִּשְׁמֹרְנָה, the suff. form, תִּשְׁמְרוּ, see § 59, (here תִּשְׁמוּרוּ), and with suff. תִּשְׁמוּרוּם; whereas we now have, instead of ־רוּם which is the normal ending, the syllable ־רֵם. But *Tseri* is the union-vowel of the suff. to the third *sing.* Imperf., and וּ to the third *plur.*, whether masc. or fem. The pointing is therefore plainly *anomalous.* Schelling (Comm. in loc.) says, that an ancient *error scribarum* has put תִּשְׁמוּרֵם for the proper תִּשְׁמְרוּם, by a transposition of the וּ. It may be so; but this does not account for the ־ֵם form of the suff., instead of ־וּם. Gesenius (Lehrgeb. s. 306, No. 10) puts the verb here in the 2d pers. sing.; against the usage of the book, which makes no such transitions of person as belong to lyric and prophetic poetry. The suff. is *masc.* plur., because it refers to *the wise.* The וּ after the ר is dropped out in writing, plainly because of the וּ inserted before it; but then it should still be written רֻם (not רֵם). Of course we are compelled to admit an error here in the vowel; or else to admit a peculiar anomaly in pointing, for which an analogon has not yet been produced. Of the meaning of the passage, as a whole, there is no room for doubt.

(4) Where there are no oxen, the stall is empty; and there is an abundance of productions through the strength of cattle.

Where no oxen are employed, the stalls are not filled; but where the strength of cattle is employed, there increase of produce will be the result. — שׁוֹר is generic.

(5) A faithful witness will not speak lies; but he who breatheth forth falsehood, is a lying witness.

That is, he who habitually indulges in falsehood. — יָפִיחַ *breathes it forth* — will do the same thing when called to testify.

(6) The scorner seeketh wisdom, and there is none; but knowledge is easy to the understanding man.

Knowledge is the gift of God to sincere seekers; but the scorner belongs not to them, and therefore may seek and not find. — נָקָל, Part. Niph. of קָלַל. But the gender is *masculine*, although דַּעַת is the subject. This brings into view an important class of *exceptions to concord* in gender. It seems that *Inf. forms*, even when fem. to appearance, are sometimes treated as *abstracts without any really appropriate gender*, and may resolve themselves of course, in such cases, into the leading gender, i. e. the masculine. So in Prov. 16: 16. 29: 25. Ps. 73: 28. See also for דַּעַת, Prov. 2: 10. Job 33: 3. And sometimes this same license is abnormally extended to other nouns, which are not fem. Infinitives; e. g. in 12: 25 above, also Job 8: 7. Ezek. 7: 25. Josh. 2: 17. See Ewald, § 174. *g*, who has more extensively developed this idiom, than any other grammarian.

(7) Go from the presence of a foolish man, for thou hast not discerned the lips of knowledge.

That is, quit the company of fools, for they can teach thee nothing. Thou hast knocked at the wrong door, to find what thou seekest, if thou goest to them. It is not there, and therefore thou hast not discerned it.

(8) The wisdom of the wary man discerns his way; but the folly of fools is deceit.

The wary consider and understand the way in which they go; but fools, through inconsideration, are deceived as to their way, and are easily misled. They have not sufficient wisdom to discern the right way.

(9) Sin-offering mocks fools; but among the upright there is ready acceptance.

Not, as most interpreters: *Fools mock at sin-offering*, for then the verb must be *plural.* — אָשָׁם is plainly the Nom.; and the meaning is, that when sin-offering is formally presented by fools, it mocks their hopes, because it is not accepted. Exactly the reverse is it with the upright. Their offerings find רָצוֹן, *good-will*, i. e. ready acceptance.

(10) The heart knoweth its own bitterness; and with its joy a stranger cannot intermeddle.

In other words: 'Men learn by experience the bitterness of suffering, better than any one can tell them; and others are not altogether adequate judges.' — And so with *enjoyment;* it is *subjective*, and therefore not fully cognizable by any intermeddler.

(11) The house of the wicked shall be destroyed; but the tent of the upright shall flourish. (12) There is a way which is right in the view of a man, and yet the end thereof are the ways of death.

For v. 11, comp. 12:7. — V. 12, לִפְנֵי = בְּעֵינֵי, *in the view of.* — *Ways of death*, plur. of intensity, = the sure way of death.

(13) Even by laughter the heart is made sad; and the end of joy itself is sorrow.

That is: 'There are cases where laughter is premature, and is quickly turned into sorrow.' So things in which we rejoice at first, sometimes become the occasion of grief.

The suff. to אַחֲרִיתָהּ is anticipative of שִׂמְחָה, and relates to it; see under 13: 4. This expresses intensity; which is also exhibited in the version above.

(14) He shall be satiated with his own ways, who turneth back with his heart; but away from him is the good man.

In סוּג לֵב, the first is a Part. pass., lit. the phrase means *turned back of heart*, which we are obliged to modify somewhat, in our idiom. — *His ways*, are evil ways, and therefore will meet with ample retribution. — מֵעָלָיו has occasioned much perplexity. Some have changed it into other words, significant of *works, retribution*, etc. It means, however, as it is translated above; and the sentiment is, that *the good man will keep aloof from him who turns back*. He will not associate with him, while in this apostatizing condition.

(15) The simple will credit every report; but the wary will give heed to his steps.

A mark of folly is excessive credulity; and by this the simpleton is misled. But the wary man will, as we say, *look before he leaps*. — אֲשֻׁרוֹ, is sing.; but our idiom requires the plural.

(16) A wise man feareth, and turneth away from evil; but the fool is haughty and confident.

מִתְעַבֵּר, usually means: *is enraged;* but here it is opposed to the modest and *humble* course of the wise, and means *to act haughtily;* see in Lex. The fool is, from self-conceit, haughty, and confident in his own opinion. He fears not evil.

(17) He who is hasty in his anger, committeth folly; and a man of evil devices will be hated.

קְצַר אַפַּיִם, is a peculiar phrase. The opposite is in v. 29 below, viz., אֶרֶךְ אַפַּיִם; lit. *short of anger*, and *long of anger*. קְצַר is the const. of קָצֵר, § 111. 2. It is singular, that the *nostrils* should have been pitched upon by the Hebrews, as the most expressive symbol of *anger*. This passion does indeed inflate and distend the nostrils, and sometimes express itself by snorting; but the *eye* is more significant of it, as we are apt to think. Yet however this may be, the secondary sense of אַף is *anger, rage. Short* (קְצַר) *of anger* means *hasty to become angry*, i. e. no delay is given to it.— In the latter clause, מְזִמּוֹת is taken by Berth. in the *good* sense = *consideration*; and he makes out the sense thus: '*A man of prudent consideration will be hated*, i. e. provided he does evil.' But whence comes this last supplement? I see no special ground for it. On the other hand, Umbreit and J. H. Michaelis render as above; and so doing, all is plain. Comp. 24:8 and 12:16.

(18) The simple inherit folly; but the wary are crowned with knowledge.

יַכְתִּרוּ, in Hiph.; but as there is no Kal, it is here used in an intransitive way, and may be rendered passively as above. So Gesenius: *coronantar intelligentia*, in Lex. Lit. it would run thus: *Make a crown of knowledge.*

(19) The evil bow down before the good; yea, the wicked at the gates of the righteous.

That is, *the wicked bow down* (from the first clause), before the gates of the righteous. The first clause represents them as suppliants in poverty, addressing the righteous; the second makes the sentiment more specific, representing them as beggars at the door of their righteous neighbors.— שַׁחוּ, Kal Perf., from שָׁחַח, Dagh. omitted in ח because of the Guttural.

(20) Even by his neighbor is the poor man hated; but they who love the rich are many.

This has respect to the negligence and coldness with which the poor are usually treated, even by their neighbors who best know their wants; while the rich find many professed friends and flatterers — a true but sad picture of what is happening every day.

(21) He who despiseth his neighbor, is a sinner; but he that showeth mercy to the poor — blessed is he!

This verse is designed as a sequel to the preceding one, which states the *fact* as to the treatment of the poor. Such conduct is sinful. But *he that showeth mercy*, will draw down blessings upon himself.

(22) Do not those err who devise iniquity? But merciful and trusty are they who devise good.

Mercy and truth, are abstracts for *merciful* and *truthful.* The *devising of good*, here refers to the good which is devised in regard to the poor. Such as devise it are *merciful* to the poor, and *faithful* or *true* to their duty as humane men.

(23) In all toil there is profit; but the word of the lips tendeth only to want.

That is: 'Every sort of doing is attended with profit; but *lip-doings* are rewarded by *want.*' *The word of the lips* means, of course, that which the lips utter. Here, *prating* is in view, i. e. the much speaking or utterance of what is useless and mischievous. This makes a man hated, and causes him to be neglected by those who might employ him in labor that would yield some profit. The consequence is *want* or *poverty*. *Is only to want*, strictly follows the Hebrew; but in our idiom we usually say: *tends only to want*, and so I have translated.

(24) A crown of the wise is their wealth; but the elevation of fools is folly.

The wealth which the wise acquire, instead of being foolishly squandered, is used in such a way as to be an ornament to them. — But high dignity conferred on fools, only makes their folly conspicuous, and serves not at all to adorn them.

That the first אִוֶּלֶת here has a different meaning from the second, seems to be nearly certain. Otherwise we must translate thus: *The folly of fools is folly;* which would be merely a tame *truism* of little significance. Truisms are not the order of the day, in this book. The proverb plays upon the two senses of apparently the same word, and its point consists in their difference of meaning. The old root, אוּל, is expressive first, of *strength, might;* hence אֵל, *God,* or *the mighty One.* Secondly, it designates, (as would naturally follow from the first meaning), *being powerful* or *having power,* as, e. g. a prince or a king. So the Arabic אול *(av-val)* means *prince, primus;* and the Heb. אוּלִים and אֵילִים mean *potentates.* Of course אִוֶּלֶת, derived from the root now in question, may mean *principatus, premiership, elevation* in rank. But the second אִוֶּלֶת comes from אָוַל, *to be foolish.* In this way, the proverbial saying becomes a striking *paronomasia;* which, in apothegms, is quite frequent in all languages. We have then this sentiment: 'While riches are so employed by the wise as to become an ornament to them, high rank bestowed on a fool, instead of serving to honor him, only manifests more conspicuously his folly. It sets him up as a mark of observation and contempt.' Bertheau has taken a different course, but, as it seems to me, a much less significant one, viz., *The foolish perversion of riches is folly.* But I do not see whence we can readily deduce the first part of this explanation.

(25) A faithful witness saveth lives; but he who breatheth forth falsehoods, is a deceiver.

Saves lives, viz., those lives which are endangered by false accusations; but he who utters falsehoods is *a deceiver,* i. e. is treacherous to the cause of truth and justice. — מִרְמָה, lit. *deceit,* but here used as abstract for concrete. The meaning is given in the version.

(26) In the fear of Jehovah is strong confidence; and to his sons there shall be a refuge.

The first clause is descriptive of a *person* who fears God, although he is not named, but only characterized. Hence, in the second clause, we find לְבָנָיו, *to his sons.* Whose? The answer must be: *The sons of him who fears God.* Sentiment: 'Piety is a ground of confidence for one's self and children.'

(27) The fear of Jehovah is a fountain of life, to depart from the snares of death.

Comp. 13 : 14. The fear of God answers the double purpose of being in itself a source of life, and also a means of escaping from death.

(28) The glory of a king is in a numerous people; but in the lack of people is the destruction of a prince.

רָזוֹן is taken by Gesenius and some otners here, as = רוֹזֵן, *prince.* Such forms, in a like sense, occur occasionally, and they are grammatically possible; e. g. עָשׁוּק and עוֹשֵׁק. But if we derive רָזוֹן from רָזָה, *to make slender* or *lean*, then we must translate the two last words thus: *Is destructive leanness,* viz., to the king. This makes good sense; but the other makes the parallelism more exact.

(29) He who is slow to anger, has much understanding; but he who is of a hasty spirit, setteth folly on high.

For אֶרֶךְ אַפַּיִם, see remarks on v. 17.—קְצַר רוּחַ, is of the like nature and opposite meaning.—מֵרִים, Hiph. Part. of רוּם, here means not to *elevate* in the usual sense of *exalting,* but *to set on high*, so as thus to make it a conspicuous object.

(30) The life of the flesh is a soothing heart; but a rottenness of the bones is passionate vehemence.

בְּשָׂרִים, plur., only here. The plur. form can hardly be here regarded as expressive of an abstract noun, or as one of mere intensity. There is no place, at least no demand, for either meaning. I should incline, with Bertheau, to put the form, in this case, to the account of designed parallelism of form, or of rhythm, with the plural עֲצָמוֹת. But perhaps בְּשָׂרִים is to be taken in the *extensive* sense of the plur., and if so, it = the *entire body*. — The Part. adjective מַרְפֵּא stands opposed to קִנְאָה — *soothing* in contrast with *exciting*. — *Rottenness of the bones*, would be a thorough destruction of the human frame; and is intensive in its meaning. — קִנְאָה, is sometimes *envy*, then *jealousy*, and next *indignation;* but here its generic meaning, *passionate vehemence*, is most congruous.

(31) He who oppresseth the poor, reproacheth his Maker; but he honoreth him, who hath compassion on the poor.

God made the poor, and ordered their condition; reproach for mere poverty is therefore out of place, and a kind of impiety. Of course the meaning is here limited, in some good measure, to such as are poor by birth or misfortune, and extends not to the poor who have become so by sloth and crime. Yet even these, although they may be made amenable to justice, ought not to be oppressed. — *He honoreth him*, i. e. honoreth God, *who*, etc. Our verb *compassionate*, used actively, would take an Acc. after it, like the Heb. חֹנֵן. Comp. 17 : 5. 22 : 2. But I have preferred the more usual phraseology in the version.

(32) In his baseness the wicked is thrust away; but the righteous hath confidence in his death.

Thrust away, viz., taken suddenly away out of life. "The wicked shall not live out half their days." The righteous man, on the contrary, חֹסֶה, *exercises trust* or *confidence*, when he dies. How? or why? are questions for those to answer, who deny that the Hebrews had any hope of a future state. If they had not, then what is the ground or source of *hope* or *confidence*, in a dying hour? This verse must be a real problem for those who have such views of the state of knowledge among the Hebrews. If there was nothing beyond the grave, in their view, on what is the hope or confidence here spoken of fixed?

(33) In the heart of the understanding dwelleth wisdom; but what is within fools shall be made known.

Dwelleth, תָּנוּחַ, *rests, quietly abides.* The Heb. is stronger than the version.—בְּקֶרֶב answers to לֵב, and means the *inner part*, the *mind* or *heart*, not the mere physical interior.—*Shall be made known*,—what? The only answer seems to be, *wisdom*, (the verb is fem.). Of course, the latter part of the verse is a pointed saying, an *oxymoron*, q. d. while wisdom dwells quietly in the breast of the intelligent, a fool parades his boasted wisdom, and makes it known to all men. The passage is well and fully illustrated by 12 : 23. 13 : 16. 15 : 2. In the second case, therefore, wisdom is implied, but the word is employed ironically = such wisdom as belongs to fools.

(34) Righteousness exalteth a nation; but sin is the reproach of any people.

חֶסֶד, *reproach*, being a sense of the word which is rare in the Hebrew, but very common in Aramaean.—לְאֻמִּים, the sing. is rarely employed; the plur. is designed to signify the *people en masse* or collectively considered, i. e. it is the plur. of extension.

(35) The good will of a king is toward a discreet servant; but he who behaveth shamefully, will be the object of his indignation.

Bertheau prefers to supply לְ before מֵבִישׁ, and translates thus: *And his anger will be to the base servant.* This is well enough as to sense and grammar; but the other method, as in the version, is more significant and energic.

CHAP. XV. 1—33.

(1) A soft answer turneth away wrath; but bitter words heighten anger.

Bitter words, lit. *a word of grievousness*, so to speak. — יַעֲלֶה, Hiph. *causes to rise, heightens.* Nothing excites anger so often and so much as bitter words.

(2) The tongue of the wise maketh knowledge grateful; but the mouth of fools will pour out foolishness.

תֵּיטִיב דָּעַת, may be rendered, *makes knowledge good.* So Bertheau; but the true idea I take to be expressed in the version. When the wise speak, it is in such a way as to make the instruction grateful to those who listen. — יַבִּיעַ, (from נָבַע), *makes to gush forth,* a very strong expression.

(3) The eyes of Jehovah are in every place, watching the evil and the good. (4) Softness of the tongue is a tree of life; but perverseness therewith is a crushing of spirit.

צוֹפוֹת, *watching,* is more intense than *beholding.* — *Softness of the tongue,* means mild and pacifying language. — *A tree of life* is a vivid image of life-giving power. — בְּרוּחַ, lit. *in spirit.* The meaning is given in the version; and in Is. 65 : 14 we have the same words, with the prep. בְּ omitted.

(5) A fool despises the instruction of his father; but he who regardeth admonition shall become wary. (6) In the house of the righteous there is much wealth; but the gain of the wicked is a trouble.

V. 5, יַעְרִים, lit. *shall act warily,* which, however, is substantially expressed in the version. — V. 6, בֵּית, Acc. of place, *in the house,* as we express it. The Heb. might use *in* (בְּ), but needed it not. — נֶעְכָּרֶת (in Pause), Part. noun, of Niph. formation, meaning *disturbance, inquietude.*

(7) The lips of the wise disperse knowledge; but the heart of the fool is not stable.

יְזָרוּ, Piel Imperf. of זָרָה.—לֹא־כֵן, may be, and often is, rendered *is not so*, i. e. is not so that it scatters knowledge. So Chald. and Vulgate; but the Sept. and Syr. render as above. This gives a better sense; for the meaning is, that the heart of the fool has not steadfastness enough to select or retain a firm position, so as to aid others by good counsel.

(8) The sacrifice of the wicked is the abomination of Jehovah; but the prayer of the upright is his delight. (9) An abomination of Jehovah is the way of the wicked; but he will love him who followeth after righteousness.

The sacrifice of the wicked, and so *the prayer of the wicked,* and *the way of the wicked,* are all an abomination to Jehovah. Why? Because he sees no sincerity or real humility in any of them, inasmuch as all is done for the sake of appearance, or at most, through terror of punishment.—מְרַדֵּף, is Piel, and intensive = *habitually pursues.*

(10) A grievous chastisement is for him who forsaketh the way; he who hateth admonition shall die.

The way is *the way of Jehovah,* i. e. that which he prescribes.—*Shall die,* is a phrase which we often meet with, in connection with commination for offences. Sometimes it is explained by phrases significant of *sudden death, early death, premature* or *violent death,* and the like. But at other times, it occurs, as here, unexplained by any additions. How much are we to attribute to it? To say that it threatens *punishment,* is saying only what lies of course upon the face of it. *But what punishment?* and *how much?* These are more difficult questions. Clearly all sinners are not punished in this world, either with sudden, or violent, or premature death. The Psalmist often complains of their *flourishing condition,* and of there being " no bands in their death." And every day we see the like at the present time. If then, under these expressions, the Hebrews did not suppose there lay some threat of *future retribution,* what did or could they make of them? That their views on the subject were somewhat indistinct, as to various particulars, no one well informed on the subject will venture to deny. But I know not who can fairly read the book of Ecclesiastes, and deny all definite views among the Hebrews in regard to this matter. Let him ponder well the following passages, viz., 3: 16, 17. 8: 11—13. 11: 9. 12: 13, 14. It is indeed true, that when the book before us was written, "life and immortality had [not] been brought to light." But can we make out anything significant, or really intelligible, in the passage before us, and in other like passages, without supposing the Hebrews to have looked to some future retribution? To say to the wicked man: *Thou shalt die*, if we mean merely a natural and ordinary death, is saying no more than Providence says, every day, to the *good* as well as to the wicked. To say that *all of the wicked die*, or *shall die*, *a sudden*, *violent*, *premature death*, is saying what is most evidently *not* a matter of fact or truth. What then did or could a Hebrew mean by such phraseology? This question necessarily forces itself upon us. I trust the phrase in question has some meaning; and if it has one which is intelligible, it would seem to be, that the idea of *future retribution* must have entered into the minds of those who employed this language. Otherwise no meaning, which is at the same time both significant and true, can well be attached to it.

(11) The Under-world and Destruction are before Jehovah; surely then the hearts of the children of men.

Sheōl and *Abaddōn* are two different names for one and the same place. *Sheol* is properly *the region of the dead;* and אֲבַדּוֹן, *the place of destruction;* and this last phrase characterizes, in another way, the world of the dead, i. e. the place where their bodies are *destroyed*, or the world which is deep beneath, and therefore dark and obscure. But God sees even this, — however dark; much more then are human hearts all open and plain before his sight. "I, the Lord, search the heart."

(12) A scorner will not love his reprover; unto the wise he will not go. (13) A merry heart maketh comely the face; but by vexation of heart, the spirit is broken.

He will not go to the wise, because he hates reproof, and expects that they will administer it. — *A merry heart* here means merely a *joyful* one. — *Maketh comely* or *fair the face,* because joy lights it up with hope and with smiles, and so makes it look pleasant.

(14) An intelligent mind will seek earnestly after knowledge; but the mouth of fools will delight in folly.

For פְּנֵי (so Kethibh) read פִּי with the Qeri; for the verb which follows is in the singular. — יִרְעֶה, in its secondary sense, namely *delight in* = רָצָה, see Lex. — *The mouth will delight in,* means that it will utter readily and in abundance *foolish* words.

(15) All the days of the afflicted are sad; but cheerfulness of heart is a perpetual feast.

It is plain that רָעִים here means *sad,* (as often elsewhere), from the contrast presented in the verse. *Cheerfulness,* which is lasting and diffuses itself over all our actions and enjoyments, is not merely like a feast which is temporary, but is like a *perpetual* feast, i. e. an enduring source of pleasure.

(16) Better is a little, with the fear of Jehovah, than much treasure, and trouble therewith.

Trouble or *perturbation* refers to the perplexity and solicitude, that usually accompany the possession of riches. The efforts for the safe keeping of them, the fear of losses and the like, occasion of course much anxiety. How insignificant then the pleasure of wealth, in comparison with that of piety, even in moderate circumstances!

(17) Better is a dinner of herbs and love therewith, than a stalled ox and hatred therewith.

A further development of the trouble which wealth occasions. If he, who can feed on stalled oxen, is exposed to hatred and envy because of his wealth, then his neighbor who feeds on herbs, in quietude and without molestation or envy, is much the happier man. — אֲרֻחַת, *viaticum, meal,* such as an אֹרֵחַ *(traveller)* takes on his journey, i. e. plain and coarse food.

(18) An angry man will stir up strife; but he who is slow to anger, will appease contention.

The sentiment is plain. See nearly the same ideas, in 29: 22. 28: 25.

(19) The way of the slothful is like a thorn-hedge; but the way of the upright is a high-way.

A thorn-hedge presents impassable obstructions to the traveller, at least very annoying ones. Not so with *the upright;* their way is *elevated;* and the idea of *elevating a way,* is that of constructing a way like what we call a *turn-pike road.* In other words: 'The way of the upright is plain and easy; that of the wicked, greatly obstructed.'

(20) A wise son will make a glad father; but a foolish man despiseth his mother.

Comp. 10: 1. The wise listeneth to parental advice; the foolish despise it, and so give pain to the adviser, instead of making him glad.

(21) Folly is joy to him who lacketh understanding; but the man of intelligence will make straight his going.

To commit *folly* is his *delight,* is the meaning of the first clause. — לֶכֶת, Inf. fem. of יָלַךְ; lit. then, the two last words mean: *Will take a straight course to go.* The sense of the words is given in the version, in a way conformed to our idiom; but the real meaning is a *moral* one = will act uprightly and not deceitfully.

(22) Plans without counsel are frustrated; but by the increase of counsellors, there shall be stability.

הָפֵר, Inf. abs. Hiph. of פּוּר, § 128. 4. *b;* lit. *there is a frustration.* — תָּקוּם is also *quasi* impersonal, and may be rendered as in the version; comp. in Is. 7: 7, for the meaning. If we render strictly, it must be thus: *It shall stand firm,* where the pronoun *it* refers to the whole concern or undertaking; or we may naturally enough supply the conjugate noun that corresponds to יוֹעֲצִים (Part.) which would be עֵצָה. The sense is substantially the same in either way.

(23) There is joy to a man in the answer of his mouth; and a word spoken in its season—how goodly!

That is, a man has joy in answering with goodly or timely words. It is a source of satisfaction, to have such an answer in his power. C. B. Michaelis and others: *There is rejoicing* (on the part of others) *over the man who answers,* etc. But לְ can hardly be brought to the meaning of *over* here, nor is the sense improved by thus translating.

(24) The way of life to the wise is upward that he may turn away from the Under-world beneath.

Upward is here employed as the antithesis of מַטָּה, *downward, beneath.* In other words, he chooses his way so as to keep himself in the *region above,* and not in the *abyss below.* — מָטָּה is in pause, for מַטָּה; and this is compounded of מַט, a *low place,* and ה־ *local,* for the regular accent of the word is on the *penult,* which shows that ה־ is *local,* and not radical.

(25) The house of the proud Jehovah will demolish; but he will establish the border of the widow.

House probably means here *family* or *household;* or it is like our familiar word *establishment.* Instead of *demolishing,* he will render *firm* and *secure*, the domains of the widow. — יַסֵּחַ, Imperf. of נָסַח.

(26) An abomination of Jehovah are the devices of evil; but words of comity are pure.

נֹעַם, *suavity, pleasantness,* or as in the version. — *Are pure,* i. e. in the eyes of Jehovah, the opposite of that which is abomination in his view. *Pure* = *acceptable*, i. e. the case is like to that of an offering, which must be pure in order to be accepted.

(27) He troubleth his house, who acquireth unrighteous gain; but he who hateth bribes shall live.

The *gain* in question is plainly that which results from *bribes,* as the latter clause shows. The supposition is that of being bribed, in the case of deciding as a judge. The honest judge who refuses such gifts, shall be prospered.

(28) The heart of the righteous meditateth on an answer; but the mouth of the wicked gushes forth with malignity.

Meditates on an answer, because he is anxious to give a right and true one. The wicked makes no scruple *to belch forth malignant things.* — רָעוֹת, plur. of intensity.

(29) Far removed is Jehovah from the wicked; but the prayer of the righteous will he hear. (30) The light of the eyes rejoiceth the heart; a good report maketh the bones to flourish.

Light of the eyes is that which the eyes see; just as *good report* is what the ears hear. There is an implied comparison here, viz.: *As the light rejoices,* etc., *so a good report* renders one's state or condition pleasant. — עָצֶם (in pause) here in the singular, but it is generic. — Of course, תְּדַשֶּׁן־ has a secondary or tropical meaning here, as given in the version.

(31) The ear which heareth the reproof of life, shall dwell in the midst of the wise.

Reproof of life, is that which leads to life, or which admonishes respecting the way of life. *Hearkening* to this, is of course the way in which the path of life and of wisdom is to be found.

(32) He who rejecteth instruction despiseth his own life; but he who hearkeneth to reproof, acquireth understanding.

Here again we meet with that peculiar and forcible idiom of the Hebrew, *despiseth his own life*, i. e. treats it as though he despised it — makes no provision for its safety and welfare. The phrase is of the same tenor as the following: *All that hate me love death; He that cometh to me, and hateth not his father*, etc.

(33) The fear of Jehovah is the instruction of wisdom; and before honor is humility.

That is: 'Without the fear of Jehovah, wisdom cannot be acquired;' or in other words: 'Wisdom counsels to fear God.' — This necessarily implies *humility;* and therefore, in order to obtain honor from him, humility must precede the gift.

CHAP. XVI. 1—33.

(1) The preparations of the heart appertain to man; but from Jehovah is the answer of the tongue.

Preparations of the heart, are what the heart devises or intends. But *answer of the tongue*, is an answer to that which the tongue utters, viz., its requests. God only can accomplish what is desired. The German maxim is very appropriate here: *Man denkt; Gott lenkt.*

(2) All the ways of a man are pure in his own eyes; but Jehovah weigheth the spirits.

Comp. 21: 2. 24: 12, the same as this verse, with only a little variation of phraseology. A man, who judges all his own conduct to be pure, judges wrongly; but he will be corrected by him who impartially weighs and scans the spirits of men, and whose judgment is unerring.

(3) Cast upon Jehovah thine undertakings, and thy plans shall be established.

גֹּל, Imper. of גָּלַל, lit. *roll, devolve;* we say, in such a case — *cast upon,* etc. Comp. Ps. 22 : 9 (10). 37: 5. In other words : 'Look to God in all thine undertakings, and he will give accomplishment to them.'

(4) Jehovah hath made everything for its purpose; yea, even the wicked for the day of evil.

לַמַּעֲנֵהוּ has been misunderstood by most of the ancient interpreters, and by many modern ones. The suff. refers to כֹּל. They render it as though the word were the same as לְמַעֲנוֹ, *for himself.* The noun מַעֲנֶה lit. means *answer;* see 15 : 1, 23. 16 : 1. The tropical sense is, *that which corresponds to,* or *is consonant with,* any purpose, design, or action. So *everything* (כֹּל) is made in accordance with its *correspondence,* i. e. with the design or purpose to which it answers. — *The wicked* are fitted, by their temper and conduct, for the day of retribution. It is an ordinance of God that they shall receive that retribution which is the *answer,* or that which *corresponds,* to their conduct. — That the Masorites had some such view of the word לַמַּעֲנֵהוּ, seems probable from their inserting the *article,* (לַ exhibits it, as also the Dagh. that follows), for either could not belong to the particle מַעַן. Of course they doubtless had מַעֲנֶה, *answer,* in view. So anxious do they seem to have been to indicate this, that they have inserted the article against the rule, which requires its *omission* when the word has a suff. pronoun, § 108. 2. This should not be overlooked; for it gives us, at least, their judgment in regard to the true state and meaning of the word.

[In respect to the *sentiment* of the text, it is a passage which has been sometimes urged to an excessive length. When the extreme Predestinarian deduces from it the sentiment, that "God made the wicked for the very purpose of punishing them and of making them forever miserable," I must regard this as pushing matters to a great extreme. And yet, there is one light in which we may view this matter, which will show that to a certain extent, or within certain limits, this sentiment may be assented to. That 'God made every thing and every man, to answer the purposes which it or he does actually answer,' cannot be denied, unless we maintain that things and men are what they are, *contrary* to his will. This would be to make the creature superior to the Creator. When the text says, that *God made the wicked for the day of evil*, I understand it as meaning, that God has so arranged things, that punishment will certainly follow the commission of sin, unless averted by repentance. He has connected together *sinning* and *suffering*, so that there can be no escape for the impenitent sinner.

There is quite a difference between the position, that *God has made sinning to be connected with suffering*, and the proposition, that God has made men sinners, and made them so in order that they might be fitted for damnation. There have been some, who have maintained the latter position, by virtually omitting, in their reasoning, a link — a very important one — which belongs to a considerate and logical train of reasoning. That link is real *free moral agency*; and with this stands connected consequentially another link, not less important, viz., *voluntary ill-desert of the sinner*, and the consequent justice of punishing him. God has so arranged his government of moral beings, that *the day of evil* will and must come, to such of them as sin and remain impenitent. *The day of retribution* is the מַעֲנֵה, *the correspondent answer* to the doings of the sinner. In other words, as before: 'He has made punishment to correspond to crime.' Further than this, I think few will now venture to go.]

(5) An abomination of Jehovah is every man of a lofty mind; should hand be added to hand, he will not go unpunished.

גְּבַהּ, adj. const. form of גָּבָהּ, with הּ Mappiq and movable. — יָד לְיָד, see under 11: 21. I take the idea here to be, that although one hand should be added to the other, i. e. although a haughty man may employ *all his power* (for this the use of *both hands* indicates) of resistance, yet he will not be able to get free from the penalty of his offence.

(6) By mercy and truth is sin expiated, and in the fear of Jehovah there is a turning away from evil.

The figurative sense of יְכֻפַּר *(atoned)* is doubtless intended here. Neither sin-offerings nor the blood of bulls and goats; neither mercy to others, nor adherence to truth; can *atone* for sin, in the higher and proper sense of this word. But *mercy and truth*, exhibited by a good man, may be a good reason why he should go free from such visitations as overtake the presumptuous wicked in the present world. In accordance with this, are the constantly recurring promises made in this book to a good and virtuous course of conduct.— *The fear of Jehovah*, is the most effectual of all persuasives to turn from evil. Without it, an evil course will never be heartily forsaken.

(7) When the ways of a man are well-pleasing to Jehovah, he will make even his enemies to be at peace with him.

A truly pious man will be blessed of God, and have peace even on the part of his enemies. They will find little to censure, and have little or no pretext for injury. Of course, this is only a *general truth;* to which are not a few exceptions. Such are the cases of persecution for righteousness' sake.

(8) Better is a little with justice, than large revenues without right.
(9) The heart of man deviseth his way, but Jehovah will make firm his steps.

בְּלֹא, lit. *with not* = *without.* — יְחַשֵּׁב, Piel, with an intensive sense — *laboriously devise* his way. But that way will not be successfully travelled, unless Jehovah shall make his steps firm and vigorous.

(10) An oracle is on the lips of a king; in judgment his mouth should not prevaricate.

קֶסֶם, usually means *sentence of a god*, or of his agent, viz., a *diviner*. What is here meant is, that what a king utters is of high import and authority. — *On the lips*, means hangs on the lips, or depends on the lips. — Since this is the case, he should look well to it, that he utters nothing *perfidious* or *prevaricating*. — יִמְעַל means, *to act perfidiously*, or *to prevaricate*. The sentence of a good king should be just, simple, sincere; and there should be in it no design of deceiving or misleading.

(11) The steel-yard and the balances of justice are Jehovah's; his work are all the stones of the bag.

פֶּלֶס is always associated with *balances*, and it would seem therefore to belong to the apparatus for weighing. Most probably it was the *rod* or *yard*, on which the figures indicating exactly the weight were marked. The Hebrew says nothing indeed of *steel*, but our English word, as in the version, gives us the familiar idea of the thing aimed at. Sentiment of the first clause: 'Jehovah employs no other than just weights;' or else: 'Only just balances does Jehovah approve.' The second is more difficult. *His work are all the stones of the bag*, refers to the stones, which were used as weights, and kept in a bag; see Deut. 25:13. Mic. 6:11. But why are *all these* called *his work?* The answer may be given thus: The *all* in this case refers to the *whole of the weights*, great and small; and as the latter are employed only in adjusting *niceties of weight*, so the idea seems to be, that the balances which Jehovah approves or employs, are adjusted with the utmost possible exactness in all respects. In this way we find the second clause to be climactic. Sentiment: 'Jehovah not only does justice, but he exacts justice of all men toward each other.'

It is evident, that if the *balances* and *weights* are spoken of as belonging to God in the sense of his employing them, the language is highly figurative. The sentiment, however, is quite plain, viz., that *Jehovah, in all his dealings, is perfectly just.* In case we interpret the passage in this way, there is plainly instruction given to men by it. The object is not merely, nor even mainly, to teach the perfect justice of God, but to hold this up as an *exemplar* for men. On the other hand, the whole sentiment may have this turn given to it: 'Jehovah acknowledges as his, viz., as that which he approves, only *just* balances and weights. He condemns all others.' I prefer the last.

(12) The doing of evil is an abomination of kings; for by righteousness is the throne established.

The sentence is capable of this meaning: *It is an abominable thing for kings to do evil;* but the next verse shows that we must understand by *abomination* here, the feeling of mind which kings have, or should have themselves, and not that which they excite in others. Why do they abominate the doing of evil? The answer is: 'Because they are exposed to lose their throne by it;' or, in other words: 'Righteousness among the people is the only thing which can render the throne stable.' The first interpretation gives a good meaning; but the second gives one in accordance with the following verse. יִכּוֹן, Imperf. Niph. of כּוּן. In כִּסֵּא, the Dagh. is *compensative*, the old form being כֻּרְסֵא, as in Syriac; see Lex.

(13) Lips of truth are the delight of kings, and he who speaketh uprightly shall be loved.

צֶדֶק, lit. *justice*, but here being in opposition to *false speaking*, it may with propriety be rendered as in the version. — יְשָׁרִים, adverbial Acc. plur., § 98. 2. § 116. 3. — יֶאֱהָב (in pause), without any express Nom. We may supply the indef. Nom. *one;* or, (which is here altogether equivalent), render the verb *passively*, as in the version. Or, with all the ancient Versions, we may supply מֶלֶךְ, as an obvious mode of *particularizing* the preceding מְלָכִים.

(14) The wrath of a king is messengers of death; but a wise man will propitiate it.

That is, when the king is angry, he commissions the messengers of death to execute his indignant sentence. The simple manner of saying this, by merely using the phrase: *is messengers of death*, is bold, striking, and pointed. The phrase is elliptical, but not obscure. — Since *kingly wrath* is attended with such bitter consequences, a wise man will seek to soften it; comp. 19 : 12. 20 : 2, and Ecc. 8 : 4.

(15) In the light of the king's countenance is life; and his favor is like the latter rain.

The *wrath* of the king (v. 14) has here an antithesis in the phrase: *the light of his countenance;* for the countenance is lighted up, when one is pleased. In this is *life;* for the object of complacency is in no danger from *messengers of death.* — *Latter rain* is that which falls just before the harvest, and fills out and completes the crops.

(16) To acquire wisdom — how much better than fine gold! To win intelligence, is to be chosen rather than silver.

קְנֹה is Inf. const., although this form is somewhat rare, § 74. n. 2. In the second clause, קְנוֹת (the normal form) is employed. *Variety* in the form of the same word appears to be here an object of choice. — נִבְחָר, *that which is to be chosen, optandum.* There is no article here before *gold* and *silver.* Usually it is inserted in such cases, (§ 107. Rem. *b*); but poetry, and especially the brevity of gnomes, may omit it.

(17) The highway of the upright is the turning away from evil; he who preserveth himself, carefully watcheth his way.

The upright will not wittingly go in the path of evil, and therefore they turn away into another and safer way. Whoever means to remain secure, must look well to the way which he takes, and adhere constantly to it. The participles here are employed to designate what is habitual and constant.

(18) Before destruction is pride; and before stumbling is haughtiness of spirit. (19) Better is lowliness of mind with the humble, than the dividing of spoil with the haughty.

" God will resist the proud." Pride goes before destruction, and is the ground or cause of it. — גֹּבַהּ, a Segholate of class iii. (§ 91. 6), and therefore when it is put in the const. state with a noun, it does not change its form. — אֶת־עֲנָוִים, (so Qeri, but without any necessity), the prep. אֶת־ has the meaning of *companionship*, *association with*; see Lex. אֵת, ii. 2. — *The dividing of spoil* implies victory, and of course exultation, the usual consequence of which is pride or haughtiness. In this way it stands virtually opposed to *lowliness of mind*. — חַלֵּק Inf. of Piel, here *nominascens*.

(20) He who is prudent respecting any matter, shall find good; and as to him who confideth in Jehovah — blessed is he!

דָּבָר may mean *command*, and then we have it thus: *He who acts wisely in respect to commandment*, etc. But the sense given above is of wider extent, or more generic. — The form אַשְׁרֵי is never employed but in the plural const. or suff. state, as here.

(21) He who is wise of heart shall be called intelligent; and sweetness of speech will increase instruction.

The Heb. lit. thus: *To the wise of heart, there shall be called* נָבוֹן. This idiom our language does not employ. I have conformed the version, therefore, to our own idiom, the sense remaining the same. — *Sweetness of speech* means *gentle and persuasive language*; for *lips*, as the Heb. has it, here means what the lips speak. This *sweetness* attracts listeners, and so increases knowledge.

(22) A well-spring of life is discretion to him who possesseth it; but the instruction of fools is folly.

There is a variety of opinion in respect to some parts of this verse. Still, there seems to be little difficulty in it. — שֵׂכֶל בְּעָלָיו, is lit. *the prudence of its possessor*, i. e. the prudence of him who is the possessor of such a virtue. We are obliged to change the manner of the expression. בְּעָלָיו has a plural form, which attaches to it in the same manner as to אֱלֹהִים (see Lex.) without a plur. meaning, constituting what is called a *pluralis excellentiae*. — *The master* or *possessor of discretion* = the discreet man. — Such a man is a fountain of life to others, because of his example and precepts. But a fool, if he undertake to instruct, can only *teach folly*; and this is no fountain of life, but of death.

(23) The heart of the wise will make his mouth skilful; and will increase instruction upon his lips.

Wisdom will cause discreet speech, which is *skill* in eloquence; and will add instruction to what is *on the lips* of such a man, i. e. to the words which he utters. It will do so, because discreet language will naturally attract listeners. — יֹסִיף = יוֹסִיף, Hiph. Imperf.

(24) Pleasant words are a honey-comb, sweet to the soul, and healing to the bones.

Are a honey-comb, that is, *are like to*, etc., for nothing is more common, than for a Hebrew to say *are* for *are like*. — מָתוֹק seems of course to have relation to אִמְרֵי, plur. — But I take it here as an *abstract noun*, like the neuter adj. in Greek and Latin. Often so in Hebrew. Lit. then we have *sweetness*, which does not require conformity of either number or gender to its antecedent. The same in respect to מַרְפֵּא. — *Bone*, in the sing., is taken in the same tropical sense, as בָּשָׂר, i. e. it here means the *person* or *whole body*.

(25) There is a way which is right in the sight of a man; and yet the end thereof is the ways of death.

See 14 : 12 for the same. In other words : 'A man may come to regard a thing as right, which in the end will prove to be destructive and fatal.' How often is this maxim still verified!

(26) The appetite of him who toils, is toilsome to him, for his mouth urgeth him on.

Is toilsome to him, i. e. makes him strenuously exert himself, for *appetite* is urgent. — לוֹ, I regard as *Dat. incommodi* here, viz., to his inconvenience. — *His mouth* = appetite. *It is urgent on him,* corresponds with the Heb. עָלָיו, the עַל being put before the thing or person urged; as often in Hebrew. Meaning: 'A strong appetite unappeased is urgent and troublesome.'

(27) A worthless man diggeth up evil; and on his lips is as it were a scorching fire.

כֹּרֶה, Part., is somewhat of a difficult word here. The verb means *to dig,* e. g. a well, pit, ditch, etc. Ges. renders כֹּרֶה רָעָה by *perniciem parat,* which gives the sense, but drops the imagery. To me it appears thus: As a man *who digs a well,* naturally and justly expects some good reward for his labor, in the water which it affords, so *the worthless man who digs up evil,* finds his appropriate reward; or, as we say, (with a small variation of the verb in Hebrew), *digs up evil,* that is, obtains it as the reward of his efforts. — *The worthless man* here seems to be described in the second clause, as a *detractor, calumniator.* — *On his lips* (= the words which hang upon his lips) is that *which resembles a scorching fire,* i. e. heated calumnious speeches.

(28) A man of perversities will stir up strife; and the prater separateth friends.

A man of perversities, is one who is very deceitful and crafty. — נִרְגָּן, with formative ָן, the root being נָרַג, *to speak rapidly.* Such a *prater* very often separates friends by tattling scandal.

(29) A man of violence will deceive his neighbor; and cause him to go in a way not good.

That is, he will allure or deceive his neighoor, so as to lead him to the commission of violence, i. e. of rapine and spoil, and thus bring him into an evil and dangerous way.

(30) He who shutteth his eyes in order to devise what is perverse, he who compresseth his lips, hath accomplished evil.

The eyes are often shut, when one designs to think closely and strenuously about anything; because notice of all that is external can thus be prevented, and one can then, as we say, *think the harder.* — *Compression of the lips,* indicates firm determination or resolution. This is taken as a sign of evil already committed; because his firm resolution, it is here supposed, will be carried into execution. Hence the declaration: *hath accomplished evil.*

(31) A crown of splendor is gray-hair, should it be found in the way of righteousness.

The image is vivid. *Gray hairs* crown the head; but that crown, in the case supposed, is splendid or beautiful. Yet this is not so in and of itself merely; for the *wicked* have gray hairs also in old age. In my version, I have made the second clause express the condition on which such a crown is splendid. This neither Umbreit nor Bertheau have done. They understand it thus: 'It is a crown of splendor, because it is evidence that the man is good; for none but the good attain to such an age.' But is this congruous with facts? With facts that always were, and still are, before every man's eyes? The version above does not contravene any laws of grammar; and certainly it comports with truth. The Nom. to תִּמָּצֵא is שֵׂיבָה, which = *old age.*

(32) Better is he who is slow to anger, than the mighty; and he that ruleth his own spirit, than he who taketh a city.

Moderation of one's own passions is better than deeds of valor; and subjugation of one's own mind, than the conquest of a city. Clearly there is a high and noble moral tone in this.

(33) The lot is cast into the lap; but from Jehovah is the whole disposal thereof.

Men may cast lots in order to ascertain their future luck; or they may embark in adventures at much risk, hoping that all will come out well; but Jehovah alone can and does decide the issue of all such matters.

[There is in this verse an idiom of which our Grammars have taken a very inadequate notice. It is this, viz., that the Acc., אֶת־הַגּוֹרָל, appears here as a *Nom.* or subject; and so it is rendered in the version—*ad sensum* indeed, yet not in such a way as discloses the idiom of the Hebrew. The real fact is, that there is a large number of cases, where the *verb passive* in the third sing., is used in a kind of impersonal way, without reference to the number or gender of the noun which seems to be its Nom., but which is actually in the Acc. The fact that such noun belongs to the Acc. seems to be evident, from the consideration that there is, in respect to the verb, no regard paid either to the *number* or *gender* of the nouns in question. This may be easily shown. We may make two divisions: (I.) *Those nouns which follow the passive verb of the third sing. masculine, which is nearly always in the Imperf.* (*a*) *Sing. masc.* with אֶת before it, the usual mark of the Acc.; e. g. Gen. 17 : 5. Ex. 10 : 8. 21: 28. 25 : 28. Lev. 10 : 18. Deut. 12 : 22. 20 : 8. Josh. 7: 15. 2 Sam. 21: 11. Prov. 16 : 33. Jer. 38 : 4. 50 : 20. Gen. 4 : 18. Num. 26 : 60. Lev. 13 : 49. (*b*) *Plur. masc.* with אֶת before it; Lev. 2 : 8. Jer. 35 : 14. Gen. 27: 42. Ex. 27: 7. Amos 4 : 2. (*c*) *Sing. fem.* with אֶת; Num. 32 : 5. 1 Kings 2 : 21. (*d*) *Sing. fem.* without אֶת, Ex. 31: 15. Hos. 10 : 6. (II.) *Nouns preceding the verb, and without* אֶת. (*a*) *Fem. sing.*, Ex. 12: 16. Is. 14 : 3. 21: 2. (*b*) *Fem. plural*, Ex. 13 : 7. Num. 28 : 17. Ps. 87: 3. Job 22 : 9.

I find but one instance of a fem. noun without אֶת, joined with a verb in the third sing. masc. of the *Perfect*, viz., Num. 26 : 62. There may be more of the like kind; but they must be rare.

With such a list before us as is exhibited above, it would be difficult to maintain with Gesenius (in Lex.), that אֵת may stand before the Nom.; for if this be admitted, it will solve only a small part of the phenomena in question. These present us with a verb sing. masc., in the Imperf. of some *passive* voice, and connected with the sing. masc., and plural masc., and fem. sing., all with אֵת, (and also fem. sing. without אֵת), all *following* the verb; then *preceding* the verb, we have, *without* אֵת, the fem. sing., and the fem. plural. Those nouns which are without אֵת (the Acc. mark), are still so conditioned, that we know they must be in the Acc. It follows from this view of the subject, since the verb remains in the same condition in all these varieties of gender, number, and location, that it must be used in an *impersonal* way, for it has manifestly no conformity to its apparent subjects or Nominatives. The Heb. employs the *sing. Passive* often in a *neuter* way, instead of the 3d pers. plur. with an indef. Nom., which the Chaldee and Syriac so often exhibit. Plainly the third sing. *pass.* in Hebrew, is equivalent to the third plur. *active* with an indef. Nom. In the latter case, (see § 134. 3. *b*), the active voice would demand the Acc.; and as the third sing. *pass.* is used in its place, since it is lighter and more facile of enunciation, it retains the same case which the act. third plur. would require.

Very much of what is usually named *anomaly* as to concord in the Hebrew, is easily solved in this way; and if this idiom be fully understood, one may thereby explain a large portion of the alleged anomalies of the Hebrew. Ewald, in § 273. *b*, has done more to illustrate this hitherto obscure matter, than I have elsewhere found; and to him I stand mainly indebted for the list of examples produced above, although he has not classified them, as has here been done.]

CHAP. XVII. 1—28.

(1) Better is a dry morsel and quietude therewith, than a house filled with slaughtered beasts and strife.

זִבְחֵים is not limited to beasts appropriate to offerings; for these מְבָחִים appropriately indicates. It means *beasts slaughtered*, either for feasts or offerings, i. e. it is generic. We cannot well imitate the Hebrew here, which lit. runs thus: *slaughtered beasts of strife.* The Gen. here —*of strife*—

qualifies the preceding noun, and indicates either that the beasts were obtained by strife, or that they are eaten with strife. — *The dry morsel* is *bread;* and this, without any fat or flesh to accompany it.

(2) A discreet servant shall rule over a son who acteth basely; and among brethren shall he divide an inheritance.

By discretion the servant will at last obtain a higher place than the profligate son, and even become his master. He will, moreover, attain to an inheritance, as if he were of the same class with the brother-heirs. The base son will become the slave of his former servant, and give up his property to him.

(3) The fining-pot for silver, and the furnace for gold; but the searcher of hearts is Jehovah.

That is, the fining-pot may try silver, and the furnace disclose true gold; but only Jehovah can explore the human heart.

(4) An evil doer listeneth to the lip of mischief; the deceitful man listeneth to the tongue of destruction.

מֵרַע, Part. Hiph. of רָעַע, final Pattah because of the ר. — שֶׁקֶר, lit. *falsehood* or *deceit;* but here the abstract is plainly used for the concrete, and is so rendered in the version. — מֵזִין, apparently from זוּן, which however I do not find in Ges. Lex.; but it may be taken as = מֵאֲזִין, Hiph. of אָזַן *to listen;* Ewald, § 141. *a.* 2. Such contractions are not unfrequent, in which א is omitted in the writing.—The plur. הַוֹּת is intensive here; which we cannot well imitate, without circumlocution.

(5) He who derideth the poor, reproacheth his Maker; he who rejoiceth in sudden calamity, shall not be guiltless.

The second clause leads us to assign *sudden calamity* as the cause of the poverty brought to view in the first. — עֹשֵׂהוּ, Part. עֹשֶׂה, with the suff. ֵהוּ.

(6) The crown of the aged is the sons of sons; and the glory of children is their fathers.

That is: Parents are honored and made happy by a numerous progeny, and dutiful children glory in their ancestors.

(7) The lip of eminence is not comely for a fool; much less the lip of falsehood for a prince.

Lip of eminence, means speech such as belongs to *eminence* (= eminent men), or is characteristic of it. *Eminence* is entitled to command, and to be obeyed. Such a place, then, is not seemly for a fool. — יֶתֶר, first *remainder;* then *abundance;* then *eminence*, as here. — אַף כִּי, after a *negative*, means *much less;* see Lex. After כִּי, נָאוָה (contracted from נַאֲוָה) is implied.

(8) A present is a precious stone, in the eyes of its possessor; whithersoever it shall turn, it will prosper

A present (שֹׁחַד) here means *a bribe* given to secure influence. He who receives such a *present*, regards it as a *precious stone*, e. g. as of value like a diamond. Hence comes the tropical language of the last clause. A diamond reflects a variety of lights, when viewed on this side or on that. Turn it how you please, it will never cease to reflect lustre; and this, the text calls *prospering* or *succeeding*, i. e. it never fails to reflect lustre. So of a *bribe* if accepted; it will influence in many ways, even without a consciousness of its power, on the part of the receiver. Turn he which way he will, the influence of it will follow him.

(9) He who covereth a transgression, seeketh love; but he who repeateth a report, separateth friends.

דָּבָר, a *word* or *saying*, means, as the sequel shows, a report which is wounding to the good name or the feelings of a friend. The repetition would show some degree of satisfaction in the thing; which of course would be offensive. — שֹׁנֶה for שׁוֹנֶה, Part.

(10) Rebuke will sink deep into an intelligent man, more than the smiting of a fool a hundred times.

תֵּחַת, Imperf. fem. Kal of נָחַת, תֵּ (with Tseri) because the Gutt. rejects Daghesh. Sentiment: 'A man of intelligence will be more influenced by mere rebuke, than the fool by severe scourging.'

(11) Only contumacy will the evil man seek; but a cruel messenger shall be sent against him.

The *contumacy*, מְרִי, here in question, is that of subjects toward their rulers. When displayed, the ruler sends his messenger of justice, who will severely punish.

(12) Meet a bear robbed of her whelps by a man, but not a fool in his folly.

פָּגוֹשׁ, Inf. abs. for Imper., § 128. 4. *b. c.* — [*Meet*] *not a fool*, etc. That is: 'It is better to meet an enraged bear, than a fool in the exercise of his folly.'

(13) He who requiteth evil for good, evil will not depart from his house.

The Kethibh reads תָמִישׁ in Hiph., the Qeri תָמוּשׁ in Kal; both are equally good. This agrees well with: "Render not evil for evil."

(14) The commencement of strife is the letting out of water; before it rolleth itself onward, let strife alone.

Where water is dammed up, a small breach in the dam occasions a rush of water, which speedily widens that breach, and then it rolls on in impetuous torrents. So with strife, which, though trifling at first, when persevered in, becomes impetuous and mischievous. Therefore, *Let alone strife, before it rolls on*, like the impetuous torrent. — לִפְנֵי, *before* in point of *time* here, Lex. D. 2. *b.* — הִתְגַּלַּע, Hith. Inf. of גָּלַע, which is like to גָּלַל, according to the older interpreters, and so Bertheau. This sense is quite congruous here, as it keeps up the metaphor of water rushing forth so that it cannot be checked.

(15) He who justifieth the wicked, and he who condemneth the righteous, are, even both of them, an abomination of Jehovah.

Even both is designed to specificate, and to speak with energy. It does not assert that both are guilty in the same degree, but represents both to be so far guilty, as to be an abomination of Jehovah.

(16) Why should a price be in the hand of a fool, in order to acquire wisdom, when there is no understanding?

That is, a man cannot purchase wisdom for any price, who is without understanding; for this is absolutely necessary to the acquisition of it.

(17) The friend loveth at all times; but a brother for adversity must be born.

A somewhat difficult passage, in respect to the last clause. — *At all times*, i. e. as well in adversity as in prosperity, a true friend will love. — *A brother for adversity*, (for so the accents indicate the connection to be), is one who will act the part of a brother in a season of adversity. Of such an one it is said: יִוָּלֵד, *he must* or *shall be born*, (possibly) *he is born*. I do not understand this last clause, unless the assertion is, that none but such as are *born brethren*, i. e. kindred by blood, will cleave to us when in distress. Yet this is true only in a qualified sense; for the most that we can say is, that comparatively few are friends in adversity, excepting one's relatives by descent. But another shade of meaning may be assigned to the passage; which is, that such a man as a friend in adversity, *is yet to be born*, i. e. none such are now to be found; thus making it substantially equivalent in sense to the expression: 'How few and rare are such faithful friends!'

(18) The man who lacketh understanding, striketh hands; he maketh a pledge before his friend.

Striking hands, is the confirming of a contract.—*He maketh a pledge*, viz., to some third person, *in the presence of his friend*, who can bear testimony to it, and therefore make it binding. The last clause is *elliptical*, viz., *he who makes such a pledge* [wants understanding].

(19) A lover of sin is a lover of strife; he who maketh his gate lofty, seeketh destruction.

The man of strife loves sin; the man of pride, who erects lofty structures, is preparing for ruin, for "pride will have a fall."

(20) The perverse of heart shall not find favor; and he who is turned hither and thither with his tongue, shall fall into mischief.

נֶהְפָּךְ, (Part.) is rendered in conformity with the primary meaning of הָפַךְ, *to turn*. The meaning is, that the *tongue* now says this, and then that, so that it is continually *turning and winding* in its course. Mischief usually and naturally ensues.

(21) Whoever begetteth a fool, it is a trouble to him; and the father of a fool will not rejoice.

See the antithesis to this in 15: 20, and comp. 18: 13.—*Will not rejoice*, =will have reason to mourn; (a form of speech which the rhetoricians name *meiosis*, i. e. *μείωσις*, *diminution*, where less is said than is meant).

(22) A glad heart will do the body good; but a mind afflicted will dry up the bone.

גֵּהָה is found only here, and seems to be a doubtful word, as to its meaning. In Hos. 5: 13, the verb evidently means *loosening* or *taking off* a bandage. On this account, *sanatio* is given here by Ges. and others, as the meaning of the noun. But the Chald. and Syr. translate the word by *body;* to confirm which, we may appeal to the kindred words, גֵּוָה and גְּוִיָּה, *body*. This makes a more congruous sense; for *body* then corresponds to גֶּרֶם, *bone*, in the other clause; which last is only a tropical appellation of *corpus*. Sept. εὐεκτεῖν, *to be in a sound bodily state.* — *To dry up the bone*, is to deprive it of all moisture and succulence, so that it becomes like the bones of those who have long been dead. The imagery is very vivid.

(23) A bribe is taken from the bosom of the wicked man, in order to pervert the ways of judgment.

Taken from the bosom, i. e. taken in a concealed or secret way. And this bribe is received, in order that a wrong decision in a court of justice may be given.

(24) Near by an intelligent man is wisdom; but the eyes of a fool are in the ends of the earth.

Near by, אֶת־פְּנֵי, lit. *with the face* or *person*, i. e. in close connection with him. Wisdom being thus at hand, he can always employ it with readiness. But a fool is looking far abroad for it, and so he never is able to find and to use it.

(25) A foolish son is a vexation to his father, and a bitterness to his mother.

Comp. v. 21 above, and 10: 1. — מֶמֶר, only here; it is a derivate of מָרַר, § 84. II. 14. — יוֹלַדְתּוֹ, fem. Part. of יָלַד, in a suff. state, § 93. D. *a*.

(26) Moreover, to punish the righteous is not good; to smite noblemen is beyond right.

Is not good, is a mere *meiosis*, i. e. a softening down of the positive mode of expression, viz., *is bad*, or *is wicked.* — So in the other clause, *is beyond right* = *is wrong*. עַל, *over*, *over and above*, i. e. beyond. See Lex.

(27) He who keepeth back his words, understandeth knowledge; and he who is of a cool spirit, is a man of understanding.

A prudent restraint in speaking, is everywhere commended in this book. — In the second clause, וְקַר in the Kethibh, is changed in the Qeri into יְקַר, *precious*. The first is altogether preferable, being more congruous.

(28) Even a fool, keeping silence, is wise; and he who closeth his lips is intelligent.

Is wise, i. e. is reputed or regarded as wise; for, so far as this goes, he acts wisely. The second clause is a more general proposition, extending the remark to all who act in the like way.

CHAP. XVIII. 1—24.

(1) One who separateth himself will seek for what he desireth; against all sound discretion will he rush on.

נִפְרָד, Part. Niph. in a reflexive sense. — תַּאֲוָה, I have translated *what he desireth*, more literally it means *desire*, which here means *object of desire*. He who separates himself from a communion of interest with others, and seeks only his own selfish ends, such an one *will rush on*, (like *the rolling on* of the current, see 17 : 14), in spite of all prudent advice to the contrary. Sentiment: 'Selfishness is apt to become exclusive and supreme, and to break through all bounds to gratify itself.'

(2) A fool taketh no pleasure in understanding; but truly in the disclosure of his own heart.

See כִּי אִם in Lex., *but truly* or *surely*, or *much more*. Here יַחְפֹּץ comes in by implication, being carried forward from the preceding clause. Thus we have this meaning: *but truly [he will take pleasure] in the disclosure*, etc. That is, since his own heart is foolish, he will take pleasure in manifesting his own folly.

(3) When the wicked cometh, then cometh also contempt; and shame will be joined with reproach.

That is, wherever the wicked comes, he meets with contempt; and shameful doings will be connected with reproach. By implication it follows, that the good and worthy are the only persons who can secure honorable regard.

(4) Deep waters are the words of a man's mouth; a gushing stream is the fountain of wisdom.

The words, in the first clause, are those of a wise and prudent man. They are like *deep waters,* because they consist of thoughts not easily sounded to the bottom, and still less capable of exhaustion; see 20:5. Ecc. 7:24.—The second image is still more lively: *A fountain of wisdom is a stream gushing forth,* i. e. it is like a stream, which, gushing forth from the earth, is always full and refreshing. Or the last clause may be thus rendered: *They* [the words, etc.] *are a gushing stream—a fountain of wisdom.* This method of arrangement puts the two last short clauses in apposition.

(5) To take part with the wicked is not good; to turn aside the righteous in judgment [is not good].

שְׂאֵת פְּנֵי, is used to designate *the acceptance of any person,* who offers presents or bribes; lit. it means *to lift up the face;* and therefore it comes to mean *to show partiality for, to take part with;* see Lex. no. 3. *b.* שְׂאֵת is the Inf. of נָשָׂא, but instead of the ordinary and later Seghol fem. form, שֶׂאֶת, it takes (by usage) the form of the older Segholates, viz., שְׂאֵת. Most plainly the last clause demands the supply of לֹא־טוֹב, carried forward from the first, else the sense would be incomplete, or even contradictory.

(6) The lips of a fool enter into strife; and his mouth calleth for stripes.

That is, his words are mingled with the spirit of strife, and he commits follies with his mouth, i. e. in his words, which deserve stripes.

(7) The mouth of a fool is destruction to him; and his lips are a snare of his life.

In other words: What he says is ruinous to him, and proves to be a *snare of his life*, i. e. his language is that by which he comes into danger of his life.

(8) The words of the tale-bearer are like sportive ones; yet they go down into the innermost parts of the body.

It is difficult to settle with certainty the meaning of מִתְלַהֲמִים. Schultens, Ges., and others, derive the meaning from the corresponding Arabic (לחם), which means, *to swallow greedily*. In this way, they bring out the meaning of *sweet morsels* or *cakes*. I prefer the explanation of Bertheau, who compares with it מִתְלַהְלֵהַּ in 26 : 18, which, as the context shows, there means *sporting*. Compare עָצָה and עָצַם, both of the same meaning. This is the more commended by its greater congruity, and the antithesis implied in וְהֵם, *yet they*, etc. That is, although his words seem to be jocose, or sportive, they are in reality malignant, and they therefore inflict deep wounds. Comp. 20 : 27, 30, for the imagery.

(9) Moreover, he who is slack in his work, he is brother to a prodigal.

בַּעַל מַשְׁחִית, lit. *possessor* or *master of wasting* = *a waster*, i. e. *a prodigal;* as in the version. Comp. אִישׁ מַשְׁחִית, in 28 : 24. By the phrase *a brother*, is meant one *very like*.

(10) The name of Jehovah is a tower of strength; the righteous runneth into it, and is protected.

The name of Jehovah, is a periphrasis (but a very significant one), which designates *Jehovah himself*. *To call on the name of the Lord*, is to invoke him by calling his name. The word *name*, in such a connection, designates all that we include under the appellation of the being addressed.— נִשְׂגָּב, lit. *is elevated*. But the *elevation* of a fort or tower, in ancient times, was that which rendered it safe or inaccessible, so that *protection* was the consequence of repairing to it.

(11) The wealth of the rich is his strong city; and like a high wall, in his own conceit.

The rich, instead of looking to Jehovah for protection, trust in their riches — which are a high wall, in their own imagination, but not so in reality. In 10 : 15, the like words are employed, but in a different relation, and therefore with a different meaning.

(12) Before destruction, the heart of man is haughty; and before honor, is humility. (13) He who answereth a matter before he heareth it, it is folly to him, and a shame.

For v. 12, comp. 16 : 18. 15 : 33, where the same may be found. V. 13 shows the folly of a hasty anticipative answer, before the examination of a question.

(14) The spirit of a man will sustain his infirmity; but a dejected spirit — who can endure it?

Spirit, in the first clause, means a firm and resolute temper of mind. — A *dejected spirit* is a *mind made sad*. *Infirmity* relates to pains of *body*; a *dejected spirit* to a *mind* sad and cast down. The first can be endured, by firmness and resolution; but the last — who can endure it, when resolution for endurance is gone? רוּחַ is *masc.* in the first clause, and *fem.* in the second.

(15) An understanding heart will acquire knowledge; and the ear of the wise will seek after knowledge. (16) The gift of a man will make room for him; and will conduct him before the mighty.

For v. 15, see 15 : 14. — V. 16 means, that the *presents* which a man may proffer, will make room for his reception, and bring him into the presence of the great or noble.

(17) He who is first in his own cause is righteous; then cometh his neighbor and searcheth him.

Not with Sept. and Vulg.: *the righteous is the first in his own cause;* for then we should have הַצַּדִּיק. — *Is righteous,* i. e. in his own estimation. — וּבָא, so the Kethibh, and rightly, for then וּ is *consequential.* The Qeri, יָבֹא is less significant. *The searching neighbor* shifts the asserted *right* to the other side.

(18) The lot maketh strife to cease, and separateth between the mighty.

An agreement to cast lots, in order to decide a disputed matter, prevents a quarrel, and separates those who were about to mingle in contest. This seems to indicate approbation of the practice of casting lots in such cases.

(19) A brother is more refractory than a strong city, and strifes are like the bars of a tower.

A brother who is in a state of strife, is meant in the first clause. Such strifes, viz., those between *brethren,* are the most difficult of all to be appeased. The attempt to appease, is like an endeavor to enter barred gates.

(20) From the fruit of a man's mouth, shall one's belly be satisfied; [from] the produce of his lips shall one satisfy himself.

Lit. תִּשְׂבַּע בִּטְנוֹ means what the version has expressed; the real idea is, *satisfy himself,* בֶּטֶן being figuratively taken for *the whole man.* — *Produce of his lips,* means what his lips utter, i. e. his words. If the verb *satisfy* is taken here in the *good* sense of the word, then the words *fruit of the mouth,* must be regarded as meaning *good fruit.* But the verse may be *ironical,* and the meaning then would be, that false or malignant words will find an ample retribution. The next verse will, perhaps, help to decide which of these is meant.

(21) Death and life are in the power of the tongue; and as to those who love it, each one shall eat the fruit thereof.

That is, a man may speak what will destroy life, or what will preserve it. — אֹהֲבֶיהָ is plur. with suff., denoting a whole class. The suff. fem. הָ refers to *tongue*; and *loving it* means expending one's care and efforts upon the employment of it, — i. e. the making of it a special object of gratification. — יֹאכַל, *each one* (אִישׁ is implied as its Nom.) *shall eat*, etc., § 134. 3. § 143. 4. This is an example of what the grammarians call *particularizing* or *merismus*. In fact, *each* means, in such a case, *any one*, or *every one*, and therefore *all*. — The predominant cast of the verse is, that the *evil use* of the tongue comes more specially into view. This may incline the scale in favor of the *ironical* meaning of *satisfy*, in the preceding verse. — As to פִּרְיָהּ, the suff. relates to *tongue*.

(22) He who findeth a wife, findeth a good thing; and obtaineth favor from Jehovah.

Of course a *good wife* is meant. This is a blessing which God gives; see 19: 14. 31: 10.

(23) The poor speaketh in a supplicating manner; and the rich answereth roughly.

Such is the usual fact; specially is the first part of the verse usually true, because the necessities of the poor force them to beg. The second also is by far too often true. — תַּחֲנוּנִים may be rendered adverbially, as above, or translated by the phrase *with supplications*. And so of עַזּוֹת.

(24) A man of friends will show himself as base; but there is a friend, who sticketh closer than a brother.

A man of friends seems to mean: 'a man who professes to regard everybody as his *friend*.' In so doing he involves himself in trouble; for he cannot serve them all, or be intimate with all; and then exceptions will be taken by those who are neglected, and they will accuse him of base desertion. Our English version, and many of the critics, translate the verb here by *show himself friendly*. But in order to do this, we must derive the verb הִתְרוֹעֵעַ from רֵעַ, *friend*. But this last word comes from the root רָעָה; and from such a root we cannot obtain the Hith. form of the text. It must therefore come from רָעַע, and this has the meaning given above in the version. Ges. renders: *periit*, which is stronger than the verb will bear. As explained above, the matter appears sufficiently clear. The man who professes to regard every body as a special friend, must bring on himself the imputation of false profession and base designs. Yet there is another and a real kind of friendship, the opposite of this; and it sometimes rises higher than that which even a brother ordinarily exhibits.

CHAP. XIX. 1—29.

(1) The poor man, who walketh in his integrity, is better than he who is perverse with his lips, and also is a fool.

The perverse and foolish man, being here contrasted with the *poor man*, shows that the fool here spoken of is supposed to be *rich*. A rich fool of perverse lips is of course inferior, in point of character, to the poor man who exhibits integrity of conduct. Compare 28 : 6, which substitutes *rich* for *fool* here. — וְהוּא, *and also is*, § 119. 2.

(2) Moreover, in the soul's lack of knowledge, there is no good; and he who hasteneth with his feet, goeth astray.

בְּלֹא־דַעַת נֶפֶשׁ, lit. *in the not knowing of the soul;* the meaning of which is given in the version. — לֹא טוֹב is used as in the neuter impersonal = *there is no good*. — *Haste* indicates the lack of proper knowledge; and this of course is apt to lead astray.

(3) The folly of a man will make his way headlong; and his heart will fret against Jehovah.

The ruin which the man brings on himself by his own folly, he will angrily charge upon his Maker. This occurs, every day even now, too often for us to call in question the truthfulness of the proverb.

(4) Wealth will make many friends; but the poor is separated from his friend.

That is, as wealth makes many professed friends, so poverty separates the poor man from even his best friend, or, in other words, the poor man is often neglected by those who ought to be his best friends.

(5) A false witness shall not be guiltless; and he who breatheth out lies, shall not escape.

Not be guiltless = shall be guilty, (meiosis). — *Shall not escape* = shall be punished, (meiosis again); for in v. 9, (exactly of the same tenor as this verse), we have, as the equivalent of the last expression, יֹאבֵד, *shall perish.*

(6) Many pay court to a prince, and every one is a friend to the man of gifts.

That is, a prince becomes popular, or obtains many friends, by virtue of liberal gifts. But instead of הָרֵעַ, the ancient Versions show that they read the text as כָּל־הָרָע, *every bad man*, viz., flatters the liberal giver. The sense given in the version seems to be preferable.

(7) All the brethren of the poor hate him; how much more do his friends withdraw from him; seeking earnestly for words — they are not.

Brethren of the poor designates his *relatives* here. Even they *hate* him, i. e. do not love him so as to show him compassion. If this be so, still less can be expected from mere *friends* or *acquaintance*. They *hold themselves aloof*, רָחֲקוּ, *plur.*, because the noun מְרֵעֵהוּ, lit. *his friendship*, (abstr. for concrete = *his friends*) is a noun generic.

The last clause is a problem. (1) It is out of proportion, the other verses of the context being bi-membral. (2) It is very difficult to make out any *congruous* meaning from it. (3) The Masorites bid us to read לוֹ (*to him*) instead of לֹא (*not*). If we follow them, then we must render the clause thus: *He who hunts after words, to him they are*, i. e. he easily finds them. But what is this to do with the preceding context? And what is *the kind of words* that he pursues? All claro-obscure. Possibly this may be the meaning: 'He who catches at *mere words* or *empty professions* of friendship, will easily obtain them.' So Bertheau, for substance. Umbreit proposes the following solution: 'He who earnestly seeks for the former words of friendship and kindness, will now find them no more.' Of course he renders לֹא as a *negative*. We might venture, perhaps, on another conjecture, like to that of Schultens: 'He who seeks for former friendly words, i. e. conversation-circles of friends, will no more find them. He is deserted, and left in solitude.' This is doubtless significant; but whether the text is of the same significance, may be doubted. A *conversazione* can hardly be found in אֲמָרִים. On the whole, I rather prefer Umbreit's solution, because it is most congruous. The Sept. has three whole clauses here, which are omitted in the Hebrew text; but they are neither very congruous or significant. The fact of such an addition, however, and the superadded third clause here, which does not seem to match well with the other verses, raises a suspicion that something has been dropped out of the Hebrew text. The Chaldee and Syriac are obscure. The Vulg. has come nearest to the present text: *Qui tantum verbis sectatur, nihil habebit.* All these take לֹא here as a *negative;* and so, in the version above.

(8) He who acquireth understanding, loveth his own soul; he who watcheth for intelligence, will find good.

Loves his own soul, i. e. does that for it which love would prompt him to do. — *Will find good*, where לִמְצֹא, the Inf., is rendered as a definite mood. See on 2 : 2, in respect to this idiom; see also § 129. 3. n. 1.

(9) A false witness shall not be guiltless, and he who breatheth forth lies, shall perish. (10) Luxurious living is not comely for a fool; much less for a servant to rule over princes.

For v. 9, see above on v. 5. V. 10, *luxury* belongs to the rich and noble only, and not to fools. More unseemly still is it, to see servants lording it over princes. Comp. Ecc. 10 : 7.

(11) The discretion of a man will make him slow to anger; and it is a glory to him to pass over a transgression.

A discreet man will forbear, when provoked. Such an one will deem it praiseworthy to pass over an insult. The Sermon on the Mount has well commented on this sentiment, Matt. 5 : 38—44.

(12) Like the roaring of a lion is the wrath of a king; but as dew on the tender herbage is his good will.

The roaring of a lion threatens destruction, and the wrath of a king does the same. The effects of his *good will* are described by beautiful imagery, which needs no explanation. Comp. the like in 20 : 2, and see 28 : 15. 16 : 14.

(13) A sore calamity to his father is a foolish son; and a continual dropping are the contentions of a woman.

טֹרֵד, lit. *driving* or *urging on*, i. e. one drop urges on another, and in this way the dropping becomes *continual*. The image is vivid. *A continual dropping* of water, e. g. on one's head, becomes, after a time, a means of the most exquisite suffering.

(14) A house and wealth are an inheritance from fathers; but a discreet wife is from Jehovah.

Comp. 18 : 22. — נַחֲלַת אָבוֹת, lit. *an inheritance of fathers,* might mean *a heritage which fathers possessed.* But as it actually means here *one which they convey to their children,* I have framed the version so as to avoid ambiguity. — *A wife from Jehovah* is a wife, the gift of whom is a proof of his benevolent regard, i. e. a good wife. But a mere *heritage* may come to a *bad* man, as well as to a good one.

(15) Sloth causeth a deep sleep to fall on one; and an idle person must go hungry.

There is no *object* expressed after the verb תַּפִּיל, in order to show who is affected by the sleep. The indefinite *one,* or *a man,* is therefore implied; which is expressed in the version. — נֶפֶשׁ רְמִיָּה, lit. *deceitful soul;* but as *soul* in very many cases means *person* or *man,* I have so rendered it here. As to רְמִיָּה, it is used, in this book, for *idle, slothful,* because it is sloth which *deceives,* or *disappoints,* the expectations of the employer. The man that is *slothful,* is of course the man who *disappoints* expectations. See in 10 : 4. 12 : 24. 20 : 13.

(16) He who keepeth the commandment, keepeth his own soul; but he who disregardeth his ways shall die.

The *commandment* is that of Jehovah. — בּוֹזֵה, lit. *despiseth,* but here in the sense of *disregard,* i. e. neglect to pay any attention to his conduct. — The Qeri bids us read יָמוּת, *shall die;* but the Kethibh exhibits יוּמַת in Hophal, which is stronger than the other form, since it = *shall be put to death.* In a gnome, this energic form is the most probable one.

(17) He who hath mercy on the poor, lendeth to the Lord; and his work will he reward to him.

מַלְוֵה, Part. Hiph., *makes a loan to,* here in the const. state, § 132. 1. *b,* — וּגְמֻלוֹ, here in its original sense, *opus* (either good or bad), i. e. *anything done.* — The לוֹ only serves to designate with intensity the person who will be rewarded. — The Nom. to יְשַׁלֶּם is of course *Jehovah*. *Seghol* here, because of the Maqqeph.

(18) Chasten thy son, because there is hope; but indulge not thy desire to slay him.

A saying adapted to angry and passionate fathers, who may be in danger of wreaking vengeance on an offending child. Sentiment: 'Merely chasten, and not kill; because there is hope, specially of a young person, that he may reform under suitable chastisement. Therefore go not beyond this, in such a case.'

(19) A man of violent anger must suffer punishment; for if thou shalt deliver him, thou must again repeat it.

The Kethibh, גְּרָל, makes no tolerable sense, even if we take the liberty, (as some have done), to make it = גּוֹרָל, *lot*, and so point it גֹּרָל. Plainly, with all the ancient Versions and the Masora (Qeri), we should read גְּדָל־, const. of גָּדֹל. The sense is given in the version. Comp. as to diction, Dan. 11: 44. 2 Kings 22: 13. — Another turn has been given to this verse by the older interpreters: 'If thou shalt deliver him from death (in reference to v. 18), yet thou must repeat thy chastisement, in order to restrain him.' This is more tame, and does not agree well with the first part of the verse. Meaning: 'An irascible man will not be held in, even by kindness in his behalf; he must therefore be given up to chastisement.'

(20) Hear counsel, and receive instruction, that thou mayest be wise in after-life.

The word אַחֲרִית signifies lit. *the latter part, the after part.* Meaning: 'Get instruction and counsel when young, that you may be wise when you grow old.'

(21) Many are the devices of a man's heart; but the counsel of Jehovah — that shall stand.

Counsel of Jehovah is Nom. absolute; הִיא resumes the subject of the sentence, and specifies with emphasis. So in the version.

(22) The desire of a man is his kindness; and better is a poor man than a liar.

To wish well, or *to desire one's good*, is a proof of *kindness*, in cases where only the *wish* can be indulged. We have a like proverb: "One must take the *will* for the *deed*."—A *poor man* who wishes well, but needs kindness or charity, is better than a man who can show it and promises to show it, but still falsifies his promise.

(23) The fear of Jehovah is unto life; he shall abide satisfied—he shall not be visited by evil.

Jehovah, who gives life to those who fear him, will cause them to possess an abundance of what they need, and to remain unharmed by evil.—The tropical sense of יָלִין is, *to abide, permanere*; which meets the demand of the present case.—שָׂבֵעַ = *satisfied*, i. e. supplied with all that one needs.—רָע, second Acc. retained by the passive which precedes it, § 140. 1.

(24) The sluggard hideth his hand in the dish; even to his mouth he will not return it.

This refers to the Oriental custom of eating, where knives, forks, and spoons, are dispensed with, and the guests help themselves by dipping their hand into the dish, and taking what they like; see John 13: 26. Mark 14: 20. Matt. 26: 3.—*Hiding the hand* is plunging it into the food, (which usually was, as to a part, in a semi-liquid state), until it is buried in it, so that the hand might come out filled with food. But the sluggard, who has thus filled his hand, will not make effort enough to bring it back to his mouth, choosing rather to go without the food, than to make the effort or exertion to feed himself. Lit. this need not be urged; nor is it said with the design of being literally understood. It is a vivid and powerful, and also sarcastic reproof of the sluggard, by making his sloth ridiculous. The irony is plainly very severe and cutting, and will be read with satisfaction by all who love to be active and industrious.

(25) Smite the scorner, and the simple will become wary; reprove an intelligent man, and he will understand knowledge.

Smite is here voluntative; lit. תַּכֶּה (Hiph. Imperf. of נָכָה) means: *thou shalt smite.* But the sense is as given in the version, viz., the conditional future or Imperative. — הוֹכִיחַ, may be a Hiph. Inf. absolute, used as an Imper. hortative, § 128. 4. *b. c;* although this form is not common here, but one with (ֵ) as final vowel, § 52. 2. n. 2. More probably it is Imper. hortative, which sometimes takes such a form, § 92. 2. n. 3, Ps. 94: 1. Is. 43: 8. Sentiment: 'Even a simpleton will grow wary by seeing scorners chastised; much more will the intelligent profit by reproof.'

(26) He that doeth violence to his father, or chaseth away his mother, is a son who acteth shamefully and putteth to the blush.

Strong precepts does the Old Testament everywhere exhibit against cruel and severe treatment of parents by their children. Even one out of the *ten commandments* is occupied with this subject. — *Chaseth away* implies such abuse, as causes the mother to fly from her home.

(27) Cease, my son, to hear the words of instruction, in order that you may wander from the words of knowledge.

Ironically said, perhaps. The meaning would then seem to be thus: 'Cease from listening to instruction, and the consequence will be, that you will wander,' etc. — The second Inf., לִשְׁגוֹת, is equivalent here to an Imperf.; see on 2: 2, 8. Or we may resolve it thus, without irony: 'Cease to hear such instruction as leads to wander from the words of truth.' This is more simple, and therefore more probable.

(28) A vile witness scorns justice; and the mouth of the wicked will greedily swallow mischief.

A vile witness will utter that which will defeat justice, i. e. he will give false testimony. *The wicked greedily swallow* injustice or wrong, as if it were a sweet morsel. But the implication of the latter clause seems to be, that still, what they devour will become noisome or poisonous to the system. In other words: אָוֶן, *mischief*, swallowed down, will be apt to breed mischief.

(29) Judgments are prepared for scorners, and stripes for the back of fools.

This verse seems to complete the preceding one. There, we have *scorners* of justice; and here we have the *punishment of scorners*. They who *swallow down* אָוֶן, must expect the consequences here threatened.

CHAP. XX. 1—29.

(1) Wine is a scorner, strong drink is boisterous; and every one who reels therewith is not wise.

שֵׁכָר, *intoxicating drink;* rarely employed alone, but generally associated with *wine*, as here. — הַיַּיִן, with the article, § 107. Rem. 2. *b.* — *Boisterous* is characteristically said of most men who are drunk. — The common idea, that *strong drink* in the Scriptures, means something *stronger than wine*, is destitute of any good foundation. Wine was the *strongest* drink among the Hebrews, if the drinks that were *drugged* be excepted. None of the Palestine fruits yielded a juice so intoxicating as that of the grape.

(2) Like the roaring of a lion is the terror of a king; he who provoketh him sinneth against himself.

Lit. thus: *A roaring as of the lion is the terror*, etc. Here, *the terror of a king* is that which he inspires in others. Such a dread of him gives an apprehension of approaching danger, like that which the roaring of the lion imparts. The same in the first clause of 19 : 12 above, with some slight variation of one particular.—מִתְעַבְּרוֹ, is a Part. in Hith., which here has an *active* sense, like Kal (§ 53. 3), and takes the Acc. pronoun after it.—חוֹטֵא נַפְשׁוֹ, one is tempted to render: *maketh himself a sinner;* but as the verb חָטָא is intrans. we can hardly give the active Part. a *Hiphilic* meaning. Yet חֹטְאִי (in 8 : 36) might justify this, for the Acc. is there governed by the word. At least we must make נַפְשׁוֹ to be a secondary Acc., indicating *manner of sinning*, etc.; and translating accordingly, we have: *he sinneth as to himself.* The sense is good; but our idiom prefers the phraseology of the version above, since it is more direct.

(3) To dwell away from strife is glory to a man; but every fool will involve himself in it.

שֶׁבֶת, the usual fem. Inf. of יָשַׁב, *to dwell*, (not a Seghol. שֶׁבֶת of the root שָׁבַת, *to cease*, which nowhere occurs). The meaning of the first is more significant than that of the second; for it imports not merely ceasing from strife, but habitually keeping aloof from it.—יִתְגַּלָּע, of the same meaning for substance as in 17 : 14. 18 : 1; the fool *rolls on impetuously* into strife, and glories in being engaged in it.

(4) Because of winter, the sluggard will not plough; and then he shall make inquiry in harvest time, and there is nothing.

The Kethibh would read יְשַׁאֵל, in Piel; but the Qeri bids us read וְשָׁאַל. Either is good; but the Qeri is the more forcible, = *and then he shall inquire.*—*Make inquiry*, viz., for produce.—וָאָיִן (Qamets in pause) is absolute, = *there is not;* which is energic here. For Qamets under ו, see § 102. 2. *d.*

(5) Deep waters is a purpose in the heart of a man; but a man of intelligence will draw it out.

Deep waters are difficult to be sounded. So a man's secret purpose or counsel it may be difficult to sound. Yet a man of skill will draw it out from its depths. *Drawing out* is a metaphorical expression occasioned by the preceding image — *deep waters*.

(6) The mass of men will proclaim each his own goodness; but the trusty man, who can find?

רָב־, *the multitude, the many,* and so *the mass.* When men are fond of boasting of their own virtues, it is ground of suspicion, and increases the difficulty of finding those who are really trust-worthy. — אֱמוּנִים, lit. *faithfulnesses* = very faithful.

(7) He who walketh in his integrity is a just man; blessed are his children after him!

Not every one who boasts is to be trusted, but he who habitually discloses (*walketh in*) integrity of character, he is a true צַדִּיק. — אַשְׁרֵי again as an exclamation.

(8) A king sitteth on the throne of judgment; he scattereth by his eyes all the evil.

Not simply a declaration of fact, (for there are many kings who do not scatter the wicked), but a declaration of what a king thus elevated ought to do. A king who sits on a throne of true and proper judgment or equity, will drive away the wicked by keeping his eye on their conduct.

(9) Who can say: I have purified my heart; I have become pure from my sin.

Purified as to this or that particular sin, or sins? Or, *purified* from sinful desires and inclinations? The latter seems to be the most significant. Meaning: 'No one can say, that he is perfectly free from sinful propensities.' "There is not a just man on earth, that doeth good and sinneth not."

(10) A double weight and a double ephah are, even both of them, an abomination of Jehovah.

Lit. *stone and stone;* where a ו, as here, comes before the repeated noun, it denotes *severalty* or *diversity*, and not plurality, § 106. 4. I have translated *double*, because this corresponds to the words repeated, and also indicates a *diversity*. Two stones of the *same* weight would be useless; at least, regarded in this way, the repetition would indicate nothing more than mere *plurality;* which, however, is not here to the purpose. See Deut. 25 : 13.

(11) Moreover, by his doings a child will make himself known, whether his work is pure and whether upright.

That is, a child's doings will be inconsiderate and rash, and thus they will show that he is but a child. *His work* will indicate, however, whether he is well or ill inclined; for early in life is the disposition disclosed.

(12) The ear which heareth, and the eye which seeth, even both of them hath Jehovah made.

The implication is, of course, that he who made the ear and the eye, both hears and sees all things. See the striking passage, in Ps. 94 : 9.

(13) Love not sleep, lest thou become poor; open thine eyes, and be satisfied with bread.

תִּוָּרֵשׁ, Niph. of יָרַשׁ *to inherit*, but here possessing a *privative* meaning, viz., *dispossess*. It is רוּשׁ.—*Open thine eyes*, that is, as we say familiarly: *Be wide awake*, or, in other words, *be active and diligent.*—שְׂבַע is Imp.; but being a second Imp., it denotes *consequence*, § 127. 2. *a.* Lit. *be satisfied with bread*, but as verbs of *fulness* govern the Acc.

of the noun which indicates the *wherewith*, the Heb. needs no preposition before לָחֶם, (Qamets in pause).

(14) Bad! Bad! saith the buyer; and then goeth away and maketh his boast.

Heb. lit. *and going away for himself, then he boasts.* This would hardly be facile English; but in Hebrew, a pronoun with ל prefix is not unfrequent, specially after verbs of motion; see לֶךְ־לְךָ, Gen. 12:1. Cant. 2:11. Job 6:19. Amos 2:13. Ewald, § 305. *a.* I have therefore slightly changed the form of the expression in the version.—For the rest; every day bears witness to such conduct on the part of purchasers. They underrate the things they wish to purchase, in order to obtain them cheaper.

(15) There is gold, and an abundance of pearls; but a precious vessel are the lips of knowledge.

That is, gold and pearls are comparatively plenty; but the lips of true knowledge are of rarer occurrence. They are like a precious and highly wrought vessel.—יְקָר is a noun in the Gen. (= *of preciousness*), but it is here used as an adjective.

(16) Take his garment, when he has pledged himself to a stranger; and because of strangers, distrain him.

The law obliged the creditor to leave untouched the necessary clothing of a debtor; but he might take all superfluous vestments. But in case of taking these, there was an apparent severity on the part of the creditor. The object of our text is to show, that in a case where a man becomes surety for others, his creditor will have to deal severely with him, in order to get his dues; and such a man is not deserving of lenity.—נָכְרִים, *strangers*, is the reading of the Kethibh, and a good one, for it is generic. The Masorites, however, bid us read נָכְרִיָּה, and have so pointed the word. This would mean *strange woman*, and this same word is employed in 27 : 13. Compare, however, 6 : 1. The sense of this would be good; but so is that of the other reading. — The last clause is plainly elliptical: *Distrain* (i. e. force by seizure) *him [who has pledged himself] on account of strangers.* — זָר is like the Latin *hostis*, and means both *stranger* and *enemy;* נָכְרִי (root נָכַר) means *a foreigner.* Sentiment: 'Take the utmost precaution to secure a debt against a man, who becomes sponsor for every body and any body.'

(17) Bread of deceit is sweet to a man; but afterwards, his mouth will be filled with gravel.

Bread obtained by fraud is eaten with a high relish by some men; but in the sequel, their mouth is filled with gravel; — no very pleasant thing either to masticate or to swallow. — אַחַר is adverbial here.

(18) Devices will be established by counsel; and with skilful management make war.

מַחֲשָׁבוֹת plur. fem. Nom. to תִּכּוֹן verb. sing., see § 143. 3. — בְּתַחְבֻּלוֹת = κυβέρνησις, *pilotage, steering, management.* It indicates here a *wary control;* and being the plur. of intensity, it of course indicates skilful management. If this be lacking, success cannot well be expected.

(19) He who goeth about as a slanderer, revealeth secrets; and therefore associate not with him who openeth his lips.

He who openeth his lips, is the same as the רָכִיל; for he speaks much and often. — תִּתְעָרָב, Hith., lit. *mingle thyself*, here used as = *join thyself*, and so it has לְ after it in לְפֹתֶה.

(20) He who treateth with contempt his father and his mother, his lamp shall be quenched in the midst of darkness.

בְּאִישׁוֹן is the Kethibh, and is right. The Qeri substitutes אֱשׁוּן for it, which is a Syr. word, meaning *darkness*. But this is designated by חֹשֶׁךְ. Still, both words might be used to heighten the intensity. The Kethibh, however, is well; for אִישׁוֹן means *midst, central point;* and hence (usually) *the pupil of the eye*, because of its *central* position. — The meaning is, that his lamp will be extinguished, when he needs it most, viz., when he is plunged in darkness.

(21) Wealth may be suddenly acquired in the beginning, but the end thereof will not be blessed.

Wealth *suddenly acquired*, is usually acquired by unjust and deceitful dealings. But to make out such a sense, we must read (with the Qeri) מְבֹהֶלֶת, Pual Part. (ה for ח). The Kethibh must come from בָּחַל, which means *to despise;* and this will give no tolerable sense. Ges. therefore proposes the same root in Arabic as our guide, which there means *to be avaricious;* and then he translates our text by *opes avaritia partae.* But to say nothing of the change of meaning from *he was avaricious* (Arabic), to *wealth acquired by avarice*, we may ask: How does such an interpretation agree with *at the beginning?* In the common course of things, *avarice* is a passion which nearly always increases by time. But in this case, we are called on to suppose, that the wealthy man was avaricious only at the outset; and this is more than we ought to believe, unless we are forced to do so. The other meaning is much better, *hastened, got hastily.* — *Will not be blessed*, which is usually verified, in regard to large fortunes acquired by improper means. The heirs commonly dissipate the whole, and that within a moderate length of time. God's blessing rests not on such wealth.

(22) Say not: I will repay evil; wait on Jehovah, and he will assist thee.

This accords well with the tenor of the Sermon on the Mount. — *Assist thee*, וְיֹשַׁע לָךְ; so we may translate, for this verb often means *opem tulit.*

(23) An abomination of Jehovah is a double weight; and balances

of deceit are not good. (24) From Jehovah are the steps of a man; how then can a man understand his way?

For v. 23, see v. 10 above. V. 24, God guides the steps of man, i. e. he chooses and arranges for him his path. — מַה is interrogative here, and equivalent to a *negative*. — Meaning: 'Man cannot know or determine with certainty his own way, since all is dependent on God.'

(25) A rash utterance of consecration is a snare to a man; and then, afterwards, to inquire into his vows.

A verse of some difficulty. יָלַע, if a verb here, seems = לָעָה, *to speak rashly* or *hastily*. With Ewald and Bertheau, I should prefer the noun יֶלַע; and so, in the version, have I rendered it. The accent is here upon the *first* syllable; and this is its natural place, if the word is a noun. But if it be a *verb*, how can we account for the accent on the first syllable? — קֹדֶשׁ, *consecration*, abstr. for concrete, and so = *something consecrated* or *vowed* to God. Here, נְדָרִים of the next clause shows the meaning to be of such a tenor. — Sentiment: 'Make no rash vows; keep those which thou hast made, and not reconsider so as to change them.' Comp. Ecc. 5 : 3 (2) — a striking parallel.

(26) A wise king scattereth the wicked, and maketh the wheel to turn upon them.

וַיָּשֶׁב, Hiph. of שׁוּב, with accent retracted, and final Tseri shortened. — אוֹפַן, *wheel;* and in this connection, a wheel employed to crush criminals. See the like in 2 Sam. 12 : 31. 1 Chron. 20 : 3. Amos 1 : 3. Perhaps the imagery stands thus: 'As the grain which is scattered, is rolled in; so transgressors are scattered and crushed beneath the earth.' As we have no direct intimation elsewhere of *punishing by the wheel*, we are left in some doubt here as to the *modus in quo*.

(27) A light of Jehovah is the soul of man; which searcheth his innermost parts.

In other words: 'A light given by Jehovah, is the soul, etc.'— נִשְׁמַת = נֶפֶשׁ, see Lex. It is the *soul*, which takes cognizance of man's most secret thoughts.

(28) Mercy and truth will preserve the king; and his throne will he support by mercy.

Such qualities as are here mentioned, will make his throne stable and secure, since they will call forth the love of the people.

(29) The ornament of youth is their strength; but the glory of old men is their gray hairs.

Each season of life has its appropriate ornament and excellence. —שֵׂיבָה, lit. *grayness.* The version follows our own idiom.

(30) Wounding stripes are the remedy for the base; and strokes of the inner parts of the body.

Ironically said. תַּמְרוּק, as the Qeri has it, means the rubbing of precious ointments over the body in the way of cleansing and decoration. Tropically, the word may mean *remedy*, in reference to the rubbing in of remedial ointments. The base man requires a different application. His ointment is a covering over with *wounding stripes.*— *Strokes of the inner parts*, are, of course, those which go down deep into the body. The bad man's remedial applications, then, are not fragrant salves or ointments, but the application of stripes over the whole person, so severe that they penetrate deep into the body.

CHAP. XXI. 1—31.

(1) As rivers of water, the heart of the king is in the hand of Jehovah; he will incline it whithersoever he pleaseth.

The Heb. omits *as;* and so oftentimes when the comparison intended is very obvious. The image of *turning*, etc., is derived from directing water-sluices, in the irrigation of land, in whatever manner the husbandman wishes. As irrigation is practised for the purpose of refreshing and rendering fruitful, so the implication seems here to be, that Jehovah will direct the heart of the king to purposes of good. — יַטֶּנּוּ, Hiph. Imperf. of נָטָה, with suffix *it*, viz., *the heart.*

(2) Every way of a man is right in his own eyes; but Jehovah pondereth hearts. (3) To do justice and judgment, is chosen by Jehovah rather than sacrifice.

For v. 2, see 16:2, and comp. 16:25. 14:2. V. 3 compares well with the thorough spiritual views of Is. 1: 11—17. Ps. 50:7—15. The לַ in לַיהוָה, coming after a passive, may indicate the agent (§ 140. 2. § 151. *e*), i. e. it is *Jehovah* who chooses.

(4) Loftiness of looks and pride of heart — the light of the wicked, is sin.

רוּם and רְחַב are both of the Inf. const., and are here used as abstracts. — *High looks*, every one understands. But the Heb. רְחַב, lit. means *being broad* or *wide* = *expansion*. We say: The heart *swells* or *dilates* with pride; and this is the Hebrew mode of expression. Hence the cause of dilation (pride), is here designated by the effects which it produces. — נִר = נֵר is properly *light;* but this has a tropical meaning, *light* being the symbol of *joy*. The word *light* is in apposition with the preceding *loftiness* and *pride*, and is a further description of the state of the wicked. It means here, *their joy*, or *that which is matter of joy*. So that not only *loftiness* and *pride* are here said to be sin, but whatever is the object of the rejoicing of the wicked, is also reckoned a sin; plainly because they delight in sinful objects. *Light* is here chosen to express this, because loftiness and pride beam forth from the eye, thus expressing the joy which they occasion. Sentiment: 'The haughtiness of sinners, although a matter of joy to them, is sin in the sight of God.' Possibly חַטָּאת may here mean *calamity*, as it sometimes does (see Lex.); and then the contrast is prominent: 'That in which the wicked *rejoice*, will prove to be their *calamity*.' This makes a facile sense. — I am aware that the word אוֹר is the one commonly employed, for the tropical signification given above; but *light* and *lamp* (נִיר) are often employed as nearly synonymous in poetry.

(5) The plans of the diligent tend only to abundance; but every one who is hasty, is tending only to poverty.

The diligent labors constantly, and in a prudent manner, with a well-concerted plan; but he who *urges on* (אָץ) with haste to acquire a fortune, becomes poor. — I have supplied the word *tends*, in the version, because, in our tongue, the manner of the verse would appear too abrupt, without some appropriate supplement. Before כָּל־אָץ, the noun מַחְשְׁבוֹת (from the preceding clause) may be supplied. This done, it will read thus: 'The thoughts of the diligent tend only to abundance; but [the thoughts] of every one who is hasty, tend only to poverty.' Comp. 28 : 20. 20 : 21.

(6) By a lying tongue is there a winning of treasures; a fleeting breath, are they who seek death.

פֹּעַל, not only *work*, but the reward of it, viz., *the winning, the revenue.* — נִדָּף, *chased, dispelled,* referring to the manner in which one breath succeeds another; consequently, *fleeting.* — מְבַקְשֵׁי־מָוֶת, usually translated as a Gen., viz., *of those who seek death.* But if this were the meaning, then נִדָּף could not stand between the const. noun and the Gen. which follows it. Grammar demands, therefore, another solution. *Rashi* read, in his exemplar, מוֹקְשֵׁי, *snares;* and this Ewald and Bertheau prefer. The objections are, (*a*) This word stands in no known text. (*b*) In this way, it is in apposition with הֶבֶל, and certainly an unexpected epexegesis of it. The *breath chased away*, would hardly match well with *deadly snares*, which are laid down and fastened in their place.

More simple seems to me the version which I have given above; not however very confidently, for the passage is obscure. I understand the sentiment to be, that 'they who use a lying tongue in order to acquire riches, are such as seek their own death, for they shall be as a fleeting breath, i. e. suddenly pass away.' The particle of comparison is indeed omitted; but this is a matter of very frequent occurrence. *Those who seek death* is fully explained by 8:36. 17:19; on which see the remarks. The meaning is, that they act like men bent upon their own destruction. The two clauses of the verse do not directly correspond, in the way either of antithesis or of parallelism; but there is a remoter correspondence, the first clause showing the evil committed, the second the sudden and fatal consequences of it.

(7) Destruction shall sweep away the wicked; for they refuse to do justice.

שֹׁד has the sense here given to it, in Is. 13:6. Job 5:22; and its root, שָׁדַד, often means *to destroy*. — יְגוֹרֵם, Imperf. Kal, of גָּרַר. The ו is a mere *fulcrum*, and is very rarely written in the Imperf. of verbs עַ״ע, § 66. n. 2. — ◌ֵם is the suffix. — מֵאֲנוּ, Piel with Tsere, because א cannot take a Daghesh.

(8) He who is altogether perverted as to his way, is a guilty man; but as to the pure, his work is upright.

הֲפַכְפַּךְ, Pealal form from הָפַךְ, adj. in reg. with the noun that follows, and intensive in its meaning, as is exhibited in the version. — וָזָר, unique, and of an unusual form. It is plainly an adjective, (comp. זָךְ which follows). The Arabic gives us light here, inasmuch as the corresponding noun there means *crime, guilt.* The older interpreters referred the word to זָר, *stranger;* but without good reason. — פָּעֳלוֹ Berth. refers to the same meaning as in v. 6, viz., *winning, gain.* But the *consequences* of actions are not here compared; it is the *actions themselves*, for these are signified by דֶּרֶךְ in the first clause. Therefore *work* is the proper translation.

(9) Better is it to dwell on the pinnacle of the roof, than with a woman of strife and a house in common.

פִּנַּת, *the turret* at the corner of the roof, elevated above the roof, and so the highest and most exposed part of the house. — Better is such a habitation, exposed to tempest and cold, than a house in common with a brawling woman. — בֵּית חָבֶר, lit. *a house of association* or *companionship.* Before *woman* we may supply שֶׁבֶת, and render thus: *than* [*dwelling with*] *a woman of strife, in one common house.* Comp. v. 19 below, where is the same sentiment, but with variations of the diction. Comp. also 25:24.

(10) The soul of the wicked greedily desireth evil; his friend will not find compassion in his eyes.

That is, the wicked is so greedy for evil, that even his friend will not be spared from being wronged. — אִוְּתָה, in Piel, and intensive. — יֻחַן = יוּחַן, Hoph. of חָנַן. In the text, the ו is omitted in the writing, and of course Qibbuts vicarious comes in its place. Lit. it means: *be compassionated.*

(11) By the punishment of the scorner, the simple will become wise; and by admonition of the wise, he will acquire knowledge.

Bertheau: *And when the wise man prospers, he* [the simple one] *will acquire knowledge.* Sine Minervâ. The contrast lies between the different ways and consequences of instruction. A simpleton learns only by being impressed with a fear of punishment; the wise man needs no more than admonition.

(12) The Righteous One taketh cognizance of the house of the wicked; he will cast the wicked headlong into evil.

As what is here said cannot be attributed to a mere righteous man, so the meaning must be as given in the version. — מְסַלֵּף, *to precipitate, to cast down headlong* — a very strong word.

(13) He who stoppeth his ear from the cry of the poor, even he shall cry aloud, and shall not be answered.

גַּם־הוּא, emphatic, *even the very same.* What he has done to others, shall be done to him, in the way of retribution.

(14) A gift in secret averteth anger; and a bribe in the bosom — strong indignation.

The word כָּפָה appears only here. The corresponding Arabic (כפא) means *to avert* or *divert.* As this sense is a good one here, we may accept it. — *A bribe in the bosom* is one clandestinely given, as in 17: 23. — Before the last two words, the verb of the preceding clause is of course implied.

(15) The doing of justice shall be a joy to the righteous; but destruction shall be to the workers of iniquity.

The meaning is, that the righteous shall have joy and peace because of doing justice; while the contrary is true of the wicked. His work brings destruction.

(16) A man who wandereth from the way of discretion, shall dwell among the assembly of the shades.

Assembly means those who are congregated in the world of the dead. — רְפָאִים means the *ghosts* or *shades* which dwell there; comp. 2: 18. 9: 18. *The wanderer from discretion* will speedily be with them, i. e. sudden death hangs over him.

(17) A poor man who loveth pleasure, he who loveth wine and oil, shall not be rich.

The reason of this is obvious. He expends his property on his objects of pleasure, and therefore lays up nothing.

(18) The wicked shall be a ransom for the righteous; and in the room of the upright shall be the treacherous.

That is, the wicked and treacherous shall bring on themselves the evil which they intended to do to the righteous, and thus their own destruction shall ransom the righteous from the doom to which they had assigned him; comp. 11: 8.

(19) Better is dwelling in a desert-land, than [dwelling with] a brawling and morose woman.

See v. 9. Here the diction only is varied; but still it is equally strong. The latter clause runs thus lit.: *A woman of strifes and of moroseness.* Here again, as in v. 9, שֶׁבֶת seems to be implied before אֵשֶׁת.

(20) Treasure to be desired and oil are in the habitation of the wise; but the foolish man devours it.

The *treasure* here seems to be an *abundance of provision*, for *treasure* here spoken of is joined with *oil.* The word extends to *stores of all kinds*, as well as to money laid up. That is, the wise man will secure ample provision for his household; the foolish man, (כְּסִיל אָדָם, *the foolish of men*, i. e. *the most foolish*), will devour all he has, instead of laying up some part of it in store. For phraseology, comp. 15 : 20. The suff. ֶנּוּ refers to *treasure*, since it is in the sing. number.

(21) He who pursueth after justice and mercy, shall find life, prosperity, and honor.

To find life, is very significant; but other words are joined with it, in order to increase the intensity of the blessing promised. The second צְדָקָה I have translated by *pros-*

perity, because this is appropriate to the nature of the promise. There is no doubt that צְדָקָה sometimes means *salus* = *prosperity;* and indeed it does so in many cases; see Lex. In this way we have a kind of *paranomasia:* 'He who practices צְדָקָה (as a matter of duty), shall receive צְדָקָה (as a matter of reward).'

(22) A wise man scaleth the city of the mighty; and he bringeth down its strong asylum.

Comp. the striking passage in Ecc. 9 : 13—16. — *City of the mighty*, is that which is defended by valiant men. — וַיֹּרֶד, (for וַיּוֹרֶד, apoc. Hiph. of יָרַד), with accent retracted and shortened final vowel, while ֹ is written for וֹ. — In מִבְטֶחָה, the ה suff. should regularly have a Mappiq (הּ), being a fem. suff. relating to עִיר. The Masora notes the anomaly, but does not explain it. — First the walls of the city are scaled; and then comes the prostration of the strong citadel within, the asylum of the inhabitants in a time of danger.

(23) He who guardeth well his mouth and his tongue, keepeth his soul from distresses. (24) A proud man puffed up — scorner is his name; he acteth with the arrogance of pride.

For v. 23, see 13 : 2. — *The inflated proud man*, well deserves the name of *scorner*, for he looks down on others with scorn. — So the last clause: *he acts*, or *demeans himself, with haughty arrogance.*

(25) The sluggard's desire will destroy him; for his hands refuse to work.

That is, the sluggard's desire to enjoy slothful repose will destroy him; for in consequence of such an inclination his hands refuse to labor, in order that he might obtain something for his support. — תְּמִיתֶנּוּ, Hiph. of מוּת, with a suffix, Gramm. p. 289, first col. B.

(26) Continually does he strongly desire; but the righteous will give, and will not withhold.

The sluggard (who is here in view) has a keen desire to obtain possession of something, but he cannot obtain it. The righteous, however, has laid up in store the fruit of his labors, so that he can give, and even be liberal.

(27) The sacrifice of the wicked is an abomination; how much more when he brings it with an evil design!

The offering of the wicked is in itself unacceptable, because he cherishes neither love nor reverence for God. But when he brings it for the direct purpose of *fraud*, it becomes still more odious.

(28) A lying witness shall perish; but a man who hearkeneth, shall speak forever.

Comp. 19 : 5, 9. — *Whosoever hearkeneth*, viz., to wise and good counsel, and so becomes instructed and steadfast — the same *may speak always*, and find confidence put in what he says. In Ps. 63 : 7 it is said: "The mouth of him that speaketh lies shall be stopped." The sincere listener to divine commands, on the other hand, will ever be at liberty to speak.

(29) A wicked man maketh up an impudent face; but as to the upright — he will establish his ways.

I prefer the Kethibh in the last clause, which must be pointed thus: יָכִין דְּרָכָיו. The Masorites (in Qeri) read: יָבִין דַּרְכּוֹ, *he will understand his way*. Either gives a good sense; but I prefer the Kethibh as most significant. The first clause says, that a wicked man will act impudently, meaning that he will utter impudent and bitter language without consideration; the second (if we take the Kethibh) says, that the upright man will choose a stable and considerate course. The Qeri, on the other hand, would solve the matter thus: The impudent man acts without consideration; the upright one understands and considers what he is about to utter.

(30) There is no wisdom nor intelligence, nor is there any counsel, like to Jehovah.

לְנֶגֶד may mean *against.* But this does not seem to be the design of the verse. The writer means to say, that compared with the divine *wisdom*, etc., there is no other to be mentioned. Probably עֵצָה is to be mentally supplied before *Jehovah;* for this will make the whole run smoothly. Many take לְנֶגֶד as = לִפְנֵי, *in the view of.* But the other sense is more significant.

(31) The horse is prepared for the day of battle; but unto Jehovah belongeth deliverance.

All the boasted preparations of man for victory in battle, are vain without the help of God, to whom belongeth victory or deliverance. This expands the sentiment of the preceding verse. — מוּכָן, Part. Hoph. of כּוּן.

CHAP. XXII. 1—16.

[It will be seen, that the series, beginning with X., ends here with v. 16. There is an admonition, in v. 17, of a transition to another category, viz., to the WORDS OF THE WISE. This last, as it appears, actually comprises several subordinate collections of Proverbs. See Introduction, § 7.]

(1) A good name is better than much wealth, and kind favor than silver and gold.

In Hebrew, שֵׁם of itself sometimes means *good name;* just as when we say in English: 'He has made for himself a *name.*' Comp. Ecc. 7:1. Job 30:8. — חֵן טוֹב, lit. means *good or kind favor.*

(2) The rich and the poor meet together; the Maker of them all is Jehovah.

נִפְגָּשׁוּ, Niph. designating *reciprocal* action, like נִלְחֲמוּ, § 50. 2. *b.* For the Qamets in נִ, see § 29. 4. b. For sentiment, compare 14:31. 17:5. Meaning: 'Men, whether rich or poor, have in common the same Creator, and stand in the same relation to him.'

(3) The wary seeth the evil and hideth himself; but the simple rush on, and are punished.

The vowels in וְיִסְתָּר belong to the Qeri, וְנִסְתָּר. The Kethibh should be pointed thus: וַיִּסָּתֵר, which is the preferable reading, since וַ is then *consequential*, as it should be here, and the verb is reciprocal.—Sentiment: 'The wary shun evil; the unwary rush into it, and are compelled to suffer the consequences.'

(4) On account of humility — the fear of Jehovah — are riches, and honor, and long life.

The fear of Jehovah, is in apposition with *humility*, and the absence of the conjunc. וְ between them, is indicative of this, for it shows that not *accession*, but *further description*, is designed. True *humility* comes only with the *fear* of God; they are inseparably connected; and such is the view of the writer, in the passage before us.

(5) Thorns — snares — are in the way of the perverse man; he who regardeth his life will remove far from them.

He keeps far away, who avoids the path of the perverse; for in that path he will certainly encounter them.

(6) Train up a child according to his way; even when he is old, he will not depart from it.

דַּרְכּוֹ is very significant here. It means *the bent of his mind* or *inclinations*, the *capacity* which he has to pursue this occupation or that. Our English version: *In the way he should go*. Many a good sermon, and much excellent advice, have been founded on the text thus translated, and one feels a kind of regret to part with a precept so excellent. Yet the Hebrew can be made to mean no more, than that the child should be educated or trained up for usefulness, in such a way as *the bent of his genius* (דַּרְכּוֹ, *his own way*, or *the way which he chooses*) indicates that he ought to be trained. In other words: *Cuique suum.** As דַּרְכּוֹ can mean only *the way of the child*, the *morale* couched under the phrase *he should go*, finds in reality no proper place here, although the sentiment in itself is excellent, and agreeable to the tenor of the Scriptures. An interpreter's business is rather to inquire what is said, than to conjecture, however ingeniously or piously, *what ought to be said.* — מִמֶּנָּה, with a fem. suff. relating to דֶּרֶךְ, which is here feminine, and is in fact of the common gender. The last clause shows the strong hold education has upon the young, when it is suited to their capacities.

(7) The rich shall rule over the poor, and the borrower shall be a servant to the lender.

This has no respect to *civil* rule, but to predominating and superior influence. — The *lender* has power to reduce the borrower to servitude, in case he delays to repay the loan which is due.

(8) He who soweth mischief, shall reap calamity; and the rod of his insolence shall perish.

The rod of his insolence, is the rod which he has employed in his insolent treatment of others. Or the more usual interpretation of עֶבְרָתוֹ, viz., *his indignation*, may be received; in which case, the *rod* is that which, when angry, he employed to chastise others. Compare Is. 14: 6. — יִכְלֶה, *consume away, perish;* but Ges. (in Lex.): *the rod . . . is prepared for him.* But כָּלָה, *to be complete, to come to an end*, can hardly be turned into the shape of *preparing* anything. *The rod of the insolent* shall perish, and leave him destitute of means to inflict farther injury. J. H. Michaelis states the sentiment thus: "tandem *consumetur*, ut vicissim caedatur," i. e. his rod shall perish, that in his turn he may be scourged. It is doubtful whether this last clause is implied here. — יִקְצוֹר־, before Maqqeph, with short ŏ, and a ו *redundant*, being retained here, because it was so written in the ground-form without the vowels.

(9) He who hath a kindly eye — he shall be blessed; for he hath given of his bread to the poor.

טוֹב עַיִן, is said of him who looks on others (as we also say) *with an eye of compassion.* He will give charities, and then he will be blessed for his beneficence by those who receive it. So the latter part of the verse explains the first clause.

(10) Expel the scorner and strife will depart; yea, contention and shame will cease.

As the scorner is the cause of strife, so his departure will make it to cease. — קָלוֹן doubtless refers to the shameful and reproachful words and doings which contention provokes.

(11) He who loveth purity of heart — is gentle of speech, his friend is the king.

Bertheau says of this verse, that it is *sehr schwer, very difficult.* So it would seem, if we look at the diversity among commentators. Yet the sentiment does not appear to be obscure. It runs thus: 'He that cherishes pure intentions, and uses gentle and decorous language, will be regarded with a friendly eye by the king.' — טְהָוֹר־ (ו redundant) in the const. state, from טָהוֹר = *purity*, whether we regard it as a noun, or as a neuter adjective, which amounts to the same thing. — There is no וְ before חֵן, and it is probably because of *apposition* that it is omitted. The words of the apposition, in this case, however, are not merely explanatory, but constitute an *accession.* The וְ might be employed here, but for brevity's sake, it can also be omitted. — *Lips = language.* Michaelis: '*Whoever loves purity, grace* [i. e. gracious or acceptable] *will be his lips, and the king will be his friend.'* Not badly; but the version above is perhaps more significant. In it, *gentleness* (abst.) is made = *gentle* (concrete). It is not a certain consequence, as a matter of course, that purity of heart will make gracious lips, i. e. gentle and persuasive language, as the version of Michaelis would seem to imply. These are sometimes separated.

(12) The eyes of Jehovah guard knowledge; but he will make the words of the treacherous to rush headlong.

Knowledge must here be the abstract for concrete = the *knowing*, the *intelligent.* A comparison with the second clause leads to the idea, that it is what the intelligent say or teach, which will be guarded and defended; while that which is uttered by the treacherous, will be frustrated or brought to ruin.

(13) The sluggard saith: There is a lion in the streets; in the midst of the broad ways shall I be slain.

Meaning: 'The sluggard will make all possible objections to exertion, and even invent ridiculous excuses for not betaking himself to active duties.'

(14) A deep pit is the mouth of strange women; he who is abhorred of Jehovah shall fall therein.

The idea is, that what the mouth of such women utters, is destructive as a deep pit to the unwary youth. — זְעוּם, Part. pass. in reg., *the abhorred*, or *object of indignation.* — יִפָּול־, Imperf. of נָפַל, with short ŏ, and ו redundant again. The ו belongs only to the form of יִפּוֹל; and even here, it is no more than a mere *fulcrum.*

(15) Folly is bound up in the heart of a child; the rod of chastisement will remove it from him.

A general truth, which shows the extent of human corruption — a corruption which can be curbed only by chastisement. — The pronoun suff. *it* refers to *folly; him* to the *child.*

(16) He who oppresseth the poor to make increase for himself, giveth to the rich—surely to his own want.

Wealth obtained by oppression, will in the end bring poverty. God blesses not such wealth, and therefore it cannot endure.—*Giveth to the rich*, i. e. to himself, who is made rich by oppression; and because it is given to such a rich person, whose evil doings will bring calamity on him, such wealth as is thus acquired, will tend only to impoverishment in the end.

PART III.

[Thus endeth the SECOND DIVISION of the book of Proverbs, containing chaps. x—xxii. 16. What follows in *Part* III., is miscellaneous down to chap. xxv. It is collected from different sources, and might have the title which is proffered to us in v. 17, viz., THE WORDS OF THE WISE. The *divisions* under this category are somewhat peculiar, and are thus distinguished: (*a*) 22 : 17—21, exhortation to hearken to the words of the wise, with reasons for so doing, and with a reference to what has already been said. (*b*) 22 : 22—23 : 11, containing *ten* warnings, mostly comprised in two verses for each. (*c*) 23 : 12—24 : 2, ten more warnings of the like form. (*d*) 24 : 3—22, consists of twenty verses, among which are seven couplets; three single verses; and three more together as one, viz., vs. 10—12. (*e*) 24 : 23—34, a small supplement, with a *separate title*, and probably derived from a different source. These are not marked by any speciality of arrangement. See a more particular account of these divisions, in the Introduction, § 7.]

(*a*) 22 : 17—21.—(Introduction.)

(17) Incline thine ear and hear the WORDS OF THE WISE; and apply thy mind unto my knowledge.

הַט, apoc. Imp. Hiph. of נָטָה.—תָּשִׁית, Hiph. Imperf. second pers. used for the Imper.—*My knowledge*, means that which I possess and communicate. This knowledge is derived from *the words of the wise*, and it is worthy of, and demands, earnest attention.

(18) For it is comely when thou dost keep them in thine inner part; [when] they are altogether fixed upon thy lips.

Keep them, viz., the words of the wise. — *Thine inner part*, i. e. the innermost recesses of the mind. — *Fixed altogether upon thy lips*, means that the words of the wise should be so thoroughly considered and learned, that the learner will have them then all as it were upon his lips, that is, be always ready to speak of them, or to recite them. We express the like idea by saying: *Learn by heart*, i. e. make them quite familiar. — יַחְדָּו, *unitedly, altogether*, i. e. the whole of them, *each and every one* of them.

(19) That thy confidence may be in Jehovah, I have made [them] known to thee, this day, even to thee. (20) Have I not written to thee heretofore, concerning counsel and knowledge?

V. 19, *Even to thee*, גַּם אָתָּה, in the same case as ךָ the suff. of the verb, and in apposition with it, being a case of the pronoun repeated for the sake of intensity; see § 119. 3. I have translated *to thee*, in accordance with our English idiom. *Even to thee* means, that his present communication is designed specially for the person addressed, and not primarily for another. — *To-day* = *now*, that is, at the time when he was writing. — V. 20, the Kethibh reads שִׁלְשׁוֹם, which, in other cases, is accompanied by תְּמוֹל, the latter meaning *yesterday*, and the former lit. *the day before yesterday*. But שִׁלְשׁוֹם is not confined to this specific meaning, but has also a more general meaning, viz., *formerly, in time past, ante hac*. That such a sense is here needed, the antithesis in הַיּוֹם shows. *The former writing* probably means the previous portions of this book. In this way, all is facile and plain. But when, with many others, we write שָׁלִישִׁים (so the Qeri), and translate it *three times* or *threefold* = oftentimes; or *three things* = the Law, the Prophets, and the Hagiography; it looks strange — the last looks passing strange. Nor is it mended, by deriving the word from שָׁלִישׁ, *third*, which is sometimes equivalent to *leader* or *prince*, and in this way the plur. in our text comes to mean *princely things* [?]. All these are unnecessary, and in fact are incongruous. — The first verb הוֹדַעְתִּיךָ, rendered as Perf., means that he has already determined on the communication to be made. If the simple Present were intended here, we should have מוֹדִיעַ אֲנִי.

(21) To make thee know the truth of faithful words; that thou mightest make answer with words which are truth, to those who sent thee.

אֲמָרִים אֱמֶת, in the second clause, are the Acc. of instrumentality or of manner, and are in apposition, as exhibited in the version. — אֱמֶת is inserted merely in order to define and qualify the preceding word אֲמָרִים. We might render it simply *true, faithful.* The version above gives more exactly the shape of the original. — לְשֹׁלְחֶיךָ is regarded by Berth. as *plur. of excellence,* as in אֲדֹנָי. It seems to refer to the king, or to some superior, to whom answer or report is to be made; see 10: 26.

[Next follow, in (*b*), *ten* warnings, the major part of which is comprised in two verses each. But vs. 23: 9, and 28, 29, each contains a complete gnome in itself; and 23: 1—3 and 6—8, each comprises three verses linked together by the sense. These artistic combinations are manifestly the effect of design and arrangement. One half of the ten consists of *couplets*, two are *triplets*, and three are single. They seem to be intermingled for the purpose of variety in manner.]

(22) Rob not the poor, because he is poor; and oppress not the afflicted in the gate; (23) For Jehovah will plead their cause; and he will despoil those, who rob them of life.

V. 22, *Because he is poor*, and therefore cannot resort to the courts of justice for retribution. — *In the gate*, i. e. in the place where courts are held, and causes decided. V. 23, If thou shalt oppress, Jehovah will be their advocate and vindicator. — רִיבָם, the plur. suff. refers to דַּל, but this is generic, i. e. a noun of multitude. — נֶפֶשׁ, Acc. of limitation, § 116. 3.

(24) Associate not with him who is prone to anger; and have no intercourse with the man who is hastily provoked; (25) Lest thou learn his ways, and get a snare for thy soul.

V. 24, תִּתְרַע, apoc. Hithp. of רָעָה; the full form would be תִּתְרָעֶה. — בַּעַל אָף, *master of anger* is said of one *prone to anger*. So אִישׁ חֵמוֹת, its counterpart, is very significant, lit. = *a man of indignations*, the plur. being plainly intensive, which is virtually expressed in the version. — לֹא תָבוֹא, is rendered by Bertheau: *come not [together] with the man*, etc. But בּוֹא, followed by *with* (as here), means: *consuetudinem inire;* Ges. Lex. 1. *e.* The version is not literal, but *ad sensum*. It is hardly necessary to insert the word *together*. — לָקַחְתָּ, *thou take, obtain, get.* But what is the *snare?* It is the example of passionate demeanor, which, if copied, will prove dangerous to a man's life.

(26) Be not with those who strike hands; with those who pledge themselves for debts; (27) If thou hast nothing to pay, why should he take thy bed from under thee?

Comp. 6 : 1—4. — מַשָּׂאוֹת, *tribute*, but here *debts*, quasi *tribute* to the creditor. — *Why should he* (i. e. the creditor) *take thy bed?* i. e. for debt. All but necessary clothing could be taken for debt. *We* should count a *bed* as a part of this; but in Palestine, a bed was merely a cushion or piece of carpet, for the most part, and it could be replaced by other substances, which would make a comfortable layer, in that warm country.

(28) Move not back the ancient boundary, which thy fathers made.

If the literal sense be intended, then its parallel may be

found in Deut. 19:14. 27:17. But I take the leading sense to be *tropical* here = 'Change not the ancient and approved usages of the fathers.' — עוֹלָם, *ancient time.* The verse here makes a sense complete in itself, and it needs no supplement. — תַּשֵּׂג, Hiph. of נָשַׂג, with shorter form, and hortative, § 52. 2. n. 4.

(29) Seest thou a man dexterous in his work, he shall take his stand before kings, and not before obscure men.

A verse of triplex form; which is unusual here. In מְלַאכְתּוֹ, the א is otiant. The word is contracted from מַלְאֲכְתּוֹ, by throwing the vowel of the א, in this last word, back on the preceding letter. In other words: 'The skilfully industrious, or dexterous, will become rich, so as to attract the notice and friendship of kings.' — חֲשֻׁכִּים Part. adj. of the Pulal form, and intensive. This verse also is complete in itself and independent.

CHAP. XXIII. 1—10.

(1) When thou sittest down to dine with a ruler, consider well what is before thee; (2) For thou wilt put a knife to thy throat, if thou hast a keen appetite. (3) Do not crave his choice viands, for they will be bread of deceit.

V. 1, בִּין תָּבִין, § 128. 3. Umbreit renders אֲשֶׁר, *whom,* i. e. consider that you are before a superior — a possible sense, but not the most appropriate. — V. 2, *For thou wilt put a knife to thy throat,* etc., that is, thou wilt incur great danger, etc. The ground of danger is disclosed, which is, that the individual who has a keen appetite, will not be likely to restrain it. בַּעַל נֶפֶשׁ, *possessor of appetite,* indicates such an individual. The danger from a keen appetite, with attractive viands set before it, is obvious. A man will almost of course feed gluttonously; and so doing, he will degrade himself, for he will appear like a starveling, in the eyes of the ruler.

V. 3, תִּתְאָו, apoc. Hithp. of אָוָה, the אָו- at the end is an unusual form, employed instead of אָי-, the latter conforming to rule, § 74. n. 9. — וְהוּא, *for it* — what? The preceding noun is *plural*, and the anomaly seems to have escaped the commentators. I see no other solution, than by supplying mentally a word which comprises the generic sense of *food;* and the context naturally supplies אֹכֶל *esca* = *viands.* — *Bread of deceit,* because the delicacies are so *appetizing* as to mislead and deceive. — Here *three* verses are closely connected, in one admonition.

(4) Do not weary thyself in order to become rich; cease from thine own understanding. (5) Wilt thou suffer thine eyes to fly toward it? It is indeed no more; for it will surely make to itself wings, and like an eagle fly away toward heaven.

V. 4, *Cease* from reliance on thine own *sagacity;* for it cannot secure the object in view. — V. 5, in הֲתָעוּף the הֲ is interrogative; and the verb, in conformity to the Qeri, should be written תָּעִיף, in Hiph. — *Wilt thou suffer thine eyes to fly to it?* viz., *riches,* עֹשֶׁר implied, or the הַעֲשִׁיר of v. 4; *and to fly to it,* means, to look at it eagerly and often, with animated or swift glances. — For עָשֹׂה וגו׳, see § 128. 3. — כְּנֶשֶׁר, without the article; which more usually stands after כְּ. — וְעָיף, Bertheau converts into וְעוֹף, = *and a bird;* but the Qeri is better, viz., יָעוּף, *will fly.* His method of construction leaves the clause destitute of any verb of motion, which should precede הַשָּׁמַיִם, i. e. *toward heaven.* The word הַשָּׁמַיִם is here used adverbially, as designating *place.*

(6) Eat not the bread of him that hath an evil eye; and desire not his choice viands; (7) For as he thinketh in his heart, so is he; eat and drink, saith he to thee, but his heart it not with thee. (8) Thy morsel which thou hast eaten — thou shalt vomit it up, and then thou shalt lose thy sweet words.

V. 6, רַע עָיִן, lit. *evil of eye*, i. e. one who has a malignant design in view. — תִּתְאָו, as in v. 3 above. — V. 7, שָׁעַר, not elsewhere in Heb. as a verb, which has occasioned some trouble among critics. The Sept. read שֵׂעָר, *hair;* the Chald. שַׁעַר, *gate;* and others have given other meanings, none of which suit the passage. The meaning given above is vouched for by the Chald. שְׁעַר, *to think.* Sentiment: 'The true character of the host is indicated, not by his language, which is all comity, but by his designs. — V. 8, תְּקִיאֶנָּה, Hiph. of קוֹא, with a suff. fem. relating to פִּתְּךָ, which is fem. — וְשִׁחַתָּ, Piel of שָׁחַת, with ת radical written by Daghesh in the suff. formative תָּ. — *The sweet words* are those, which invited and which caress the guest at the feast. They are lost to the guest, since he vomits up his food, through disgust, and loses all pleasure in the entertainment. Sentiment: 'Beware of flattering and deceitful men, who show you special civility only to mislead you, and to put you off your guard. Their courtesies will be loathed, when their real design comes to be known.' — Here are *three* connected verses again.

(9) Speak not in the ears of a fool, for he will despise the wisdom of thy words.

That is, waste not your time in addressing him, who despises all you have to say. "Cast not your pearls before swine."

(10) Remove not the ancient boundary; nor go into the fields of orphans; (11) For their Redeemer is mighty; he will plead their cause with thee.

V. 10, Take not possession of the orphan's field by enlarging the bounds of thine own, so as to encroach upon him. Think not that he has no vindicator; for an Almighty One will plead his cause. — *With thee*, i. e. in contest with thee. — Here again is the *couplet*, i. e. two connected verses; and this completes the first series of ten admonitions.

(c) *Ten more admonitions, of unequal length*, 23 : 12—24 : 2.

(12) Apply thy heart to instruction, and thine ear to the words of knowledge.

This is merely an exhortation to attend diligently to the instruction which he is about to communicate, and does not belong properly to the *ten admonitions*. — לַמּוּסָר, with the article, because the specific instruction of the teacher who warns, is here meant.

(13) Withhold not chastisement from the child, for shouldest thou smite him with the rod, he will not die. (14) Do thou smite him with the rod, and thou shalt deliver his soul from the world beneath.

The child, with the article, which refers to the child of the person addressed; and so *with the rod*, i. e. the appropriate rod of a teacher. — מוּסָר has the sense of *chastisement* here, as the sequel shows; in v. 12, the meaning is different. — תַּכֶּנּוּ, 2d pers. Imperf. Hiph. of נָכָה, with a suffix. — *Deliver his soul*, etc., i. e. save him (by amending his life) from sudden and unexpected death. — (*Two* verses in admonition *first*.)

(15) My son, if thy heart is wise, my heart will be glad, even mine. (16) And my reins shall exult, when thy lips shall utter things upright.

גַּם אָנִי, a repetition of the suff. ־ִי in לִבִּי, see § 119. 3, and comp. Prov. 22 : 19. — *Reins*, is only a variation of the diction, the meaning being equivalent to that of *heart*. — *Things upright*, can be spoken only by the truly wise. — (Admon. 2, in *two* verses.)

(17) Let not thy heart envy sinners; much rather, be in the fear of Jehovah continually. (18) For if there is a hereafter, thine expectation shall not be cut off.

Umbreit renders יְקַנֵּא by *being zealous for*; but this would demand לְ after it, while here we have בְּ, which gives the verb the sense disclosed in the version; see in 3:31. 24: 19. — The כִּי אִם, in v. 17, there meaning *much rather*, differs from the same in v. 18, where כִּי is *causal*, and אִם means *if* conditional, not dubitative. Suppose we say: 'If God lives, we will do so and so,' we mean not to express a doubt of his existence, but a conditionality which we regard as a certainty. So here, *if there is a hereafter*, implies that the writer regards it as certain that there is one. — But what is אַחֲרִית? *A hereafter* is the literal sense. But is it *the hour of death?* Or that which comes *after that hour?* *The end*, or *hereafter*, must at least mean here, *the end of trials and of sins.* But this comes only with the end of life. *The hereafter*, then, seems to be that of the *future world.* If not, what is that hope which will not be disappointed? All hope of stable peace and joy in this world, is surely fallacious; but the hope now in question is not so; see and comp. 24: 14, 20. — (*Two* verses again in division 3.)

(19) Do thou hear, my son, and be wise, and make thy heart go onward in the way. (20) Be not among those who greedily swallow down wine, among those who are prodigal of flesh for their gratification. (21) For the drunkard and the glutton shall come to want; and slumbering shall clothe with rags.

V. 19, *The way*, with article, i. e. the way which he is marking out. — V. 20, זֹלְלֵי, *prodigal*, i. e. consuming large quantities. — לָמוֹ, lit. *for them*, i. e. for their own gratification, *Dat. commodi.* — קְרָעִים, second Acc. after תַּלְבִּישׁ, § 135. 3. *a.* The direct Acc. of the main object is omitted in the Hebrew, but is easily supplied, viz., *one, man.* Our idiom obliges us to supply a *with*, in such cases of second Acc. We may, however, imitate the Hebrew here, by translating thus: *shall put on rags.* (Three verses.)

(22) Hearken to thy father who begat thee; and despise not thy mother when she is old.

זֶה, *who*, a *relative* here, which is unusual; see Lex. No 2. — *Who begat thee*, describes the relation, and implies the consequent obligation to hearken. This is implied, too, in the case of the *mother*. — *Despise not* is *meiosis*, i. e. a negative for a positive precept. It means therefore the same as, *Pay her all the deference which is due.* (No. 4, one.)

(23) Buy the truth, and sell it not; wisdom, and instruction, and understanding.

Buy, means *acquire, obtain*, קְנֵה. — *Sell it not*, i. e. prize it so highly, that no consideration will induce you to part with it. — The last three nouns have קְנֵה implied before them; and the description thus becomes cumulative, in order to include every species of wisdom and instruction. (No. 6, one verse.)

(24) The father of the righteous will greatly rejoice; and he who begetteth one that is wise, shall verily have joy in him. (25) Thy father and thy mother shall rejoice; yea, she who bore thee shall have joy.

V. 24, גִּיל יָגִיל is the Qeri, and also in several Mss. The Kethibh must be pointed thus: גּוֹל יָגוּל. Both forms are normal, that of the Qeri is more common. The intensity which this phraseology designates, is expressed in the version. — The יוֹלֵד here reads in the Qeri, וְיוֹלֵד; hence the *Sheva* in the text, which now stands without any consonant, is designed for the marginal word. That consonant, (וְ), the Qeri supplies; and rightly. Hence, in the Qeri, the וְ before יִשְׂמַח (now written in the Kethibh) is dropped. The sentiment of v. 24 seems to be repeated in v. 25, for the sake of emphasis on intensity. (No. 7, two verses.)

(26) My son, give me thy heart, and let thine eyes take pleasure in my ways. (27) For a deep ditch is a harlot; and the strange woman a narrow pit. (28) Yea, she like a robber will lie in wait; and the treacherous among men will she increase.

V. 26, the Kethibh would be pointed תִּרְצֶינָה = תִּרְצֶנָה, from רָצָה. But the Qeri has תִּצֹּרְנָה (from נָצַר), which means:

shall watch over, or *observe*. The last is more congruous; the first more intense. — V. 27, *a narrow pit*, into which if one falls, he cannot get out. — V. 28, חֶתֶף, lit. *robbery*, but here the abstract is put for the concrete = *robber*. Or we may suppose that it stands for אִישׁ חֶתֶף. — *The treacherous will she increase*, i. e. by her wily arts of allurement, she brings her wooers within her influence, and subjects them to her demands; so that they betake themselves to fraud and treachery, in order to procure wherewith to pay the price of their unlawful pleasures. (No. 8, three verses.)

(29) Who hath wo? Who hath sorrow? Who hath strifes? Who hath solicitude? Who hath wounds without cause? Who hath blurred eyes?

The designed *assonance* in אוֹי and אֲבוֹי is very palpable. אוֹי is our exclamation *Oh!* in the way of expressing anguish. — אֲבוֹי is first *poverty* (root אָבָה, No. 2), then *misery* or *sorrow*. — שִׂיחַ is *deep and earnest thought* or *reflection*, when the mind is agitated; and so, *solicitude*. — *Wounds without cause*, are such as a man in any way inflicts on himself, by his own folly. — *Blurred eyes*, are the unfailing accompaniment of drunkenness. חַכְלִלוּת, lit. means *obscurity*, *darkness*. — The repetition of לְמִי, *to whom?* gives energy and vivacity to the questions.

(30) Those who tarry long over the wine; those who enter in to make trial of mingled drink.

For the first clause, comp. Is. 5:11, where the same expression occurs. Long sessions for compotation, is the usual custom of drunkards. — בָּאִים, *enter in*, i. e. into the house where wine is kept. — מִמְסָךְ *wine mingled*, viz., with intoxicating spices or drugs — a common resort of drunkards. This is wholly different from the mingled wine of Wisdom in 9:2. The mixture there is with water or milk, or with both of them. — In Heb., the ל is prefixed to both of the participles, in order to answer the previous question, לְמִי? But we need not follow out this as to the *form* of the answer, since we have not adopted it in translating the questions; for these are rendered by: *who hath?*

(31) Look not on the wine, when it seemeth beautifully red, when it sparkleth in the cup, when it goeth down smoothly.

תֵּרֶא, apoc. Imperf. Kal of רָאָה; see § 74. n. 3. *b.* — יִתְאַדָּם, *shows itself as ruddy.* In the version, an additional shade is given to the meaning, which seems here to be indicated by the verb. — *Sparkleth,* Heb. *gives its eye,* which tropically designates what we call *sparkling.* The sparkles resemble the pupils of little eyes. — The Kethibh כִּיס, *purse,* would make no tolerable sense here. The Qeri כּוֹס is the true reading. — יִתְהַלֵּךְ, *goes along,* i. e. goes down the throat. — *Smoothly,* lit. *evenly,* i. e. with no roughnesses; Vulg. *blandê.* The smoothness here spoken of, is highly appreciated by wine-drinkers, and is called by them *mellowness.*

(32) In its sequel, it will bite like a serpent, and sting like a viper.

יִשָּׁךְ (in pause), Imperf. Kal of נָשַׁךְ. In this verse, the article is twice omitted after the כְּ of comparison; which seems to be poetic or gnomic license. The images of the *sequel* of drunkenness, are vivid and impressive.

(33) Thine eyes shall see strange women; and thy heart shall utter perverse things.

Intoxicating drink excites to lust. Hence *strange women* will be sought after. — Of course, the heart of an intoxicated person utters he knows not what, and usually all manner of *perverse things.*

(34) And thou shalt be as one who lieth down in the midst of the sea; as one who lieth on the mast-head.

The *lying down,* means *sleeping,* or *endeavoring to sleep.* — *Midst of the sea,* implies the *midst of a rolling sea,* which is agitated by the wind. In such a condition, a stupid, careless sleeper may easily be rolled overboard. — More exposed still is he, if *he sleep at mast-head*, where the rocking or reeling is much more violent. — The imagery here is more impressive and terrible, than that of the preceding verse.

(35) "They have smitten me, [saith he], but I am not sick; they have beaten me, and I have not known it; when I shall wake up, I will seek it yet again!"

Words put into the mouth of the inebriate. He does not apprehend any danger. His friends warn him of sickness and blows and wounds; but he derides them in the language of the text. 'They have smitten me, (you say), but I am not made sick; they have beaten me, (you say), but I have felt no bruises. No; I will not hear your advice; but as soon as I have slept, I will again seek the cup.'— This seems to import, that what he utters, is said under the influence of much wine; for he calculates on a *sleep*, before he shall be able again to seek his מִמְסָךְ. What he says, is in contempt or ridicule of the admonitions of friends; and the resolve to *seek the cup again*, shows in a striking manner the indomitable appetite of the inebriate. — אוֹסִיף here simply makes the sense of *again*, or *repetition*, being put before another verb, § 139. 3. *b.* — עוֹד, *farther*, strengthens this assertion, in respect to renewing his potations. — A vivid picture of the dangers and progress of the drunkard. (No. 9 has seven verses.)

CHAP. XXIV. 1, 2.

(1) Be not envious of evil men; desire not to be with them. (2) For their heart meditateth violence; and mischief do their lips speak.

V. 1, for the first clause, comp. 23: 17. — תִּתְאָו, see on 23: 3. V. 2, for יֶהְגֶּה, comp. 15: 28. (No. 10, two verses.)

(*d*) *Chap.* XXIV. 3—22.

[This division is separated from the preceding one, by no definitive mark, excepting that it begins anew the subject of wisdom, and continues it more or less directly through seven verses. The rest is miscellaneous; but there are here fewer of simple parallelisms in which the sense is completed, than is usual elsewhere in this book; see the composite sentences in vs. 3—9; 11, 12; 13, 14; 15—18. With v. 23, another addition, a new one, evidently commences.]

(3) By wisdom shall a house be built up; and by understanding shall it be established. (4) And by knowledge shall the chambers be filled — with all wealth precious and pleasant.

V. 3, *house*, not the edifice merely, but its tenants also included. Discretion will establish a family. — V. 4, *precious*, i. e. of great value. — *Pleasant*, i. e. such things as administer to the pleasure of the indwellers. — כָּל־הוֹן, Acc. after a verb of *filling*, § 135. 3. *b*.

(5) A wise man is strong; and a man of knowledge maketh firm his strength.

בַּעוֹז, lit. *in strength* = *strong*. — מְאַמֶּץ, *renders firm* or *robust*.

(6) For with skilful management must thou make war for thyself; and there is discretion in much counsel.

תַּחְבֻּלוֹת, not simply κυβέρνησις of some kind or other, in this case, but in the sense exhibited in the version; comp. 20:18. — לְךָ, *Dat. commodi*, i. e. for thine own benefit. — רֹב־יוֹעֵץ = *many a counsellor*. I have given the substantial idea in the version, and turned the *concrete* into the *abstract*, in conformity to our idiom. — In other words: 'Success in war depends on well digested plans, made by the advice of much counsel.

(7) Wisdom is very high to a fool; he openeth not his mouth in the gate.

רָאמוֹת, *elevations*, plur. of intensity. The א is a mere

fulcrum; root רוּם.— חָכְמוֹת, see on 1 : 20. It is here a plur. *abstract*, and of course with the meaning of a singular. It also comprises an idea of intensity, quasi *sound wisdom*. Wisdom being *very high*, the fool cannot attain to it.— Therefore he must not *open his mouth in the gate*, for there causes are tried and decided; and, consequently, much wisdom is needed there.

(8) He who contriveth to do evil—men shall call him master-schemer.

לוֹ, although it stands first, for the sake of emphasis, in reality is constructed with the verb of *calling*, which takes לְ before the person or thing named.— The name itself is in the Acc.; and so it is here, as to בַּעַל־מְזִמּוֹת. The exact idea of this phrase is given in the version, with the exception, that here מְזִמּוֹת is taken in the *bad* sense, so that the phrase is equivalent to *trickish, crafty*.— Before יִקְרָאוּ, the indef. Nom. *they*, or *men*, is of course to be supplied.

(9) The device of folly is sin; and a scorner is an abomination to a man.

A fool devises something in accordance with his own views and feelings, and therefore something sinful.— In לְאָדָם we have an example of לְ after the const. form, § 114. 1.

(10) If thou hast become relaxed in the day of distress, thy strength is straitened.

Relaxation is the opposite of strenuous *exertion;* and for the latter, the day of distress calls. In such a state, viz., one in which a man feels but little power to make effort at a time when much is needed, that small power is of course *reduced to straits*.— צַר, third Kal Perf. from צָרַר.

(11) Deliver thou those who are drawn away to death; and those who are tottering to the slaughter, O do thou keep back!

לְקֻחִים, *taken off, dragged away*.—*The death ... the slaugh-*

ter, with the article in Hebrew, i. e. death by the executioner, which is specific. — אִם, here a particle of *wishing;* like εἰ γάρ in the New Test. I have so translated it; see Lex. אִם, C. 3. This particle demands the Imperf. after it, which accordingly here makes its appearance. — This refers, of course, to an interference on the part of the humane, in order to deliver those who are unjustly accused and sentenced to death.

(12) Although thou shouldest say: "Behold! we know not this;" he that pondereth hearts — doth not he know? Yea, he that guardeth thy soul, doth know; and he will reward every man according to his work.

הוּא, *he* above all, or *he knows*, although there be no other one who knows. וְנֹצֵר וגו׳, Bertheau renders *interrogatively.* But then we have to bring forward הֲלֹא. This may be done; but I prefer the affirmative sense as given above. — *He who guards the soul*, must of course know all the deeds of man.

(13) My son, eat thou honey, for it is good; and honey-comb upon thy palate is sweet; (14) So do thou obtain knowledge of wisdom for thy soul; if thou hast found it, and there is a hereafter, then thine expectation shall not be cut off.

V. 13. Of course, the *literal* sense of this, as a command, would not at all comport with the ultimate design of the writer. It is merely the first member of a comparison; the second of which is introduced by כֵּן, *so*, in the next verse. — V. 14. *So*, i. e. in like manner as honey is good and sweet, let a knowledge of wisdom be pleasant and precious. — דְּעָה, with ה‎ָ‎ paragogic, instead of ה‎ֵ‎, Imp. of יָדַע; (which in a few instances takes place, see 1 Sam. 28: 15. Ps. 30: 4. § 48. 3. remarks). — *And* ⌊*if*⌋ *there is a hereafter;* see 23: 18 above, where the same phrase occurs, and with the same meaning, and also 24: 20. Here, as there, the apparent conditionality is not one of doubt, but a case supposed, the reality of which is taken for granted 'as surely as there is a hereafter.'

(15) Lie not in wait, O wicked man, for the dwelling of the righteous; destroy not his resting-place; (16) For should the righteous fall seven times, yet will he rise; but the wicked shall be made to stumble upon evil.

V. 15. רִבְצוֹ, lit. *his layer, couch*, or as in the version. V. 16. וָקָם, Kal Perf., *then will he rise*, with ו consequential. As to *seven times*, it of course means *a good many times*. The sense here does not point us to *moral lapses*, but to *misfortunes*. Still, it seems to be true of moral lapses also, if we may credit the apostle Paul, Phil. 1: 6. Rom. 5: 5—10. 8: 35—39.

(17) When thine enemy falleth, rejoice not; and when he stumbleth, let not thy heart exult; (18) Lest Jehovah should see, and it should be evil in his eyes; and he should then turn away his anger from him.

The Kethibh reads *enemies*, plur.; the Qeri, with more concinnity, *enemy*, sing. — יָגֵל, Hiph. Imperf. of גִּיל. — *Be evil in his eyes*, i. e. displeasing in his view. — וְהֵשִׁיב, with ו consequential, which is expressed in the version. — Sentiment: 'If evils come upon a man who is your enemy, and you feel that he deserves them, do not exult in his sufferings. If thou displayest such a temper of mind, the Lord will rebuke thee by removing the cause of thine exultation, i. e. by ceasing to inflict chastisement upon thine enemy.' A noble sentiment, and indicative of high moral views on the subject of kind feeling toward our fellow-men! "Love your enemies."

(19) Be not enraged against evil doers; be not envious in respect to the wicked.

Comp. v. 1 — תִּתְחַר, apoc. Hith. of חָרָה.

(20) For there shall be no hereafter to the evil; the lamp of the wicked shall be quenched.

That is, there shall be no *hereafter of reward*, such as is described in v. 14, and in 23 : 18. The question here is not about a *future existence*, but about a *future retribution* or *reward*. This is a good reason why we should not envy the wicked, or be angry with them, since they, in view of their doom, are objects of compassion rather than of vengeance.

(21) My son, fear Jehovah and the King; with revolters do not mingle.

שׁוֹנִים means *those who change*, viz., their dutiful and loyal opinions and feelings, and make revolt.—In תִּתְעָרָב, the first Qamets comes by reason of Dagh. being excluded from the ר; the second, because the word is in pause.

(22) For their calamity shall suddenly rise up; and the destruction of them both, who knoweth?

Here the idiom is very Hebraistic. *Their calamity* means the calamity which they (God and the king) inflict or send. This is made clear by the latter clause: *The destruction of them both*, that is, the destruction which both Jehovah and the king will bring on the wicked.—This, *who knoweth?* i. e. no one can tell when or how it will come—it will come *suddenly* and *unexpectedly*, for מִי יוֹדֵעַ = פִּתְאֹם in the first clause.

[Thus end the twenty verses which constitute this fourth portion of Part III. of the book. Another addition is still to be made, by subjoining some other things which *wise men* have composed or uttered. So the title to the next, and *fifth*, portion of Part III. informs us. This distinguishes the last portion from the other four.]

(*e*) *Chap.* XXIV. 23—34.

(23) THESE ALSO ARE OF THE WISE: Partiality in judgment is not good.

In לַחֲכָמִים, we have, apparently, the so called לְ *auctoris* — like מִזְמוֹר לְדָוִד. See Introd. § 7.—הַכֵּר־פָּנִים, verb Hiph.

Inf. from נָכַר, with Tseri shortened because of the Maqqeph, lit. *to consider persons* or *faces ;* which expression the Hebrews used to designate *partiality.* — בְּמִשְׁפָּט, without the article here, because the sense is generic. — בַּל־טוֹב might be לֹא טוֹב, or *vice versa.* But בַּל is *poetic,* and not employed in prose.

(24) He who saith to the wicked: Thou art righteous; the people shall curse him, nations shall abhor him. (25) But to those who admonish, there shall be pleasure; blessings of good shall come upon them.

יִקְּבֻהוּ, Imperf. third plur. of נָקַב, with suff., and בּ for בּוּ. — V. 25, *blessing of good,* i. e. the thanks and kind wishes of those who have been benefited by their admonitions; or it may mean *an excellent blessing,* i. e. a good reward.

(26) One will kiss the lips of him, who answereth with upright words.

This verse also has a relation to what is said respecting the sentence given in judgment, v. 1, seq. When the judge *speaks upright words,* every one is ready, as it were, to salute him with affection and respect.

(27) Prepare thy work without, and get it ready in thy field; then afterwards thou shalt build thine house.

בַּחוּץ, lit. *in the without,* i. e. abroad in the field. — בַּשָּׂדֶה, with the article, because it is here a specific field. — וּבָנִיתָ, with ו consecutive. Sentiment: 'Prepare, first of all, for your necessary sustenance; accommodations follow.'— With us, in our climate, a house comes early into the list of our necessaries; much less so in Palestine. The proverb: "First bread, then family," applies well there.

(28) Be not a witness against thy neighbor without cause; for wilt thou deceive with thy lips?

חִנָּם may mean *inconsiderately* or *rashly ;* but the version gives a more extended sense. — In וַהֲפִתִּיתָ, the הֲ is an interrogative; which, however, nowhere else has a ו before it. Yet the וְ plainly adds to the significance here, as the version shows. The question implies, that the speaker takes it for granted, that the witness in question may have honest intentions, but needs caution as to what he is about to do. *Wilt thou?* = *thou shalt not*, in such a connection, and after a preceding negative. In Greek, *καί* often adds to the intensity of a brief question. So here.

(29) Say not: As he hath done to me, so will I do to him; I will reward the man according to his work.

An admirable principle, and one which comports entirely with the Sermon on the Mount.

(30) I passed over the field of the sluggard, and over the vineyard of the man who lacketh understanding; (31) And behold! it had all of it shot up with nettles; and its surface was covered with thistles; and the stone-wall was broken down.

A vivid picture of the effects of sloth! Both corn-field and vineyard all overgrown with noxious weeds! — עָלָה, lit. *ascended;* but here as in the version. The field *mounted up* by the growth upon it. — כֻּסּוּ, Pual of כָּסָה, § 61. 2. n. 4. — *Nettles and thistles* are the secondary Acc. of means; we must supply the prep. *with.* — נֶהֱרָסָה, fem. in Niph., and of course its Nom. גֶּדֶר is here fem.; so Ewald, § 174. *d. γ.*

(32) Then I looked, I considered; I beheld, I received admonition. (33) A little more sleep, a little more slumber, a little more folding of the hands for sleep; (34) So shall thy poverty come as a traveller, and thy pressing want as an armed man.

V. 32, *I considered*, Heb. lit. *I set my mind* upon it. — V. 33, שֵׁנוֹת, lit. *of sleeps;* and so תְּנוּמוֹת, *of slumberings.* To avoid this plural in English, (for it would be bad usage here), I have inserted the word *more;* as our Eng. version has done. The Heb. plurals have an intensive meaning in themselves, indicating a succession of sleep and slumber. — חִבֻּק,

a noun, is also of an intensive Piel form.—V. 34, מִתְהַלֵּךְ, implies a כּ before it, at least it needs the particle *as*, in an English version. The real shape of the Heb. is thus: *So shall thy poverty—a traveller—come*, etc. But here our word *traveller* hardly does justice to the meaning. *A highwayman*, seems to be here plainly meant, of which the Heb. is very expressive, viz., *one who goes hither and thither.*—Then the concinnity with *an armed man*, (which follows, and which lit. is *man of the shield*), is very plain. *Highwaymen* come suddenly and unexpectedly; they come to rob and to kill, and of course they come armed; and sloth and slumbering will do the like for the sluggard, by reason of the consequences which they bring upon him. The word מַחְסֹרֶיךָ is a plural of *intensity;* and is so translated, viz., pressing want.

Thus ends the fifth and last subdivision of PART III. We come next to,

PART IV. CHAPS. XXV—XXIX.

[Again we have a specific title or introduction to the piece which follows; comp. 10:1. As this consists of *Solomon's compositions*, we might expect, that it would accord, as to manner, with Part II. of the book, which clearly belongs to him. And such is the case. But the discussion of these matters would hardly be appropriate here, and the reader is therefore remitted to Introd. § 8. The larger portion of what is now before us, has only two members in each gnome; and these are commonly either in contrast, or else they exhibit comparisons of similitude. Commonly, also, each member has eight or else seven words; more rarely six. Even the parallelism is not always kept up; but in general it is somewhat equable. This composition has so many traits of resemblance to Part II., as already intimated, that they seem enough to persuade an attentive and discerning reader, that Parts II. and IV. came originally from the same hand.]

CHAP. XXV. 1—28.

(1) These, moreover, are the PROVERBS OF SOLOMON; which the men of Hezekiah king of Judah collected.

גַּם, *moreover, besides*, seems to look back to 10 : 1, seq., which has the like title with v. 1 here. — הֶעְתִּיקוּ, lit. *transferred.* It is hardly to be supposed, that the proverbs which follow were already embodied in some little book by itself, which came into possession of Hezekiah's friends; for what can *transferred* mean, in such a case? The probability is, then, that these regal coöperators found the following gnomes in this collection and in that; and that they *copied them out*, or *transferred*, i. e. *collected*, them into one little volume. The Sept., therefore, have well translated by *ἐξεγράψαντο, copied out.* By what *indicia* they determined the question of authorship, we have no information. The probability however is, that some title, bearing the author's name, was connected with them, whenever they were found; or tradition, it may be, had brought down a report of the authorship. — By *the men of Hezekiah*, we are doubtless to understand his friends, who were *literary courtiers.* It matters not, whether the service was performed at the king's suggestion, or at theirs. It was an important, and doubtless a very acceptable, service; and it is no wonder that such an excellent king as Hezekiah, should forward such a compilation.

The fact that there are repetitions of the same proverb in Part IV. itself, and a great many repetitions of the proverbs in Part II., either exact, or with slight variations, seems to be a good voucher for the fact, that Part IV. was made up from different sources, which seems to have embodied, here and there, portions of Part II. When the transfer was made, they were taken as they stood in their original sources. One and the same continuous writer, or a mere selector of choice portions, would hardly have introduced repetitions so numerous as are found here. His memory would have guarded him against them.

For the critical discussion of the subject, the reader is referred to the Introduction, § 8.

(2) The glory of God is to conceal a matter; but the glory of kings is to search out a matter.

That "God's ways are *unsearchable*," is one of his high and awful prerogatives. "Verily he is a God who *concealeth* himself," says Is. 45 : 15. This deep mystery serves to make a solemn impression, and to silence all impertinent inquiry. On the other hand, kings should never proceed in a hidden way, but do all by inquiry and counsel, respecting what they are called to decide. Without *searching out a matter*, in this sense, they can never decide properly. It is a king's *glory* to get all the light he can.

(3) The heavens for height, and the earth for depth; even so is the heart of kings — there is no searching it out.

That is, the heavens are so high, and the earth so deep, that we cannot explore them thoroughly. So is it, too, with the heart of kings. When they keep their own secrets, no one can venture to draw them out, or no one is able to do it.

It is one thing for kings *to search out* a matter before they judge of it; and quite another to keep their own secrets. *Kings* are introduced here, because of the difficulty that lies in the way of probing them. Their rank and their relation to the community exempt them from ordinary injury.

(4) Remove dross from the silver, and there will come forth for the founder a vessel.

הָגוֹ is Inf. abs. of הָגָה, No. II., and is used for the Imp hortative; for *form*, see § 74. n. 2; for *syntax*, § 128. 4. *b* — *A vessel*, i. e. a silver vessel, which can be shaped as may be required, the purification having rendered the metal malleable and ductile. Of course this is not said for its own sake, it being an ordinary and familiar fact, but for the sake of what follows, and in such a way, that a comparison may be tacitly made. The sequel runs thus:

(5) Remove the wicked from the presence of the king, and his throne shall be established by righteousness.

That is, remove wicked counsellors and companions from the king's presence, and the dross will be taken away. The consequences will then be, the establishment of his kingdom by justice and equity, since evil advisers are rejected.

(6) Do not make display of thyself before the king; stand not in the place of the great.

The presence of a king is not an appropriate place for one of his humbler subjects to display splendor and pomp, which belong only to his courtiers. — *Great* = *nobility* or *courtiers*. Meaning: 'Be not emulous of taking thy place among those who are above thee in rank;' for this seems to be the admonition contained in the verse.

(7) For it is better for thee, that one should say unto thee: 'Come up hither,' than that one should degrade thee in the presence of a prince, whom thine eyes behold.

That is, it is better to be invited to a place of honor, than to thrust thyself into it without invitation. For if thou doest thus, thou wilt be *degraded*, i. e. sent down to a lower place by the officer of arrangements, and thus put to shame before the very king, to see whom thou hast officiously thrust thyself in. Comp. Luke 14: 8—10. Matt. 23: 12.

(8) Go not forth to strive hastily; lest thou shouldest do something in the end thereof, when thy neighbor hath put thee to shame.

The consequence of entering *hastily* into strife, is to enter into it unprepared, and so the way is open and easy. —

There is an emphatic use of the מַה here, for it indicates *something very bad*, or *something very dangerous*. A man *hasty in strife*, or *easily provoked*, and who readily enters into a quarrel, if he gets *worsted* in any respect, i. e. *put to shame*, becomes so enraged, that he is apt to do something desperate, either what is very wicked, or is fraught with danger. For the latitude of meaning in מַה, compare Prov. 9 : 13. 2 Sam. 18 : 22. Job 13 : 13.

My first impression, on reading this verse attentively, was, that the tenor of its meaning in the latter part runs thus: *Lest thou mayest not be able to do anything at the end of the strife, when thy neighbor hath worsted thee.* In other words: 'A hasty contest may end so much to thy disadvantage, that thou mayest be quite crippled in thy power to make any farther resistance.' For this, we must make מַה = *anything, quidquid*, and פֶּן must be taken as a simple negative. Neither of these are impossible; see Lex. מַה, and for פֶּן comp. Prov. 5 : 6, where seemingly (but not really) it is = אַל, *not*. The first view is the more simple and certain. The latter would make a good sense, but not so true to Hebrew as the other.

(9) Contend earnestly with thy neighbor; but still reveal not the secret of another.

Not a command to enter into contention, but the hypothetical supposition of such a case = Let us suppose that thou art even earnestly contending with thy neighbor, still, be not so dishonorable as to reveal a secret which he has confided to thee, and the disclosure of which might be hurtful to him. — The word *another* here means the friend with whom one is contending. — תְּגָל, in pause, for תְּגַל, which is apoc. Piel Imperf. of גָּלָה. Some good editions exhibit תְּגַל; but the other is normal in pause.

(10) Lest he who heareth should reproach thee; and so thine ill fame shall not depart.

That is: 'Do not reveal secrets; for he who hears the revelation will *reproach* thee for making it; and *ill fame* will follow thee, yea, even such as will not depart from thee.' — תָּשׁוּב, lit. *return*, and then, *turn away*, *desistere*, *recedere*. Meaning: 'By the disclosure of secrets, an ill name will be given to thee, which will continually cleave to thee.'

(11) Apples of gold among picture-work of silver, is a word spoken in proper season.

In the first clause, the idea is that of a garment of precious stuff, on which is embroidered golden apples among picture-work of silver. Costly and precious was such a garment held to be; for besides the ornaments upon it, the material itself was of high value. — דָּבֻר, Part. pass. Kal is found nowhere else. — עַל אָפְנָיו, has received many interpretations. Kimchi, Schultens, Bertheau, and others, have made it the plur. of אוֹפָן, *wheel*, and so construed it as conveying the idea of *haste*, *alertness*, *readiness*, because wheels run swiftly. It seems to be a conclusive objection against this, that אוֹפָן, *wheel*, has a long immutable Hholem, which is nearly always written ו in the sing., and always in the plur., whether absolute or const. Besides this, the *plur.* always doubles the radical ן, e. g. אוֹפַנִּים, showing that the word is a Pilel form. *A word on its wheels*, moreover, at least sounds strange to our ears. We must resort to another root, which is אָפַן, prob. = פָּנָה, *to turn*; and hence, with reference to the revolutions or vicissitudes of time, it comes to mean *time*, i. e. *period of revolution*. From the Segholate אֹפֶן, we here obtain אָפְנָיו, instead of אֳפָנָיו; but this is nothing strange, for the shortened plurals here, like the first of these two words, are not uncommon; see § 91. 6. 2, plur. abs. and const. Ges. Lehrgeb. s. 575, (which has a fuller exhibition of the shortened plural forms). — *A word in its time*, is a word in the time appropriate to it. It seems plain, that this last signification is wellgrounded; for in

Arabic, the same word (written אִפָּן) means *time.* The exigency of the case, and the testimony of the Arabic, seem sufficient to guide us in this controverted passage.

(12) A ring of gold, and an ornament of pure gold, is a wise reprover to a hearing ear.

נֶזֶם lit. means, *a nose-ring*, or *an ear-ring*. The less specific sense sounds better to us. — So חֲלִי properly means a *necklace* or *collar;* but sometimes it designates an *ornament* for any part of the body. Here, too, the generic sense is preferable. — That '*the listening ear* is better than the ear adorned with gold rings,' seems to be the gist of the proverb. In other words: 'Knowledge is better than ornaments.'

(13) Like the cold of snow in harvest time, is a faithful messenger to those who send him; for the soul of his masters will he revive.

צִנַּת, const., from צִנָּה, a word of very peculiar and diverse significations. The custom of mixing *snow* with drinks, during the hot season, is here alluded to; and it is a vivid image of refreshment. *A faithful messenger* refreshes in like manner. The two words שֹׁלְחָיו and אֲדֹנָיו may both be considered as cases of the *pluralis eccellentiae*, and therefore can be translated by the *singular.* The case supposed, is that of a faithful emissary on important business, which he transacts with success, to the gratification of his employer.

(14) Clouds and wind without rain, is he who boasts himself of a deceitful gift.

וְגֶשֶׁם אָיִן, lit. *and yet no rain;* the version gives the sense truly. — *Boasts himself* of an *intended gift*, and consequently of his *liberality*, and yet the gift is a deception, being never actually made. — The comparison is very striking, and the sentiment pungent. Clouds and wind sometimes promise rain, and do not give it; so the boasting man promises, and perhaps parades, his so-called gifts; but he does not bestow them.

(15) By delay of anger a prince is persuaded; and a soft tongue breaketh the bone.

When any one restrains his indignation at a wrong done him, even a prince, who is very likely to persist in his own way, becomes softened, and persuaded to do justice. — *A soft tongue*, is one which speaks mild and gentle language. — *Breaketh the bone*, is a vivid image of the power which softness and mildness have in overcoming obstinacy. *The bone* is a hard substance; but hard as it is, the *soft tongue* has power to break it. Meaning: 'Forbearance and gentleness have great power in subduing self-will and obstinate persistence in wrong-doing.'

(16) Hast thou found honey, eat [only] what sufficeth thee; lest thou become satiated with it, and vomit it up.

דַּיֶּךָ, דַּי in the suff. state takes this form; in the const. it is דֵּי, from דַּי. The idea is: 'Eat only so much as will be innocent and useful. Beyond this, satiety and loathing follow, even to vomiting.'—The two suffixes to the two last verbs refer to דְּבַשׁ, and are in the Acc. As to the first, it is governed by the verb of *filling*, § 135. 3. *b*. We are obliged to employ, in English, a preposition after such verbs, (e. g. *with*), but not so the Hebrews. — הֲקֵאתוֹ, Hiph. Praet. 2 pers., with suff., from קוֹא. The final ת of the verb loses its own vowel (ָ), because it must be joined to the vowel-suffix. Sentiment: '*Ne quid nimis*. Moderation in luxuries is essential to comfort and health.'

(17) Keep back thy foot from the house of thy friend, lest he should become satiated with thee, and hate thee.

הֹקַר — הוֹקַר, lit. *make scarce* (see Is. 13:12), from יָקַר. Here again, we have a *Ne quid nimis*, in another form. Sentiment: 'Do not pay too frequent visits to thy neighbor. Satiety, and at last disgust, will ensue.'— Here again is the Acc. pron. suff., after a verb of *filling*, as in v. 16.

(18) A maul, a sword, and a sharp arrow, is the man who answereth against his friend as a false witness.

That is, such a man is *like* to those destructive weapons, כְּ, *as*, being omitted, as often elsewhere. — *Answereth*, e. g. the questions put to him by a magistrate, acting as a judge. — עֵד שָׁקֶר is in apposition with אִישׁ, and is designed to characterize or farther describe.

(19) A broken tooth, and a foot which is a-wry, is confidence in a treacherous man, in a season of distress.

רֹעָה, fem. Inf. as a noun, from רָעַע, Inf. רֹעַ, lit. *a tooth of breaking.* — מוּעָדֶת (in pause), Part. Pual of יָעַד. Gesenius, and many others, make the word a pres. Part. of מָעַד, and suppose מוּעָדֶת to be a shortened form here of מוֹעָדֶת. But the Hholem, in such a case, is *immutable*, and this solution, therefore, cannot be accepted. No analogy is even appealed to, in defence of this latter opinion. The other solution is an obvious one, as to the *form;* and as to the *meaning*, see Ezek. 21: 21, where the word plainly means *turned aside;* which in the version I have expressed by *a-wry.* — In the next clause, the Heb. lit. taken, stands thus: *confidence of a treacherous man*, which we express by *confidence in him.* — Meaning: 'A treacherous man will not only fail you in a time of distress, but will annoy you like a broken tooth or a sprained foot.

(20) [As] he that taketh away a garment in a cold day — [as] vinegar upon nitre — even so is he that singeth with songs to a sad heart.

The two first clauses are designed as the basis of comparison; the last shows that with which they are compared. — The second clause, *vinegar upon nitre*, is a *constructio praegnans*, the verb *pouring*, or some equivalent word, being implied before עַל. To expose *incongruities* of action, is the object here. 'It would be *mal apropos* to strip off clothing on a cold day; vinegar and nitre are opposite to each other, and combination spoils them both; and equally incongruous as this, is the making merry to a heart which is saddened.

(21) If thine enemy hunger, feed him with bread; if he thirst, give him water to drink; (22) For coals of fire wilt thou heap on his head, and Jehovah will reward thee.

V. 21, comp. Rom. 12: 20. Matt. 5: 43, 44. — *Bread . . . water*, are in the second Acc., i. e. the Acc. of *means*. — V. 22, חֹתֶה, lit. *to take* or *to gather;* but here it seems to convey a sense appropriate to the עַל that follows, as in the version. As to the sentiment; some of the ancients construed the *coals of fire* as indicative of *vengeance, destruction*. But this is not congruous with the sequel: *Jehovah will reward thee*. Reward for *vengeance*, inflicted by man, is surely not a matter of promise in the Bible. The meaning then must be, that the *coals* will melt his enmity; or else, perhaps, that they will enkindle his shame. It seems to be as much as to say: 'The reception of undeserved kindness must make him blush deeply for his enmity;' for this is plainly the general sentiment aimed at. The whole two verses are worthy of "Him who spake as never man did speak."

(23) The north wind bringeth forth a shower; and a concealed tongue — a rueful countenance.

It is a matter of fact, that a *north-west* wind, from the Mediterranean Sea, brings rain in Palestine. In the language of Scripture, this is a *north wind*, inasmuch as the Hebrews have only four cardinal points. — In the second clause, the verb יְחוֹלֵל is implied, where the dash is inserted. — נִזְעָמִים, Part. Niph., *affected with anger*, or *with abhorrence* or *disgust* = *rueful*. Meaning: 'Concealed or private slander excites anger and disgust.'

(24) Better is it to dwell on the pinnacle of a roof, than with a brawling woman who is a house-companion.

See 21: 9, 19, where stands, verbatim, the same proverb.

(25) [As] cold water to a weary soul, even so is a goodly report from a distant country.

The ו before שְׁמוּעָה, is that of comparison, § 152. B. 3. The meaning is, that both of them are quickening and refreshing. — *The report from a distant country*, doubtless refers to good news from a friend, absent in a foreign country.

(26) A disturbed fountain and a spoiled well, is a righteous man tottering before the wicked.

נִרְפָּשׂ, lit. *trodden with the feet*, and so *disturbed* or *roiled*.— *A spoiled well*, מָשְׁחָת Part. Hoph., is one into which impure substances are thrown, which destroy the quality of the water. These are disagreeable objects; and so is it revolting to our minds, when we see a good man succumbing to a bad one.

(27) To eat much honey is not good; and searching after one's own glory is burdensome.

There is a great variety of sentiment in regard to the exposition of the last clause, כְּבֹדָם כָּבוֹד. Eng. Version: "To search after their own glory *is not* glory;" i. e. the liberty of supplying *is not*, is taken in order to avoid an absurd sentiment. The verb *is*, we know well, is implied some twenty times where it is inserted once; but as to supplying *is not*, unless a previous parallelism contains a negative *expressed*, I know of no authority for it, and no grammatical precedent.— Arnoldi, Ewald, and others, appeal to the Arabic חקר, which means *to despise*, and so they render thus: *To despise their glory* [that of men], is *glory*. The sense is well; but the resort to the Arabic for the meaning of a word so frequent as חָקַר and its derivates in Hebrew, (it is used some forty times), is aside from sound philology. That the second כָּבוֹד differs in meaning here from the first, seems quite plain. I would refer the second to the original sense of כָּבֵד, viz., *to be weighty, grievous, troublesome* or *burdensome*, which last word preserves the exact shade of the original; see in 27 : 3. The examples of this sense are abundant; see Lex. s. v. No. 4. We have then here a *paranomasia;* exactly like that of אִוֶּלֶת in 14: 24. *The search after* כָּבוֹד (in one sense), is כָּבוֹד (in another sense). So the version above. — The only seeming difficulty is the suff. in כְּבֹדָם. But this I take to be a pronoun indefinite, and as it were impersonal. If the *plur.* be insisted on, then the implied antecedent is אֲנָשִׁים. In impersonal verbs, the third sing. and plur. are both used indifferently. So here — *their glory* is the glory of those who make the search in question. I have translated in the sing. by *one's glory*, which gives for substance the same sense, and runs smoother in English than the plural. — Thus we obtain the sentiment in substance, of our English version, without trespassing, as that does, upon the integrity of the text.—We see, moreover, in this way, the force of the comparison. The first clause declares, that we may have too much of a good thing, so that it becomes virtually an evil to us. As for the second; *glory*, i. e. an honorable name, is a good thing; but to seek after this as an object, and with solicitude, becomes a burden.

(28) A city with breaches — without a wall — is a man who has no control over his own spirit.

פְּרוּצָה, lit. *broken, cast down.* — *Without a wall,* is an epexegetical clause, in apposition with the other, defining still more particularly. Such a city is liable to be attacked and plundered; and so the man, who has no control over himself, is always exposed to doing or saying something which will be injurious to himself.

CHAP. XXVI. 1—28.

(1) As snow in summer, and rain in harvest-time, so honor is not comely to a fool.

Snow in summer, and showers in harvest-time, are very incongruous with the season, i. e. they are untimely. So is it with *honor bestowed on a fool.* It does not fit him.

(2) As a sparrow in respect to flitting away, as a swallow in regard to flight, so a curse without cause will not take effect.

The sparrow and the swallow are remarkable for rapid flight. They not only fly swiftly away, but one cannot make them abiding or stationary. So shall the curse, which is causelessly uttered, be dissipated. It will not hit the mark, *will not enter into* (לֹא תָבוֹא) the object aimed at; or, *it will not arrive, happen,* take effect; for בּוֹא sometimes has this meaning. This is much better than the Qeri לוֹ (for לֹא), which runs thus: *will come upon him,* viz., on the fool who utters it. The *comparison* is lost by this. 'The birds swiftly vanish; and so does the causeless curse, i. e. it will not light.' I take this to be the gist of the comparison; and after this tenor is the version above.

(3) A scourge for the horse, a bridle for the ass, and a rod for the back of fools.

That is, a rod is as appropriate for fools, as a whip for the horse, or a bridle for the ass. Comp. 10 : 13. 19 : 29.

(4) Answer not a fool according to his folly, lest thou be like unto him, even thou. (5) Answer a fool according to his folly, lest he be wise in his own view.

Both true or correct, with appropriate limitations. In the first case, one is *not to answer a fool* in a way that accords with his folly, i. e. by saying silly things as he does; for this would make one turn fool himself. In the second place, *one should answer him as his folly deserves,* i. e. with reproof, or (it may be) with a wise moderation; for otherwise he will indulge the conceit, that he himself is as wise as others.—The play of words here, consists in giving to כְּ in the two cases a meaning somewhat diverse, although both come within the range of the particle. The first כְּ means *in accordance with,* i. e. *after the tenor of;* the second, *according to the desert of,* i. e. in such a way as one ought, as a matter of justice, to answer folly. There can be no doubt that these seemingly discrepant gnomes are here put together, for the sake of point or paronomasia.

(6) He cutteth off feet, he drinketh in wrong, who sendeth a message by the aid of a fool.

Cutting off the feet of a messenger, would of course deprive a man of any advantage from his service. He who sends a fool, does the like, as to getting any good from his service. Nor is this all; *he drinketh in wrong*, who sends such a messenger, because he will do or say something, which will bring mischief upon him who sent him, so that he will be the sufferer.

(7) Take away the legs of a lame man; and so — a proverb which is in the mouth of fools.

דַּלְיוּ can be made only in the Piel of דָּלָה; not = דָּלְלוּ (so Ges. in Lex. and others) *are weak;* for how would this meaning suitably compare with the next clause? The Dagh. in ל is omitted, because the ל is virtually repeated by inserting the *Yodh;* as in French, where in *mouiller* (moul-yé), etc., the second *l* is pronounced as an *i*. The legs of the lame are useless, is the meaning; and so they may as well be taken away, as it respects any good from them. So a proverb in the mouth of fools is useless; for they know not how and when to use it. It is a *lame* proverb. — בְּפִי, *which is in the mouth*, not מִפִּי, *from the mouth;* i. e. take away that which is in the fool's mouth, and which he is about to utter. In other words: 'Lay restraint upon a fool's uttering what he has made ready to speak, for it will be useless.'

(8) As the binding of a stone in a sling, so is he who giveth honor to a fool.

It would be absurd *to bind a stone to a sling*, and then expect it to do execution. Equally so is it, *to bestow honor upon a fool*, and then expect any good consequence from it.

(9) As a thorn-bush which is elevated in the hand of a drunkard, so is a proverb in the mouth of a fool.

As a drunken man, who holds a high thorn-bush in his hand, will be very apt to injure others or himself; so a fool's words will injure himself or others.

(10) An arrow which woundeth every one, is he who hireth a fool, and he who hireth vagrants.

רַב from רָבַב, No. 2. Lex., *an arrow.* — The man who employs fools and vagrants to do his work, and pays them wages, will injure himself. Such *hiring* is like an arrow, which, if poisoned, may wound those who handle it, as well as those against whom it is sent. In other words, the employment of fools and vagrants is very mischievous, in its consequences, to him who needs to have work well done. — עֹבְרִים, *passers by, vagrants,* or if not these, at least it implies persons who are mere passers by, i. e. not well known.

(11) As a dog returneth to his vomit, a fool will repeat his folly.

The Heb. shape of the last clause is thus : *A fool will make repetition with his folly,* i. e. will repeat his nonsense. — קֵאוֹ, *his vomit,* (not *the act of vomiting*), is the *filthy food* on which the dog feeds, even the sight of which produces loathing and abhorrence. The dog eats such a nauseous morsel greedily; and the fool repeats his nonsense in a like manner.

(12) Seest thou a man wise in his own view, there is more hope for a fool than for him.

Self-conceit and vain-glory are more hopeless (in their tendencies) than folly.

(13) The sluggard saith : There is a lion in the way ; a lion in the midst of the broad streets.

Almost an exact repetition of 22 : 13. Sentiment : 'Sloth invents even the most absurd things, as an apology for inaction.'

(14) The door turneth upon its hinge, and so the sluggard upon his bed.

Comp. 6: 10. 24 : 33. The point of comparison is not very obvious at first, and opinions differ. The matter, however, seems to be thus: The door is turned upon its hinges by others; it does not turn itself. Even so the sluggard. He will not so much as turn himself in bed, but needs others to help him. A biting sarcasm indeed; but there are many such, respecting sluggards, in this book; see the next verse. For the Chaldaizing form תִּסּוֹב, from סָבַב, see § 66. 5. E. g.

(15) The sluggard plungeth his hand into the dish; it is wearisome to bring it back to his mouth.

With slight variations, this verse is the same as 19 : 24. q. v. — נִלְאָה may be rendered, *he is wearied.* The sense is the same, for substance, as in the version.

(16) The sluggard is more wise in his own view, than seven men who can render a reason.

That is, he is, in his own view, wise in forging excuses for his sloth; even more wise than those who can give intelligent answers. — *Seven* is of course the *perfect* number; and here it is merely an indefinite number. — מְשִׁיבֵי, Part. plur. const. in Hiphil.

(17) [As] one who graspeth hold on a dog's ears, [so] is he who, passing along, rusheth into strife which belongeth not to him.

I have supplied the particles of comparison, which are plainly implied, in order to render the passage more explicit. He who grasps strongly a dog by the ears, provokes him to an attack. Like to this, is intermeddling with a quarrel which does not belong to us.

(18) Like a silly jester, who shooteth forth darts, arrows, and death; (19) So is the man who deceiveth his neighbor, and saith: Am I not sporting?

V. 18, מִתְלַהְלֵהַּ, in Hithpalpel, from לָהַהּ, verb עַ״ע, and found only here. The account of the word in Ges. Lex. is hardly satisfactory. Bertheau compares it with the Arabic לַהא, which means *to joke;* and in its intensive form (as in our text), it means: *to be always employed in silly joking.* This agrees well with the exposition of the meaning, as made in the next verse, by the well-known word מְשַׂחֵק, *sporting. Madman* is a meaning, that seems not capable of satisfactory proof. — זִקִּים comes from זָנַק, and has the נ assimilated. But the verb means *to cast, to throw far,* and so the noun comes to mean *a dart,* (not *firebrands,* as in our Version). — *Death,* tropically used as here, means *deadly weapons.* — V. 19, *the man who deceives,* and calls it *sporting,* gives deadly wounds, like the weapons before mentioned.

(20) Where there is no wood, the fire goeth out; and where there is no tattler, strife is silent. (21) As charcoal for glowing coals, and wood for fire, so is the man of strife for kindling contention.

V. 20, Strife goes out, without tattling and slander; even as fire goes out, without wood. V. 21, On the other hand, a man who loves strife will excite a heated contest; just as charcoal makes glowing coals, and wood makes the fire to burn. — לְחַרְחַר, Inf. Pilpal of חָרַר, *to inflame.*

(22) The words of a slanderer are like sportive ones, yet they go down into the deep recesses of the belly.

See on 18:8, where are the same words, which are there explained at length.

(23) Drossy silver spread over an earthen vessel, are burning lips and an evil heart.

That is, metal of little worth is used to cover a mean vessel, although it appears splendid like silver. Even so, *burning lips,* (i. e. lips which give warm kisses that seem to indicate much affection), if connected with an evil disposition, are no better than the splendid dross.—Meaning: 'Pretension of friendship, where real malice is harbored, is utterly worthless.'

(24) By his lips doth he who hateth make himself known; and in his inner-part doth he lay up deceit.

Internal hatred will disclose itself by words. When bitter feeling is prepared or laid up in the heart; then it will disclose itself by the lips.

(25) When he maketh his voice pleasant, trust him not; for seven abominations are in his heart.

יְחַנֵּן קוֹלוֹ, *utters sweet* or *lovely tones.*—*Seven* = many.—*Abominations*, things abominable to be done.

(26) Hatred concealeth deceit; the malice thereof will be revealed in the great assembly.

I do not find the word מַשָּׁאוֹן either in Ges. or in Fuerst's Concord. Heb. But there can be no doubt, that it is a derivate of נָשָׁא, *to deceive*, and so means *deceit.*—רָעָתוֹ, with a masc. suff. referring to the masc. noun מַשָּׁאוֹן.—The meaning seems to be, that although hatred may conceal deceit while it is privately indulged, yet by intercourse with men a development of it will be made, so that the malignity of the hater will become known.

(27) He who diggeth a pit, shall fall into it; he who rolleth a stone, it shall turn back upon him.

Comp. Ecc. 10:8.—The last clause runs lit. thus: *It shall return to him.* But the real idea is given in the version. Meaning: 'He who devises mischief to others, it shall come upon himself.' Not perhaps the same identical mischief, but at least an equivalent.

(28) A lying tongue will hate those who are crushed by it; and a flattering mouth will bring about ruin.

לְשׁוֹן is *fem.*, while the verb that follows is *masc.*; but as *a lying tongue* here = *liar*, so there is a concord *ad sensum*. The case may be solved in another way; most names of the members of the body are employed in both genders. — Nothing is more common than to *hate* those whom we injure. — דַּכָּיו, plur. of דַּךְ, with suff. *masc.*, for the same reason that the verb is masc. — *A smooth tongue* may be employed, while efforts are made, at the same time, in order to overthrow or bring to ruin.

Chap. XXVII. 1—27.

(1) Boast not thyself of to-morrow, for thou knowest not what a day may bring forth.

Rely not confidently on plans for the future, however well they may be concocted; for God only knows what may happen. — יָדַע, *Qamets* because of the smaller Distinctive Rebhia. — יֵּלֶד for יֵלֵד, because the accent is thrown back by reason of the tone-syllable which immediately follows, § 29. 3. *b*.

(2) Let another praise thee, and not thine own mouth; a stranger, and not thine own lips.

זָר I have rendered *another*, because *stranger* must otherwise be repeated. Indeed, the actual idea is not that of a *foreigner*, but only of another and different person from one's self. — Meaning: 'Indulge not in self-gratulation and applause.'

(3) A stone is heavy, and sand is weighty; but vexation by a fool is more burdensome than both of them.

Hebrew lit. *a stone is heaviness*, and *sand is weightiness*, abstr. for concrete. — *Vexation of a fool*, is the shape of the Heb., but the meaning is: 'The vexation which he occasions.' This idea is expressed in the version. — It would seem as if the writer's store of characteristics applicable to the description of *fools*, had been already exhausted; but this is a new development, expressing strongly the disgust which a fool's demeanor occasions. This verse throws light on כָּבוֹד in 25 : 27.

(4) Cruel is wrath, and anger is overwhelming; who then can stand before envy?

Heb. *cruelty . . . inundation*, which I have made *concretes* in the version. — Both *wrath* and *anger* are fraught with evil, which is hard to be borne; but much worse still is the passion of *envy*, or (perhaps) *jealousy*. Either of these excites to deeds the most atrocious.

(5) Open admonition is better than secret love. (6) Faithful are the wounds of a friend, but the kisses of an enemy are multiplied.

V. 5, Love, kept entirely secret, profits not the object of it. — *Admonition* shows the better kind of friendship. — V. 6, the *wounds* of a friendly monitor are salutary; they make us see and feel our faults. — *The many kisses of an enemy*, however much of love they may seem to promise, are of course deceitful, and the multiplication of them only aggravates the wrong. — I see no way to get the meaning of *deceitful* from נַעְתָּרוֹת, root עָתַר; compare Ezek. 35 : 13. — The point of comparison here, is that of *wounds* on the one hand by a friend, and *kisses* on the other by a secret enemy. A friend, open and ingenuous, admonishes and wounds, or reproves for our good; but nothing of this do we get from a crafty enemy. Instead of *wounding* for salutary purposes, he bestows nothing but *kisses often repeated*, i. e. *multiplied*. And all this — that he may render his victim unsuspicious and unguarded; and so strike the surer blow.

(7) An appetite satiated loathes the honey-comb; but [to] the craving appetite — every bitter thing is sweet.

That is: 'The pampered glutton loathes even luxurious food; but he who is really hungry, will eat even indifferent food with a high relish.'—I have supplied the prep. *to*, where our idiom demands it. In the Hebrew, *the craving appetite* is Nom. absolute. We might translate thus: *as to a craving appetite.*

(8) As a bird which hath wandered from her nest, so is the man who wandereth from his place.

His place = *his home.* Such a wandering bird is restless and unsatisfied; and so is a man, while absent from home, specially if he has a good home.

(9) Oil and perfume exhilarate the heart; so the comity of one's friend, which springs from set purpose of the soul.

Oil here doubtless means *scented* or *perfumed oil.*—מֶתֶק, *sweetness*, applies either to words or demeanor, or it may include both = *comity.*—The suff. in רֵעֵהוּ is altogether indefinite, having no antecedent, and therefore I have rendered the word *one's friend.*—*Which springs from the set purpose of the soul,* lit. *is from the counsel of the soul;* but the literal version hardly makes an intelligible sense, and therefore I have translated *ad sensum.* The word עֵצָה may imply *set purpose*, for the root has the meaning *to decree.* Comity makes glad when it proceeds from the real design and intention of him who manifests it, or when it is what his soul counsels him to exhibit, and not mere conventional politeness. We say: "When it comes from the bottom of the heart," when we mean to convey such an idea as the Hebrew here comprises.

(10) Thine own friend, and thy father's friend, forsake not; into the house of thy brother enter not, in the day of thy calamity; better is one that dwelleth near, than a brother afar off.

That is: Go to well and long-tried friends in the day of calamity; for "there is a friend, that sticketh closer than a brother," Prov. 18 : 24. The last clause in our text, makes all plain. Sentiment: 'Only long-tried friends are to be trusted, above all in a calamitous time. Even the ties of consanguinity are not always to be relied on.' — בֵּית may be an Acc. of *place;* or we may consider תָּבוֹא here as a kind of transitive verb, § 135. 3. *d;* as in fact it sometimes is by usage.

(11) Be wise, my son, and gladden my heart; that I may have somewhat to answer him who reproacheth me.

This may be interpreted in two ways: (1) If a child is wise, through the instruction and example of a father, this gives good testimony against any slanderer of the father's character. (2) If the son is actually wise, then he may aid and counsel his father, and defend him against unjust reproaches. Bertheau prefers the latter; the former strikes me as more obvious and natural. — דָּבָר, *thing* (as often); and here it means *something*, or = our English *somewhat.*

(12) The wary seeth the evil — he hideth himself; the simple pass on — they are punished.

נִסְתָּר (in pause), in a *reflexive* sense, § 50. 2. *a.* In both clauses, the second verb is *asyndic*, i. e. וְ is wanting. I have made the dashes to perform a part in imitating the Hebrew mode of expression. In our idiom, we should say: 'The wary man, seeing the evil, hideth himself; the simple, passing on, are punished.' But the Hebrews seldom employ *participles*, in such a case. They prefer the verb; and doubtless their mode of construction has more life and energy. In 22 : 3, we have the same text, with וְ inserted in each clause.

(13) Take his garment, when he hath become surety for a stranger; and on account of a strange woman, do thou distrain him.

See 20 : 16, where are the same words, fully explained.

(14) He who blesseth his friend with a loud voice, early in the morning, it shall be counted to him as a curse.

גָּדוֹל, *great*, when applied to *voice*, of course means *loud.* — הַשְׁכֵּים, Inf. Hiph. as a noun or adverb, in apposition with בֹּקֶר, and the Acc. of time; compare הַרְבֵּה, as an adverb. The reason why it will be counted as a curse, rather than a blessing (which it would seem to be), is, that such unusual or extraordinary developments of gratuitous zeal, of course excite suspicion of fraudulent design. They are not natural, but assumed.

(15) A continual dropping in a rainy day, and a brawling woman, are much alike.

For the first clause, see 19 : 3. — סַגְרִיר occurs in Hebrew only here, but it occurs in the Syriac and Chaldee, in the sense here given to it. The root שׂגר (in Arabic) means: *to fill with water.* — נִשְׁתָּוָה, a difficult word as to its *form;* at least we must think so, if we look at the criticisms upon it. Yet the solution is attended, as I apprehend the matter, with but little difficulty, in case we allow (with Ewald, § 132. c), that the Hebrews had a *Nithpael* conjugation. Examples of this are נִכַּפֵּר = נִתְ״, Deut. 21 : 8; נִוַּסֵּר = נִתְ״, Ezek. 23 : 48; also the word now before us. This word seems then to be a fem. Part. of Nithpael, root שָׁוָה, masc. Part. נִשְׁתָּוֶה, fem. ־וָה, referring to *woman*, its nearest antecedent. — The שׁ of the root is transposed, as usual, in Hithpael. The only trouble here is, that we should expect נִשְׁתַּוָּה instead of תָּוָה. — But is not the Dagh. here resolved into the long vowel, Qamets, and so the reduplication omitted? See § 20. 3. *a. b.* See also פִּלֶּגֶשׁ, פִּילֶגֶשׁ, and comp. § 20. 3. c. Note. Bertheau does not here recognize the participial form in question, and so he has made it in the Imperf. first pers. plur. voluntative; in other words, according to him, it should be נִשְׁתָּוָה, i. e. accented on the penult, and it has a paragogic ָה, which may reject the accent from the ultimate. (But only a portion of the copies so accent it.) He confesses that the meaning thus brought out, is strange, viz., *let us compare.* Truly it is so, for there is no *analogon* in the whole book. Moreover, it seems to be unnecessary. Compare Ewald, § 132. *c.*

(16) He who restraineth her, restraineth the wind; and his right hand cometh upon oil.

The *wind* or *air* is incapable of such restraint by any ordinary means, as will prevent its escape; and like to this is the brawling woman, who cannot be restrained. — *Right hand cometh upon oil,* is explained by considering, that oil makes a thing so slippery that it cannot be held fast in one's grasp. So she cannot be held fast or restrained. — יִקְרָא, see the root No. II., *occurrit, obviam venit, meets with.* That is: 'A brawling woman is incapable of being tamed.'

(17) Iron may sharpen iron; and so a man may sharpen the countenance of his friend.

יָחַד (Qamets in pause) is Hiph. Imperf. apoc. of חָדָה = חָדַד. Ges. makes it from the verb ע״ע, but with much difficulty. Much better is it, with C. B. Michaelis, Bertheau, and others, to suppose a root חָדָה. For יַחַד, Imperf., abridged, see § 74. IV. note 14. — We can easily understand how a *knife* can be sharpened by a *steel;* but what means the other clause? *To sharpen the countenance,* is hardly susceptible of any other meaning than that of making the visage look stern or severe, i. e. to be angry. We say of a frowning man: '*He looked sharp* at his enemy.' But then comes the question: Why should one man provoke another? — This, however, is not the real meaning. It is not a command to excite or provoke, but a supposed case; and when this occurs, then let a man enter the list of controversy (if he must do so) with a man like himself, and not with a child, or an inferior; see Judg. 8 : 21. In other words: 'If men must enter into contest, let the antagonists be worthy of the strife.' Or it may be taken *passively;* viz., let not a man be angry at the mischief done him by a *child*, and not by a *man*. Should he so do, then he would act *childishly*. So Bertheau. I prefer the preceding exegesis; but the verse is somewhat obscure.

(18) He who keepeth the fig-tree, shall eat the fruit thereof; he who guardeth his master shall be honored.

That is, the master will reward the *keeping* or *guarding*, by suitable retribution; just as the fig-tree feeds him who keeps it, and thus makes him a retribution for his labor.

(19) As in water face answereth to face, so doth the heart of man to man.

בַּמַּיִם, art. before the name of a substance; the Acc. of place = *in water*, and designating the *where*. — *Face to face*, i. e. water reflects back the image of the face. — *The heart of man* is reflected back (so to speak) by the heart of another man; i. e. each has corresponding views and sympathies, so that one can reason from his own heart to that of others, at least in many respects; for the properties of human nature are common.

(20) The under-world and destruction are never satisfied; and so the eyes of man are never satisfied.

The grave swallows up all, and yet remains ever unsatisfied, for it is always craving more; and so the eye is never satiated with seeing. — The Qeri אֲבַדּוֹן is the more usual form; but this may be abridged, as in the Kethibh אֲבַדֹּה, the ה being merely a *fulcrum*.

(21) A fining-pot for silver, and a furnace for gold; so is a man in respect to his praise.

A fining-pot will disclose the true silver, and the furnace the true gold; and so a man's praise will disclose his true character. Praise is apt to puff up men, and make them self-conceited. If it does, or does not, produce this effect, it will, in either alternative, make their true character known. "It is a fining-pot."

(22) If thou shouldest beat a fool in a mortar, in the midst of crushed grain, with a pestle, his foolishness will not depart from him.

Another of those stringent sarcasms with which fools are assailed, in this book above all others in the Bible. — Sentiment: 'No chastisement, however severe, will cure a fool of his folly.' Such is the obstinacy of the men, who are here characterized by the appellation of *fools*.

(23) Look well to thy flock; attend carefully to thy herds; (24) For abundance will not be perpetual; not even a diadem [will be] for generation after generation.

Precepts economical, addressed to husbandmen. — יָדֹעַ, not unfrequently, as here, means *to take knowledge of* in the sense of *caring for, looking to.* The Inf. abs. here, joined with the definite mode, gives intensity to the expression. Hence the version, *look well.* — שִׁית לֵב, means *to fix one's mind* or *attention* on a thing. — Take good care of your property, for although there now is an *abundance* of wealth, it will not last always, not even a *diadem*, i. e. regal domain or authority, will be permanent. — אִם is a strong *negative*, when it follows לֹא in a preceding clause; see Lex. s. v. C. *c*. — After *diadem*, the verb of *existence* or *continuance* is plainly implied, as inserted in the version. In plain words: 'Not even regal wealth is secure and lasting.'

(25) The grass passeth away, the tender herbage showeth itself, and the herbs of the mountains are gathered.

גָּלָה sometimes designates *going away into exile;* here, it denotes the passing away of the grass from its location, when the time to harvest it is come. Then spring up the *tender shoots* (דֶּשֶׁא) from its roots, supplying pasture. Fodder, moreover, is laid up in stock, which comes from the mountain-bushes and grass, עִשְּׂבוֹת. Such is the provision to be made for flocks and herds. Then follows their thrift.

(26) Lambs are for thy clothing, and the price of a field is bucks.

That is, *lambs*, when sold, purchase thy clothing; and *bucks* will fetch a sufficient price to purchase land. *Bucks* are the males of either sheep or goats; so the German: *Böcken*. In this way, permanent property may be acquired,

(27) Moreover, there will be a sufficiency of goat's milk for thy nourishment, for the nourishment of thy household, and means of living for thy maidens.

חַיִּים, lit. *life*, here, *means of life* or *of living*. In other words: 'If you look well to your farm, it will yield whatever you may want for food, or clothing, or even for the purchase of more land. It will, in a word, make you truly rich.'

CHAP. XXVIII. 1—28.

(1) The wicked flee, when no one pursueth; but the righteous are bold as a lion.

נָסוּ, *plur. of* נוּס, because the Nom. רָשָׁע (sing.) is generic. —*Are bold*, lit. *are confident;* but here the verb יִבְטַח is *sing.* with a Nom. in the plural—a case, therefore, of *specializing* or *individualizing*, where the idea is, that *each one* of the collective (plur.) body is, or does, so and so, § 143. 4. Comp. Gen. 49: 9, as to the simile.—Meaning: 'The wicked are full of fears; while the righteous repose in quiet safety, not being apprehensive of any danger.'

(2) Because of the transgression of a land, many are its princes; but because of a man of understanding, he who regardeth what is right shall prolong [his days].

When a nation transgresses, God gives them up to the conquest of invaders, and to a partition of territory, or to internal factions which divide and distract the country.—The last clause is difficult. Berth.: "So soon as men [the people] become intelligent and knowing, then he [the prince] lives long," i. e. the one and only prince of the country reigns long and undisturbed. — I doubt this exegesis. It is plain that בְּפֶשַׁע and בְּאָדָם מֵבִין are two opposites, which are contrasted; the one leads to division and partition, and consequently to uncertainty of life and happiness; the other governs the country in such a way, that all who know and practise what is right, have a prolonged season of quiet under him. — כֵּן I take to be a noun-adjective here; and יֹדֵעַ as designating another person (i. e. a *citizen* or subject) than the *intelligent man*, who seems plainly to be the *ruler*. The two clauses are partially, but not fully and directly, antithetic. *Many* princes occasion a state of things, where all is unsafe. But a *sole* and intelligent ruler will *prolong* the life and safety of those who cleave to rectitude. — יַאֲרִיךְ, *prolong* = *live long*, for *days* are implied after it, which are elsewhere expressed. See Lex. under Hiphil, and Prov. 29 : 16.

(3) A poor man, and yet an oppressor of the poor, is a shower sweeping so that there is no bread.

Probably an *indigent ruler* of a subordinate class is here meant, who oppresses the poor in order to enrich himself; a thing very common in the East and also the West. But he can no more become rich by such means, than a violent shower, which sweeps away the surface of the ground, can bring forward prosperously a crop of grain which has been sown. In other words: 'Overdoing, in both cases, prevents a crop from being gathered.'

(4) Those who forsake the law, praise the wicked; but they who keep the law, rouse up themselves against them.

The word רָשָׁע is used generically here. Hence the plur. suff. in בָּם. Meaning: 'The impious eulogize the wicked; the pious oppose them.'

(5) Evil men do not understand justice; but those who seek Jehovah understand everything.

Do not understand, i. e. have no adequate and proper sense of it. — *Understand everything*, viz., everything that relates to right and duty.

(6) Better is the poor man, who walketh in his integrity, than he who is perverse by double dealing, although he is rich.

דְּרָכַיִם, dual, *two ways*, because such a man now pursues this course, and then that, in order that he may deceive. The version gives the sense aimed at, although not literal. — וְהוּא, *and yet he is*, here = *although he is*. Sentiment: 'An upright poor man, is better than a perverse rich one.'

(7) He that keepeth the law, is a discreet son; but he who delighteth in prodigals, will bring his father to shame.

רֹאֶה, *delighteth in* = רָצָה, Lex. s. v. No. 3. He will behave in such a manner as to put his father to shame.

(8) He who augmenteth his wealth by usurious increase, he shall gather it for giving alms to the poor.

The two words נֶשֶׁךְ and תַּרְבִּית are both applied to the *interest* of money. United, as here, they are either intensive = *excessive interest*, or else a Hendiadys in which one acts the part of an adjective, as in the version. — *Gather it*, viz., his wealth. — לְחוֹנֵן, lit. *for compassionating*, i. e. in the way of administering to their wants. The usurer meant not so, in amassing his property; but Providence orders things in such a manner, that this wealth will come into the hands of some liberal and compassionate person, who, by means of it, relieves the wants of the poor.

(9) He who turneth away his ear from hearing the law, even his prayer shall be an abomination.

The impious cannot be sincere in their prayers; and consequently, they are rejected because they are hypocritical.

(10) He who leadeth astray the upright in an evil way, into his own pit shall he fall; but the upright shall inherit good.

That is, he who leads the good astray, in order to do them mischief, shall himself fall into mischief. Instead of perishing in the pit which was dug for them, the upright shall become possessors of good.

(11) A rich man is wise in his own view; but the poor man, possessed of understanding, will search him out.

A conceited wise man is easily understood by an intelligent poor man, and easily exposed. His riches will not save him from such disgrace.

(12) When the righteous rejoice, great is the glorying; but when the wicked rise up, a man hideth himself.

תִּפְאָרֶת, (in pause), not only *glory*, but *glorying*. — יְחֻפַּשׂ, lit. *is made to be sought after*, that is, he withdraws himself so that one cannot easily find him = *hideth himself*. So Ges. in Lex.

(13) He who covereth his sins, shall not prosper; but he who confesseth and forsaketh [them], shall find mercy.

See a striking exposition of this, in Ps. xxxii. Concealment of sin exempts not men from punishment by a Being who knows all things; confession and repentance are indispensable to the obtaining of mercy. — יְרֻחָם, (Qamets in pause), in Pual, *shall be the subject of mercy*.

(14) Blessed is the man who feareth always; but he who hardeneth his heart shall fall into evil.

Feareth, viz., to offend God. — *Hardeneth his heart*, means: 'Renders it insensible to admonition or reproof.'

(15) A roaring lion, and a ranging bear, is a wicked ruler over a poor people.

That is, by his rapacity he crushes and devours them, even as those wild beasts do their prey.

(16) As to a prince who lacketh understanding, and multiplieth oppression — he who hateth covetousness shall prolong his days.

In other words: 'As to a foolish and greedy oppressor — I have only to say, that the man of an opposite character shall obtain the blessing of long life.' Of course, he (the oppressor) cannot obtain it. — The Kethibh reads: שֹׂנְאֵי, const. plur.; the Qeri, שֹׂנֵא, in the sing. const. The latter is rather preferable, because the verb which follows is singular.

(17) A man oppressed with life's blood, let him flee to the pit, let no man stay him.

Murder demands suitable retribution. No one should interfere to prevent it. The precept is older than Solomon, or even Moses; see Gen. 9: 6. In the older editions, אָדָם is, by Rabbinic conceit, printed thus: אָדָם, i. e. with a minute ד. See Mich. Bib.

(18) He who walketh uprightly shall be safe; but he who is perverse in double ways, shall fall in one [of them].

Integrity is safety; double-dealing will end in a fall. — בְּאֶחָת in pause, *in one*, fem., as דֶּרֶךְ (to which it refers) occasionally is. The Seghol (instead of Pattah) in אֶחָת, comes by reason of the Qamets after it under a Guttural, § 27. n. 2. *b*; the Qamets (for _) because of the pause.

(19) He who tilleth his field, shall be satisfied with bread; and he who followeth after vain persons, shall have plenty of poverty.

Industry makes adequate provision for our wants; but an idle and profligate man will suffer much from want.

(20) A man of great faithfulness is rich in blessings; but he who hasteneth to become rich, shall not be innocent.

אֱמוּנוֹת, plur. intens., and so translated. — רַב, an adjective here, as the Maqqeph indicates, = *abundant, rich.* — *Hasteneth to become rich,* that is, by fraud, or violence, or oppression, instead of faithful and steady industry. Cupidity always tempts to fraud or oppression.

(21) To respect persons is not good; for because of a piece of bread a man will become a transgressor.

הַכֵּר־פָּנִים, lit. *to know* in the sense of favoring; root נָכַר, and it is here in the Inf. Hiph. הַכֵּר, with the Tseri shortened because of the Maqqeph. By this phrase, (as we have seen above, 24: 23, q. v.), is meant *to show partiality for*. — *Because of a piece of bread*, (spoken ironically, and it means as much as to say, *for an insignificant bribe*), a man will show partiality in judging. That (partiality) cannot be *good*, i. e. it must be very evil, when even a small bribe will purchase it, and thus occasion much mischief.

(22) A man of an evil eye hasteth for wealth; and he knoweth not that want shall come upon him.

The man of an evil eye, is the envious and covetous man. — נִבְהָל, Part. Niph., lit. *is urgent* or *hastening*. In Piel this sense is more clearly developed; but we find it also in Niph. No. 3, in the Lex. — לַהוֹן, with the art., either because it is abstract, or else because it is the specific name of a thing.

(23) A man who reproveth shall afterwards find favor, more than he who flattereth with his tongue.

אַחֲרַי = אַחַר, an adverb. Ges. thus: "*after me*, i. e. following my precepts;" for he regards it as the plur. with suff. ־ַי, *my*. To say the least, this is a doubtful solution — certainly a very unusual one, in Hebrew. Sentiment: 'Those who are reformed by admonition, will afterwards feel grateful to their monitor.'

(24) He who robbeth his father and his mother, and saith: No harm! he is a companion to a destroyer.

No harm! because, forsooth, the property is going to be his own, ere long. — Such a man is to be ranked with *destroyers* or wasters, i. e. with men who desperately do every kind of violence and wrong. Compare Matt. 15 : 4—6, which is quite analogous.

(25) He who is of a haughty spirit will stir up strife; but he who trusteth in Jehovah shall have an abundance.

רְחַב, lit. *ample, expanded.* The imagery is borrowed from *inflation;* just as we say, *puffed up*, in a tropical way. Hence *haughty*. — יְדֻשָּׁן, Pual, lit. *shall be made fat.*

(26) Whosoever trusteth in his own heart, he is a fool; but whoever walketh wisely, he shall be delivered.

The הוּא, in both cases, makes intensity of specification. — *Be delivered*, viz., from the evils which self-confidence occasions. — *Walketh wisely*, here seems to mean as much as *puts his trust in God, and not in himself;* for this is true wisdom.

(27) As to him who giveth to the poor — there shall be no lack; but as to him who hideth his eyes — there will be plenty of curses.

The version discloses the form of the original, as to the Nom. independent. — The liberal giver shall not come to want, because God will bless him. — *Hideth his eyes*, viz., from noticing the wants of the poor. — רַב, with a Maqqeph following, shows itself to be an *adj.* here. But an adj., taken as neuter, makes the abstract noun, as in the version.

(28) When the wicked rise up a man hideth himself, and when they perish the righteous increase.

בַּאֲבֹדָם, Inf. Kal. with suff. — The wicked, by their oppression and violence, strike such terror into the good, as to make them withdraw, in order to seek a place of refuge. When such oppressors are removed, then the righteous are multiplied.

CHAP. XXIX. 1—27.

(1) A man who is often reproved and hardeneth his neck, shall be suddenly destroyed, and there shall be no remedy.

תּוֹכָחוֹת, develops strikingly the plur. intens. The meaning is not that of a man who has been only *once* reproved, but plainly that of a man *often reproved*, i. e. one to whom many reproofs have been directed. — *Hardening his neck*, means *pertinaciously going on* in his evil ways. His neck does not feel the yoke of reproof to be galling; for it is so hard that he heeds not the yoke. — יִשָּׁבֵר is intense = *shall be shivered in pieces.*

(2) When the righteous increase, the people rejoice; but when the wicked bear rule, the people bemoan themselves.

The righteous are a blessing to any community, and the people have reason to rejoice in their increase; but the domination of the wicked will make them grieve. יֵאָנַח, Niph. Imperf. reflexive, *bemoan themselves.*

(3) The man who loveth wisdom, shall make his father glad; but he who hath pleasure in harlots, will waste wealth.

רֹעֶה, Part. of רָעָה = רָצָה, see in Lex. It is so far transitive as to put the object of pleasure in the Acc. after it. — *Waste wealth*, viz., his father's wealth, and so make the latter *sorrowful*, instead of making him glad.

(4) A king by justice will establish the land; but a man of presents will destroy it.

Man of presents, is one who loves them and gladly accepts them, as bribes for partiality. Such a ruler will ruin his country. — The last verb, with suff. ֶנָּה.

(5) A man who speaketh smoothly against his neighbor, spreadeth a net over his steps.

That *the smooth speaking*, in this case, is *in malam partem*, is made clear by עַל, *against*. The basis of the idea is that of *smoothing* (חָלַק) *a thing by rubbing it against another.* — *A net over*, etc., means a net so spread, as to entangle him and arrest his steps, or make him fall.

(6) In the transgression of a bad man there is a snare; but the righteous shall sing and be glad.

By transgressing, a man brings on himself a snare, in which he may be caught and made to stumble; but the righteous shall go on and prosper, and so they shall sing aloud for joy. Not that they rejoice because the wicked are ensnared, but because God gives them safety and prosperity. — יָרוּן (from רָנַן) is an uncommon form; but there is a number of such in the Hebrew Bible; see § 66. n. 9.

(7) The righteous taketh knowledge of the cause of the poor; the wicked will not understand knowledge.

The righteous design to aid the poor, by taking cognizance of their cause, when they claim their just dues; the wicked will never take proper pains to gain a knowledge of it.

(8) Men of scorn blow up a flame in the city; but the wise cause anger to abate.

יָפִיחוּ, from פּוּחַ, *to blow, puff, to blow up*, e. g. a fire, that is, *to enkindle* it. Hence the tropical meaning, *to inflame*, i. e. *to blow upon* or *enkindle* the passions or prejudices of a city, for the sake of leading the people to rash proceedings. — יָשִׁיבוּ, *cause to return, to turn back*, and consequently it is equivalent to *abating*.

(9) Doth a wise man contend in a cause with a fool? He will be angry, and will laugh, but there is no pacification.

That is, he will at one time be agitated with rage, at another with scornful laughter; a quiet and considerate state of mind he will not come to.

(10) Men of blood will hate the man of integrity; but the upright will seek anxiously for his life.

יְבַקְשׁוּ, Piel, with Dagh. in ק omitted, because this would require a movable Sheva, § 20. 3. *b.* It is a very common method of abridging words. Lit. *seek his life;* which usually means: *seek it in order to take it away.* Here, *in bonam partem,* in order to preserve it; but to avoid the *equivoque,* I have slightly changed the manner of expression, while the sense is retained.

(11) A fool will pour out all his indignation; but a wise man will afterwards try to appease it.

רוּחוֹ, as in our English phrase: "He showed much *spirit.*" The wise man will deal gently with such an one, and try to soften and appease him. The Piel form of the last verb gives room for the version, *try to appease;* for *to appease* is the primary sense of שָׁבַח.

(12) Doth a ruler listen to a false report? — all his servants are wicked.

That is, if the ruler loves to deal in slander and falsehood — then all his underlings will learn to imitate him in his vices, and thus become wicked.

(13) The poor and the man of exactions meet together; the eyes of them both Jehovah enlighteneth.

Meet together in a hostile way, or in conflict, seems to be the idea. The hardly *exacting* man is resisted by the oppressed *poor* man. — Jehovah has given to both *the light of life,* here designated by *enlightening the eyes,* i. e. making them to sparkle with living power. Of course, both are equally dependent on him, and both under his supervision; and therefore the one can have no right to bear hard on the other, and the oppressed may hope for vindication.

(14) As to the king who judgeth the poor with faithfulness — his throne shall be established forever.

A faithful discharge of duties toward the poor and oppressed, will result in the firm establishment of a throne.

(15) The rod and reproof will give wisdom; and the lad who is freed [from them], will cause shame to his mother.

Compare 23 : 13, and also 13 : 24, where the same sentiment is found, with some little variation of phraseology.

(16) When the wicked increase, transgression increaseth; but the righteous shall look on when they fall.

Be the wicked ever so flourishing, to appearance, yet the time of their fall will come, which the good will witness. — רָאָה בְּ has usually the meaning of *looking on anything with satisfaction*. But we should not associate with this the idea, that the good have any delight in the plagues of the wicked, in themselves considered, but that they rejoice because the time of their deliverance has come. Comp. Rev. 11: 17, 18. 18: 20.

(17) Chasten thy son, and he shall give thee rest; yea, he shall give delight to thy soul.

יַסֵּר, Piel, Pattah in the ultimate, because of the ר. — מַעֲדַנִּים, of an intensive form and meaning; which is expressed in the version.

(18) Where there is no vision, the people become dissolute; but he who keepeth the law — blessed is he!

Vision means here *prophetic vision* or *revelation*. — *Dissolute*, i. e. loosed from restraint in a moral sense; compare Ex. 32: 25, which fully confirms this sense of יִפָּרַע. In such a case, when deprived of prophetic teachers, the only recourse is to the Law; the which, if a man will diligently attend to it, will render him happy.

(19) By words a servant will not be corrected; although he understands, yet will he not make answer.

Something more than *mere words* must be employed, to

secure the ready obedience of some servants. The words they may understand; but they will regard them as mere words and nothing more, unless some more effectual corrective be applied. — The *answering* does not here mean *a reply only in words*, but also in doing the things which are correspondent with the commands given, i. e. making a practical answer.

(20) Seest thou a man hasty in his words, there is more hope for a fool than for him.

See the proverb in 26 : 12. It seems to be the same gnome in all, but still it was a little modified when it was inserted in the different sources of selection, which "the men of Hezekiah" had before them.

(21) As to him who bringeth up delicately his servant from childhood, at last he will surely be a son.

מְפַנֵּק, not elsewhere in Hebrew, but frequent in Aramaean, in the sense here given by the version. — מִנֹּעַר, the abstract form, i. e. *childhood ;* נַעַר means *lad.* — אַחֲרִיתוֹ, lit. *in the end*, or *sequel of it ;* for I take ו here as relating generally to the whole affair. It is the Acc. of time. If the pronoun suff. must be made more definite, then it must relate to *servant*, and mean *the after-part of his life.* The sense is virtually the same in both cases. — מָנוֹן, is unique, being found nowhere else in the Bible. It is probably made from נִין, *offspring*, by prefixing a formative מ. So the Rabbins; and the sense is good. The ancient versions seem to have read a different word here. The Vulgate only approaches our text. This renders מָנוֹן by *contumacem ;* and so Ewald, and others, who compare the Arabic מנון, which means *ungrateful.* The sense of this is not bad; but the other meaning given above, has more point.

(22) An angry man will stir up strife; and a man enraged abounds in transgression.

בַּעַל חֵמָה, means *an irascible man*, one who easily and often becomes enraged. — Anger, of course, prompts to do wrong.

(23) The haughtiness of a man will bring him low; but humbleness of spirit will obtain honor.

Compare 25: 6, seq. 16: 19. For יִתְמֹךְ, compare 11: 16. Lit. this means *to grasp, to lay fast hold of.*

(24) He who maketh a division with a thief, hateth his own life; he heareth the curse, and yet will not reveal.

Hateth his own life, see remarks on 8 : 36, respecting such *meiosis*. He acts as though he hated it, by thus wickedly exposing it to danger. — *The curse*, namely, that which is pronounced on him *who concealeth a theft;* see Lev. 5 : 1, and comp. Judges 17 : 2. — But although he is brought under this curse, in case of concealment, still he will not reveal the thief, with whom he has become a partaker.

(25) The fear of man will lay a snare; but he who trusteth in Jehovah shall be protected.

Men will through fear do that which they disapprove; and so they are ensnared. — *Trusteth in Jehovah*, viz., trusts that he will protect those who do right, and fears not the consequences. — *Be protected*, lit. *be elevated to a high place*, and therefore safe from attack.

(26) Many seek the face of a ruler; but from Jehovah cometh the right of a man.

Many repair to rulers, in order to obtain their favor by flattery; but it is God only who will and can do perfect justice to all. That is: 'Look more to heaven, and less to rulers.'

(27) An abomination of the righteous, is the man of mischief; but the abomination of the wicked, is he who is upright in his way.

The righteous abhor wrong-doers; but the wicked abhor the upright.

PART V. CHAP. XXX. 1—33.

(1) THE WORDS OF AGUR, *the son of her who was obeyed in Massa.* Thus spake the man: I have toiled for God, I have toiled for God, and have ceased.

So far as I know, Hitzig (in Zeller, Theol. in Jahrb. 1844, s. 283) was the first to propose this new modification of the verse before us. It is adopted and finely commented on, in Bertheau. — There can be no doubt, that יָקֶה, לְאִיתִיאֵל, and אֻכָל, were regarded by the punctators, by the Chald. and Syr. translators, and by nearly all of the modern commentators, as *proper names.* Not so the Sept. and Vulg. — "quae in omnia alia abeunt." Nothing can be learned from them about the true original here. Is the version above correct? Will the words fairly admit of a different and more intelligible construction than that which has been the usual one? are questions fairly before us, since the critics of other times are not agreed.

The reasons for doubting the correctness of the present vowel-points are several. As they stand, we must translate thus: *The words of Agur, the son of Jakeh, the oracular message, the declaration of the man for Ithiel—for Ithiel and Ukal.* Here then, (*a*) We have conveyed to us the idea of *words* (a part of the title) virtually repeated three times, viz., first in דִּבְרֵי, then in הַמַּשָּׂא, and lastly by נְאֻם; the like of which can nowhere else be found, and which seems to be not only altogether unnecessary, but in a measure even unmeaning. This awakens suspicion. (*b*) The names *Jakeh* and *Ukal* occur nowhere else, as proper names; that of *Ithiel* only once, viz., in Neh. 11: 7. This would not indeed be proof of itself, that they might not be used as proper names here; but if the consideration of them as proper names, would make the passage appear very singular and tame; and specially, if the interpretation of them as usual words, and not proper names, makes a good and congruous sense; then all this is proper to be thrown into the balance of adjustment. (*c*) If *Ithiel* and *Ukal* are both proper names intimately associated, why is it that the first is repeated, and the last not repeated? Both appear, from our present point of view, to stand on the same level. (*d*) It seems singular, that the *oracular message* and *the declaration* should both be addressed to one person twice; to another person once; and moreover to two persons, who are elsewhere (if in fact they are persons) wholly unknown, and who, so far as the sequel is concerned, are never addressed or recognized in that sequel. At least, we can discern nothing specially appropriate to them, in what follows. (*e*) Quite strange is it, in case the whole of verse first is title merely, to find כִּי, in verse second, at the very beginning of a discourse. (*f*) In the usual mode of interpretation, הַמַּשָּׂא and נְאֻם are both in apposition, and therefore both are in the const. before הַגֶּבֶר. But this cannot be, for the *article* before the first would be inadmissible, at least by any of the ordinary laws of grammar. (*g*) After נְאֻם, in all other places, comes merely the person whose *word* it is (i. e. the subject or agent who speaks), but not the one *to whom* the address is made (the indirect object). At least this is the case universally in the Heb. Scriptures. Therefore "the word (נְאֻם) of the man *to Ithiel*," is without any parallel. (*h*) מַשָּׂא is not congruous in its meaning, with the matter which follows; for this is not, (like what follows הַמַּשָּׂא in other cases), *one connected oracle*, or *one connected and judicial sentence*, but *many sayings* on different topics. Nor does the matter of the sequel, i. e. the *tenor* of it, at all agree with the proper meaning of מַשָּׂא. — These are serious difficulties indeed; and if they can be well avoided, it seems desirable to shun them. Let us see whether this can be fairly done.

(1) מַשָּׂא is probably here the name of a *place*. This may be argued, from its necessary meaning in 31: 1, a passage

altogether parallel with the one before us, as every one will see. There we have the following: " *The words of Lemuel* מֶלֶךְ מַשָּׂא, i. e. (as usually rendered) *the words of Lemuel the king, an oracle*, etc. But this is an impossible construction. The Hebrews could say: הַמֶּלֶךְ לְמוּאֵל, or לְמוּאֵל הַמֶּלֶךְ; but they did not and could not say: לְמוּאֵל מֶלֶךְ. Of course, then, מֶלֶךְ without the article is necessarily here in the *const.* state; and if so, then מַשָּׂא is *the name of the country* over which Lemuel was king. This follows by a grammatical necessity. —But where is such a place or country? In Gen. 25:14 and 1 Chron. 1:30, Massa is mentioned, and is coupled in each case with דּוּמָה; and this latter name occurs again in Is. 21:11. In Arabian geography, we find two Dumahs, viz., the Syrian one called *Dumah el G'ondol*, and the Arabic one named *Dumah of Iraq;* but there is also another one, on the western slope of the highlands of Arabia, about some fifty to sixty geographical miles from Akaba, which is at the head of the eastern fork of the Red Sea. Near this latter *Dumah*, (in all probability, as it would seem, because of the junction of the two names elsewhere), was *Massa*. Moreover, both Dumah and Massa were probably inhabited by a colony of Jews, i. e. Simeonites; about five hundred of whom marched into that country, and expelled the former inhabitants, in the time of Hezekiah, as we are informed in 1 Chron. 4:41—43. After possessing themselves of Mount Seir, in Edom, they extended their conquests over all the remainder of the Amalekites, who are reckoned among the ancient Arabians by their own geographers. In view of those facts, it is easy to account for it, that a messenger was sent to consult Isaiah the prophet, out of the land of *Dumah*, Is. 21:11. Doubtless, the messenger and those who sent him were Hebrews.

(2) Taking the above historical events into view, it will be easy to see how it comes about, that a writer in Massa should develop an acquaintance with the Heb. Scriptures,

and a high reverence for them ; which is plainly shown in 30 : 5, 6, and also in the word *Jehovah* in 30 : 9. Whatever might be the difficulties we should meet with, in case Massa was inhabited by *heathenish* Amalekites, we are now freed from them by the historic notice above referred to, in 1 Chron. 4 : 41—43. Dumah, and Massa its neighbor, in all probability were a portion of the Amalekitish country, if we may judge from their localities ; and after the conquest of them by the Simeonites, we never hear any more about Amalek as an existing nation. It is plain, then, that chaps. xxx. xxxi. might have been written at Massa ; and this not very long after the Hebrew conquest of it. Thus far our path seems to be open.

(3) The main difficulty respects *Massa;* and this being now removed, we come to the word which precedes it, and which, if we are in the right, should (with Massa) be pointed and read thus : יִקְהָהּ מַשָּׂא. By this mode of writing, the ה, which appears in our text as an article before מַשָּׂא, is attached to the preceding word as a suff. pronoun. That this ה does not belong to *Massa* as an article, has already been shown, (see (*f*) above, and comp. *Massa* in 31 : 1, which has no article). Written in this way, the meaning stands thus : *Agur, the son of her whose domain is Massa.* The ground-form of יִקְהָהּ is יְקָהָה, and this appears in Gen. 49 : 10, in the const. state, and there means *domain*, or *dominion ;* in a like sense it occurs in v. 17 of this present chapter ; or, if we follow the Arabic root וקה, lit. it means *obedience*, i. e. (in the concrete) *those who obey. Domain* is therefore a good word to convey the idea intended to be conveyed. We might expect, that יְקָהָה would, in the suff. state, make יִקְהָתָהּ ; and so it would in its full form, but Hitzig (loc. cit.) has shown, that the form of nouns that have a double ה, drops one of them before a suff. which consists of another הּ-ָ, so as to prevent the occurrence of three *He's* together ; and consequently, that the abridged

form here, יִקְּהָה, is within the rules of Hebrew normal usage. — Only one question remains, then, in regard to such a phraseology, as here follows the const. noun בִּן (from בֵּן, see in Lex.), viz., Can the const. state precede not only *nouns* in the Gen., but also *a whole clause*, as in this case? Ewald has fully answered this question in § 323, *b*, with many examples of such a construction. Our way then seems clear. בִּן is often employed for בֶּן in the const.; see Fuerst, Concord. Heb. We have then the following idea: *The words of Agur, the son of her whose domain is Massa.* — So much is the proper title or inscription of the book; and here that title ends, as we shall soon see.

The same *queen of Massa* seems to reappear, in 31 : 1. *Lemuel, the king of Massa*, is going to utter *things which his mother taught him.* It seems probable, then, that he was a successor to his mother in her domain; and also that Agur (in 30 : 1) was a brother of his, being the progeny of the same queen. A person of remarkable endowments this mother would seem to have been, thus to instruct her sons; and fortunate, as the world say, in having such sons.

(4) We come now to the latter part of the verse. This I should write and render thus: לָאִיתִי אֵל לָאִיתִי אֵל וָאֵכֶל, *I have toiled for God, I have toiled for God, and have failed.* The Acc. אֵל is hardly governed by לָאִיתִי, a verb intrans. It is rather that kind of Acc. which indicates *in respect to, in reference to*, § 117. 3; of which there is a multitude of like examples. The sequel shows, that the toil in this case consisted in endeavors to find out God. After toiling in vain to accomplish this, *he desisted*, or *failed*, as to making more efforts. So stands it in our text, as pointed above, וָאֵכֶל. This is the apoc. Imperf. of כָּלָה, which does not simply imply the fact of *desisting*, but desisting because of a *failure* of strength and resolution to pursue the matter. The sequel will show why he failed, i. e. it develops the impossibility of accomplishing such an object. — That this

is not a forced or improbable construction, when we point the word וָאֵכֶל, is plain from the fact, that anciently the Sept., the Syr., and the Vulgate, all treat it as a *verb* in the Imperf.; although some of them derived it from יָכֹל, *to be able*, and read it וָאֻכַל = the full form וָאוּכַל. So Cocceius, who translates thus: *Laboravi propter Deum, et obtinui.* But the verb יָכֹל elsewhere always makes its Imperf. in the full form, אוּכַל. We must go then to כָּלָה as the stem, or to כָּלַל = כָּלָה in respect to meaning. J. D. Michaelis came near the true sense, in his translation: *Concerning God I have toiled, and given up the investigation.* He must have pointed the word as proposed at the beginning of this paragraph. Forms like וָאֵכֶל we have in וָאֵפֶן in Deut. 9:15. 10:5, see § 74. n. 3. *b.*

If it be objected to the pointing in לָאִיתִי אֵל, that the name of God in the form אֵל or אֱלֹהִים never appears elsewhere in the book of Proverbs; the fact is conceded, with the exception of אֱלֹהִים in 2:5, 17. We always have *Jehovah*, through the whole book elsewhere; and just the contrary of this is the usage in Ecc., where *Jehovah* is never employed. This is a strong circumstance against identity of authorship in respect to the two books. But in the present case, it is of no weight as an objection against the use of אֵל here, because the ground taken is, that the authorship belongs to a man out of Palestine, and one who cannot be regarded as bound by Solomonic usage.

Thus we obtain a facile and congruous sense for the clause under examination; as we shall more fully see in the sequel. If the Acc. אֵל, after לָאִיתִי, be a matter of difficulty to any one, (which surely it cannot be, if he well understands the Hebrew idiom), let him consider what license the Greeks take, with this same tense, after intrans. verbs; e. g. *Βαίνειν ὁδόν — ἀλγεῖν τοὺς πόδας — κάμνειν τοὺς ὀφθαλμούς* — and even *χορεύων Φοῖβον, dancing Apollo*, i. e. in honor of him — *ἑλίσσειν Ἄρτεμιν, to dance Diana,* —

and many more of the same tenor. But the Heb. employs the Acc. even more extensively than the Greek. Most of the *adverbs* of *manner*, are made by nouns in the Acc. case.

The version above, viz.: *I have toiled for God*, must of course be here understood, (if we retain the word *for* in the translation), as meaning, that he had toiled *for the acquisition of a knowledge of God;* but yet, not in the ordinary sense of acquiring a *saving knowledge* of him, but in order to obtain a speculative knowledge, either ontological or physiological. That he failed in this toil, is not a matter of wonder; compare the striking passages in Job 11 : 7. 36 : 5, 26. 37 : 23. Rom. 11 : 33.

If our conclusion above is correct, then the two chapters, Prov. xxx. xxxi., came from the hand of a *Jewish Arabian writer*. The manner in which his composition begins, reminds one of the usual manner of commencing any composition in Arabic. Here we have נְאֻם הַגֶּבֶר; in Arabic, قَالَ (*dixit*) is the preface to any piece, with the name of the author following this verb; and this is exactly = נְאֻם, with the speaker's name after it.

No apology, I trust, is needed for the length of a discussion, which proposes so much of a change in the ordinary version of the passage before us. Not a single consonant, let it be noted, has been changed or omitted, in making out this alteration, but merely a different vocalization is employed. The difficulty of the passage doubtless occasioned the punctators to make *proper names* of those words, which they did not well understand.

(2) For stupid am I more than any man; and I have not the understanding of men.

Here we see the full force and propriety of כִּי. — He *failed*, because God cannot be searched out to perfection; and then he *desisted*, because he found himself altogether unable to comprehend God. He was even made to feel, that he was stupid beyond the common measure, yea, more than any other man. The phraseology need not, however, be urged to rigid exactness of statement, for it is poetical, and specially is it the language of feeling, rather than that of exact philosophizing or logic.

(3) For I did not learn wisdom ; nor did I become acquainted with a knowledge of the Most Holy.

The וְ at the outset is *causal* in a measure. Because he did not learn, etc., is the reason why he has said, that he was uncommonly stupid. The second וְ, following a negative, means *nor.* — קְדֹשִׁים, lit. *the holy ones*, plainly a *plural intensive*, and it is so rendered in the version.

(4) Who ascendeth to heaven, and then descendeth? Who hath gathered the wind in his fists? Who hath bound up the waters as in a garment? Who hath established the ends of the earth? What is his name, and what is his son's name, that thou shouldest know him?

That is, God ascends and descends, and is everywhere. He holds the winds in his grasp, and restrains them or causes them to blow at his pleasure. — *Bound up the waters*, i. e. the waters above the firmament (Gen. 1 : 7), which of course, according to Hebrew views, needed to be *bound*, in order to keep them in place. — בַּשִּׂמְלָה, *as with a garment*, the כ being omitted because of the בְּ, that is, as a man girds a garment around him so as to make a complete covering, so are the waters above confined. The רָקִיעַ seems to be the covering in question here, which, being regarded by the Hebrews as a *solid* expanse, affords a check upon the descent of the waters. Hence "the opening of the windows of heaven," at the time of the deluge, Gen. 7 : 11, 12. — *What is his name?* etc., are questions which imply, that no one knows him, or his family, (so to speak). — *That thou shouldest know him*, i. e. *so that thou*, etc. In other words: Not even his name, or that of anything which pertains to him, is such that thou canst know it. To think of the *Logos* here, under the name of בֵּן, would be "travelling very far out of the record." — The sentiment plainly is: 'We cannot know *him* or *his*, so as to satisfy speculative inquiry.'

(5) Every word of God is pure; a shield is he to those who trust in him.

Compare the original of this, in Ps. 119 : 140. 12 : 7 (6). All which God has said is free from dross or imperfection; and he will protect all who trust in him.

(6) Thou shalt not add to his words, lest he reprove thee, and thou become a liar.

Compare Deut. 4 : 2. 13 : 1, (Eng. Vers. 12 : 32). The quotation here is so plain, that one cannot doubt the familiarity of the writer with the Jewish Scripture. — For the form תּוֹסְףְּ, from יָסַף, see § 74. n. 3. *c.* — *A liar* is any one who falsifies God's truth, either by addition or diminution.

(7) Two things have I asked of thee; withhold them not from me before I die. (8) Falsehood and lying words remove far from me; give me neither poverty nor riches; feed me with the bread of my allotted portion.

טֶרֶם demands the Imperf. after it, as here in אָמוּת. — *Give me neither*, etc., the Heb. runs thus: *Poverty and riches give not to me!* — הַטְרִיפֵנִי וגו״, lit. *pluck food for me — the bread of my portion.* — חֻקִּי, is his *ration*, so to speak, i. e. what is allotted or suffices to satisfy his wants. — There appears, at first view, to be *three* things instead of *two*. But the last two clauses combine in the following way: 'Let me be neither rich nor poor, but merely one who has a sufficiency.'

(9) Lest I be satiated and deny [thee], and say: Who is Jehovah? and lest I be poor, and steal, and violate the name of God.

Great plenty usually produces pride and sensuality, and, of course, forgetfulness of God, and of our dependence on him. — *Poverty* tempts men to steal what they want, and which they cannot otherwise obtain. Moreover, in consequence of this condition, some men often assail the divine Being with charges of partiality, severity, and injustice.—*Assail* or *violate the name;* the verb תָּפַשׂ lit. means *to take hold of, to grasp, to seize rudely* for the sake of treating any one roughly. It is difficult to find an adequate English word. *Assail* has of course a bad sense, (which is required here), as commonly employed; but the idiom is unusual. *Violate*, seems to come as near to the original, as we can well manage to come. *Name of God* is = *God himself;* as often elsewhere.

(10) Thou shalt not cause a servant to slander his master; lest he should curse thee, and thou shouldest be guilty.

תַּלְשֵׁן is in Hiph., and so has the meaning given to it in the version.—*Should curse thee*, viz., because he has incurred punishment for his crime of slandering, to which thou didst move him.—And since thou hast done a wrong, and made thyself *guilty*, the curse will light on thee, for thou hast deserved it. It will not be a קִלְלַת חִנָּם, but a curse with a good reason for it.

[Next follows a specification of *four* classes of people, each one independent of the other; and what is remarkable in the case is, that nothing is predicated of them, as to what they are to do or will do, (except in one case), or even as to any retribution which awaits them. They stand in no connection with the context; and they apparently represent prevailing vices, inasmuch as whole classes are specified. It seems to be taken for granted, that each of these classes will be looked upon by the reader with high disapprobation.]

(11) There is a generation, which curseth its father, and blesseth not its mother; (12) A generation pure in its own eyes, and which is not washed from its filthiness; (13) A generation—O how lofty are their eyes, and their eyebrows lifted up! (14) A generation whose teeth are swords, and their grinders knives, to consume the wretched of the land, and the needy among men.

V. 11, *blesseth not* = *curseth;* a case of *meiosis.*—V. 12, *pure in its own eyes,* although still unclean. רֻחָץ, Part. Pual, with מְ omitted, § 51. n. 5. — V. 13, *Lofty eyes* and *eyebrows elevated* are the usual marks or signs of pride or haughtiness. — V. 14, *swords* and *knives* are instruments of destruction. Here the image is that of wild beasts, which are ready to devour, and so we have לֶאֱכֹל. — מֵאֶרֶץ, *out of the land,* it might be rendered, i. e. to clear the land of them; but I take מִן to denote *a part of,* or *belonging to.* So also in מֵאָדָם. — But, what of all these? and what is to become of them? the writer does not say. He merely proffers them to our notice, doubtless anticipating our disapprobation of them.

(15) The vampire hath two daughters, give, give; three there are, which are never satisfied, four which never say: Enough! (16) The under-world, the barren womb, the ground never saturated with water, and fire which never says: Enough!

The vampire, עֲלוּקָה, is perhaps a somewhat doubtful translation. The ancients render *leech* or *blood-sucker;* our English version, *the horse-leech.* In one respect this is congruous; for these creatures are in a measure *insatiable;* which makes the gist of the comparison. But they do not seem to be sufficiently significant, or of importance enough, to constitute the basis of comparison here. *Vampire* comes much nearer, in this respect. This is an *imaginary spectre* or *ghost,* in the popular mythology, which sucks human blood, specially that of children, and is insatiable for it. The word עֲלוּקָה is found nowhere else in Heb.; but the Arabians have the same word, and in the *Kamus,* their standard dictionary, it is defined by another Arabic word, viz., غول, *Ghool.* This latter word, the Kamus again defines, as meaning, (1) *Calamity.* (2) *Forest-devil.* (3) *A demon anthropophagous* or *man-eating and insatiable.* The Arabians, down to the present hour, maintain that it is often met with in the forests of Arabia; and they stand in great terror of it, when entering a thick forest. The Syrians had a like tradition; but, like the

Hebrews, they more generally named the *Sprite* לִילִית. In Is. 34: 14, this last word occurs, and it is amply and finely illustrated by Gesenius, in his Comm. on the passage. In fact, the *popular* mythologies of hither Asia correspond very near with those of the West. We have, or have had, spectres, sprites, hobgoblins, elves, imps, vampires, and — what not? Of all these, the last named, i. e. *an insatiable blood-sucking spectre*, comes the nearest to the Arabic *Ghool*, and probably the Heb. עֲלוּקָה. Such a creature is of sufficient magnitude to correspond with the exigency of the passage. *Insatiability* in its highest development is required; and the *vampire* or *Ghool* furnishes an example in point. Bertheau does not translate, but *transfers*, and writes *'Aluqa*. I should do so likewise, if I were not satisfied that *vampire* comes sufficiently near to the original. — Whether the being in question be real or imaginary, is of no importance to the writer. The simple object is, to get a good basis of comparison in respect to *insatiability*. The popular notion of the vampire's *insatiability* afforded him one; like to the popular notions which Isaiah assumes as the basis of his representation, in chaps. xiv. and xxxiv.

Has two daughters, not in the way of *descent* or *generation*, but (in conformity with the Heb. idiom), *daughters* so called from *similitude*. Thus Jesus said to the Jews: *Ye are of your father the devil* (John 8: 44), i. e. his children, because they were like him in malicious intentions. — The *vampire*, then, has *daughters* in this sense, and in this way. There are *two* in number who are preëminent for insatiability, and so, on this account, are called the *daughters* of the vampire. These are named הַב הַב, i. e. *give, give*. These names are in apposition with בָּנוֹת, and partly exegetical of it. The names indicate the *qualities*, i. e. *insatiable desire and the lack of any adequate satisfaction of it*. To the two *daughters*, הַב, הַב, is added another thing of like character; and of all these three in common it is said: *They are never satisfied.*

Then, finally, comes another thing which makes *four*; and none of these ever say: *Enough!* Thus one common trait, i. e. *insatiability*, belongs to the whole; although the first two are preëminent above the rest, and so are called *daughters of the vampire*. The apparently masc. numerals have of course a fem. meaning in both cases, § 95. 1. The first clause in the verse seems to preclude the idea, that the third and fourth are reckoned as *daughters* of the vampire.

Next comes the specification of the *four*. (1) *The underworld* or *grave*; which is always receiving, and never satisfied, but continually says: *Give!* (2) *The barren womb*, or *restraint of womb*, viz., restraint from child-bearing. It is a generally acknowledged physiological fact, that barren women are the most vehement in their passion for offspring; see Gen. 30: 1, seq., which illustrates the subject. (3) *Ground not to be saturated with water*, i. e. a sandy or gravelly soil, which speedily drinks up all the rain, and is ever needing more. (4) *The fire*, which is ever consuming, and ever needing to be replenished.

Thus it appears, that the עֲלוּקָה, the mother-monster, is not herself reckoned as one of the number here produced, but only as a specimen to which the four are compared. It farther appears, that the two first are regarded as the most insatiable; for *give! give!* applies specially to them, since they are so named. But what is the object of producing these similitudes? On this the commentators have generally shown a prudent silence. It is clear, that not one of these *insatiabilities* is in itself of a moral or criminal nature. They either belong to things not moral, or they are involuntary. If the context developed a *miser*, all would be plain. His appetite resembles the *insatiability* here described. But no miser makes his appearance in the context. One, therefore, can hardly help supposing, that this passage contains an extract from some other book, where, as it stood, it had proximate objects in view, and furnished similitudes to illustrate them. As the objects are here presented, the passage seems designed rather to be classed with striking descriptions, or similes, than with *gnomes* of a moral or prudential character. This constitutes a striking particular of difference, between this and the preceding parts of the book. All heretofore has some *practical* bearing. Here, the object seems rather to gratify the love of similitudes, than directly to inculcate prudence or morals. We must suppose, however, at least, that the writer left it to his readers to apply these illustrations of an insatiable appetite to something within his own knowledge; for example, it was easy to apply them to the miser, the glutton, the drunkard, and the debauchee; although the writer has not himself expressly made such an application.—On the whole, there is good reason for reckoning this passage among the חִידוֹת (*enigmas*) of the book, mentioned in 1: 6 as a part of the contents of the book.

(17) The eye that derideth a father, and despiseth the control of a mother—the ravens of the valley shall pick it out, the young eagles shall devour it.

That *eye* here represents the person who sees, is plain. Yet the image of the *eye* is carried out, in the closing part of the verse.—לִיקֲּהַת, is the same word which stands in the title of the chapter, and there means *domain*. The Dagh. in ק is a mere compensation for the Yodh which is made *otiant* here, for the sake of a more rapid pronunciation. Regularly written it would read, לִיקְהַת; comp. examples in § 20. 2, which are of the like kind.—This *eye, the ravens will pick out, the young eagles will devour it*—vivid images are these of severe punishment.

(18) Three things are too wonderful for me; and four things I do not understand; (19) The way of an eagle in the air; the way of a serpent on a rock; the way of a ship in the midst of the sea; and the way of a man with a maid.

V. 18, What is it which is matter of wonder? The things themselves, or *the impossibility of tracing the way once gone over?* Certainly not the things themselves, for they are familiar and every-day matters. But that all these transitions can be made, without leaving any marks or signs of their having taken place — that seems to be the nucleus of the thing. — For examples of the phraseology, by which *three* are designated, and then a *fourth* is added, see Amos 1: 3, 6, 9, 11, 13. 2 : 1, 4, 6, = eight examples in succession. — As to the last clause, lit. it runs thus: *As to four, I know them not.* — V. 19, בַּשָּׁמַיִם, *in the air*, see Lex. The eagle leaves no trace of his lofty flight in the air; the serpent, no trace of his passage over a rock; a ship, no trace of its division of the waters. But the main thing is yet to come, because it has a special bearing on v. 20. — *The way of a man with a maid;* so our Eng. version, and I have followed it *causâ verecundiae.* The Heb. בְּעַלְמָה means *in puella*, i. e. "homo vaginam pertransiens."— Of this no traces are left upon the man; for it is *the way of the man*, in this case, and not of the woman. Whether עַלְמָה here means *virgin*, or *maid*, i. e. young woman, is not what the writer is here concerned with, although *virgin* is the more probable sense. In either case, the thing asserted is equally true. No traces of intercourse are left upon the man. The case of the maiden may be physically different from this, and must in fact be so, although it may not be apparent. But this is not what the writer intends to assert. The *woman*, who makes pretences to *incolumity*, comes before us not here, but in the next verse. — The three first, then, are mere *similars;* the fourth is not merely so, but it also prepares the way for what is said of the adulteress.

(20) So is the way of the adulterous woman; she eateth, and wipeth her mouth, and saith: I have done nothing wrong.

She eateth, means that she indulges her passion or appetite for venery. — *Wipeth her mouth*, is a continuation of the imagery of *eating*. The ancient (and indeed the present) Orientals fed themselves merely with their hands; they were of course obliged to wash or wipe after eating, for the sake of cleanliness. When this was done, no visible sign of having eaten was left. — So the adulteress takes all possible precaution to remove any *indicia* of her criminal intercourse; and when this is done, she claims to be guiltless. She would fain have others believe that she is innocent, and challenges any one to point out the least index of crime. But the manner in which she comes to make the claim, seems to imply, that pains-taking was necessary in order to render it credible. Were it not for that pains-taking, it would seem to be implied, that the thing done might be traced or suspected. The whole taken together serves to show, that although nothing palpable in the way of proof remains in the case of the *man*, by which his doings might be ascertained, it is different with the *woman*, unless special pains be taken to remove or conceal every trace of crime.

The moral of the whole seems to be, that not all guilt can be discovered, in consequence of its leaving palpable evidence behind it. The writer would seem to say: 'Trust not mere appearances too much. Remember, that neither professions of innocence, nor even appearances of it, do always prove the existence itself of innocence.' — The passage thus considered, however, is not designed to inculcate a proneness to suspicion, but merely to throw in a caution against unlimited credulity in first appearances. — It may well be reckoned as one of the חִידוֹת.

(21) Under three things the land trembleth, and because of four, it cannot lift itself up; (22) Under a servant, when he hath rule; and a fool, when he aboundeth in bread; (23) Under a hateful woman, when she getteth married; and a servant-maid, when she becometh heir to her mistress.

Three and *four* again perform the same part here as

above.— The numbers being to appearance masc., are in fact fem., agreeing with *things* implied.— שְׂאֵת, contracted from שְׂאֵת, fem. Inf. of נָשָׂא. The idea is that of *bearing up*, under the weight of what presses it.— V. 22, וְנָבָל implies the תַּחַת of the preceding clause before it; and so of וְשִׁפְחָה in the next verse.— לָחֶם (in pause), Acc. after a verb of *fulness*. Our idiom supplies a preposition.— V. 23, שְׂנוּאָה, fem. part. noun, *under her who is hated* = a hateful or ugly woman.— גְּבִרְתָּהּ, suff. form of גְּבֶרֶת. *To inherit her mistress*, means to come in her place, i. e. to become the wife of her master. The writer plainly deems such things as are here mentioned, to be *odious incongruities*.

(24) There are four small things in the world; and yet they are very wise.

The sequel shows, that *the four small things* are animals of the smaller kind. Heb. lit. *small things of the earth*, i. e. belonging to it.— *Very wise*, lit. *wise made wise*, the last word being Part. Pual; of course if the *wise* are made *still wiser*, then they become *very wise*, quasi *be-wised*; so in the version.

(25) The ants are not a strong folk; and yet they prepare their food in summer. (26) The mountain-mice are a folk not mighty; and yet they fix their habitation in the rock.

V. 25, *The ants* are a conspicuous example of activity and diligence; comp. 6 : 6—8.— V. 26, שְׁפַנִּים, not *conies*, for they do not build among the rocks; and it is doubtful, moreover, whether they are indigenous in Palestine. But the proper *mountain-mice* have some resemblance to them, although they are smaller. In Arabia, and other places, they are gregarious, and very abundant among the rocky hills; and withal, they are remarkably swift, and dexterous in escaping danger, by retreating into the crevices of the rocks where they live.— בַּסֶּלַע, with the article, as being the name of a substance.

(27) The locusts have no king; and yet they march on, all of them divided into bands.

In the Heb. אַרְבֶּה is sing. *generic;* and of course the suffix in כֻּלּוֹ is the same. Our idiom demands the plural.—וַיֵּצֵא is often used in reference to the orderly marching forth of an army.—חֹצֵץ, *dividing, sundering,* i. e. into regular bodies of march, like soldiers under their leaders. This they do spontaneously, without any king; which shows their instinctive sagacity.

(28) The lizard layeth hold with both hands, and she is even in the palaces of the king.

שְׂמָמִית, not *spider* (as in our version), as Bochart has fully shown, but the *lizard,* i. e. the *house-lizard,* which is very frequent in Palestine, and gets into every kind of dwelling. Its principal food is *flies;* and these it springs upon, and grasps with both its prehensiles, as if they were *hands.* They are tolerated in palaces even, because they help to clear them of vermin.

The *activity* and *dexterity* of these four classes of insignificant animals, gave occasion to the gnomic sayings before us. The hue of the whole chapter is very remarkable. In the present case, there is no *moral* suggested. To the mind of the reader is left the application. In the present case, the moral seems to be, that however insignificant a man may be in the eyes of the world, who have much regard to birth and outward circumstances, there is after all abundance of room for him to be active and sagacious, and to accomplish important ends thereby.

(29) There are three things which excel in step; yea, four which excel in gait.

מֵיטִיבֵי וגו׳, Part. Hiph., lit. *make good the step,* or *make goodly steps;* which means what the version expresses. The last clause repeats the same idea, in another form, viz., *maketh goodly the gait* or *going.*— לָכֶת (in pause), fem. Inf. of יָלַךְ.

(30) The lion is mighty among the beasts, and he will turn back from the face of no one. (31) The greyhound, and the he-goat, and a king who cannot be withstood.

V. 30, The majestic and fearless gait of the lion has been often remarked.— V. 31, זַרְזִיר מָתְנַיִם, lit. *compressed* (root זַר) *of loins.* Probably it is the *greyhound,* which is here characteristically so called, whose gaunt loins are conspicuous. Then the *gait* of this animal answers well to the writer's object, for it is at once graceful and rapid. To translate *war-horse,* with Gesenius, and others, seems incongruous. Of himself, he is not *compressed of loins;* nor are his *belts,* to which they appeal, bound on his *loins,* but on the fore-part of his body. Others translate *Zebra;* but this is not a Palestine animal.— אוֹ is a particle which seems hardly in place here. To translate *or* (the usual sense) makes no tolerable meaning, for this would be merely to say, that זַרְזִיר and תַּיִשׁ are two names of one and the same animal. In that case we should have only *three* of the whole, and not *four* as v. 29 demands. With J. H. Michaelis, then, we must here translate אוֹ as = *and;* and so, all the ancient Versions. With Michaelis we may refer to Num. 15: 6. Mal. 2: 17, as supporting such a translation.— תַּיִשׁ means the *he-goat* who is the head of the flock, and leads and controls its movements. The ordinary gait of goats among us certainly has little of the טוֹב in it; but the larger Oriental *he-goats,* at the head of a flock, march along with much affected dignity and stateliness.— אַלְקוּם, see on אַל־מָוֶת, in 12: 28. In the book of Psalms, קוּם is often used in the sense of a *hostile rising up;* and here אַלְקוּם appears to be a compound word, viz., קוּם and the negative אַל. Hence it means *no withstanding,* i. e. there is nothing of opposition which avails *with him.* So the Jewish interpreters. The usual stately movement of such a heroic sovereign, is here the point of allusion.

And now for the *moral*. What is it? These stately gaits are surely not proposed as *objects of imitation*; nor yet, of repugnance. I see no more in them, than the presentation of remarkable things, to witness which impresses the mind in a pleasing manner. They seem to be made prominent here, principally as *mirabilia*.

(32) If thou hast played the fool in exalting thyself; if thou hast craftily devised, with thy hand to thy mouth.

For הִתְנַשֵּׂא, see 1 K. 1: 5. — יָד לְפֶה, *with hand to mouth*, (Acc. of manner), denotes the action of a man in deep thinking, who often spontaneously puts his hand to his mouth while making mental effort. In other words: 'If thou hast, with much pains-taking, devised evil.'

Thus far is protasis, in both clauses introduced by *if*, but without any apodosis expressed to either of them. We must therefore suppose one; which would be as follows: 'Thou hast acted wickedly or foolishly.' Or, we may take אִם in a negative way, implying that one *ought not* to engage in such things. In accordance with this last implied idea, is the tenor of the next verse.

(33) For the pressing of milk produceth cheese; and the pressure of the nose produceth blood; so doth the pressure of anger produce contention.

That is: 'Indulge not evil devices, *because* (כִּי) this will bring you into contention and mischief.' *Milk pressed* becomes another substance, viz., *cheese*, which is harder and more solid; *the nose pressed* in anger, (our vulgar idiom is, *pulling one's nose*), *produces blood*; and then comes the main point aimed at, viz., *the occasion of strife*. — אַפַּיִם (lit. *nostrils*) has here its secondary sense, viz., that of *anger*. If one urges and presses hard on an angry man, the consequence of such a course is a *quarrel*. — If we look back, we may now see a connection. *Mischievous devices*, which bear hard or *press* on others, will be certain to produce strife and do mischief.—In the two last clauses, the paronomasia in אַף and אַפַּיִם is very conspicuous.

[Thus end the words of Agur. The difference between the style and manner of sentiment here, and in the preceding part of the book, must be obvious, at once, to every discerning reader. In the latter, we have no such continued and multiplied similes; and besides this, we are scarcely, if ever, at a loss to see the *moral*, that is, the prudential principle or sentiment aimed at. It usually lies on the surface. But in the present chapter, in several cases, we have no small difficulty to find any *moral;* and in some, we cannot, as we have seen, find it at all. In some cases, we have מְשָׁלִים of mere similitudes, adapted more to surprise or to please, than to impart ethical instruction. See Introd. § 1.]

PART VI. CHAP. XXXI. 1—9.

[These nine verses contain the instructions of Lemuel's mother; (1) Caution against incontinence. (2) Against drunkenness. (3) Monitions in respect to doing justice, and vindicating the oppressed.]

(1) THE WORDS OF LEMUEL, KING OF MASSA; which his mother taught him.

See on 30:1, where the first part of this verse is fully discussed.—מֶלֶךְ, (without the article) must be in the const. state; and if so, then *Massa* is the name of the king's *domain*. As *Agur* is called *the son of the queen of Massa* (30:1), and here the *king of Massa* is represented as being taught by his mother; so it seems quite probable, that this mother of the king of Massa, is the queen referred to in 30:1; and consequently, that Agur and Lemuel were brothers. The two compositions are probably contemporaneous, or nearly so.—יִסְּרַתּוּ, Piel fem. Perf. with suffix; see Parad. Suff. p. 292.

(2) What, my son? and what, the son of my womb? yea what, the son of my vows?

That is: 'What shall I say to thee?' Or: 'What oughtest thou to do?' The repetition denotes earnestness in demanding attention. *The son of my vows,* probably refers to vows uttered before his birth, that she would do so and so, in case she should bear a son; comp. 1 Sam. 1: 11. Perhaps the name of that son, לְמוּאֵל (in v. 4), *for him is God,* or *he belongs to God,* may indicate a consecration of him to God as his. — בַּר in Ps. ii., and in other places, shows that the word is not merely Aramaean, but belongs to the older Hebrew.

(3) Give not thy strength to women, nor thy ways to the destruction of kings.

חֵילֶךָ may mean *wealth;* but here this meaning is less probable. *The destruction of kings* seems to refer to the enervating power of excessive venery, and the premature death which it usually brings. *The destruction of kings* = that which destroys kings. לַמְחוֹת, Inf. Hiph. ה prefix being *elided,* and its vowel thrown back under the ל, § 52. 2. n. 7. *Strength,* therefore, i. e. physical vigor, seems to be the true idea of חֵיל. — The plur. ־ִין, in מְלָכִין, is not alone. Other like cases are found in Hebrew, § 86. 1. *a.*

(4) Not for kings, O Lemuel, not for kings, is the drinking of wine; nor for princes, the desire of strong drink.

שְׁתוֹ, the apoc. form of שְׁתוֹת, Inf. of שָׁתָה, § 74. n. 2. — Before the second clause, וְ means *nor,* because it follows a negative. — אַוֹ, Qeri אֵי, which would be an interrogative; and then we must translate: *where is strong drink?* A possible, but not a probable sense. Ges. (Lex.) reads אֹוִ, which he makes the const. of אַוֹ, just as מוֹת is const. of מָוֶת. I prefer this solution to the Qeri. The root then is אָוָה, *to desire,* and אֹוִ is const. of אוֹ = *desire.*

(5) Lest he drink, and forget that which is decreed, and pervert the judgment of all the afflicted.

מְחֻקָּק, Pual Part. form, used as a neuter noun here.— Heb. *all the sons of the afflicted*, means merely what is expressed in the version.—It is a king's business to sit as a court of ultimate appeal for the oppressed. But how can he judge rightly, under the influence of intoxicating drink? It is assumed that he cannot.

(6) Give strong drink to him who is ready to perish; and wine to those who are in bitterness of spirit. (7) Let him drink, and forget his poverty, and no more remember his toil.

לְמָרֵי, plur. const. of מַר adj.—V. 7, רֵישׁ, also written רִישׁ and רֵאשׁ, root רוּשׁ. It has an unusually fluctuating orthography. *The bitterness of spirit* seems to be regarded here as brought on by *poverty* and *excessive toil.*

(8) Open thy mouth for the dumb; for the cause of every orphan.

That is, plead for those who cannot plead for themselves. —Advocate *the cause of the orphan*, lit. *of all the sons of bereavement.*

(9) Open thy mouth, to judge righteously; yea, vindicate the afflicted and the poor.

צֶדֶק, Acc. adverbial.—דִּין may be a noun=*judgment;* but the verb makes a more energetic sense. *To judge* is generic, and may mean *to acquit* or *to condemn.* Here it means *to acquit*, and thus to vindicate the cause of the afflicted, that is, of the *oppressed.*

[These precepts are brief, but very expressive. The cautions are directed against those vices, into which kings are most apt to fall. Wine, women, and oppression in order to collect much money from the people, are things about which kings usually need very impressive instruction. The excellent mother, who seems to have understood these matters well, has here given salutary advice, with great kindness and much earnestness. How different would the conduct of most kings be, should they hearken to the admonitions originally addressed to the young king of Massa!]

CHAP. XXXI. 9—31. *Eulogy of the prudent and industrious housewife.*

[This is one of the *alphabetical* songs. The style differs strikingly from that of chap. xxx.; for here, all the verses are nearly of the same length. The parallelisms have a close resemblance to those in the book of Psalms; and especially to those in the alphabetical Psalms. It results from the texture of an alphabetic song, that the connection of the thoughts should be somewhat looser than in free song, because such words must be introduced as will chime with the order of the alphabet. This is strictly observed in the present case. But the second parallelism in such verse is free, and is not bound by any order of the alphabet at all. Whoever was the author of the piece, (it purports to have come from the queen-mother), an extensive acquaintance with the laws and nature of the more artificial Heb. poetry is manifested. It is a song which is at the same time both beautiful and noble. The picture is certainly very attractive, and shows the hand of a skilful artist. It is a striking specimen of the *simplex munditiis.*]

(10) A woman of energy who shall find? For her value is far removed from pearls.

Who shall find? i. e. such a woman is rare, but well worth searching after. — *Far removed from pearls,* because she is worth much more than pearls. Thus we say: 'Such a person distanced another,' when we mean that he far exceeded him.

(11) The heart of her husband trusteth in her; and gain will not be lacking. (12) She rendereth him good, and not evil, all the days of her life.

שָׁלָל, usually *spoil,* but here tropically, that which is equivalent to it in value, viz., *gain, profit.* In other words, she brings him that which takes the place of spoil, and supersedes it. — After גָּמָלַתְ comes two Accusatives, viz., that of the object given, and of the person to whom the gift is made § 136. 2.

(13) She seeketh wool and flax, and manufactureth them with willing hands. (14) She is like to the ships of the merchant; she bringeth from afar her sustenance.

V. 13, בְּחֵפֶץ כַּפֶּיהָ, lit. with the *desire* or *good pleasure* of her hands. The real meaning is given in the version, i. e. she labors readily and cheerfully. — *She bringeth from afar*, etc., that is, she sells her manufactures, and purchases with the price of them that food which is imported from abroad, whether necessaries or luxuries. The implication is, that she sends the products of her labor to a foreign country, and thence brings, in the way of exchange, what she needs for her household.

(15) She riseth up, moreover, while it is yet night, and giveth food to her household, and a due portion to her maidens.

The meaning of טֶרֶף (*food*) here is derived from the Hiph. of טָרַף, which means *cibum discerpere.* — בֵּית here probably means her own family; while חֹק, (lit. *statute, law, decree*), designates the *determined portion* of food allotted to her maidens; comp. 30 : 8, where is a like instance of חֹק employed in this way. Were it not for this, I should be inclined to refer חֹק to the *allotted task* of the servant-maids.

(16) She setteth her mind upon a field, and procureth it; from the fruit of her hands is the planting of the vineyard.

זָמְמָה, *thinks upon, revolves in her mind*, i. e. she thinks out a plan of purchasing the field. — *The fruit of her hands*, means the products of her labor. With these, she, by selling them, procures money to purchase a vineyard. The Kethibh should be written נְטַע, const. of נֶטַע (see Is. 5 : 7), which makes a better sense than the verb נָטְעָה, which is proffered by the Qeri.

(17) She girdeth her loins with strength, and maketh strong her arms. (18) She well understandeth that her merchandize is good; her lamp goeth not out, through the night.

V. 17, She is active and energetic.—V. 18, She knows how to appreciate and to relish the good or comforts which her merchandize procures. Heb. lit., *She tasteth that her merchandize is good.* I have endeavored to preserve the idea, while expressing it in our current idiom.—As to לַיִל, the Masorites bid us to turn it into לַיְלָה, which last is the usual form. But the other is good, and is elsewhere employed.—The idea here is, that she works through the night, in order to accomplish some favorite task of her industry, and so needs a lamp during that period.

(19) Her hands she putteth to the distaff; her fingers grasp the spindle-wheel.

כִּישׁוֹר is found only here. Ges. refers it to the root כָּשֵׁר, and so it would seem that it must be referred, as to its form. But there is nothing in the *meaning* of this verb, (*to be right, prosperous*), which indicates any relation to the subject. We depend on Jewish tradition for its meaning; which, however, is uniform.—פֶּלֶךְ is rendered *spindle* by most. But if her hands took hold of that, it must be something very different from our spindles. As the word means *a little wheel* or *pulley, orbiculus*, I take it as here designating the wheel which the hands turn, and which is connected with the motion of the spindle.

(20) She openeth wide her hand to the afflicted; she putteth forth her hands to the needy. (21) She feareth not for her household because of the snow; for all her house are clothed with purple.

V. 20, *Opens wide her hand*, i. e. dispenses liberally.—*Putteth forth*, etc., i. e. she stretches out her hand for the sake of succoring. V. 21, *Because of the snow*, i. e. because of the wintry cold.—שָׁנִים, *purple*, is probably to be understood tropically here; for the mere color of a garment would not defend from the cold; nor was the color in question limited merely to garments of woollen cloth. The meaning, therefore, seems to be, that she furnishes handsome and warm clothing for her family. *Purple garments* were of course of the better sort, and also the highest in price; hence the tropical meaning here.

(22) Coverlets doth she make for herself; fine linen and scarlet is her clothing. (23) Her husband is known in the gates, because he sits with the elders of the land.

V. 22, מַרְבַדִּים seems to be confined to the *clothing of beds.* We cannot well give it the generic sense of *covering*, although it would fit well here. — The *literal* meaning of *scarlet* here, need not be urged. The general idea is, that she furnishes the best kinds of clothing. — V. 23, By thrift, her husband attains to a place among the magistracy, who sit by the gates in order to decide causes. Accordingly, he is said *to sit with the elders.*

(24) Linen vestments doth she make and sell; and girdles doth she present to the merchant-man.

סָדִין is *the inner linen vestment* = *shirt.* — *The girdle* is a necessary part of oriental costume, because of the loose outer vestments, which it is employed to draw close to the person.

(25) Strong and beautiful is her clothing; and she laugheth at the time to come.

Lit. *strength* and *beauty*, abstract for concrete. — *Laughs at the time to come*, because she has abundant provision for it, i. e. clothing and stores of every kind; and therefore she is cheerful (laughs), not having any solicitude.

(26) Her mouth she openeth with wisdom; and the law of kindness is on her tongue.

She speaks discreetly, and her speech is kindly.

(27) She watcheth the ways of her household; and the bread of sloth she eateth not.

צוֹפִיָּה, fem. Part. Kal of צָפָה, § 74. n. 5. — The Kethibh makes no sense, in the next word, without another vowel-pointing; but הוֹלְכוֹת, would be a fem. Plur. Part., and then the meaning would be: *she watcheth over the goers of her house*, i. e. over her servants — a possible, but rather improbable sense, as no example of the like kind anywhere occurs. We must (with the Qeri) read הֲלִיכוֹת, *goings*, i. e. *ways* or *demeanor*. — *Will not eat the bread of idleness*, means that she will not sit down inactive, and be fed merely by others who are active, while she is idle herself.

(28) Her children rise up and call her *blessed;* as to her husband — he will praise her: (29) Many daughters have done virtuously, but thou hast excelled them all!

בַּעְלָהּ is put first for emphasis' sake, and stands here as Nom. independent. — V. 29 is the eulogy which the husband utters. — *Virtuously*, in the older sense of the word, i. e. *efficaciously* = בְּחָיִל. We say still: "This herb has no *virtue* in it," i. e. no *potency* or *efficacy*. — אַתְּ, *thou* fem.; the Dagh. stands for נ; and the reason of the Sheva at the close will be seen at once, by writing out the full word אַנְתְּ, § 10. 3. *b*. — עָלִית, second fem., *hast risen up*. Then follows עַל, *above;* so, *thou hast excelled*. — כֻּלָּנָה, כֹּל with plur. suff. fem.

(30) Loveliness is deception, and beauty is vanity; but a woman who fears God shall be praised.

That is, loveliness and beauty of person merely are fleeting, evanescent, and unsatisfying. *Piety* is everything. — יִרְאַת, Part. fem. in the const. state, masc. יָרֵא, fem. יְרֵאָה, const. יִרְאַת, § 132. 1. *b*.

(31) Praise ye her according to the fruit of her hands; yea, men shall praise her in the gates for her deeds.

תְּנוּ most make from נָתַן, in the Imper., and so, they translate by *give*. But another way is open. תָּנָה, in Piel, means *to praise*, and perhaps the same in Kal. If not, then the vowel-points may be changed to תַּנּוּ, Piel Imper. That this is the more probable sense, seems to be indicated by the corresponding יְהַלְלוּהָ, in the next clause. In Judg. 11: 40, לְ is inserted after תַּנּוֹת, as it is in לָהּ here. — In מִפְּרִי, מִן has the sense of *according to, secundum;* see Lex. s. v. A. 2. *f.* — מַעֲשֶׂיהָ, Acc. of *in respect to, in regard to.*

It may not be amiss to suggest here, that the verb תָּנָה originally means *extend, porrigere, spread out,* (the root of the Greek verb τείν-ω), and that the much controverted תְּנָה of Ps. 8 : 2, may be easily explained by pointing it תֹּנֶה, which makes the passage read thus : *Who spreadest out thy glory* עַל הַשָּׁמַיִם, *over the heavens.* In this way, all is easy and natural ; for עַל (*over*) is altogether appropriate after such a verb or participle, but not at all after תְּנָה as derived from נָתַן. Hence the perplexity of commentators, who derived it in this way. If the sense proposed be altogether congruous, (as it plainly is), and at the same time we are liberated from all grammatical straits, I know of no good reason why we should not adopt it.

One must go back to the simplicity of ancient times, in order to enter fully into the spirit of this eulogy ; and every one who does this, cannot fail to perceive the admirable beauty, congruity, and simplicity of the whole.

CONTENTS.

I. Introduction.

II. Special Remarks on peculiar Forms, Syntax, and Meaning of Words, etc., in reference to Grammatical Difficulties and Exegesis.

[The design of the following notices is to guide the reader, in any particular researches after specialities in Hebrew Grammar or exegesis. They may assist him in finding examples for the illustration of peculiar idioms and meanings of words and phrases, and also peculiar constructions.]

(1) Infinitives with לְ instead of a definite Verb, 1: 2. (Variety in the construction), 2 : 2, 8. 8 : 21.
(2) Gender of Infinitive Nouns of fem. form may be masculine, 14 : 6, (cases quoted).
(3) Inf. construct admits a qualifying or object-noun, between its subject and itself, 1: 26.
(4) Inf. Mode continued by a definite Mode and Tense, 1: 26. 2 : 2, 8. 19 : 8.
(5) Speciality of כִּי, Prov. 1: 17, (initial), 2: 3.
(6) נָה– added to third person fem. of the Imperfect, to distinguish it from second pers. masculine.
(7) Use of Perf. and Imperf. distinct, 1: 22, comp. 1: 24.
(8) Difference between וּן– ןְ– and נָּה– נָה– in the Imperf. forms, 1: 28.
(9) Preposition מִן meaning *without*, 1: 30, fortified by examples.
(10) Discrepancy of. Gender between a Verb and its subject, Introd., § 11. chap. 2 : 10. 1: 20. 9 : 1. 12 : 25. 14 : 1. 16 : 33, (Exc.).
(11) Plural Nom. having a *Sing*. predicate, — i. e. case of individualizing, 3 : 18, (cases cited), 4 : 22. 28 : 1.
(12) בְּ *essentiae*, 3 : 26, (with references), 8 : 8.
(13) לְ after verbs of Motion, 20 : 14.

www.ingramcontent.com/pod-product-compliance
Lightning Source LLC
LaVergne TN
LVHW021140110826
845150LV00005B/1079

* 9 7 8 1 4 2 5 5 4 7 7 0 7 *